Theatrical Direction
The Basic Techniques

Figure 1. The director at work. During a rehearsal of *Stop the World, I Want to Get Off*, presented by the civic theater of Winston-Salem, the director, Errol C. Cahoon, demonstrates a gesture for Mark I. Feldman, while other cast members watch. [Photograph by Dorothy Welker]

Theatrical Direction
The Basic Techniques

David Welker

Wake Forest University

Allyn and Bacon, Inc., Boston

I would like to mention first my indebtedness to my wife

Dorothy Welker

for her encouragement and assistance throughout the preparation of this book.

My interest in directing was stimulated by the fine directors under whom I worked as an actor. I have learned most, however, from the many outstanding performers whom it has been my privilege to direct in the fields of public address, television, and the theater; I am sure that they taught me far more than I was ever able to teach them. To list them all would be impossible; each name must be understood as representing a dozen others.

(*In Television*)

Vice President Hubert H. Humphrey
Governor Orville L. Freeman
Governor Karl Rolvaag
Professor James Jones
Mrs. Kathy Olsen Tyler

(*In the Theater*)

Miss Laurel Dane
Mr. William Duell
Mr. John Figlmiller
Miss Caymichael Patten
Mrs. Paula Starks Wilson

Contents

Preface

Of all the subarts that combine to form a theatrical production, none is more demanding, more exciting, or more rewarding than directing. At the same time, none is more difficult to teach or to learn.

A very large number of discussions of directing theory are in print; reading them in succession is a bewildering experience, however, especially for the student, because they seem contradictory fundamentally and in detail. The discussion presented here does not attempt to resolve the contradictions, something which is apparently impossible at present. Rather, it focuses on the practical questions of the specific procedures and activities that a director must carry out in working with his playscript, his production staff, and his actors. Special emphasis is placed on the ultimate goal of any production, the creation of an experience for the audience, which can serve as a guide to the director in making decisions throughout his work on a play.

The discussion is aimed at the beginning director, and methods and techniques are described in detail, including many examples of specific instructions that can be used in working with the actors. It is hoped that the book will serve almost equally as the basis for formal classroom study or for the amateur who finds himself suddenly thrust into a directing assignment and who needs the assistance of an organized treatment of the art.

The discussion is necessarily based on personal experience in working with many hundreds of actors, as well as in teaching directing courses on the undergraduate and graduate levels. This is supplemented by the accounts in the standard literature and by numerous interviews with other directors. I would especially like to express my appreciation to the many directors who have freely shared their experiences, problems, and methods with me.

The anecdotes scattered through the book are fictionalized distillations from the many experiences of a number of directors. Anonymity has been furthered by substituting names adapted from the plays of Plautus.

The theater seems to pass through alternating cycles of consolidation and fluidity. The current period is one of change and experiment, and the concept and function of directing are altering along with other aspects of drama. It is hoped that this text will provide a solid footing of theory and technique that will serve as a support for the new director in assessing and adapting to the changes as they occur.

David Welker
Winston-Salem, North Carolina

1

Introduction

1/The Role of the Director

It is early autumn in North Carolina. Dusk settles down, forming pools of shadow under the trees and bushes. The loud and varied songs of southern birds fill the air as latecomers hurry to the university theater for the opening performance of the season.

Inside the building, brightly lighted activity contrasts with the peace of the scene outdoors. In the auditorium, the sound of hundreds of separate conversations blends to form a busy hum; ushers lead the latecomers to their seats; programs rustle as the members of the audience scan the cast list and the program notes.

Backstage, the bustle is still more intense; an apparently disorganized but carefully controlled sequence of activities is drawing to a climactic conclusion. For the last quarter of an hour the house manager has been watching the stream of incoming patrons, trying to forecast the critical time when the audience will be complete, so that the play can start at the psychological moment—not so early that the opening scene will be disrupted by late arrivals, and not so late that there will have been time for the audience to become

> The prompter's hand is on his bell;
> The coming heroes, lovers, kings,
> Are idly lounging at the wings;
> Behind the curtain's mystic fold
> The glowing future lies unrolled.
> BRET HARTE

3

restless. He has just sent word to the stage manager: "Ten minutes." The single message has been multiplied. A member of the stage crew has been sent to warn the actors. The light crew, in its soundproof booth at the back of the auditorium, has been alerted by telephone. The conductor of the orchestra has been notified by intercom.

Soft chimes sound in the lobby as a signal to the last members of the audience to take their seats. Starting at the back of the auditorium, the lights begin to fade imperceptibly, and although the viewers at the back may not be aware of the reason, their voices become quieter, and their conversations gradually stop. As the last lights fade and the wave of silence moves slowly toward the front, the spotlights above the ceiling of the auditorium come up, and when they have been brought up full and the auditorium is darkened, when the hubbub of conversation has ceased and the attention of the audience is directed toward the stage in single focus, the members of the orchestra enter and take their places in the pit. The conductor moves toward his position at center, acknowledges the burst of applause, turns and raises his baton, and the overture begins.

Any great work of art is great because it creates a special world of its own. It revives and readapts time and space, and the measure of its success is the extent to which it makes you an inhabitant of that world—the extent to which it invites you in and lets you breathe its strange, special air.

LEONARD BERNSTEIN

The magic of the theater is concentrated with special clarity in this ritual prolog to opening night, a bridge to the special world of the theater, a bridge that the audience has eagerly crossed. The randomness of experience in any large group of people, the various directions of their attention, have been organized and focused, and the special excitement and anticipation, which seem the essence of theater, provide a momentum that accelerates as the curtain rises and the first actors enter.

All over the nation, similar rituals are in progress, on university campuses, in high school auditoriums, off Broadway, on Broadway, in remodeled barns, in magnificent civic theaters. And everywhere the ritual is the same, in nearly all of its details, but especially in its spirit.

THE DIRECTOR

For each production, on whatever level, a second drama has taken place, one of which the audience is at most only dimly aware. The star of that drama is the director. Even historically, the two dramas seem in contradiction. The actor has been a recognized part of theater for thousands of years; the position of the director has been clearly defined for hardly more than a hundred. For actors and audience, when the curtain rises at the conclusion of the overture, the play begins; for the director, when the curtain rises, his performance is over.

The actor, moving through the pattern of spotlights on the stage, is maximally visible; the director's work is hidden, so much so that not even an experienced theater person can assess it with much confidence, unless he has been present at the performance of the private drama—the one in which the director has starred.

VARIETY IN DRAMA

The complexity of the theater can be illustrated by a particular production of Shakespeare's *Antony and Cleopatra* presented at a midwestern college. Forty actors appeared in the play, and fifty-three different people participated in the technical work for the production. Some of the actors played more than one role each, and some of the technical workers functioned in more than one capacity.

Each member of this group, totaling almost a hundred people, brought to the production his own point of view, his varied attitudes, tastes, interests, experiences, and skills. In addition, Shakespeare's script is one of great scope. It portrays the cultures of two great nations in conflict, emotions ranging across a wide gamut, and a variety of personalities—all expressed in a vivid and constantly changing style.

It is obvious that the kind of staff described provides variety in abundance. If each of the elements were listed, for each person involved in the production, in all of the degrees of variation in which they occur, it would be clear that an enormous number of different factors were involved in the work of preparing the play. But the functional number is even greater, because each factor functions in relation to every other factor. The actual effective number of elements involved in such a production, then, is not the total of the factors, but their permutations—which, if figured mathematically, would result in a number of unimaginable astronomical size.

UNITY IN DRAMA

Since the complexity of a theatrical production as a whole is impossible to visualize, let us consider only one small element: the problem of deciding where each actor is to stand and move throughout the play. As will be seen in a later chapter, the arrangement of the actors is of great significance in the effectiveness of a play. If each actor involved in a scene were to plan his own positions and movements independently, the result would be so chaotic a tangle that it would fail to contribute meaningfully to the play. If this aspect of production is to be fitted together with all the other production elements to produce a single unified esthetic effect, one member of the production staff must be assigned the task of coordinating them; in the contemporary theater, that person is the director.

> *If there is no focusing, organizing intelligence behind it, there is no art in any meaningful sense of the word.*
>
> SYLVIA ANGUS

The production staff as a whole, then, including the playwright, is the major source of variety in a theatrical production; the director is the major source of unity.

THEATRICAL ORGANIZATION

Nontheater people, on their first experience in the theater, often express surprise and puzzlement at the methods of operation they observe, which seem very different from those with which they are familiar in other types of activity. Work procedures often look chaotic to them, although they are clearly effective. Staff members seem to operate almost completely independently, and yet their work is closely coordinated. Staff organization looks excessively rigid on paper, and yet in operation it seems extremely loose.

The methods, policies, and organization, however, are the logical results of the special theatrical purposes, materials, and personnel. The various activities and skills which must be incorporated into the production of even a simple play are so diverse that no one person can master them all. To achieve the maximum variety and diversity in the production, the taste, experience, and skill of each worker must be utilized to the fullest. Both those facts require that each staff member be encouraged to display maximum initiative, and to work freely without harassment or interference. At the same time, if the finished production is to display unity—in fact, if the separate elements are to be fitted together so as to function at all—they must be coordinated carefully, and by a single overseer.

PRODUCTION POLICIES AND PROCEDURES

The result of those apparently contradictory requirements is the pattern of working which prevails in the theater today. In the first place, the staff positions are filled with the most effective people available—the best set designer, the most skilled construction workers, the finest costume designers, the best actors, the best director. In the educational theater, a vital part of the program consists of training inexperienced people; they are placed on the production staff in positions where they can work with the close assistance of experienced supervisors.

At the beginning of the work on a play, the staff members in the supervisory positions meet for conferences, in which the factors are emphasized that it is hoped will produce the intended unity in the final production—the style and spirit of the production, the major theme of the play, the relationships between such elements as set, costumes, lighting, makeup, and acting. Following such conferences, the supervisory staff members then work independently in preparing plans for particular areas of the work for which they will be responsible; these plans are prepared without supervision.

A second conference is then held, either with the supervisory staff as a whole, or in groups, or even individually, in meetings with the director. At these conferences the plans are discussed, and approved or rejected; additional suggestions may be made in either case. Further planning, again by the staff members independently, typically follows, the work being discussed again in additional conferences. Eventually the plans will be completed, and approved by the director.

Each member of the supervisory staff then meets with the production workers who will serve under his direction. The plans for their area of work are studied in detail, and specific work assignments are made. The properties supervisor, for instance, might have listed all of the properties needed for the show in five groups, assuming that he has a five-man crew; each person would then be given one of the lists, as his own particular assignment. Such patterns of assignment are not rigid, however, and can be expected to vary from crew to crew and show to show. In one play, for instance, it might be desirable for the property crew members to work together in pairs rather than individually.

Following the assignment conferences, the crews separate to carry out their assignments. Some of the work will be done independently (as property work is often done); other work is more likely to be done by groups of people (usually set construction is handled in this way). If the crew members are inexperienced, their supervisor is likely to work with them closely, although they will be encouraged to assume initiative as quickly as is practical. If they are skilled and experienced, they are more likely to work essentially without supervision. In any case, the supervisor will occasionally check to make sure that the work is progressing on schedule.

THE DIRECTOR'S RESPONSIBILITIES

Most of the work of production, then, is done without supervision. It is understood that if any staff member has difficulty with his assignment his supervisor is always available for consultation and assistance; and as a corollary, it is assumed that if no problems have been reported none exist and the work is proceeding smoothly. If a problem should arise that the crew chief could not solve, he would probably consult with the supervisor next above him on the organizational chart. A problem might be carried up the chart until it reached the director; since he occupies the top position, in such a case he must assume responsibility for handling the problem.

Rarely are production problems carried to the director; nearly always they are solved at some other level of the organization. The director must evaluate the technical work that has been done, and give it his final approval or indicate what must be altered. Usually one rehearsal is set aside for checking the work of the staff; this is called the "technical rehearsal," and occurs about a week before opening night.

The Director's Relation to Theater Administration

One agency appears on the organizational chart above the director. The character of the top supervisory position varies in different types of theater; on Broadway, the position is occupied by the producer; on college campuses, it is likely to be held by the chairman of the Speech or Theater Department; in community theaters, it is usually made up of a Board of Directors, who are elected by the full membership of the theater. Some functions that are of essential importance to the continuing theater program lie entirely outside the authority of the director; these are customarily supervised independently by the controlling person or board. Examples of such areas are financing, publicity, the preparation of playbills, ushering, theater maintenance and cleaning, and the selection of the season's plays. Even in some of those areas the director is likely to be consulted, especially in working up publicity and in choosing the plays; organizationally, however, the final authority for decisions in such matters rests with the people at the top administrative level. A glance at the chart will demonstrate that this division is a logical one: the director is in charge of all of the work that has aesthetic significance, which affects the experience that the audience will have in viewing the play; all nonaesthetic decisions are left in the hands of the administrative supervisors.

The principle that theater workers essentially work without interference is customarily applied in its extremest form in the relationship between the administration and the director. As at every level of organization, the administration select for their production the best director available. They will provide him with general guidelines for his work—a statement of the purpose and philosophy of the producing group, a description of the type of audience they customarily attract, the schedule of productions, and the budget for the play. And then they let him alone. Traditionally they do not involve themselves in the actual work of production; they do not interfere with the director's functioning; they do not pass on his decisions so long as he stays within the guidelines which they have given him. If these guidelines are breached, for example, if it develops that the play cannot be presented by the scheduled date, or if the expenditures exceed the budget, then special conferences will be called with the director for working out acceptable solutions. They would become involved in production problems only if some crisis should arise that could not be handled at the director's level. If, for instance, the director should find himself unable to complete his work because of ill health, or if a personal conflict should arise between production workers and the director so severe that it could not be resolved among themselves and the work of the play could not be continued until it had been resolved, the administrative board would be called into extraordinary session to handle the situation. Such crises, however, are so rare as to be phenomenal when they occur. Certainly, the assumption is that no such problem will occur during any particular season, and it is entirely possible for a director to spend a lifetime in the theater without ever having been involved in one.

PLANNING THE SEASON

The one area of top-level administration in which the director is most likely to be invited to participate fully is the selection of the season's plays. Usually the program for the following year is planned a month or two before the end of the current season.

Choosing the plays is strongly influenced by broad policies and factors that must usually be accepted as given—the general purpose and philosophy of the theater organization, the character of its audience (their age range, education, tastes, and interests), the traditions that have been established, and the restrictions of budget, facilities, and personnel.

Within that framework, the selection should probably be guided by three major considerations: the quality of the plays to be presented, their practicality for the organization, and the provision of maximum variety.

One college theater adopted a formula that was used for many years as a guide in planning their seasons. Of the four plays regularly presented, one was chosen from the modern period and one from the premodern; one play was selected primarily for its entertainment value, and one included some unusual or experimental aspect. These categories were not mutually exclusive; among the "entertaining" plays appeared Molière's *The Imaginary Invalid* and Shakespeare's *The Taming of the Shrew,* both premodern, as well as Tom Jones and Harvey Schmidt's *The Fantasticks* and Mary Chase's *Harvey.* In the "experimental or unusual" category were included Mozart's *Marriage of Figaro* (a premodern opera), Ionesco's *Rhinoceros,* Pirandello's *Six Characters in Search of an Author* (an early modern play), and a specially commissioned original play and an original opera, both given their premières at the college.

Unless the audience has extremely unified tastes, it will be impossible to select plays that will appeal equally to all viewers. Incorporating as much variety as possible in period, mood, style, and type will ensure the broadest choice for the audience and will itself add interest to the season.

The members of the administrative board give most of their attention to fitting the season to the tastes of the audience; they are likely not to be greatly concerned with the practicality of the selections and may be unable to assess it accurately. The director must consequently be extremely careful that the plays chosen can be produced without straining the resources of the staff. Mozart's *Marriage of Figaro* should not be included unless it is certain that adequate singers are available and that the orchestral work can be handled properly; to include *Aida* or *Die Meistersinger* would require still larger musical resources. Even with musical productions that are more narrowly theatrical, the practicality of scheduling *Oklahoma, Oliver,* or *The Boy Friend* should be examined carefully before they are announced as part of the season's bill. The number of sets required for each play, the expense of costumes, the sizes of the casts are all important factors; for most theaters, it is not wise to schedule more than one lavishly costumed multiset show a year. Since educational and community theaters are designed to serve the actors and staff almost as fully as the audience, balance in casting is often an important consideration; if *Waiting for Godot* is scheduled, it should be matched by a play which provides several good parts for actresses; if one play with a very small cast is chosen for the season, the other plays should have larger casts to ensure adequate opportunities for the potential actors.

When theater programs seem improperly planned, it is most often because they offer their audiences too restricted a range of choices. Season after season of light contemporary comedies quickly become cloying; a long series of Greek and Elizabethan tragedies might well drive the audience from the theater. A program including all periods and types of plays is likely not only to be more popular but even esthetically more defensible; variety is the spice of theater, as of life.

THE ORGANIZATIONAL CHART

Strange as theater organization often seems to nontheater people, it has the very great virtue that it works. It combines the kind of freedom and independence without which artists cannot function effectively with the kind of control and supervision that makes possible the smoothly coordinated functioning of an enormously diverse group of people, working in very different areas, so as to produce a unified work of art.

The preceding discussion, and a study of the organizational chart shown in Figure 2, will demonstrate that the organization of the staff is extremely clear-cut. The responsibility, authority, and assignment of each member of the

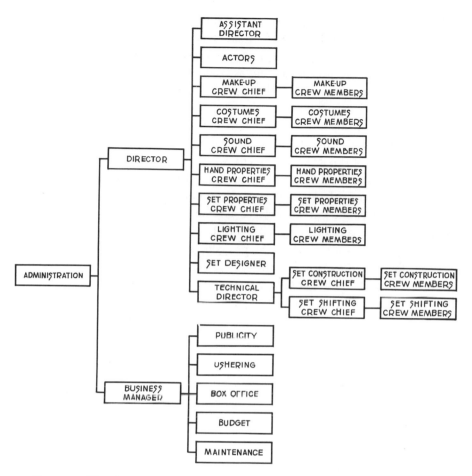

Figure 2. The director's place in the theater staff. The chart shown is typical, although many theaters introduce minor changes to adjust the pattern to their special conditions and personnel.

staff are unmistakable. In addition, it is clear who is authorized to give instructions to whom. With a staff that is thoroughly familiar with the organizational plan, it is impossible for one staff member to be given conflicting instructions by many different people. That actually happened at one college production, in which the organizational chart was not being followed. The result was an explosion so shattering that the rehearsal could not continue; it was dismissed for twenty-four hours to give actors and crews time to recover their self-control. If the chart had been followed, the conflicting instructions would never have been given, but even if they had, the crew members would have known immediately which one it was their responsibility to follow.

Another practice is not evident from the chart itself: as a policy the organizational pattern is followed very informally. In union theaters, work assignments are rigidly restricted, but elsewhere lines are crossed at will. Thus, if a member of the properties crew needs assistance in building a property, any knowledgeable member of the set construction crew will be glad to assist. Often, in small theaters, one person may be assigned to handle two or three of the positions shown separately on the chart.

The chart, then, functions to some extent like a safety net. As long as the work is proceeding smoothly it is not necessary. If a property cannot be found during a performance, the crew member who is laying out the properties, or the actor who must use it, knows exactly whom to consult: the property chief. If an actor faints back stage just before the rise of the curtain, not only the cast but every member of the production staff knows who has authority to handle the crisis, to order the curtain delayed and to make any other necessary decisions: the stage manager.

For all its paradoxes, theatrical procedures meet the test of practicality. They combine clarity with flexibility, responsibility with independence, and they make possible the highest degree of efficiency and achievement of which the actors and staff are capable.

The Director as Executive

It is clear from the preceding discussion that a director must have outstanding executive ability. He must be able to see the work of the theater in the large, in terms of broad philosophy and purpose; at the same time he must understand clearly the relationship of each detail to the pattern as a whole. He must have the ability to work realistically with the conditions, restrictions, and particular personnel available to him: he must be intensely practical. He must be able to make detailed plans and schedules that will result in the efficient progress of the work toward completion within the deadlines that have been set for him. And he must be able to work smoothly with a variety of specialists, many of them highly expert, each with his own interests and attitudes, and nearly all of whom display the intensity—and potential explosiveness—that characterizes artists. He must be able to assess precisely when they need guidance, and how much, but also when they should be allowed to work independently.

It may seem too much to expect that any one person would display all of those characteristics; but administrative skill is only one of the abilities necessary for theatrical direction, and it is perhaps the least difficult.

The Director as Teacher

The director must also be a teacher. His educational work is largely confined to training actors, with whom he spends a large part of his work time in rehearsal (from a third to two-thirds of the entire time he devotes to a play). His work with them is more clearly visible to the audience than any of the other work he does, and has more influence on the success or failure of the productions.

It is assumed that the other artists and technical workers (at least at the supervisory levels) will already be skilled, and in fact, they are likely to be more skilled in their areas of specialization than the director himself. For example, his set designer will know more about designing scenery than the director; the construction supervisor should have command of the techniques of building the scenery, so that the director need not have mastered them; the director is not handicapped by being unable to repair electrical equipment, so long as his lighting crew has the necessary skills. Even with the technical staff, the director may occasionally engage in incidental teaching, and his ability as educator may be significant in his relations with his administrative superiors, with the community in which his theater operates, and with his audiences.

EMPATHY AND THE DIRECTOR

In his functions as executive, teacher, and artist, the director especially needs one quality of mind and personality: the ability to understand the thinking of other people, to look at things from their points of view. That quality, which is called *empathy*, is characteristic of all artists, but it tends to be especially characteristic of theater artists; and of all theater artists, the director must develop it most fully.

Since the foundation, the framework, the skeleton of a play is the script, the director can function effectively only if he is able to sense the playwright's viewpoint, to see life from his special angle: that is, he must empathize with the playwright. And since the play involves the experiences of its characters and their reactions to those experiences, he must be able to empathize with the characters, even the unsympathetic ones.

The ultimate result of the entire process of theatrical production is to produce an experience for the audience. If the play is to be successful, the director must know how they will react to what is presented. He must know what will make them laugh, what will move them, what will attract their attention, what will interest them, what will be clear to them. The director must be able to empathize with his audience.

The director combines the involvement of the actor with the detachment of the spectator, the practicality of the performer with the critic's interest in the whole.

ERIC BENTLEY

But his ability to share other people's attitudes is most crucial during rehearsals. Each actor is unique, with his own set of experiences, skills, frustrations, and fears. All of those things in large part constitute the raw material out of which he creates his performance, and the director can train the actor only if he takes them into account. In an extreme degree an effective director must be able to empathize with his actors.

The Development of Skill

Administrator, teacher, artist, with an extraordinary ability to share others' experiences: the list seems to describe an unattainable ideal. Ideals, of course, are more often aimed at than reached. Probably no director in all the history of the theater has mastered all of the areas equally. From the discussion it is clear why truly great directors are so rare, and why this is perhaps the most difficult of all the positions on the theater staff.

A beginning director can expect to find that his skill is at a different level in each of these areas. Perhaps he has excellent taste as an artist, with a warm understanding of the actors' experiences, difficulties, and fears, but less ability in predicting audiences' reactions. He may flounder as a teacher, not because he cannot understand the actors' problems, but because he cannot put them into words that the actors find meaningful. As an administrator, he may have great difficulty in scheduling the work effectively. He may find that he is attacking his tasks in the wrong order, or that he schedules too little time for one part of the work and too much for another. A second director, of course, might display another pattern of skills.

But even though the description of an ideal director makes the work seem extremely difficult, it should also suggest one optimistic conclusion. It is clear that in each of the four areas (and particularly the first three) improvement is possible. Simply to be aware of what is needed will help the director function more effectively. And the description of the ideal should assist in a director's continued growth throughout his career.

After each production it is suggested that he sit down and think over his work in the light of the four-sectioned ideal. The first step consists of ranking his performance in the four areas: in which was he most effective? in which least effective?

Then each area should be analyzed separately. Most importantly, he should attempt to identify his moments of success and try to determine what made them successful. Only slightly less importantly, he should note his failures, the moments when things went wrong, and then try to find other techniques that might have produced success.

The conclusions reached through such analysis can be applied to his next directing assignment. Further experience may demonstrate that not all of his conclusions were correct: the techniques that seemed successful in the first production may fail in the second; the alternative techniques developed as substitutes for those which had been ineffective may themselves prove ineffective. If the analysis is done carefully and objectively, however, the director's work on his second play is almost certain to show some improvement, and continued analysis and experiment will produce steady growth in effectiveness and skill.

Improvement in directorial skill can be accelerated by using two other sources of assistance to supplement the method of analysis and trial and error. The first is to take advantage of every opportunity to observe skilled directors at work, in particular directors who have varying methods. Experience as an actor will help expose the beginning director to a range of techniques, especially if he is able to work with several directors. Acting, however, tends to interfere with learning direction, since the actor must necessarily give his major attention to his role. Perhaps the ideal position from which to study the work of a director is that of assistant director. Almost equally effective is simply to attend the rehearsals as an observer. Many theaters have a policy of "closed rehearsals," from which casual visitors are barred. Even in such theaters, however, a serious student of directing is likely to be given permission to attend.

To benefit from such observation, the student must remain constantly alert; he must watch all that goes on with the greatest intensity and must subject it to constant analysis and evaluation. At every moment, he must ask: "What problem is the director concerned with? How would I handle it? How has he handled it? What specific techniques is he using? Which techniques are effective, and which seem not to produce the desired result? What other problems are present? Why has the director chosen to work on this particular problem at this moment and ignore the others?"

That kind of concentration is difficult to maintain; much of the work of rehearsal involves drudgery, and often progress seems very slow. The advantage of serving as assistant to the director, rather than as an observant visitor, is that the assistantship supplies him with responsibilities that keep the mind active without distracting his attention from the directorial process. To be maximally valuable, it is also necessary that a visitor attend every rehearsal. The month's work of training the actors is broken into short segments, usually three hours long, but the separate rehearsals are not discrete units. Often the instructions given to the actors at one rehearsal will not be carried out fully until a much later rehearsal. In fact, the pattern of direction, and of the actors' growth, may not be fully clear until the last week before the play opens. Often the director's work on Wednesday evening will be related to what occurred at the rehearsal on the previous Friday, or even earlier. Consequently, a visitor who skips a single rehearsal, even one at which very little progress seems to have occurred, may find it impossible to analyze the later rehearsal sessions and the methods of the director with complete accuracy.

The second supplement to the trial-and-error technique consists of a systematic study of the art of direction, as presented in a textbook and in a course in the art. No such study would produce much improvement by itself, but when used as the basis for planning practical direction and analyzing what has been done after the completion of a production, it is invaluable, and it can enormously speed up the rate of improvement in mastering the art of direction. It is the aim of this text to provide the materials for such a systematic study.

2/The Director as Artist

A director's work is even more diversified than was suggested in the previous chapter. During his month and a half of preparation and rehearsal, he engages in a number of activities of many different types. At one moment, he may be consulting with the scenic designer; at another, with the makeup designer; and throughout rehearsals, he will find himself closely involved in work with the actors. But all of his decisions are guided by the same purpose: the ultimate production of a work of art. In order to function effectively, then, a director must first develop the clearest possible understanding of the art of the theater and of his place in it.

This is also his most difficult task. Many of the greatest thinkers of history have struggled unsuccessfully to define the nature of art; many different theoretical analyses and formulations have been proposed, but they are bewilderingly contradictory. Even such apparently simple questions as "What is a tragedy?" have not been satisfactorily answered, although theoreticians have worked with them for over 2,500 years. Each director, then, must develop his own approach to art, basing it on all of the evidence now available, and each working hypothesis will differ somewhat from that sketched here. Following one path may help the student find his bearings and perhaps make it easier for him to mark out his own route, even if it should be a very different one.

DRAMA AS ART

The art of the theater is unique among the arts in its dependence on an audience. In other arts, an audience may be highly desirable, but it is not

17

necessary. If Robinson Crusoe had amused himself on his island by painting pictures, he might have become a very fine artist; and his effectiveness as a painter would have been the same even if Friday had never shown up and they had never been rescued. Emily Dickinson wrote poetry throughout her life, but she published almost nothing, and few of her poems were seen even by friends until they were discovered after her death. But the poems existed before publication, even before anyone but herself had read them; if they had been permanently lost, they would still once have existed complete, and her achievement as a poet would have been the same. A poem is a poem whether it is read by one person, or a million, or no one at all.

You need three things in the theatre—the play, the actors and the audience, and each must give something.

Kenneth Haigh

But in the theater, a play cannot exist without an audience. Drama involves communication as an essential element. A script unperformed is not a play—it is only a proposal or a blueprint from which a play might be constructed. If it has esthetic value in itself, it is as literature, not theater. But not even performance is enough to transform a script into drama. Actors often perform without an audience; if a count could be made, it is quite possible it would show that more performances are given without audiences than with them. But such a performance is not a play, it is a rehearsal. A short story is a short story, whether it is read or not, whether it is published or not; but a play is only a rehearsal until an audience has been assembled to watch it.

Not only is the presence of an audience essential to a play, the quality of the audience is a vital factor in the success of a play. In every theater, on every level from the smallest high school to Broadway, there is one question that is asked over and over again. An actor has just exited from the stage, early in the play; another actor, waiting backstage for his first entrance, whispers to him, "How's the audience?" The question is instantly understood; it is a request for information. The first actor typically stops and gives a report, which may be only a single word, but which both recognize as important: "Cold" or "Great" or "A little slow." So important is the audience that every actor who is past his first play quickly develops the habit of concentrating intensely throughout a performance on the responses of the audience, of interpreting them, and constantly, though subtly, adjusting his performance to them. This interaction between audience and actor is one of the distinctive characteristics of the legitimate stage, and a major source of its special excitement.

Drama is unique among the arts, not in having an audience, but in the degree to which it is audience-centered. It not only is designed to provide an experience for the audience, but it consists only in that experience: the only elements in drama are what the audience can see and hear.

THE EXPERIENCE OF THE AUDIENCE

The analysis of drama as an art must fundamentally be concerned with the experiences of the audiences in the theater, and the director's responsibilities can be described as the' identification of the particular experience that it is hoped will be created for the audience and the supervision of the work necessary to produce it.

> *Men who love humanity have all dreamed at least once during their lives of bringing all their fellow men together in a state of carefree happiness. And only the world of the theatre ever really succeeds in doing this. For a minute or perhaps two—and this is a long time—the theatre makes men better and happier on this earth. That is why I love the theatre.*
> JEAN-JACQUES GAUTIER

People attend the theater for a variety of reasons. A dramatic performance may distract the audience momentarily from the drabness or irritations of daily life (escapist drama). It may help them relieve emotional tensions—give them a hearty laugh or "a good cry." It may give them pleasant experiences, with charming music, colorful costumes, and delightful stories. All these are familiar to anyone connected with the theater.

DRAMA AS A PSYCHEDELIC EXPERIENCE

But other and more important values are possible. On the next higher level, drama is often, perhaps usually, what it is now fashionable to call "psychedelic"—enriching, mind-expanding. One of the startling experiences of working in the theater is the discovery of how much more vivid ordinary objects and actions seem when placed on stage. It is interesting to watch the process called "setting lights." The lighting designer typically sits in the center of the darkened auditorium, while the members of his crew adjust one spotlight after another. At first no meaning or pattern will be visible, but as the session continues, more and more lights are focused on the stage, colored by gelatine filters, forming an integrated pattern. As a final test, the designer will ask one of the technicians to take up various positions on the stage, to stand in a doorway, to sit in one of the chairs, so that the effect of the light falling on an actor can be estimated. At that moment something unexpected happens. The technician, sitting casually in a chair, perhaps turning his head mechanically in different directions as instructed by the designer, suddenly takes on a vividness that he had not had before. The distractions of the auditorium itself are removed by the fact that it is in darkness; the attention of a visitor is powerfully attracted to the stage itself and to the person sitting there. The brilliance of the stage lighting intensifies the drab colors of his work clothes. So vibrant is this effect that it operates even with ordinary objects. A ladder, left accidentally in the middle of the stage, takes on a special quality under the lights; its neutral color becomes a pattern made up of strips of warm, bright gold where the lights catch the tops of the steps, and strips of velvet darkness where shadows are cast.

> *I love acting. It is so much more real than life.*
> OSCAR WILDE

That intensification of experience operates still more fully when what appears on stage is not random or esthetically meaningless, but has been carefully selected and designed for maximum effect: when the furniture is not an accidental ladder but has been selected to fit into the pattern of the play, when the people on stage are actors engaged in communicative actions and costumed to support the mood of the play. People are often surprised to discover how ordinary and unimpressive stage properties seem offstage in the light of day; how quiet and unassuming actors appear who had seemed so striking on stage. The difference between the theatrical experience and the ordinary experience is a measure of the special intensification, the psychedelic effect, that characterizes all the arts, and the theater more than any other. All of the technical aspects of production assist the director in achieving this intensification of experience—lighting, costumes, even the architectural definition of the acting area. Nevertheless, in working with his actors the director needs to be constantly aware of the necessity of raising speech and action from the relatively low-keyed and understated level of ordinary life to the intensity that is an essential part of the art of the theater.

EXTENDING EXPERIENCE

But beyond the intensification of ordinary sensation, the theater expands awareness in another way: it provides the audience with experiences that they could not have as part of their ordinary life. The importance of empathy for the director has already been mentioned, but it is not restricted to the director; set designers, costume designers, sound men, actors—all theater workers must use empathy as a fundamental part of their resources. It is, in fact, so central to drama that, with a very few possible exceptions, it is a very large element in the experience of all audiences. They do not simply observe the actions and emotions of the play, they share them, so that the events presented become part of their own experience.

What was it like to be a teen-age girl, hiding from the Nazis in an attic in Denmark, during the second world war? What is the experience of a child who is deaf and blind on learning her first word? How would it feel to be pushed by unexpected cruelty and contempt, by the discovery of one's own defects, to the edge of madness and beyond? Few people can, or would want to, go through those experiences in ordinary life, but the theater offers them an opportunity to share them safely, by attending performances of *The Diary of Anne Frank, The Miracle Worker,* and *King Lear.*

> *When I buy a ticket to the theater I make a contract to leap the gulf of unreality and join the company in creating a greater reality. Therein lies the magical lure of the theater for playwrights as well as audiences. A great play can make the incredible seem credible. It can stimulate the mind, touch the heart and comfort the soul. A great drama is not only a mirror of life—it magnifies the human spirit.*
>
> RICHARD RODGERS

The simple intensification of sensory experience may be exciting and satisfying. The extension of general experience satisfies a deeper need, the universal curiosity about life, the desire to live as fully and broadly as possible. In addition, it enlarges human sympathy, increases the ability to empathize, which is not only immediately enriching, but which may even affect behavior outside the theater, long after a performance has finished—and almost certainly for the better.

DRAMA AS AN INTELLECTUAL EXPERIENCE

Much drama also operates in a third area, which is at least as important: the area of intellect. Some years ago, psychologists engaged in a kind of game of trying to list all of the "basic motivations" of people, such as food, security, approval, and sex. But at least one item seems never to have appeared on the lists, although it is surely one of the strongest of human drives: the desire to

> *The highest moral purpose aimed at in the highest species of the drama is the teaching the human heart, through its sympathies and antipathies, the knowledge of itself.*
>
> PERCY BYSSHE SHELLEY

understand—to understand ourselves, to understand each other, to understand life itself, to understand the universe and our place in it.

It is interesting to read a twenty-year-old newspaper, perhaps found at the bottom of an old trunk. Here is a segment of life: one day's events, selected for their interest and importance. And yet they seem to have no significance at all once their context has been forgotten. Some politician made a trip; another made a speech; a search was on for a missing child; women's hemlines were higher— or lower; there was some possibility of tornadoes later in the week. The items are unrelated, except by the accident of time; what caused various events, or what results they later produced, it is impossible to guess. What is presented is chaotic and essentially meaningless; only if we could unearth the earlier and later newspaper accounts could we hope to make any kind of sense of the reports, to find the other events that were meaningfully related.

Life hurries by, but the stage offers us the privilege of seeing it a second time and at one remove.

ERIC BENTLEY

Yet life is lived in even smaller units, a fraction of a second at a time. In a famous incident, a scientific law suddenly became clear to a researcher while he was riding through London on the open top deck of a bus. A melody he had been trying to write flashed into Noel Coward's mind while he was in a taxi, stalled in a traffic tangle in New York City. The scientist's discovery had no meaningful connection with the fact that he happened to be at the top of a bus; it was related to all of the research which he had done before, at moments widely separated in time. An understanding of how to write popular songs would not be furthered by an attempt to relate composition to taxis or traffic jams. To find significant correlations with Coward's development of his melody in a New York street, it would be necessary to ignore many of his activities that were closely associated with it in time—a thousand random experiences— and to analyze what had happened to him at widely varying times and in far countries: his long experience in the theater, the many musical comedies that he had composed, events that had occurred in his childhood.

Ordinary people, not scientists or artists, pass through a sequence of experiences each day at least as bewildering, unpatterned, chaotic, and apparently meaningless. What happens at three o'clock Tuesday afternoon may be almost unrelated to what happened at two. The decisions made Wednesday morning may depend on experiences that were analyzed and stored in the mind twenty years before.

Each life, then, tends to be lived close up, from a point where "you can't see the woods for the trees." One of the commonest of human feelings is a strong need to trace relationships among experiences that will be more valuable than the coincidences of time and place, to discover and mark whatever rationality and meaning it is possible to find in life.

> *Life is terribly deficient in form. Its catastrophes happen in the wrong way and to the wrong people. There is a grotesque horror about its comedies, and its tragedies seem to culminate in farce.*
>
> OSCAR WILDE

Works of art, however much they differ, generally share this characteristic of greater clarity, greater unity, and often greater significance than comparable sections of ordinary experience. It is seldom possible to point to any two-hour period in life in which experiences have occurred that are rounded, harmonious, clear, and meaningful, yet those characteristics are typical of drama. Even if such a period could be identified in ordinary experience, it would be likely to be only the climax or last step in a sequence, the full meaning of which would become apparent only if previous events were studied, extending over a long period of time. In the theater, human experience is reworked so that a complete pattern is introduced, developed, and analyzed within a single two-hour period.

ACHIEVING SIGNIFICANCE

Two methods are available to the theater artist for achieving this greater clarity and significance. The first is selection. Out of all of the varied experiences of life, the playwright chooses only those that have a part in the pattern he is trying to communicate to the audience. In a neglected and overgrown garden, the outlines of the flowerbeds, the locations of the paths may all still be present, but detectable only from a distance, or by patiently checking each weed and flower, each stone and fallen leaf. The playwright clears out the overgrowth, sweeping up the leaves and twigs that have fallen at random across the paths, clearing out the weeds, and revealing the hidden pattern, so that it is possible even for a casual visitor to see that one flower bed repeats the shape of another on the other side of the garden, and that all of the paths join in the center.

All of the trivia of life are cleared away, unless they are themselves part of the pattern with which the playwright is concerned. Selection alone, emphasizing the essentials by pruning away the accidental foliage, may produce so much greater clarity and meaning that the material retained acquires the status of art without further alteration.

But typically the playwright subjects his materials to a further step. This consists of an analysis of the relationships to be found in them. In what way is one incident in a character's life related to another? What experiences lead to the development of cruelty in a human being, what to kindness and sweetness? What are the effects of being insulted, of being spit upon, as Shylock was by Antonio?

Genius is a perception of the obvious which nobody else sees.
ANONYMOUS

A great artist analyzes the interrelationships among experiences, seeking relationships that are so subtle, so separated in time and space, or so familiar that others have missed them precisely because they are so obvious.

Magicians report that it is much more difficult to fool an audience of children than an adult audience. Adults have been trained to follow directions —to look at the right hand rather than the left, to imagine that they have seen all sides of a box when in fact they have been shown half the sides twice; to a great extent, magic consists of giving the audience the wrong directions, in confidence that they will follow instructions. But children have not yet learned to follow such orders. The magician may point significantly to his breast pocket; never mind that, each child instead watches his left hand, where the glass ball was last seen, and consequently they see him slip it into his side pocket.

A special characteristic of the great artist is that he typically does not follow orders; he has for some reason not been brainwashed. He asks the questions "What?" and "Why?" when no one but a child would ask them, because everyone else has been trained to assume that he already knows; he is not afraid of the obvious. He retains the directness and clarity of vision of a child, although he combines it with the larger fund of experience and the analytical ability of a thoughtful adult.

HUMAN VALUES IN ART

But the intensification of experience and its clarification through selection and analysis are not the only resources of the artist; at least one important one remains.

Each artist has an individual viewpoint, a particular set of standards and values. His analysis of life is seldom simply objective; at the most significant level, he not only analyzes, he evaluates. He asks himself: "What is good about life, or about this segment of life that I am studying?" "What is wrong with life?" "How might it have been handled so that it would have been better?" Simply to ask those questions is of significance, and may on occasion require

> *Art is the controlled structuring of a medium or a material to communicate as vividly and movingly as possible the artist's personal vision of experience.*
>
> *This definition, be it noted, allows for weak art or for great art, depending on the skill or stature of the artist. It does not allow any place for the random or totally unstructured. The key words are "controlled structuring." Experience, emotion, communication are all ingredients, but all are insufficient without the controlling mind which, alone, is capable of producing art.*
>
> SYLVIA ANGUS

great courage, but sometimes the artist provides answers as well. "This is the way life is," he may say early in his play, and "This is the way it ought to be" before the play is over.

How much effect have artists' prescriptions for the ills of life had? Have audiences ever found lessons in the drama that they could put to use in their lives outside the theater? Arguments over that question have been going on for centuries, and in numbers and brilliance the advocates of the two sides seem almost equally balanced. Plautus, long before the birth of Jesus, remarked that he had often heard the Roman audiences enthusiastically applaud noble sentiments expressed from the stage by actors in plays, but he noticed that as soon as they left the theater they reverted to their customary scoundrelly ways.

> *But the past is of no importance. The present is of no importance. It is with the future that we have to deal. For the past is what men should not have been. The present is what men ought not to be. The future is what artists are.*
>
> OSCAR WILDE

On the other hand, it has been argued by distinguished critics that the works of Henrik Ibsen have discernibly transformed human society. Ibsen had been subjected to neglect and cruelty as a child, or at least he thought he had. When he became a playwright, he took a long look at human relationships, especially within the family and in small towns, and when he wrote his startling study of what was wrong with marriage, *A Doll's House,* the audience felt as though a bomb had been exploded in the theater. One critic remarked that when the heroine, Nora, walked out of her house at the end of the play, and slammed the door, the sound echoed in every home in Europe. It has even been claimed that family relationships throughout the western world, in America as well as Europe, were changed by Ibsen's dramatic studies, that many social changes which have taken place during the last thirty years of

> *A lively and lasting sense of filial duty is more effectively impressed on the mind of a son or daughter by reading* King Lear *than by all the dry volumes of ethics and divinity that were ever written.*
>
> THOMAS JEFFERSON

the present century resulted indirectly from Ibsen. These claims seem extravagant to some, but the fact that they can be made at all demonstrates that the theater is at least potentially a social force which must be taken seriously. Certainly, Ibsen was the idol of the young during his own time, and his plays formed the basis for the nineteenth-century version of the perennial demand that the world be made better. His play *Ghosts* became a symbol of youth in revolt and was presented as the first play in a number of new theaters that sprang up throughout Europe, most of them given the same defiant name, "Free Theater."

The theater artist, then, uses the experiences of ordinary life as his raw material. He may handle it in various ways. Basic to any treatment is selection; a two-hour section cut from life at random might or might not have interest, but it would be no work of art at all. But beyond selection, the artist may simply vivify and intensify his material. He may subject it to careful analysis, so as to find meaningful relationships in it. He may evaluate it and present his judgments for the consideration of the audience. Or he may rework it in harmony with his own scheme of values, as a demonstration of how life itself might be improved.

THE FUNCTIONS OF DRAMA

Stated more briefly, the functions of drama can be summarized as follows:
1. To entertain (here is a two-hour section of life to enjoy).
2. To inform (here is a two-hour presentation which will show you more clearly what life is really like).
3. To stimulate evaluation (here, in two hours, is a picture of life; what do you think of it?).
4. To persuade (this is what life might be if only we would handle it better). Often this may be presented negatively (this is what we are doing with life, and this is what will happen if we don't stop it.)

Fine drama can be produced at all of those levels. For example, Shakespeare's *The Merry Wives of Windsor*, Molière's *The Doctor in Spite of Himself*, and Mary Chase's *Harvey* seem primarily intended to entertain. Ibsen's *Hedda Gabler*, a study in idiosyncratic neurosis, serves both of the first two purposes listed; although far from pleasant, it is an absorbing, fascinating,

> *The purpose of playing, both at the first and now, was and is to hold as 't were the mirror up to nature; to show virtue her own feature, scorn her own image, and the very age and body of the time his form and pressure.*
>
> SHAKESPEARE

unforgettable theatrical experience. While it may seem to offer little that is applicable to our own lives, it says very clearly, "Here is one type of person; this is what she was like." It seems that a whole civilization is frozen in some of Chekhov's plays, as if a single frame had been printed from a movie film taken with a wide-angle lens. Around the turn of the century, a school of playwrights advocated presenting on the stage "slices of life," in a style that they called "realism," designed to show life as it actually is, primarily aimed at portraying the audience themselves—or their neighbors. Shakespeare's history plays are informative as well as entertaining, and his two supreme love dramas, *Romeo and Juliet* and *Antony and Cleopatra,* seem intended both to interest the audience and to say to them, "This is what love is like—for the young and for the old."

> *Poetry is man's rebellion against being what he is.*
>
> JAMES BRANCH CABELL

Thousands of plays, while entertaining and informing, also invite the audience's evaluation of what is presented. Plautus's *Truculentus* is a picture of slavery at its worst in Roman times. He is not only saying "This is how it is," but also, by clear implication, "What do you think of it?" Brecht's plays, for example *The Good Woman of Setzuan,* raise disturbing questions. Euripides' play *The Trojan Women* seems to say, "You think war is glory and bluster and victories? Well, here's what it really is—suffering for women and children; and you've got to change it, or live with it." Albee's *Who's Afraid of Virginia Woolf?* presents an equally vivid picture of a private hell, with no apparent solution, but with an open invitation to the audience to analyze it for themselves.

And finally, innumerable plays, such as Shaw's *Mrs. Warren's Profession, Pygmalion,* and *Back to Methuselah,* express the dramatists' ideas not only of what is wrong with the world, but what might be done about it. Aeschylus's masterpiece, *The Oresteia,* is clearly designed to persuade the audience to accept his views about crime and punishment; several of Aristophanes' plays are arguments against the war in which Greece was then engaged; nearly all of Euripides' plays are persuasive, and it is at least arguable that those of

> *We spend our days, each of us, in looking for the secret of life. Well, the secret of life is in art.*
>
> Oscar Wilde

> *An actor is a public instructor.*
>
> Euripides

Sophocles are also. The liturgical drama of the Middle Ages was strongly didactic, as well as such secular plays as *Everyman*. It has been the fashion in recent years to attack didacticism, but this persuasive element appears almost as strongly in recent drama as in classic. *A Man for All Seasons* clearly presents conflicting philosophies, one of which we are asked to admire and presumably to adopt as our own.

The examples cited suggest that although a playwright may stop at any level as he moves down the list, he is unlikely to skip items. All plays must entertain, in the sense of providing the audience with an interesting experience that will hold their attention. A play may in addition communicate significant information about life, or it may go further and invite the audience to evaluate the aspects of life that the playwright has chosen to present. But no play can successfully present a philosophy or persuade the audience to adopt a new view of life unless it also entertains, informs, and stimulates evaluation.

The Reduction of Intellect

In recent decades there has been some tendency to reduce the intellectual content of the arts. Beginning in painting, this reduction has affected sculpture, music, and other arts; the drama was the last to be influenced. The effect of the movement has been to remove subject matter, so that paintings and sculptures are produced that are not representations of anything, but simply manipulate the various characteristics of the materials. In drama, the result was a reduction in plot, the suppression of logical sequences and analyses, and the disappearance of didacticism. At its extreme, plays were written with long passages without denotation, as for example Lucky's nonsense speech in *Waiting for Godot,* and *The Bald Soprano,* which ends with a quarrel in which the actors, instead of insulting each other with meaningful words, scream the letters of the alphabet. The name of this play itself is nonsense, being a record of a slip of the tongue made by one of the actors during rehearsal.

Since intellect is an important element in life, and traditionally an important factor in art, the omission created new problems, while avoiding some old ones. To hold the attention of an audience for a full evening, without

> *To leave out the intellect, the element of thought, is to deprive oneself of a great part of human awareness.*
>
> ERIC BENTLEY

the support of intellect, requires that the playwright be almost superhumanly inventive, and all "absurdist" drama tends to create an impression of thinness, especially when the scripts are read silently; these plays have been most successful when they were presented by virtuoso actors who could supplement the weakness of the scripts with their vividness of personality and inventiveness of business. Even such a delightful play as *The Bald Soprano* seems somehow wearisome, although it is too uniformly charming to want to cut any of it.

In the past, plays which have attempted only to entertain have depended heavily on plot, on brightly posteresque characterization, and on a variety of familiar theatrical devices, including suspense, to sustain interest. The type of performance which is currently called a "happening" dispenses with most of those supports, and relies primarily on sensory variety and intensity, surprise, and shock. All of the elements are intensified as far as possible: music is electronically amplified to the upper limit of endurance, lighting effects are exaggerated, with changes in lighting emphasized and contrasts made extreme, and elements of shock have been exploited as far as imagination could invent: nudity, taboo words, and simulations of sexual behavior of various kinds have been employed, *Macbeth* has been turned into a *drame à clef,* and symbols which have been commonly respected have been ridiculed (even Mom and apple pie).

Many viewers have found such performances exhilarating, but as one contemporary playwright has remarked, it is very difficult to sustain such material at a pitch of intensity necessary for maintaining interest and persuading people to come to a series of productions. Once you have presented an actor in the nude, he said, what do you do for his next entrance?

Of all effects in the theater, nothing is easier to achieve than a moment of meaningless shock and sensory intensity, and nothing is more difficult to maintain throughout an evening, much more throughout a series of productions. In spite of the best efforts of theater artists, such performances keep slipping into sense. It is at least possible to argue that *The Bald Soprano, Waiting for Godot,* and *The Chairs* are as ordinarily didactic as Thornton Wilder's *Our Town* or *Everyman,* and that their "absurdity" is simply a stylistic veneer, used, as in Wilder's *The Skin of Our Teeth,* to conceal a message which otherwise would be either too obvious or too trivial to justify buying a ticket to hear. In fact many viewers of happenings and such productions as *Hair* express their reactions to them by reporting that they experienced feelings of excitement, of liberation, of release from the drabness and stifling restrictions of ordinary life; that they were filled with an enthusiastic sense of the vividness with which life might be lived, at its best. And with those reactions, we have returned precisely to item four on our list above, and the aggressively plotless, subjectless, purely sensory theatricality has suddenly become the didactic.

Absurdist drama has already faded, and plays like *Hair* have come to seem almost conservative. The absurdist reminder that much of life is absurd, and the demonstration by more recent plays of the level of excitement that it is possible to reach are valuable indeed—and both are didactic ideas of the most traditional type, and ideas which have been expressed by other plays in other times, even though any new and fresh expression is welcome.

PATTERN IN DRAMA

The widespread delight in pattern is of special significance in drama. Man is a pattern-making creature, who takes pleasure in organization for its own sake. An ancient Greek remarked that even kitchen utensils had a kind of beauty when they were neatly arranged, hanging on the wall in a series according to their sizes.

> *The random, the formless, is basically impossible and uninteresting to man, who is, willy-nilly, a pattern-making animal. Given a blank wall, man will form its cracks into a design. Set down in chaos, man will separate the whirling from the stationary, for chaos and meaninglessness, as the existentialists have discovered, are the hardest of all things for man to endure.*
> SYLVIA ANGUS

This delight in pattern was a major source of effectiveness in the "well-made" plays of the nineteenth century, such as those of Feydeau and Henry Arthur Jones; it was standard in the construction of plots in the late nineteenth-century melodramas, and it dominated the western movies of the thirties and forties, as it still dominates many of the comedy and dramatic series on television. The desire for the discovery of meaning and the related pleasure in pattern, unity and balance are so strong that this element alone will do much to strengthen a play. This factor can be used to support plays aimed primarily at other values.

A director who intends to base a performance on a script that is intended only to entertain must work within severe restrictions. Noel Coward's *Blithe Spirit*, for example, is not a great play, and the script is not an unusually rich one. To direct it effectively requires assembling a cast of actors of more than ordinary skill, and the director must use all of his ingenuity to enrich the script with as much variety of interpretation, as much imaginative business, and as much verve and style as he can supply or elicit from his cast and staff.

If the playwright has constructed a weaker plot or written an essentially plotless play; if the characters are less vivid, less varied, and less interesting; if the dialogue lacks brilliance; then a still greater burden will be placed on the director's ability and inventiveness, and the ingenuity of the staff—set designer, costumer, lighting and sound crews—must be utilized to the full.

A stronger script, and particularly one that serves more of the four dramatic functions listed, will present somewhat different problems; but on the whole, the stronger the script, the lighter the burden that must be assumed by the director in order to achieve an acceptable production.

Throughout the long history of the theater probably more plays have aimed at all four of the goals listed than have attempted to serve three or two or only the first; certainly that is true of the great masterpieces that form the richest section of the available scripts. The primary concern of playwrights operating on the broadest scale is the discovery, through observation and

> *The most important thing in a work of art is that it should have a kind of focus; that is, there should be some place where all the rays meet or from which they issue.*
>
> LEO TOLSTOY

analysis, of a pattern of meaningful relationships in the tangle and apparent chaos of experience. Once he has cleared away the accidental, the trivial, and the irrelevant, the artist hopes to demonstrate a unifying pattern that will serve as a kind of skeletal organization among the related data. In order to achieve status as a work of art, then, the final production must show a central unity, to which each detail is related, and the closer that goal is approached, the more clearly unified the play is, the higher is its status as a work of art.

UNITY AND VARIETY

Such unity, if it is to be valuable, depends on close observation and painstaking analysis, both difficult activities. A great writer, in selecting the aspects of experience that he will use in constructing his play, chooses on the basis of significance: he retains the relevant and important, and discards the trivial. It is possible, however, to achieve an impression of unity by either of two devices that avoid the difficulties of the legitimate method. One involves developing a preconceived pattern, which is then imposed on the material. A writer may select not on the basis of significance, but rather what will support his previously defined pattern; what he discards is not simply the trivial or the irrelevant, but whatever contradicts his preconceptions.

The identifying mark of such drama is that the philosophical or ethical proposals it makes are spurious; when they are tested against the experiences of life, the evidence contradicts them. Such identification, of course, depends on the ability of the critic to read the evidence with accuracy; if he happens to share the spurious philosophy of the playwright, the false philosophy will seem real. The melodramas of the nineteenth century form a large group of such plays. They expressed a highly simplified view of life that was false; even a brief comparison with ordinary experience demonstrates that life does not operate in harmony with the picture presented in the plays. Even while they were popular, their spuriousness was obvious to anyone who looked at them with clarity and objectivity (Bernard Shaw and Oscar Wilde, for example). And yet to many of the audience, who did not do such checking, they seemed profound and accurate analyses of life; they were praised again and again for their "truth."

The second unsatisfactory method of achieving unity is to narrow the scope of the work of art so extremely that there is little left to unify. Obviously, the broader the area of experience the artist chooses to deal with, the more difficult it is to trace its underlying pattern. As an analogy with the art of architecture, to organize the space in a small closet is so easy that few people would regard planning a closet as lying within the field of art at all; but to organize the space to be included in a large and complex building is regularly recognized as an artistic achievement.

We see now and again in the theatre great decor, great acting, great drama, but only two or three times in our lives do we see a quality expressed down to the last element in the theatre art, a perfect unity in idea, plot, and every other medium of theatrical expression, the music, the setting, makeups, costumes, voice, gesture, and group movement. Such completeness, such unity in essence and form, is the living principle in every work of art, the supreme soul and test of it, first and last.

STARK YOUNG

A legitimate work of dramatic art, then, must display a central unity: without that it is not a work of art at all. The unity must be derived from the areas of life with which the playwright is concerned; if it is externally imposed on them, and then life twisted to fit the imposition, the result is not art but *kitsch*—something which displays the surface manner of art, but without its substance. And if the work of art is to have importance, it must deal with an area of life of significant breadth.

The larger the area encompassed in a work of art, the greater the variety of elements included in it. This analysis, then, leads us back to the familiar formula: a work of art must display both unity and variety, and the greater the unity and the greater the variety, the greater the stature of the work of art.

No method has been devised by which unity or variety can be expressed in mathematical terms. And individual critics differ on the importance of the two factors; such differences cannot at present be resolved. A critic who values unity highly will admire such plays as Racine's, which are highly unified but restricted in scope. A critic who places a higher value on variety will prefer the plays of Shakespeare, which are somewhat less unified than Racine's but which are so much broader in scope that they seem like large mural paintings as compared with Racine's delicately carved cameos. Shakespeare's *Comedy of Errors* is a reworking of Plautus's *Menaechmi;* a comparison of the two plays would be interesting in this connection. Both have essentially the same characters and plot, but one of the significant differences is the greater complexity and variety of Shakespeare's version. In this case, some critics prefer one play, some prefer the other, and the choice seems to depend primarily on each critic's preference for unity or variety.

As has been seen, the conditions of theatrical production tend to provide variety in abundance, although of course the number of elements varies greatly from play to play; Shakespeare's plays are bewilderingly rich in variety, Chekhov's are less varied, and with such plays as *Waiting for Godot* and *The Chairs,* the director may well find that he must devote a considerable part of his attention to supplementing the bareness of the scripts with a variety of business and interpretation.

Drama as a Composite Art

The theater is a composite art to which almost all other arts contribute. It seems impossible to find a recognized art that does not play some part in theatrical production. Some of the arts are used only very incidentally in the theater; other arts, however, and some of the most important, reach their highest pitch of achievement there. The speech arts fuse in the theater at their highest esthetic level; dance, music, decorative design are fundamental in good theater.

In his capacity as artist, the director will make use of all of the sources of variety that are available to him, including the script itself, the contributions made by the other arts to the theater, and the abilities and resources of his cast and staff. His primary concern, however, will be with unity: defining the central theme or pattern that has been developed by the playwright and controlling the other elements of production so that they harmonize to form a single esthetic effect. Unity cannot be effectively achieved by committee; it must be the work of a single mind. In order to facilitate that achievement, theater artists in the nineteenth century created the position of director and placed it at the head of the chart of theater organization.

The essence of artistic effect is unity.
OSCAR WILDE

2

*The Design
of the Production*

3/Analysis of the Script

The standard directorial procedure is to start with the script as the basis for planning. The director's first task is to study the script closely and repeatedly, to make himself an expert in the script; only then can his own work begin, and only then can he make effective suggestions to his technical staff.

> The dramatist not only charts out a plan of procedure, he conceives and realizes a work of art which is already complete—except for technical reproduction—in his head, and which expresses by verbal image and concept a certain attitude to life.
>
> ERIC BENTLEY

Actors, technical staff, and playscript constitute the resources out of which the director must build his production. He is concerned with how to make the most of all of them and how to fit them together into a harmonious whole. The script is the unifying element in this construction.

SCRIPT REVISION

The priority of the script in theatrical production rests on esthetic and practical bases; it does not presume that the script is flawless or cannot be improved. In probably more than half of theatrical productions, the scripts are subjected to some cutting, rearrangement, or rewriting.

Such revisions raise delicate questions of ethics; what alterations are legitimate and acceptable and what are unethical has never been clearly defined. As a result, many experienced directors, and nearly all beginning directors, tend to feel an uneasy discomfort as they pick up their blue pencils and start to work on a play.

The clearest of the problems involved is the legal one. The author of a script subject to copyright restrictions has complete control of what is done with his play, a control that can be enforced by legal authority. Sometimes a notice is included at the beginning of each playbook indicating which types of revision are permissible and which are forbidden; of course, every ethical director will follow such restrictions to the letter.

Typically, directors are forbidden to change the title of a play, and they must include the name of the author in advertising and playbills. In addition, they are forbidden to revise whole scenes and to make even minor revisions that will change the theme, plot, or esthetic effect of the play; for instance, it would be unthinkable to rewrite the last act of *The Death of a Salesman* to save Willy Loman from his suicide attempt and provide a happy ending.

Even under the most stringent restrictions, however, certain alterations are nearly always considered permissible. For example, if the play calls for more actors than are actually available, it is acceptable to ask one or more actors to "double," that is, to play two parts each, if the action of the play allows. An actor who appeared as a butler in the first act might also, with alterations of costume and makeup, appear as a soldier in the last act. Sometimes, instead of doubling, one or more characters' speeches can be assigned to other actors. A drinking party takes place in Scene Three of the third act of Sheridan's *The School for Scandal;* five characters are specified by the script, Charles Surface, Sir Harry Bumper, Careless, and two unnamed characters identified as "1st and 2nd Gentlemen." In one production of the play, actors were not available for the two anonymous parts; instead, their speeches were divided among the other characters.

Occasionally, auditions may provide the director with an oversupply of women but a shortage of men; in that case it is often possible to assign minor men's parts to women: a butler is replaced by a maid, a clerk in a store scene appears as a woman instead of a man.

Two other types of alteration are usually felt to be acceptable, both designed to adapt a play to the special local conditions of production. If the script prescribes technical work or effects beyond the resources of the producing company, it is ethical to cut them or to make practical substitutions, so long as the esthetic intention and general effect of the play remain constant. If the script specifies five different settings, three of them representing different rooms in the same house, examination may reveal that the three scenes can all be placed in the same room, perhaps by changing a few words in the speeches that refer to the locale; sometimes such alteration can be made without any dialog revision at all. If the set crew can build three sets but not five in the time available for construction, such revision would seldom alter the play significantly and might make it possible to produce a play that would otherwise have to be dropped from the season's presentations.

And finally, plays written for one type of audience may be unsuitable for the audiences who patronize a particular theater. Local customs and attitudes may produce in the audience reactions to scatology, to sexual allusions, even to the simulated act of drinking that are very different from those of the audiences for whom the play was written. Of course, if such elements are esthetically significant they must be presented as written, or a substitute play must be chosen. If on-stage drinking happens to be tabooed in a particular theater, then *Harvey* cannot be presented. Often, however, such elements have no essential relevance to the central theme or intention of the play, but function simply as surface decoration. In that case, they can be cut or replaced without esthetic damage.

All theatrical decisions are difficult, and they can be made soundly only by exercising the greatest taste and judgment. Some of the scenes in *Romeo and Juliet* are intensely sexual; some of them are light-heartedly vulgar; to weaken any of them would be unthinkable. *Lysistrata* is one of the outstanding masterpieces of dramatic literature, a devastating attack on war, uproariously funny, and incorrigibly bawdy; to attempt to revise it so that it would be acceptable to everyone's maiden aunt would be to destroy it. It does not have to be presented, but if it is presented it must be played as written, with the bawdry emphasized, not glossed over—and let Aunt Eppie march angrily down the aisle in the middle of the first act if she must. Even the famous line in *Peter Pan*, which has become an improper joke never intended by Barrie, should not be cut. But to present *Peter Pan* in the nude is to fail in judgment and taste (that is not an invented example: one such production was actually performed). For a director to threaten to resign unless he is allowed to do Euripides' *Bacchae* with nude actors and thereby distract the audience from the play is to raise serious questions with regard to his good sense. Even though nudity was familiar on the Greek stage in Euripides' time, he intended *The Bacchae* to be presented by fully clothed actors, and until this decade it had always been so performed. For a director to threaten resignation when it is suggested that *Tobacco Road* is unsuited to his audience is to suggest a failure of taste on his part; *Tobacco Road* is not worth interrupting a career.

COPYRIGHT RESTRICTIONS

The copyright law is so complicated that its full implications have never been precisely defined. The essential fact for a director to remember is that an American playwright is legally given total control of what is done with his play for a period of fifty-six years, starting with the date of publication. When the copyright period has expired the play is said to be "in the public domain" and is no longer subject to the author's control. The same protection is provided for an adaptation or translation. Thus, a translation of Plautus's *Rudens* (*The Rope*) copyrighted in 1956 can be produced only by special arrangement with the owner of the copyright and is subject to whatever fees and restrictions he chooses to place on its use until the year 2012. The original play, however, was written before the beginning of the Christian era and is consequently in the public domain; it can be presented freely in the original Latin, or in a translation older than fifty-six years, without permission and without the payment of royalty. In the same way, if an adaptation of Shakespeare's Roman plays were made, selecting and combining passages from *Julius Caesar, Coriolanus,* and *Antony and Cleopatra* to form a new production, such an adaptation would be copyrightable and subject to the control of the adapter; the source plays, however, are in the public domain and can be presented freely without permission. (An unpublished play is subject to the author's control in perpetuity; the age of the play is not significant here; the author of an unpublished play has the same rights in it as the author of one which has been published, even though the manuscript play has not been registered for copyright.)

PLAYS IN THE PUBLIC DOMAIN

In the programs of theaters on all levels, from Broadway to high school stages, plays in the public domain bulk very large. Many plays in the early modern period and all of the plays of the premodern period are in the public domain; many theaters, perhaps most, present at least one play from this group each season. Such plays are free of legal restrictions; no director can be sued, however much he revises, rearranges, rewrites, mangles, or mistreats them.

Even with such plays, however, the director is bound by moral, ethical, and esthetic considerations. Certainly, simple honesty requires that productions be presented for what they are; if two plays of Plautus are combined to form a new dramatic work, it should be identified on the playbills and in advertising as "adapted by Abraham Sceparnio from Plautus's *Aulularia* and *Trinummus*"; the production should not be claimed to be "by Plautus."

A candid admission of the fact of adaptation, however, does not necessarily justify the action. When should a director revise a script, assuming that he has the legal right to do so?

If the prevailing technical or casting restrictions prevent presenting a play as written, and it can be adapted without serious damage so as to make it practicable, such adaptation is desirable. Plays of the ancient Greek and Elizabethan periods were written for theater structures very different from those of today. When Shakespeare had an actor refer to the theater as "this wooden O," the spectators could look around them and see an essentially circular structure that fitted the description. If the play is to be presented in a modern theater of different shape, it is at least defensible to cut or rewrite the line, which otherwise might seem meaningless. In Greek tragedy the performers were divided into two groups, the actors and a group called the chorus. The two groups were generally physically separated throughout most of the tragic performances (although they mingled freely in the comedies). Especially with a proscenium theater, but even to some extent on a thrust stage, clearly defined spaces are not provided which can be used by the two groups in the same way as in the ancient Theater of Dionysus. It is seldom possible to build a neoGreek theater for a production of one of the plays; if they are to be presented at all—and as one of the richest periods of our dramatic heritage they must be presented—then they must be revised, at least in the physical arrangement of the performers, and occasionally even in some of the speeches.

Even a totally accurate translation of a script may still distort the audience's experience. In Plautus's *Rudens,* the villain, who is perhaps in his fifties, tries to escape from a contract by telling the person with whom the contract had been arranged, "You'll have to prove that I'm over eighteen!" The point of the joke is that in ancient Rome contracts made by a minor under the age of eighteen were not enforceable. The Roman audience, looking at the villain's bald head and grey beard, and being familiar with the law, would have understood the joke immediately. In America, where the age of legal maturity is not eighteen but twenty-one, the figure must be changed.

Even with premodern plays written in English, topical allusions may need expansion for a modern audience. Scenes that once were delightful may now seem tasteless or tedious, and individual words may have changed meaning so as to make nonsense out of a line, or even to reverse its meaning. "Let" in Elizabethan times meant to stop or to prevent, not to allow, as it does now; "prevent" meant to go first, not to stop someone; "to ear" meant to plow, and "marry" was a swearword. Whether such words are to be translated from Elizabethan to modern English depends on the judgment and taste of the individual director; but even if they are retained as written, they must be given special treatment by the actor—they must be accompanied by illustrative gestures or must be specially pointed to make their meanings clear; they cannot be spoken casually, as they might have been for their contemporary audiences. In some sense, then, the production must be revised, not to alter the experience intended by the playwright, but to preserve it.

And finally, a director is justified in revising a script if he can improve it.

Some few directors seem to operate on the basis of an arrogant conviction that they are better playwrights, or at least play doctors, than anyone in the galaxy of great masters of the theater. Most directors are likely to display the opposite attitude—a respect for the playscript amounting to an excess of humility. The truth is, of course, that the quality of artistry among the plays produced, even excluding contemporary drama, varies over an extremely wide range, from masterworks to badly written claptrap. It might seem surprising that, with masterpieces available, plays of lower quality would ever be produced, but there are many reasons for presenting plays besides their esthetic quality. Some are of historical interest; some are presented as what has come to be called "camp"—their very defects make them amusing; some are played because they provide gratifying starring roles for actors; and some are simply good fun. One of the most engaging aspects of the theater is that it has room for all kinds of artistry, good, bad, solemn, funny, inspiring, and simply entertaining. Certainly, in a lifetime of play production, a director is likely to work with a number of plays where his critical sense is superior to the playwrights' and where judicious revision can produce clear improvement. Only a rash director would casually attempt to improve on Shakespeare at his best, or Sophocles, or Shaw; but a director who treated *Our American Cousin,* or *The Drunkard,* or the plays of Feydeau or Henry Arthur Jones with the same high respect would be displaying a deficiency of judgment or an excess of humility.

But plays written even by the masters of the theater vary greatly in quality; no artist works always at his highest pitch. A director who might properly hesitate to alter *Antony and Cleopatra,* or *Hamlet,* or *The Tempest,* might reasonably feel freer in working with *The Merry Wives of Windsor, The Taming of the Shrew,* or *Richard III.*

Even with a lesser playwright, a director is wise to revise only with great caution. No alterations should be made until the script has been studied in detail and the play analyzed as a whole, both in its original form and as revised, to make sure that it is actually better in the new version. The last and climactic speech of Oscar Wilde's *The Importance of Being Earnest* repeats the title of the play, which is given an ironic twist amounting to a pun; Jack turns to the others and says, "I've now realized for the first time in my life the vital Importance of Being Earnest." The director who cut that line from his production of the play had a legal right to do so (the play is in the public domain), but he was not showing good judgment. The university director who pulled a long speech out of the middle of Euripides' *Medea* and used it to open the play, although it was incomprehensible in the new context, and who crossed out the last line of the play, again a climactic line for which all of the rest of the play is a preparation, was not showing sound esthetic sense.

One particular type of questionable alteration of classic plays springs from the belief, perhaps subconscious, that well-known plays, however great, tend to lack interest for an audience. If they are to be presented, perhaps for reasons of prestige, some substitute must be provided—something for the audience to watch or listen to, something titillating and novel, that will occupy the attention long enough for the actors to grind out the too familiar lines. The distracting element most frequently chosen is anachronistic costuming; if *Hamlet* has finally run down, lost its steam, used up its supply of interest, then dress the actors in space suits, and hope that the novelty will keep the audience from paying too much attention to the threadbare script. Or use costumes in the style fashionable in the gay nineties, or the roaring twenties. Set *Macbeth* in the African jungle, and turn the weird sisters into witch doctors. Transfer *The Taming of the Shrew* to the American frontier in the early part of the last century and make a western out of it. Imagine that *King Lear* takes place not in the primitive past but in the future, following a world-wide nuclear war. An extreme example of that kind of treatment was the television production of *Twelfth Night* some years back, in which actors hung upside down from trees, had their noses tickled with straws, sat in wheel chairs pushed by actors dressed in monkey suits at top speed, careening in wild circles around the set.

> It was a great discovery for the mentally indigent that you can costume a Shakespeare play in any period. You choose the one that has not been chosen.
>
> ERIC BENTLEY

Such gimmicks are justified only if their addition to the play results in a better play than the one planned by the author; in none of the examples cited was that the case. A clue to the weakness of the costume-it-in-the-wrong-period treatment of drama is the ease with which it can be adopted. Sound art is the product of careful analysis, judgment, and selection—a laborious and often painful task. Easy tricks designed to revivify plays that are in no need of such assistance are worthless or destructive.

In summary, then, any handling of copyrighted plays must conform to the letter of whatever restrictions are set up by the playwright; scripts in the public domain are not subject to legal restrictions, but honesty requires that an adaptation be labeled for the audience for what it is, and esthetic standards suggest that revision be done only if the result is an improvement on the original, or if it is intended to fit it to local conditions and resources. Most often, when revisions seem desirable, they are undertaken by the director.

THE DIRECTOR'S SCRIPT READINGS

The script in its final form normally constitutes the working basis for the entire production. The first step in the preparation of the play consists of a detailed study of the script by the director. When he has mastered it as fully as possible, general plans and assignments are made in consultation with members of the production staff on the level immediately below the directorship, and the work of detailed planning and design is then begun by those staff members and by the director himself.

The director's first script reading is likely to be fast and general; he treats the play in about the same way as someone who was reading it simply for pleasure. From this reading he will learn the plot of the play, its mood and style, and the personalities of the characters.

His second reading will be somewhat more concentrated, and will be intended to define more precisely the various elements that go to make up the general impression he has received. This reading will attempt to answer a number of questions about the play.

What are the sources of interest in the play: plot? the personalities of the characters? verbal style? What is the range of all of the elements in the play: how varied are the characters? what range of emotion is presented? what is the range of tension or excitement in the play? What is the fundamental pattern of the play, emotionally, structurally, ideationally? What special problems does the play present: are there any especially difficult roles? can the sets be provided practically within the local limitations of manpower and facilities? are there any special technical problems?

The questions listed are illustrative, not exhaustive. The director, in fact, does not guide his study by such a list, externally imposed on the play; rather, he searches the script to determine what is there in order to fix in his mind as clearly as possible exactly what demands the play will make on the staff and what resources the playwright has provided with which the staff can work. These points are essentially technical; they assist in identifying the raw material out of which the play was constructed.

THE POINT OF VIEW OF THE PLAY

The playwright's philosophy, his values, his special point of view of life are basic, since the purpose of the selection and handling of his material is to express and support his conclusions about life. The coloring of the picture as a whole, as well as the interpretation of individual lines, depends on the director's identification of the playwright's special slant. A third study of the script should be carried through in order to define this fundamental factor.

Is *Waiting for Godot* an amusing collection of vaudeville turns, or is it a somber analysis of human frustration? Is *The Madwoman of Chaillot* a sober commentary on twentieth-century life, a crypto-fascist apology (as one critic has claimed), or a delightful fantasy about four charming lunatics?

The Merchant of Venice was apparently first understood as a bright comedy, with Shylock as a major comic figure; later it became the fashion to interpret him as a tragic character embedded in a romantic play with minor comic overtones. *Romeo and Juliet* was intended as a tragedy, although it is a very unusual one; at one time the last act was rewritten to provide a happy ending, and the play was performed for decades as a comedy.

Obviously, every decision made in preparing these or any other plays for production would depend on the director's interpretation of the philosophical implications of the script. It cannot be expected that different directors will always agree in their analyses, but each director must identify the point of view of his play as precisely and accurately as he possibly can, in order to make any decisions about how it is to be presented. If Shylock is comic, then the actor who plays the part should read his speeches in one way; if he is tragic, then the lines should be read differently; and of course it is always possible that he is both comic and tragic, like Falstaff, in which case they should be read in still another way.

The theme of the play is its major source of unity. Every play is made up of a multitude of different elements; if the script is a good one, they are all fitted together so that each forms an essential part of a single pattern. In some cases that pattern will be immediately clear; in others, tracing it may require close study. Usually it will be seen that a single idea or effect occupies a central position in the play, serving to organize all of the elements that combine in the total pattern. We have seen that plays may serve at least four different purposes, as indicated in the list given earlier. Usually the organizing center of the play will fit into the item that is farthest down on the list of purposes.

RECORDING THE THEME

When the director's organizational analysis of the play has been completed, he will find it helpful to record the basic theme in writing. His statement should be in the form of a single sentence, as short and clear as possible. A beginning director is likely to be disturbed by the baldness and apparent obviousness of such a statement. It is of course not a work of art itself, since it presents only the unifying element in the play and omits the elements of variety. Also, as has been remarked, to see the obvious clearly—what is so obvious that most people overlook it—is as much the mark of a great artist as to see relationships that are overlooked because they are subtle and obscure. Sometimes playwrights have left records identifying the fundamental themes of their plays, either in prefaces (Shaw) or in the notebooks used in working up the plays (Ibsen). Such statements may be helpful, but they must be used with caution; particularly in the case of preliminary notes, a playwright's thinking may change while he is working on his play, and early notes may not match the finished product.

A few examples of directors' statements of the themes of plays are given below, with some hesitation. Even though other directors might disagree with one or more of the analyses, at least they illustrate the type of conclusion at which a director should aim.

> Euripides' *The Bacchae*: Emotion and the irrational are powerful elements in life, and when they are too rigidly suppressed by decorum a tragic explosion results.
>
> Shaw's *Pygmalion*: Class distinctions are based on superficial differences.
>
> Shakespeare's *Twelfth Night*: Honest emotion, especially true love, is more powerful than fashionable affection.
>
> Maxwell Anderson's *Joan of Lorraine*: A too rigid devotion to principle is disastrous; even a saint must be prepared to compromise in small things.
>
> Ionesco's *The Bald Soprano*: Too often people talk but do not listen, so that real communication does not occur.
>
> Aeschylus's *The Oresteia*: An evil act is repaid by an evil act, which is then answered by a third; the continuing chain of evil can be broken only by the application of both justice and mercy.
>
> Ibsen's *Hedda Gabler*: The inability to feel emotion, or to empathize with the emotions of others, brings tragedy.
>
> Thornton Wilder's *The Skin of Our Teeth*: The human race has always been on the brink of disaster and has always escaped "by the skin of its teeth."
>
> Sheridan's *The School for Scandal*: Selfishness and a delight in the misfortunes of others, however fashionable they may be, are destructive of happiness, which can be achieved only through good will and true affection.
>
> Giraudoux's *The Madwoman of Chaillot*: The ruthlessness with which success is pursued has filled society with such evil that goodness is no longer to be found except among the unsuccessful and the insane.
>
> Arthur Miller's *The Death of a Salesman*: Every human being, however inept and unsuccessful, is important, and the courage that leads a man to push forward with the last ounce of his strength, in spite of fear and failure, ennobles him.
>
> Ibsen's *Ghosts*: The familiar falsehoods that society has woven into a code of conduct are tragically destructive, and must be replaced by truth and goodness before life can be made worth living.

The Meaning of the Lines

The director's fourth reading carries him to a still more specific level, at which he analyzes the meanings of the individual speeches. This study should begin at the simplest level, working out their obvious surface meanings. With a play from an earlier period (the Elizabethan, for example), the director must either have already mastered the dialect of the period or he must study with a good glossary at his elbow. But even with contemporary plays the meaning may not be so obvious as it seems. Figures of speech must be identified, and not interpreted literally; technical language must be analyzed: for a courtroom drama it may be necessary to look up legal terms in a dictionary.

THE PERSONALITIES OF THE CHARACTERS

Once the surface meaning of the lines has been determined, the director can turn his attention to a closer study of the personalities of the characters. Each script provides four sources of information about each character: what he says about himself, what other characters say about him, what he does, and how he reacts to what happens to him and what is said to him—what he notices and chooses to discuss, and what attitudes he displays toward it.

All of those elements are likely to be clearer than for real people in life outside the theater, since they have been especially selected and arranged by the playwright. In real life, people often reveal the most conflicting characteristics: a savage murderer may treat a wounded animal with the greatest tenderness; an excellent marriage counselor may be totally unable to solve his own marriage problems or to raise his own children well. Some of the same contradictions and complexities appear in drama; only in melodrama are characters painted with a single color, with heroines purely heroic and villains totally depraved, like Squire Cribbs in *The Drunkard,* who when encouraged to reform replies defiantly, "Never! I have lived a villain; a villain let me die!" The personality of any character in a play must display a central unity, but one that is broad enough and complex enough to make credible the full range of his actions in the play; if he is decisive in one scene and hesitant in the next, cruel at one moment and tender at another, his outline must be drawn large enough to include all of his various characteristics. One of the first things to look for, then, in working out the personality of one of the characters in a play is the range of attitudes, emotions, and actions that he displays during the progress of the story.

Every statement made by a character, or about him by other characters, must be examined for its accuracy. Not only may he be misinformed (the letter Cleopatra assumed came from Antony's wife Fulvia actually contained the news that she had died), but he may be consciously lying, or unconsciously distorting the truth. When he talks about himself, he may be trying to make himself look better than he really is, or he may be beating his breast and shouting an unjustified "Mea culpa!" He may be speaking with total sincerity and yet express opinions with which others might disagree. Was Oedipus completely innocent of any wrongdoing, as he fervently insists in *Oedipus at Colonus?* Is Satan or Don Juan right in their analyses of mankind in *Man and Superman?* Is Shaw's Candida a noble and self-sacrificing woman, as she sees herself, or is she a scheming monster who revels in her ability to manipulate other people's lives?

Characters' truthfulness can be tested by the same methods that are useful in ordinary life: Are their various statements contradictory? Do they say one thing and do another? When Witwould protests in *The Way of the World,* "Petulant's my friend, and a very honest fellow, and a very pretty fellow. . . . I'll do him justice. I'm his friend, I won't wrong him," and then proceeds to tear Petulant's character to ribbons, his insincerity is obvious. What is said about one character by another often reveals something about both: Witwould's attacks on Petulant tell us a good deal about Petulant, but they reveal Witwould himself almost more fully.

A special note should be made of what the characters do not do or say, especially when they go to some lengths to avoid what might be expected. The fact that Higgins does not consider marrying Eliza is a clue to his real feelings about class distinctions. That Shaw felt it to be important is demonstrated by his long footnote to *Pygmalion* justifying Higgins's failure; the fact that the marriage was arranged in the musical version of the play, *My Fair Lady,* obviously produced a significant alteration in Higgins's personality. Crichton's refusal to renew his engagement to Polly after they have returned to England, in *The Admirable Crichton,* is also essential to an understanding of the part and of the play as a whole.

Although the director cannot devote as much time to any part of the script as the actors, each of whom can concentrate on his own role, the director should try to achieve as full a realization of the reading of each line as possible. He should absorb its meaning, identify its accompanying emotions, and attempt to create the performance in his mind vividly, imagining how the actor should move and how the line can be read most effectively.

Each speech should be analyzed by asking a series of questions. What is the situation in which it is set? What has preceded it? what speech or action is it a response to? What are the character's relationships, factual and emotional, with the others who are on stage at the same time? Is he dominant, or dominated by one or more of the other characters? Given his basic personality, what emotions is he likely to be feeling? What precisely does the line mean? What is the character thinking about when he speaks it? Is his mind focused on what he is saying, or is he actually thinking about something different? Does he mean what he is saying, or is he lying, or speaking ironically? Does he express any emotions in the line itself? If so, do they match the emotions he is likely to be feeling at the moment, or are they different in kind or degree? Is he feeling a single emotion or more than one, and if more than one are they harmonious or do they conflict with one another?

Are there any particular difficulties in the line? any points that must be made clear to the audience but that are stated obscurely or casually and that might be missed? What style of speech does the character use? Especially, how closely does it match the style of ordinary speech? Does it seem natural or mannered and artificial? If it does not seem natural, is the artificiality especially characteristic of the speaker, or is it a general style used by all of the characters in the play? Is the speech flat and ordinary, or does it include figures of speech, puns, or other decorations?

What techniques will come closest to producing the desired effect, in reading the line? How should the line be phrased, what words should be emphasized? How can variations in pitch, time, and loudness be used to express it most fully and clearly? What crosses, turns, gestures, or business can be used to reinforce the meaning and emotions?

SUBDIVIDING THE SCRIPT

Throughout his study of the script up to this point the director has been concerned with the play as a whole. His study will have resulted in the preparation of a mental map showing the extent and shape of the play, the network of paths through it and the central point to which they all lead, and the variety of terrain and vegetation appearing within the territory covered by the play. Throughout, his view has been that of a helicopter pilot hovering above the area, low enough to see the individual details but high enough to see its outline as a whole. The work of design must be carried on from a much closer point of view: the helicopter must land, and the director follow every path on foot.

Much of his later work consists in the application of his general conclusions in specific terms, defining the exact position of each actor on stage at each moment in the play, determining the readings of the individual lines, training the actors in learning to use their voices and bodies most effectively. The director's work on this level is discussed in the chapters on blocking and those on training the actors.

The director's broad analyses are also essential to his preliminary instructions to the technical staff, especially those members of the staff who are responsible for designing specialized aspects of the production.

As a final preliminary to his own designing, the director should examine the script a fifth time, trying to divide it into the smallest meaningful sections. Since the purpose of such division is to make the play easier to handle, different directors might be expected to draw the dividing lines at different points, adjusted to their own tastes and habits of thinking. For the beginning director, it is better to mark more rather than fewer divisions.

The basis of the sectioning will differ from play to play, so that only illustrative suggestions can be made. In the scripts for French drama it is customary to mark the end of a scene whenever any character exits from the stage, and the beginning of a scene whenever any character enters. Often such divisions are artificial rather than meaningful: the entrance and exit of a butler bringing tea may not interrupt the flow of a scene, and a break marked at that point in the script might be misleading to the director rather than helpful. Often, however, the entrance or exit of an important character does turn the dialog in a new direction, and if so, the point of shift should be marked in the script.

A change in mood or in the subject of conversation should also be marked. Any long speech (for example, Lucky's in *Waiting for Godot* or Enobarbus's "barge" speech in *Antony and Cleopatra*), even if it is occasionally interrupted by other characters, constitutes a unified section of the script to which the director must turn his attention as a whole while he is preparing his designs, and should be marked so as to separate it from its context.

In ancient Greek drama such sections are easy to identify. Greek tragedies, and to a lesser extent the comedies, tend to be constructed as a series of conversations among small groups of characters, with occasional choral interludes. Thus in Sophocles' *King Oedipus*, the personality of the king is developed by setting it in contrast with a number of other characters in clearly separated brief scenes: with the priest of Apollo; with the blind seer Tiresias; with Creon; with the queen Jocasta; with an old slave.

Numerous scenes are marked in the scripts of Shakespeare's plays, and the scene divisions nearly always coincide with meaningful breaks in the action. Fairly often, however, it is convenient for the director to divide still further. The script for *Antony and Cleopatra* is divided into forty-two scenes; however, Act V is printed as only two scenes, which can be handled more easily if they are subdivided.

Act I of Sheridan's *The School for Scandal* is written in two scenes. The director will find it easier to work with if the first scene is divided approximately as follows:

1. An expository conversation between Mr. Snake and Lady Sneerwell.
2. Joseph Surface enters, and after a short time Snake exits.
3. Joseph and Lady Sneerwell discuss Snake.
4. Maria enters and converses with Joseph and Lady Sneerwell.
5. Mrs. Candour enters and reports the latest gossip.
6. Mr. Crabtree and Sir Benjamin Backbite appear and contribute more gossip, which so upsets Maria that she leaves.
7. The others continue to discuss Charles; Mrs. Candour leaves to spy on Maria, and Crabtree and Backbite eventually leave.
8. Joseph and Lady Sneerwell discuss Crabtree and Backbite.

Having completed his preliminary study of the play, the director is ready to make assignments to the designer specialists on his staff, to describe his fundamental concept of the play to them as a guide for their work, and then to turn to his own work as designer of blocking and readings, in preparation for the work of rehearsals.

4/The Evaluation of Technical Designs

One of the director's most important concerns as an administrator is making sure that the production work is characterized by practicality, especially that it can be done comfortably within the available time limits.

The dates of performance are usually set by the administrative authority immediately above the director on the organizational chart, although he may often be asked to take part in the conferences at which the season's schedule is planned.

The time available for the preparation of a production varies, as well as the conditions under which the staff must work. Plays may be irregularly spaced in order to adjust to holidays, to the schedules of nearby theaters, or to other local events. Less time is often provided for preparing the first play of a season than for later ones. The production requirements of plays also differ greatly; one play may involve numerous and complicated sound effects, another may not even need a sound crew; costuming one show may involve hundreds of hours of work, while another show may require only a few hours. Consequently, although a typical schedule can be described, individual productions are likely to deviate from it.

THE PRODUCTION CONFERENCES

Usually a period of six or seven weeks is available for preparing a play. The director's preliminary analysis extends over about a week. At the beginning of the second week, key members of the technical staff should be assembled for a conference. The precise makeup of this group will vary according to the demands of the particular play and according to the director's preferences in working methods. Usually all staff members will be included who supervise the work of others, that is, the technical director and the chairman of each crew. In addition the set designer must be included, although in some theaters the execution of his designs is supervised by the technical director or crew chiefs rather than by himself. It is common to delay the selection of an assistant director until the beginning of rehearsals; however, this position is so important and the value of the assistant's work is so dependent on his total familiarity with the planning of the play that it is highly desirable to appoint him early enough that he can be included in the first conference.

Throughout most of the production period, these members of the staff will work independently, without supervision. Each will make hundreds of decisions, some of them many thousands, all of which, when ultimately joined, must fit together to form a clearly unified pattern. The major purpose of this conference is to define that pattern, so that each designer or supervisor will understand it fully. The first half of the conference session consists of a description by the director of the fundamental concept of the play, which he has developed during his preliminary study.

In this discussion the director should not hesitate to point out the most obvious facts; clarity is vital, and few staff members are likely to be offended even by being reminded that *The Bald Soprano* is a comedy, or that Pirandello's *Right You Are If You Think You Are* deals with the ambiguities of life. The underlying theme of the play, which the director has already summarized in written form, should be presented, the mood of the play, its range, its period and style, and its special problems.

The second half of the conference period will be used for a general discussion; the staff is likely to ask for a repetition of points about which they are not certain, for clarification of what has been said, and for a discussion of items that have been omitted.

The technical work, like that of the director, involves two steps, planning and execution. The last part of the conference should be devoted to working out a practical schedule for the planning. Since the staff members will be able to estimate the speed at which they can work much more accurately than the director, each one should be asked in turn to suggest his own deadlines. Realistic dates for the completion of the production work should be developed during the conference, but the detailed scheduling can be handled better by the individual supervisors.

The play may impose a special sequence on the work. For example the staff may feel that the design of the costumes for the play should be delayed until the set designs have been completed, so that the colors chosen for the costumes can be coordinated with the colors of the set. It may seem more efficient to delay the selection of incidental music for the production until rehearsals have progressed to the point that an accurate timing of key scenes can be done.

THE PRODUCTION SCHEDULE

On the basis of the complexity and sequence of the various areas of planning, a schedule should be drawn up listing a series of deadlines and conferences. How many deadlines are included in this schedule depends on the work habits of the staff and on the director's familiarity with their work. When a director and set designer, for instance, have worked closely together on a number of productions, and when it has become clear that their thinking is usually harmonious, they may feel it desirable to delay a second conference until the set designs have been nearly completed. On their first play together, it may seem preferable for them to schedule several conferences while the designing is in process, perhaps first to examine the designer's exploratory sketches, then again to check his scaled ground plan, a third time to discuss his perspective drawing of the set, and a final conference to evaluate his plans for the decoration and color scheme. An additional factor is the difficulty of the play; if it seems to need a set with many platforms and stairs, arranged in a complex pattern, the director and set designer are likely to want to meet more frequently than for a show that seems best suited to a simple and fairly familiar pattern of scenery, with no variations in level.

After the schedule has been agreed on, copies should be duplicated and distributed to the staff members involved as soon as possible after the close of the session.

On pages 54 and 55 is the schedule for a particular play; it illustrates the adaptation of the generalized plan that has been described, to fit the needs of a special play. To facilitate rehearsing the dancers, the deadline for supplying platforms is earlier than usual, and the technical rehearsal has been moved back to the next to the last week of rehearsals on the assumption that more than the usual number of technical problems are to be expected. There are almost no sound effects in the play, so that it was possible to omit the sound crew altogether; instead the director of the orchestra was included in the planning conference. The term "rehearsal properties" indicates properties to be used especially during the rehearsals; some of them may be the properties that will actually be used in performance, but others may be substitutes that can be used by the actors but that will be replaced for performance.

LATER CONFERENCES

During the following weeks, the director meets as scheduled with the members of the staff. These will usually not be group conferences; often only

PRODUCTION SCHEDULE

A Funny Thing Happened on the Way to the Forum
by Burt Shevelove, Larry Gelbart, and Stephen Sondheim

1. General conference to discuss the basic
   concept of the play and to plan the production
   schedule .... Friday, October 2

   > Director
   > Assistant Director
   > Technical Director
   > Musical Director
   > Choreographer
   > Set Designer
   > Costume Designer
   > Costume Crew Chief
   > Makeup Crew Chief
   > Properties Crew Chief
   > Lighting Crew Chief

2. Conference to discuss sketches for the
   scenery .... Wednesday, October 7

   > Director
   > Set Designer

3. Conference to discuss designs for properties ...... Thursday, October 8

   > Director
   > Properties Crew Chief

4. Conference to discuss sketches for costumes .... Friday, October 9

   > Director
   > Costume Designer
   > Costume Crew Chief
   > Set Deisgner

5. Conference to check the final set designs .... Monday, October 12

   > Director
   > Set Designer
   > Technical Director

6. Conference to check makeup designs .... Tuesday, October 13

   > Director
   > Makeup Crew Chief

7. Deadline for delivery of a ground plan of
   the set to the director .... Wednesday, October 14

8. Deadline for delivery of the working drawings
for the set to the Technical Director .... Monday, October 19

9. Deadline for completion of the major functional
elements of the set, especially platforms;
they are to be in place on stage by the
beginning of rehearsal, 7:00 P.M. .... Monday, October 26

10. Conference to check lighting designs .... Friday, November 6

Director

Lighting Crew Chief

11. All rehearsal properties to be available at the
beginning of rehearsal, 7:00 P.M.; they will
be used at all following rehearsals until
replaced by the performance properties .... Monday, November 8

12. Deadline for the completion of set
construction .... Friday, November 13

13. Deadline for the erection of the set on stage;
to be finished by the beginning of rehearsal,
7:00 P.M. .... Monday, November 16

14. Technical rehearsal. Makeup and costume
parade at 7:30 P.M. Performance properties
and lighting to be used during the rehearsal.
(Costumes, properties, and lighting to be
used at all following rehearsals; makeup to
be omitted until November 24 unless further
makeup sessions are added to the schedule.)

15. Full orchestra at this and all following
rehearsals .... Tuesday, November 23

16. Makeup used at this and all later
rehearsals .... Wednesday, November 24

17. Schedule of performances

> Opening night, Friday, November 27, 8:15 P.M.
> Saturday, November 28, 8:15 P.M.
> Monday, November 30, 8:15 P.M.
> Tuesday, December 1, 8:15 P.M.
> Wednesday, December 2, 8:15 P.M.
> Thursday, December 3, 8:15 P.M.
> Friday, December 4, 8:15 P.M.
> Sunday, December 6, 3:30 P.M.

18. Strike (all technical crews), 7:00 P.M. .... Monday, December 7

the director and the individual designer or supervisor will be involved. However, other members of the staff may be included whenever it seems desirable. For example, one of the conferences with the set designer might include also the technical director and the head of the scene-shifting crew. Set properties and hand properties, although they are theoretically separate, may be affected by similar factors, such as the style and period of the production, so that it might be desirable to confer with the heads of the two crews at the same time.

After the major part of the work of planning or design has been completed, it may be helpful to expand the production schedule by adding further deadlines for the execution of the designs, as developed by the production supervisors. The technical director may want to set up a series of deadlines for different parts of the work; the chief of the scene-shifting crew may want to schedule special shifting rehearsals. Whether these additional dates are added to the master schedule or not depends on the preferences of the director and his staff.

The conferences at which the plans and designs are discussed serve two purposes; they enable the director to determine that the work is proceeding on schedule; and they provide for the evaluation and eventual approval of the plans before they are carried out by the production staff.

At each conference the designer or planner submits his work to the director; it is discussed in detail, not only the actual designs but the thinking on which they are based. Typically perhaps half to two-thirds of the plans will be acceptable to the director as submitted. For the others, he may simply reject the proposals and ask that new ones be prepared. Most commonly, however, he will analyze the weaknesses that he senses in the designs and will make suggestions for revision. Following the conference, the designer will rework his plans and then resubmit them; this procedure is repeated until the plans are approved. Since it is not possible to predict which plans or designs will require revision, these further conferences cannot be included on the master schedule.

Handling the evaluating conferences effectively depends on the director's skill in two of his three capacities: as an artist, he must be able to judge the effectiveness of the proposals submitted to him; and as an administrator, he must be able to judge their practicality, and to carry on the discussion in such a fashion that the staff member's willingness to cooperate in the production work is not reduced.

No problem arises when the proposals can be approved as submitted; a rejection that goes beyond a very minor suggestion for revision can produce unfortunate results if it is handled improperly.

The Director's Relations with the Production Staff

Theater artists differ from other people not so much in kind as in degree; they too take pride in their work, they bring to it enthusiasm and dedication, concentration and time—but all of those things, typically, in greater degree than most workers in other fields of activity. Like all artists, they tend to be less sure of their decisions and more sensitive to criticism than nontheater people. In addition, it is the assumption that as specialists they have a firmer command of their own area of theater than the director: it is most likely that the set designer is better informed and more skilled in planning the scenery than is the director. Thus the director who must reject a proposed design is in the position of a generalist evaluating the work of a specialist who is his superior in the particular area in question.

All of those considerations to some degree constitute difficulties for the director. Two facts, however, are of assistance to him. One is the firmly grounded acceptance of the traditional organization of the theater staff, with the director at the head of the chart; the authority of the director is so generally accepted that even a novice in the theater is likely to assume it without question.

The second source of strength is the fact that the director's purpose in evaluating the designs of his staff is to make sure that they harmonize with the production as a whole: that the costume, properties, and lighting designs not only harmonize with and supplement each other, but that they are all fitted precisely to the spirit and pattern of the script. Since he is almost certain to have studied the script more intensively than any other member of the staff, and since one of his major concerns has been to identify the sources of unity in the script, in this respect he is the superior expert, even though his skill in the specialized area being evaluated may well be less than that of the designer whose work is under consideration.

And finally, even if there should be a diametric and irresolvable difference of opinion, both the director and the staff member have at least one goal in common, the desire to produce the finest, strongest, most effective performance of the play possible; if they do not share that goal, then at least one of them does not belong in the theater at all.

In his relations with his staff, as in his associations with his administrative board, with his audiences, and with his actors, ordinary courtesy and tact are vital for the director. Beyond simple good manners, for a theater program to continue effectively, the relationship between the director and the other artists must be one of mutual respect. The focus of any discussion should be on the plans themselves, not on the artist who has prepared them. If the placement of an entrance or the arrangement of platforms is unacceptable for some reason, a frank discussion of the problem is always in order; a criticism of the designer is not only irrelevant, it distracts attention from the essential consideration, which is how to correct the difficulty, and it will almost certainly make the designer's later work less effective. Perhaps the only circumstance in which a criticism of the staff member himself is excusable is when, without any reason except indolence or carelessness, the designer has simply failed to do his work; and even in such an instance, it is important for the director to be absolutely

certain that the inadequacy of the work is not due to illness or external interference or to a fear of failure.

The most effective assistance in handling unsatisfactory technical work is
a careful analysis of the reasons why the director objects to it. If a flight of stairs
as designed for a set has risers so high that an actress descending them would
look awkward, thus spoiling a climactic scene, the designer is likely to agree to
their rejection as soon as that fact has been pointed out to him. If a costume
will prevent an actor from moving freely during a sword fight, few designers
would fail to agree that it should be replanned. If a property is scaled so as to
be ineffective from the middle of the audience, the crew chief is likely to recognize immediately that it must be replaced. A director who simply says "No, I
don't like that; you'll have to redesign," not only gives the artist no assistance,
but he creates a conflict of taste, his own against the designer's, and by not
exploring the reasons for reworking a design, if he happens to be wrong in his
evaluation, something which does happen, he cuts himself off from a discussion of the designer's reasoning, and consequently makes it unlikely that he
will discover his error in time to correct it. It is at least as important to identify
those aspects of the designs which are acceptable, which have been well done,
as those that need revision. A careful analysis of what is right with a design,
explaining why it is effective, is often the best possible guide to the designer in
reworking the details that are not acceptable.

The Certification of Approval

Good relations are promoted by the director's initialing designs that he has
approved. No director can carry all of the details of the plans submitted to him
permanently in his mind, and disagreements of considerable violence have
sometimes developed when a designer was certain that his plan had been approved and the director was certain that his approval had been provisional, on
the assumption that additional changes would be made; if he routinely indicates his approval by initialing the designs, such arguments can never arise.

Such marking is a protection for the director, since he will not indicate
his acceptance until the designs are actually submitted in finished form; it is
also a protection to the designer, since he can then proceed with full confidence
in assigning the production work to his crew. If the director has approved designs that later are found to be unacceptable, the presence of his initials puts
responsibility for the error clearly where it belongs. No director can demand
that a costume, or a pattern of lighting, or any other production element be
reworked after he has approved the designs and they have been followed; not
only does he not have the authority to make such a demand, he should not have
it. Theater artists are among the most understanding and cooperative people,
and hardly ever would they reject a request for revision, even though the

changes were necessitated by the director's own faulty judgment; but for him to demand such a change with even an oblique suggestion that it was the designer who was at fault might well precipitate a crisis. The director's mark on the designs in such a case will prevent the possibility of misunderstanding, with an attendant explosion. If all designs are routinely initialed when they are accepted, the absence of such marking constitutes an unanswerable demonstration that the design in question had not been approved.

Evaluating the Designs

The production of a play has some resemblance to a jigsaw puzzle; it is made up of a very large number of pieces of various shapes, colors, and sizes, each meaningless by itself, but so designed that they will fit precisely together. In the play, the various pieces are designed and constructed by many different people, individually and in groups, each specializing in one particular aspect of the finished work of art. Instead of being two-dimensional, the structure is multidimensional, combining vision and sound, each in multiple forms, as well as all of the ideational and meaningful resources of dialog. A skilled jigsaw-puzzle fan usually begins by sorting out the straight edge pieces, and fitting them together to form the outline of the picture, which can then be used as a guide for the placement of the other pieces. The script serves something of the same function, defining the outline of the play, although it also traces essential parts of the picture within the frame. Nevertheless, the picture presented by the script has many missing parts; these must be supplied by the director and his staff, and it is his primary responsibility to make sure that the added pieces fit precisely into the gaps left by the script.

In making his evaluations, he must be constantly aware that there are many alternative pieces that could be fitted into any particular gap in the picture; it is not enough to find one piece that will fit, but instead, from many such pieces, to select the one that will contribute most to creating the effect—the experience for the audience—that will be most exciting, most vivid, and most meaningful.

In order to evaluate proposals that are submitted to him, the director should have the broadest possible familiarity with the range of possibilities. In examining a proposed lighting design for his play, he should be able not simply to imagine the effect of the lighting as planned, he should in addition be aware of all of the other effects and arrangements of light that might be used.

It might seem that the achievement of that ideal would contradict the assumption that the lighting designer, or set or costume designer, should have a superior expertness in his own area. Such a contradiction is only apparent; in the first place, the ideal is never achieved, although the closer the director approaches it the more effectively he can function; in the second place, one enormous area of competence, which is an essential part of the equipment of every technical worker, the director has no need to master. Ideally he should be thoroughly familiar with the range of effects that can be achieved in each of the technical fields, but he does not need to know how to produce those effects. He needs to know as much as possible about the ways in which scenery can contribute to the play as a whole, but he does not need to know how to design scenery, to prepare working drawings or ground plans or perspective paintings of the set. He needs to know the range of styles and effects available in costumes, and how actors can use their costumes, but he does not need to know how to sew a costume, alter a pattern, or even redesign a costume in order to alter its effect. Even in these areas, some degree of skill is useful to a director in helping him avoid requests of the technical staff that may be esthetically desirable but which are impractical under the restrictions of time, equipment, or degree of skill available; but a director who is thoroughly familiar with the esthetic range of each technical area of production is at least adequately prepared to work with a skilled technical staff.

Such familiarity can best be acquired by experience in the theater, by observing lighting, properties, makeup, sound, scenery, and the other elements of production in a series of plays, and preferably by working as a member of various technical crews. The second best training is a formal course in technical theater; many such courses combine both training and practical experience, which is better than either alone. The discussion here can give only a hint of the range of the technical arts of the theater and the bases on which the director can evaluate either the design proposals or the finished work.

The technical aspects of play production can be thought of in three groups: personal (costume and makeup), environmental (set, properties, and lighting), and sound (effects and music).

The first two groups function visually; of the five divisions, the set constitutes the largest area in the stage picture, although its importance is less than that fact would suggest, since it is the background and environment of the action; the focus of attention is on the actors, who are consequently much more important than the relatively small portion of the stage picture that they occupy would imply.

EVALUATING THE SET DESIGN

The design of the setting, however, is an important factor in the effect created by the actors. Which particular actor attracts the attention of the audience depends on how the actors are arranged on stage and the pattern of movement of the actors about the stage. Both the arrangement and movement of the actors are strongly dependent on the arrangement of the elements in the set. The placement of entrances, of windows, of fireplaces and furniture are major factors in the arrangement and movement of the actors. In addition, the presence or absence of variations in level of the stage floor greatly influences the type of movement that the actors can display and affects the degree to which actors on the different levels attract the attention of the audience. Such variations in level, provided by stairs and landings, by balconies, by raised areas, by trap doors, and by abstract platform arrangements, seem almost to add a further dimension to the stage picture, or at least to make its three-dimensionality more expressive.

This function of the set has been described figuratively by saying that a well-designed set should be a machine that will facilitate the effective arrangement and movement of the actors about the stage. This is not only the most important function of a set, but overwhelmingly so: the other functions are all minor in comparison.

The set also underlines or expresses the fundamental mood of the play—"mood" being used here to indicate all of the emotions which the playwright hopes to arouse in the audience as part of the experience of watching the play.

In addition, the set gives the audience information about the locale and period in which the play takes place and provides an effective esthetic experience for the audience.

Designer-director relationships vary more than those of any other staff members. Because the blocking plans are so dependent on the arrangement of the scenery, directors are often reluctant to accord set designers the same independence as costumers, property chiefs, or makeup artists. They may even be tempted to try to work out the ground plan of the set, leaving only the preparation of the construction drawings and decorative decisions to the scenic artist. One designer reports having worked with directors over the entire range of treatment; one made numerous detailed suggestions about scenery, including color schemes, the size and placement of scenic units, and even the angle of slant for a ramp. "At the other extreme," the designer said, "I did the scenery for sixteen plays with a second director who made no suggestions in advance, and asked for only two alterations in sets after they had been designed, in one case that a tree have fewer branches, and in the other case that a door be omitted so that actors could walk through the opening more easily."

The ideal relationship seems to lie between those two extremes. It is the director's responsibility to define the style and tone of the production and to describe them as clearly as possible to the designer. Advance suggestions about specific details of the scenery are more likely to handicap the designer than to help him, and violate the principle of the separation of areas of responsibility. Assuming that the designer is a competent artist, placing such restrictions on him results in less effective scenic designs. After the designer has completed his initial analysis and is ready to submit proposals to the director, such suggestions may be helpful.

Beginning directors sometimes assume that the designer's function is

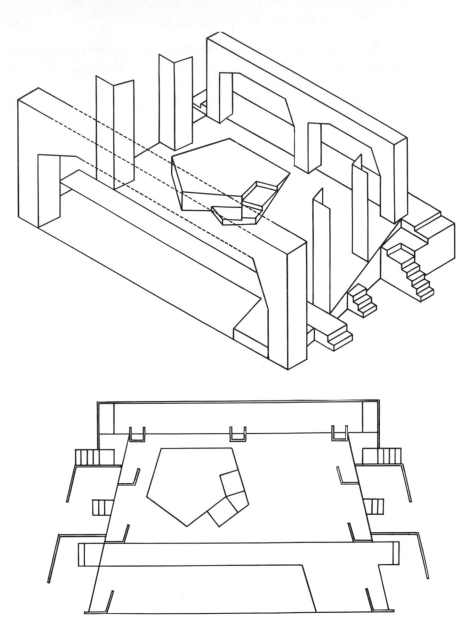

Figure 3a. The set as a machine for organizing the action of the play. The designer submits his plans for scenery in the form of a ground plan (the bottom drawing) and a perspective or an isometric drawing (top). The director's first concern is with the usefulness of the scenic elements in helping him arrange the actors and plan their patterns of movement.

The design for *Macbeth* shown here provides a large ramp, covering most of the stage, two level runways at the front and back of the set, and two level platforms, one at the down-left corner of the stage and a pentagonal platform in the right half of the ramp. Multiple entrances permit the director to move actors on with great speed and with dramatic use of processional effects.

Figure 3b. This set, for Anouilh's *The Lark,* includes broad arches for processional entrances, and varying levels that assist the director greatly in arranging his actors. [Directed by Donald Wolfe; photograph by Douglas R. Hux]

simply to reproduce the set used in a previous production of the play, perhaps the one illustrated in the play book. Such sets are seldom well suited to the local theater, and their use is likely to be inartistic, and possibly unethical. The set design, like all other aspects of the production, should constitute a new work of art, fitted to the special conditions of the producing organization.

Often a set designer submits his plans to the director at the ground-plan point in the form of a scaled drawing showing the location of the walls of the set, doors and windows, furniture, and the height of any areas raised above the level of the stage floor. Even if the designs are carried beyond this point before submission for approval, the director should start his evaluation of them by a study of the ground plan. Since he is primarily concerned with the assistance the design will provide him in arranging the actors and planning their movements about the stage, he should note first the details in the ground plan that will affect his planning, especially the location of entrances and the placement of the furniture. Next he should check the variations in level, so that he has a basic picture of the three-dimensional arrangement of the set.

As soon as he has the functional pattern of the design in mind, he should recall the most important or most difficult scene in the play and attempt to arrange the actors on the ground plan in imagination so that the scene could be effectively performed. Other critical scenes should be tested in the same way. This analysis can be carried as far as seems desirable.

If the set has been well designed, the arrangement of the actors should be easy; with an outstanding design, actors often seem to fall almost automatically into effective arrangements: the design creates a feeling of ease and inevitability.

Most directors find it difficult to imagine the completed set from a ground

Figure 3c. This set, for *Rosencrantz and Guildenstern are Dead,* is designed in the form of a complicated maze, decorated in somber colors and matching the mood and complications of the play. The various levels, as well as the barrels that pop up magically out of the platforms, provide valuable resources for imaginative exploitation by the director and the actors. [Directed by Harold Tedford; photographs by Douglas R. Hux]

plan with any confidence, even with regard to those details which are accurately recorded on the plan; consequently the perspective drawing should be used to recheck the analysis of the ground plan. The placement of a door may have seemed adequate for the actors' use in ground plan; but how does it look from out front (in perspective)? If one actor must jump off a four-foot-high platform, it may be easier to check the practicality of his leap in a perspective drawing than in a ground plan which showed the outline but not the height of the level. The relative dominance of the various areas can also be checked with more confidence.

Assuming that the perspective view passes this test, it can be examined for the effectiveness with which the other functions are handled. The communication of information about the locale of the play will be most evident. Are the architectural details authentic? Does the style of the furniture indicate locale and period? The drawing will give only minimal information about the expression of mood and esthetic effectiveness, but in so far as they can be determined, they should harmonize with the spirit of the play.

After the perspective drawing has been accepted, the designer will prepare a full-color painting of the set from the viewpoint of the audience, showing not only the color scheme he has designed, but the effect of light on the set. Since the lighting can be expected to change frequently throughout the play, only one momentary pattern can be shown in the painting; however, the designer will select a typical one that reveals the form of the set clearly. The director can evaluate the effectiveness of the set in expressing the fundamental emotional tone of the play by concentrating on his own reactions to the painting, trying to pull them up to the level of consciousness and matching them against his memory of the element of emotion in the playscript. The esthetic effectiveness of the set can be tested in much the same way, turning the attention to the interest of the pattern of light, form, and color that has been recorded in the painting, and checking not only its effectiveness in itself, but comparing it in imagination with the total esthetic effect of the script, to make sure that they harmonize.

In judging both mood and esthetic effect, the director must imaginatively supplement the painting in two ways. The first is in the addition of the third dimension; although the painting attempts to represent the actual appearance of the finished set, it does so in monocular and two-dimensional terms; the actors, however, do not simply move across the plane surface of the picture: they will move back and forth within it, in front of other actors, through doors, and around furniture. The three-dimensionality of the set itself is a factor in its expression of mood and in its esthetic effect, but the use that the actors make of the space is even more important. In the main, the absence of depth from the painting is only a slight handicap; when the intended space appears in the final set, it is most likely to make the stage picture more effective, so that if the design

Figure 4a (facing page). The set as expressive of mood. When a set design is submitted to the director as a finished full-color painting, his main concern is determining how effectively it will assist him and his actors in communicating the emotions implied in the playscript. This set, for *A Funny Thing Happened on the Way to the Forum,* with its bright colors and lively shapes, clearly supports the play's mood of lighthearted farce. [Directed by Harold Tedford; photograph by Douglas R. Hux]

Figure 4b. The oppressive stuffiness of the locale of *Hedda Gabler* is suggested by the fussy decoration and dark colors of the scenery. [Photograph by Dorothy Welker]

Figure 4c (facing page). The details of this set for Martha B. King's *Peter, Peter, Pumpkin Eater,* including the pumpkin house and the stylized building, help express the general tone of this play for children. [Photograph by the Austin-Everest Studio] is acceptable as shown in the painting, it can be expected to be still more striking in reality.

The director must also bear in mind that the painting is incomplete. The major emotional and esthetic elements—the actors—are missing. Since they are the subject, accent, and focus of the stage picture, and the set itself is background, the design as submitted, if it is a good one, should look unfinished. If it forms an esthetically satisfying pattern in itself, it will look confused and overdecorated when the actors appear. Many designers for that reason include

Figure 4d. This unit set for Lorca's *Blood Wedding* helps the director and actors express the starkness and simplicity of the Spanish peasant life (top), and the tragedy of the last act (bottom). [Photographs by Dorothy Welker]

paintings of the actors in their set designs. But as with lighting, only one arrangement of the actors can be shown, and even that arrangement is deceptive, since it omits the actors' movements, which constitute an extremely important element in the visual aspect of the production. The pattern of movement is only slightly less important in the expression of emotion: an actor crossing the stage in a direct line, or tracing a broken path around scattered pieces of furniture; an actress gliding gracefully down a flight of low, broad stairs, or climbing with effort up a series of platforms almost too high for her to manage—such variations in movement have a powerful effect on the emotional responses of the audience.

Whether the designer has included actors in his painting or not, the director must supplement the picture by imagining the actors using the set and by attempting to assess the esthetic and emotional effects of the types of arrangements and movements for which the set provides.

After the set design has been approved in the form of the perspective painting, the designer turns his attention to the preparation of working drawings to be used as a guide in building and painting by the construction crew. These drawings are not usually submitted to the director, since they are purely technical and are simply implementations of the decisions which he has already approved. Judging them is likely to be outside his sphere of competence.

EVALUATING THE LIGHTING DESIGN

Lighting is closely related to the set, so much so that in many theaters the lighting and set are both designed by the same artist. Lighting serves four functions that are analogous to those of scenery; in addition, it provides visibility.

Lighting, like the set, gives some information about time and place. The time of day is suggested by the angle and color of light shining through windows in the set. The types of light sources used, and their decorative accessories, will help indicate the period of the play, as well as its specific locale: primitive torches and oil lamps, elaborate chandeliers of crystal and silver, floor lamps of various styles, the light of a glowing fire, votive candles glowing dimly against the walls, the harsh overhead lights of a hospital corridor—all of these help the audience identify time and place.

Lighting also can be used to express the mood of the play; cold moonlight streaming through the trees of a forest, dim lights thrown on layers of scrim to simulate fog, a warm flood of sunlight washing over a weathered stone wall, can all be used to underline the emotions incorporated in the script and expressed in the set design.

As currently used, the pattern of spotlights, floods, and strips, which differs considerably from the lighting patterns common outside the theater, is frankly

Figure 5a. Lighting the stage. The effectiveness of lighting in controlling the attention of the audience is illustrated by the prominence of the actor standing on the platform, who attracts the eye immediately even though the actor at the left is closer to the audience. [*We Bombed in New Haven;* directing and lighting design by Donald Wolfe; photograph by Douglas R. Hux]

revealed, in contrast with the former practice, which tended to obscure it; such a pattern, often consisting of pools of light along the walls of a set, around major pieces of furniture, and in important acting areas on the stage floor, may have an esthetic interest in itself. Many other lighting effects having esthetic implications are available—the shadows of leaves falling across an outdoors scene, the color of a sunset on a skydrop, the glitter of decorative candles.

The most important function of lighting, however, besides its fundamental purpose of making the actors visible, is related to the most important function of the set: the control of the audience's attention. The assistance that lighting gives in leading the audience to turn to the actor who is carrying the story of the play forward at any particular moment depends primarily on the fact that a viewer automatically tends to turn his attention to the most brightly lit area of the stage.

Actors usually perform on the stage floor; even if various levels are provided by the set, the action is usually confined to the lower half or two-thirds of the stage space. To assist in focusing the audience's attention on this most important part of the stage, it is usually much more brightly lit than the upper half of the space. This variation is most visible on the walls of the set; the bottom third is brightly lit, with the light fading gradually up to the top third, which is lit almost entirely by light reflected from the stage floor. (Incidentally, this is a marked deviation from the pattern of light found most frequently outside the theater, where the sky is the major source of light outdoors and the ceilings are often the brightest areas of rooms.) This general difference in brightness firmly restricts the attention of the audience to the lower half of the stage space, where the actors perform.

Still more specific control of attention is provided within the acting area. Usually it is divided into a series of sections, traditionally six, although the exact number and arrangement vary with the shape of the set and the placement of furniture, entrances, and other elements influencing the positions of the actors. At each moment of the play, it is intended that the audience turn their attention to one particular actor. The lighting is used to facilitate that focus of attention by slightly dimming all of the stage areas except the one where the key actor is standing, which is made slightly brighter. As the attention shifts to another actor in another area, the lighting is readjusted, so that at each moment the area toward which it is hoped the audience will look is brighter than any other on stage. Occasionally such shifts in brightness are revealed

Figure 5b (facing page). This scene from *The Lark* reverses the pattern shown in *Figure 5a*; emphasis is thrown on the nearer actors by the skillful use of light, even though the three judges are placed on a higher platform directly facing the audience. [Directing and lighting design by Donald Wolfe; photograph by Douglas R. Hux]

Figure 5c. The use of light is especially subtle in this picture from *The Lark*. A different level of illumination is used for each character, producing three distinct degrees of emphasis, with major attention placed on Joan, and the executioner hovering in the background as a presence felt rather than consciously seen. [Photograph by Douglas R. Hux]

frankly to the audience; in the majority of cases the cross-fading is done smoothly and minimally in the hope that the audience will be unaware of it. The key area is pulled up very slightly, and the other areas pulled down, just enough to shift the balance toward the important section of the stage. The attraction of the brightest area is so great that the attention of the audience can be controlled very effectively even when the differences in brightness are so minimal that they operate subliminally. Visible sources of light are usually avoided on the stage, or are used only with the greatest care, because even a tiny candle flame becomes the brightest point in the stage picture and is likely to draw the attention of the audience irresistibly from the actors.

Evaluating Properties

The term *properties* is used in two ways in the theater (and often abbreviated to "props"). Stage properties consist of the furniture included in the set, and sometimes also of such easily removable decorative additions as drapes and pictures. Hand properties are objects such as trays, coffee cups, cigarette lighters, and guns, which the actors pick up during the course of the play. Practicality requires that props of both types be designed so as to be suited to whatever use is made of them in the play; thus, if an actor must climb up on a table to crawl through a window, the table must be constructed to bear his weight; if a tray is used to bring breakfast dishes and food on stage, it must have sufficient size and strength to serve the purpose.

In addition, properties should be suited to the spirit of the play, and should harmonize with the style and period adopted for the set and costumes, as well as fitting into the esthetic pattern established by the other visual elements. A throne, scepter, and other symbols of royalty designed for the White Queen in *Alice Through the Looking Glass* would undoubtedly be entirely unsuited for Lady Macbeth, or Jocasta in *King Oedipus.*

Stage properties (especially furniture) are probably selected from available sources about half the time in the American theater; about a fourth of such properties are produced by rebuilding existing furniture in varying degrees; in the remaining instances, the furniture is especially designed and constructed in the scene shop. Hand properties follow approximately the same pattern. When storage space is available, it is desirable to collect as large a supply of properties as possible. Even with a large collection some reconstruction is usually necessary, although often it consists simply of added decoration and repainting.

Even if the director has not mastered property work, he can usually rely fairly safely on his reactions to the properties or designs which are submitted to him. Often the props chairman will bring half a dozen trays, from which he is asked to select one. The director can make his selection by checking to make sure that the property will support whatever use is to be made of it in the play, and by checking its appearance against the effect that he hopes to achieve in the production as a whole. Usually, in examining half a dozen trays, he will quickly identify a couple that are clearly unacceptable, three or four that might do, and two or three that look best; after having discussed his evaluations with the props chairman, the director might well leave the final selection to the chairman himself.

Evaluating Costumes

Very much the same method of evaluation can be used by the director in judging costumes or costume designs as in judging properties. However, because they are part of the audience's view of the actors, because they move with the actors, and because they are likely to be more vivid in color and design than other parts of the stage picture, costumes are usually more important to the production as a whole than stage properties, and very much more important than hand properties, and consequently must be judged with special care.

Clothing is seen by the audience from a much greater distance in the

Figure 6. Style in costume. Although decorative details vary, the character of the style depends most on the silhouette, so that in evaluating costume proposals the director first studies this aspect of the designs.

The two undated drawings in the bottom row show adaptations of the Elizabethan style designed for Shakespeare's *Twelfth Night*. Both dresses are basically modern, but have been given something of an Elizabethan flavor by the imitation of details of the Elizabethan silhouette, including the farthingale and the ruff.

theater than in ordinary life; the average member of the audience may be forty feet from the nearest actor. Fine details of construction or decoration either change in appearance or become totally invisible at such distances; for example, an all-over pattern of flowers on a dress fabric may become simply a textured blur when viewed from the audience, and light-colored embroidery may become almost invisible. Shapes must therefore be simplified, decorative areas and motifs enlarged, and colors made more vivid. Ordinary clothes can sometimes be used in the theater if they have sufficient simplicity and contrast to function effectively. Occasionally an effect of drabness and unobtrusiveness may be suited to a particular character or play, so that, for example, it might be possible to use an ordinary dress for Birdie in *The Little Foxes.*

When plays are set in earlier periods, costumes are an important means of identifying the style of the time. Even authentic clothing from the proper period, however, generally fails to function satisfactorily for the reasons given. The major factor in expressing style on stage is the silhouette or outline of the costume: the broad farthingales of Elizabethan England, the tubular shape of dresses in the 1920s, the bustles and padded blouses of the 1890s, the exaggerated square shoulders of dresses from the 1930s, are more expressive and more meaningful in the theater than fine details of construction or decoration.

In addition, the costumes, like hand properties, are *used* by the actors, and they must be adapted to whatever use is to be made of them. They must be strong enough to withstand a duel or a fall down a flight of stairs, if those actions are required by the play, and conversely, if they are to be torn or removed, they must be constructed so that they can be used without delaying the action of the play and without permanently damaging them. An extreme example appears in *Finian's Rainbow,* where the costume of the leprechaun must disappear magically, an effect produced by a member of the costume crew off stage jerking on a wire attached to the costume, which must be especially designed for such treatment.

The comfort of the actors is of vital importance. An actor whose costume is too tight in the armpits, or who is choked by his collar, could hardly deliver one of Hamlet's soliloquies effectively. Each period, however, develops a characteristic style of movement, to which its clothing is adjusted. Effective performance requires that the actors master that style, so that the requirement that costumes seem easy to the actors assumes that their postures and movements are fitted to the period. If an actor who is appearing in a play set in one of the more formal periods complains that his costume is uncomfortable when he slouches or lounges, he should be instructed to restudy his movements, rather than asking the costume crew to remake the costume. A costume that makes the wrong style of movement difficult and the right style comfortable is an advantage, not a handicap.

The colors used in the costumes are of extreme importance in the stage

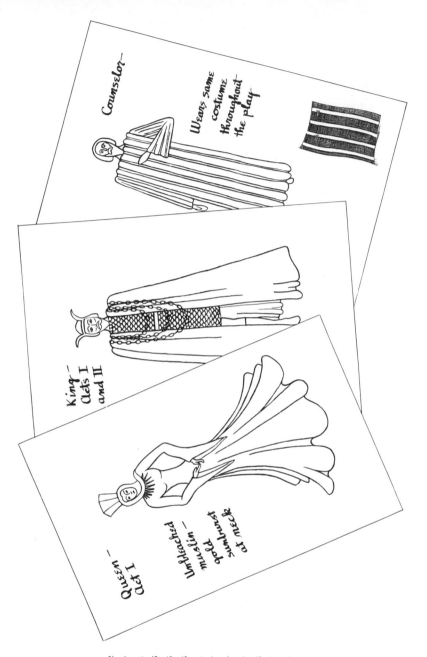

Counselor—

Wears same
costume
throughout
the play

King—
Acts I
and II

Queen—
Act I

Unbleached
muslin—
gold
sunburst
at neck

Figure 7. Costume sketches. The drawings illustrate the form in which the costume designer is most likely to submit his plans for the director's evaluation. Usually, each sketch is accompanied by brief notes describing details of decoration and construction. When samples of cloth are available, they are often clipped to the drawing, as in the design for the counselor's robe, at the right.

picture, including the variations in reflectivity of the various materials—the rough texture of burlap, the sheen of satin, the brilliance of gold embroidery or jewels. In evaluating the effectiveness of the colors used in the costumes it is important to remember that they are the most visible parts of the total picture; they are accents and points of special interest; consequently they should fit harmoniously with the color scheme of the set but should generally be more vivid and attractive; in fact, in a well-designed set the color scheme should be incomplete without the actors in costume.

As with properties, a well-stocked costume wardrobe is of great value to a theater. Costumes are sometimes rented for plays. Often it is possible to use the actors' ordinary clothing, if it is carefully selected. Costumes may be taken from stock and resewn or redecorated, or they may be especially designed and built for the play. The director may consequently be asked to evaluate costumes in any stage of completion—colored drawings of new designs, costumes that will be redecorated, clothing that will be selected unchanged from what is available.

Essentially the same questions should be asked in judging proposals by the costumer as with properties. Will they function practically in the play? Will they be comfortable for the actors to wear? Will they be effective under the special conditions of lighting and viewing distance in the theater? Are they clearly expressive of period? Are they harmonious with the mood of the play? Will they function effectively as accents in the stage picture? As with all of the technical aspects of production, a full mastery of costuming would be ideal for the director. In its absence, his own taste and impressions, supplemented by the expert knowledge of the costumer, should enable him to make generally sound decisions.

About a week before opening night, one rehearsal is set aside for a final check of all technical work. Before the rehearsal begins, the actors appear for what is called a costume parade, during which the director judges the effectiveness of the costumes as the actors stand on stage, with the lighting that is to be used for the performance. The director views them from a seat in the middle of the auditorium, and indicates his approval or makes suggestions for changes to the chief of the costume crew. Often the costume parade is combined with the makeup check, described in the following section.

Evaluating Makeup

The unfamiliar viewing distance from which the audience watches a play alters the actors' appearance in two ways: the stereoscopic effect is reduced, so that the actors' faces seem less three-dimensional; and the perspective reduction in the size of the image tends to obscure facial features, just as it does decorative details in costume. The brilliance of stage lighting, as contrasted with the darkened auditorium, exaggerates both effects.

Figure 8a. Character makeup. The photographs demonstrate the extreme degree to which an actor's appearance can be altered by makeup. John David Lokke is shown at the left without makeup, and at the right as made up for the part of the villain in Plautus's *The Rope*. For the part, his nose has been broken, his eyes bagged, his features coarsened, and his head made bald. [Photograph by Dorothy Welker]

Figure 8b. Tim Moyer is shown in the roles of Senex in *A Funny Thing Happened on the Way to the Forum* (left), and Macbeth. [Photographs by Douglas R. Hux]

Normal appearance can be restored by the skillful use of makeup. Skin colors are brightened, greater contrast is provided (for example by reddening the lips and darkening the eyebrows), and the shape of the features is emphasized by darkening the shadowed areas and painting the highlighted areas more brightly.

Makeup used simply to counteract the alterations in appearance due to the special theatrical conditions is called *straight makeup*. If it is done skillfully, an actor wearing straight makeup will seem to the audience not to have any makeup on at all: his appearance will match that of people without makeup in ordinary life. Of course the members of the audience sit at different distances from the stage, so that makeup can be ideally adjusted only to one row of spectators. Usually it is designed to look most effective from a position about two-thirds of the way back in the auditorium. It will then seem slightly understated from the back row and somewhat overdone from the front row; it will look crude to the other actors on stage, because they view each other from a closer distance than that of any member of the audience.

In addition to compensating for the effects of distance and lighting, makeup can also be used to make an actor look very different from the way he looks in ordinary life; he can be made to appear older, younger, fatter, thinner,

Figure 8c. Randy Perryman as a murderer in *Macbeth*. [Photograph by Douglas R. Hux]

Figure 8d. Gerald McGowan as the executioner in *The Lark*. [Photograph by Douglas R. Hux]

happier, sadder, more heroic or more villainous. A discussion of the techniques by which such alterations are produced is beyond the scope of this book, but they should be part of the skill of the makeup designer and crew. Makeup intended both to compensate for the special conditions of theatrical viewing and to alter the appearance of the actor is called *character makeup*.

The head of the makeup crew will have taken part in the first conference on the play. He may also want to confer with the director about such matters as the age of the various characters, where it is not clearly indicated in the script, and their personalities and emotional attitudes. It is a great help to an actor who must play the part of a villain to wear makeup that expresses the basic emotions of the character; and an actor who must play a happy-go-lucky comic will find it easier if the emotions he is to express can be supported by his makeup.

Following such a conference, the makeup designer will plan the makeup for each cast member. Since the normal appearance of the actor is a major factor in designing his makeup, the crew chief will want to delay making his plans until the play has been cast; usually they are completed by the end of the first week of rehearsal.

The plans are recorded in the form of a list of the colors and types of makeup to be used for each actor, a diagrammatic sketch marking the shape and placement of details, and written notes about how and where they are to be applied ("naso-labial folds strongly emphasized"; "nose narrowed by darkening the sides and adding a sharp vertical highlight down the center").

A second conference is usually held after the designs have been worked out and recorded. It is difficult to evaluate them from the notes and sketches, which are likely to be technical and diagrammatic rather than pictorially representative. If gross errors appear, the director may be able to discover them. The designs at this stage, however, are almost always considered highly tentative, even by the makeup crew chief, and are thought of as the basis for experimentation rather than as final decisions.

Makeup is not customarily used until late in the rehearsal period. It can be judged effectively only after the stage lighting has been completed, and the lights cannot be placed and adjusted until the stage set is in place.

For a show that opens on a Friday night, it is customary to ask that makeup be used on Monday of the same week. The head of the makeup crew works out a schedule for applying the makeup, arranging the actors in the order of the difficulty and length of time needed to make them up. By prearrangement with the director, he explains the schedule to the cast during a break in one of the rehearsals and distributes copies of the schedule. Usually the beginning of rehearsal is delayed on makeup night by half an hour or an hour so that the cast does not have to come inconveniently early for their makeup calls.

When the makeup has been completed, the director takes a seat in the

```
                        MAKE-UP INSTRUCTIONS
                        Plautus, The Rope
                           T R A C H A L I O
```

Trachalio is 23. Although he is a
slave, he is something of a dandy.
He has a mercurial wit and a sharp
tongue, and is given to dramatiz-
ing himself.

Materials Needed

Base: Stein's grease paint 28D
Shadows: Stein's grease paint 10
Highlights: Stein's grease paint 21
Liner: Stein's liner 1
Rouge: Stein's moist rouge 2
Mascara: Brown
Powder: Stein's face powder 10
Hair: Brown crepe hair

Application

The face is lengthened and narrowed in the shape of an inverted triangle.
Hair: Brown
       Combed to the sides so as to broaden the head; slightly unkempt
       Eyebrows arched two-thirds of the way from the nose
       Thin mustache
       Moderately short beard with a curved point
Forehead: Light horizontal wrinkles
Eyes: Eyes lengthened
      Crowsfeet
Nose: Thinned and straight
Cheeks: Slightly hollowed
        Naso-labial folds faintly strengthened
Mouth: Thin lips, pointing up at the corners

Figure 9. Specifications for makeup. Makeup designs are most often submitted
to the director in this form, with a list of the materials to be used, a description
of their application, and a sketch of the character.

center of the auditorium, about two-thirds of the way back, and the makeup
chief sits beside him with his sketches and notes. The auditorium is darkened,
the stage lights brought up to playing level, the curtain is raised, and the actors
are asked to come on stage one at a time or in small groups. After checking
their appearance in the center of the stage, the director may ask each one to

take up different positions in which he will appear during the play, especially those positions he will occupy at climactic moments, standing on a stair landing, sitting on a sofa, moving from one spot on stage to another. If the makeup appears satisfactory, the director will indicate that fact to the crew chief, and call for the next actor. If the makeup is not acceptable for readily identifiable reasons, he will dictate instructions for alteration to the crew chief: "Trim his beard a little more to a point"; "Try a little darker base"; "The lipstick is too red; get a darker color, or mix a little brown with that," etc. If the makeup is unsatisfactory but the director is unable to specify exactly what should be done to improve it, he is likely to report his emotional responses to the appearance of the actor: "Tom looks a little too pleasant to me"; or "It seems to me Theda ought to look just a little more artificial; you've got her looking attractive, and that's fine, but she ought to look phony, as if the attractiveness had been externally applied." In such cases, the crew chief may make suggestions of techniques by which the desired effect can be produced. Since such discussions require the actors to wait on stage, they must be brief, but usually agreement can be reached very quickly.

If the director approves the makeup or has only a few minor changes to suggest, it is customary to omit makeup from the next few rehearsals, perhaps including it next at the last rehearsal before opening night. If major changes must be made, it is safer to announce a second makeup call for the following night, so that the changes can be checked. Nearly always the second call will result in nearly or entirely satisfactory makeup, but if important problems persist, makeup can be repeated on successive nights, at least for the actors involved in the difficulty.

Besides the makeup parade before the rehearsal begins, the director should remain aware of the makeup throughout the entire rehearsal; not only will he be able to check the actors in many more positions on stage, but he will be able to judge their appearance in groups. Most importantly, he will emerge from the rehearsal with a generalized impression that may be sounder than his judgment of individual actors' appearance.

Evaluating Sound

Playscripts often specify sound effects and music as incidental details of production. They are nevertheless seldom exploited to the full in the theater. Much of the effectiveness of radio drama depended on sound effects, and background music is a major factor in strengthening movies. Noel Coward's use of music, even aside from his revues and musical comedies, is one of the brightest aspects of his plays. The imaginative use of animal trumpeting was a major factor in the success of Ionesco's *Rhinoceros*.

Nearly all sound effects are now played from tape recordings, which permits precise cuing. The work requires not only taste and ingenuity, but considerable technical skill in recording and tape editing. If a composer who is theatrically sensitive is available, the best method of supplying background, incidental, and overture and intermission music, is to have it specially written. It can be performed by a live orchestra or ensemble, or it can be prerecorded and played from tape.

In order to fit specially written music as closely as possible to the general style of a production, a conference should be held with the composer to discuss the director's interpretation of the play. The composer should be supplied with a script in which the position and duration of each separate musical passage is marked. It should be clear whether music is needed to accompany a song by an actress, as a bridge between scenes, or continuing through a scene to help support the mood.

In addition, a complete list of all the passages of music needed should be given the composer, numbered to make it easy to match them with the script markings. The type of music and the mood or feeling which it should express must be stated as clearly as possible in a brief description, and the duration of each passage should be indicated, in minutes and seconds. Estimating the length of a musical passage in advance is difficult, but no composer can be asked to write background music for a scene without an indication of how long it will last. The director should take the script and a stop watch and read the dialog that is to be accompanied by music out loud, attempting to read at the rate at which he expects the actors to perform. If the dialog is interrupted by pauses or by actions performed in silence, they should be included in the timing. Other passages of music can be timed similarly by imagining whatever takes place during the interval, and most accurately by actually carrying on the activity. For instance, if the curtain must be closed between scenes while minor rearrangements of the furniture take place and the interval is to be covered with music, the passage should be timed by going to the theater with a few assistants and asking them to go through the procedure of closing the curtain, rearranging the furniture, and reopening the curtain.

Often music can be unobtrusively faded out at the end, rather than rising to a recognizable conclusion; for example, the music covering a scene break might start full, continue as long as the curtains are closed, and then fade simultaneously with their reopening. In that case it is more convenient to prepare a considerably longer passage of music than will be needed, avoiding the necessity for hairline precision in timing. Also if some accident were to occur back stage and the interval extend longer than had been planned, sufficient music would be available to cover. In such cases, the composer should be given both timings, the precise estimate of the length of the passage needed, and the total length with the extra music intended to serve as a cushion against an emergency. A composer cannot be expected to write music that matches the director's suggestions with absolute precision, but the preparation of specific guidelines will make his work much easier and can be expected to result in a score that can be fitted effectively to the action of the play.

Following are the specifications provided for the composer of music for the second act of a college production of Shakespeare's *Twelfth Night*. In this case, the play was divided into three acts, so that the act and scene numbers do not correspond to those which appear in the printed scripts.

ACT II				
Page in Script	How the Music is Used	Mood of Music, Etc.	Dynamic Pattern	Minimum Length
47	Opening music before Scene 9	Sweet	Fades on, plays to end	1 minute
48–50	Accompaniment for song, "Come Away, Death"	Wistful, melancholy	Starts full, plays to end; repeat to fill the time specified	2 minutes and 30 seconds
53	Bridge music between scenes 9 and 10	Bright, humorous	Could fade on or start full; fast fade off	1 minute
62	Bridge music, scenes 10–11	Bright, humorous, sharp	Fades on and off	1 minute
69–71	Background music, used at the end of the scene as bridge music between scenes 11 and 12	Sweet, a little sentimental	Slow fade on, played to end	2 minutes
75	Bridge music, scenes 12–13	Bright, with strong rhythm	Fades on and off	1 minute
77	Bridge music, scenes 13–14	Nervous music, with strong rhythm	Fades on and off	1 minute
99	Finale music, end of Act II	Humorous, bright music, with climactic finish	Fades on, played to end	3 minutes

If original music is not obtainable, it is possible to select passages from recordings, or to have selections especially performed and recorded for the production. Sometimes it is intended that the audience notice and recognize the passages played, for instance the *Lohengrin* wedding march, or "Yankee Doodle" for a Revolutionary War play. More often, the music is intended to function unobtrusively, supporting the mood of a scene without drawing attention to itself. In that case it is important to choose music with which the audience is likely to be unfamiliar. Furthermore, music of the first rank is generally unsuited to this purpose, since it is likely to be so vivid and interesting that it will attract undue attention; unobtrusive, understated music, even though it may abstractly be of a lower quality, will be less likely to compete with the actors for the audience's attention.

The whole subject of sound in the theater is so complex and so technical that few directors become experts in it. An effort should be made to find or develop highly skilled specialists in this area, whose good judgment can be relied on to plan the sound for a play so as to make the most effective contribution possible to the production.

PRODUCTION DEADLINES

The schedule of deadlines controlling the work of the technical staffs depends on the difficulty of their assignments and on the needs of the director and actors. Since all of those differ from play to play, each production schedule varies somewhat; however, a kind of basic pattern can be described.

The set design must be completed well in advance of the first rehearsal, since the director needs it to plan his blocking; the critical elements, however, are the ground plan and the arrangement of levels. The work should be done so that the director will be able to approve these aspects of the design not later than a week before the beginning of rehearsals. The design of decorative aspects of the set may be delayed a week or two longer, but it must be completed early enough to allow the set builders and painters to do their work comfortably. It is helpful to have a full-color painting of the set to display to the cast at the first or second rehearsal, in which case the design must be entirely finished, except for working drawings.

Before the first blocking rehearsal of the play (usually the second rehearsal) the ground plan of the set should be marked on the stage floor, with paint or adhesive tape; the heights of any levels above the stage floor should be indicated. If at all possible, any stairs and platforms that will appear in the set should be provided, or substitutes of similar dimensions.

Properties are a handicap rather than a help so long as actors must carry their scripts on stage. However, a full set of properties should be provided for all of the rehearsals following the completion of memorization, at least through the last two weeks of the rehearsal period. Especially in the first few rehearsals with properties, substitutes are acceptable, although they should match the final hand props as closely as possible in size and weight, and they should be fitted to whatever uses the action of the play requires. The use of substitutes gives the props crew a longer time for assembling and building the actual props and makes it possible to protect fragile or valuable props that might be damaged by extended use during the rehearsal period. As the final properties are located or constructed, they are used to replace the rehearsal props. The actual props to be used in the performances should be available not later than the last Monday before opening night, assuming that the play opens on a Friday or Saturday.

The set should be in position on stage, and complete, by the last Saturday before opening night. Often it is not possible to assemble it until it is finished; however, if parts can be erected as they are built, it will help the actors to have them in place, especially those sections affecting the action, such as flats containing doors and windows, fireplaces or bookshelves.

Lights cannot be set until the scenery is in place, although the lighting pattern can be designed in advance on the basis of the set designer's drawings and painting. At least a full day should be available for setting the lights. If the scenery is scheduled for assembly on Saturday a week before opening night, the light crew may have late Saturday afternoon and evening to work, and they will have all of Sunday and most of Monday. The lighting should be finished by the beginning of the Monday rehearsal.

It is desirable to have sound effects available as soon as the actors drop their scripts. Background music is an irritating intrusion so long as scenes are being interrupted for directorial comments; it becomes a help when the rehearsals reach the point where scenes are played through without interruption. Sound effects, then, should be provided for rehearsals during the last two weeks, and music should be introduced about a week and a half before opening night.

Especially for period plays, actors must become accustomed to wearing their costumes, so that they will not be distracted by them during the later rehearsals and performances. Not all costumes need to be provided early, but any that affect the actors' posture and movements, such as armor, dresses with trains, or long, tight-fitting coats, should be available for at least the last week and a half of rehearsals.

THE TECHNICAL REHEARSAL

One rehearsal, well in advance of opening night, is set aside for checking the technical aspects of production; this is known as the "technical rehearsal," and it is usually scheduled for the Monday preceding a weekend opening. At this rehearsal, although the actors give a full performance, it is understood that the director will concentrate not on them but on all of the technical aspects of the production. All technical work should be completed by the time of this rehearsal and displayed in performance for the director's evaluation. The director dictates notes to his assistant, discusses problems with members of the technical crews during intermissions, and may stop the rehearsal occasionally to work out difficulties in sound, lighting, or other technical areas. The actors should also be asked to report technical problems, such as a property placed on the wrong side of the stage.

If the technical staff has done its work well, the technical rehearsal will be sufficient for discovering and solving all difficulties. When it seems necessary, special meetings can be arranged for additional work. If scene shifts take too much time, for example, a special rehearsal may be called for the shift crew alone, either immediately following the technical rehearsal, after the actors have been dismissed, or the next day. At such a session, the director and the head of the shifting crew can analyze the shifting procedure and replan it for greater speed, and supervise the crew as they rehearse the shift.

Makeup is usually omitted from the two or three rehearsals following the technical rehearsal, and added for the last rehearsal before the opening performance. All other technical elements are retained for all rehearsals following the technical rehearsal. In later rehearsals, the director returns his attention to the actors, and is likely to focus on the technical aspects of the production only in order to check what has been done to correct the problems he has noted, or whenever any new difficulty appears.

At the end of most rehearsals, the actors are assembled "down front" for evaluations and comments by the director. At the end of the technical rehearsal, the actors are dismissed to remove costumes and makeup, and the technical staff is assembled for discussion. Most of the comments will concern only individual crews or crew chiefs, and each crew can be dismissed as soon as its special problems have been discussed. A few general comments are always in order: an assessment of the smoothness of the rehearsal, and a discussion of problems involving more than one crew. It may have been discovered, for example, that the work of the properties crew is delayed undesirably by the shifting of scenery. Or a few light and sound cues may need to be reversed, with a change in lighting taking its cue from the beginning of a sound effect, rather than the opposite.

In discussing their work with the technical staff, as in commenting on acting and design, it is as important to express appreciation of good work, to identify especially skillful performance or the effective handling of unusually difficult problems, as it is to analyze errors. The director need not minimize technical breakdowns, but it should be clear that he is an evaluator, not simply a fault-finder. A generous recognition of real achievement is most likely to encourage the staff to attack the remaining problems with enthusiasm. Creating the impression that only mistakes have been noticed is more likely to produce the feeling "There's no satisfying that guy; what's the use of trying?"

The technical elements of production are background and environment, the accompaniment to which the actors provide the melody. The attention of the audience will be focused on the actors, but even so the technical effects will powerfully, even if obliquely, influence the success of the production. Certainly, the audience will instantly notice—and remember—any technical error. Often, the efficiency of the technical staff constitutes the difference between a smooth, professional production and sloppy amateurism.

5/The Functions of Blocking

The aspect of the director's work that is most closely related to the work of the technical staff is planning the arrangement and movement of the actors on the stage. So important is this aspect of production that a special term has been assigned to it: *blocking*. It indicates the work of planning the arrangement and movement, the resulting pattern, and the process of teaching it to the actors.

The importance of blocking is second only to that of the dialog in its effect on the total production. The preparation of the blocking design is so important a part of the director's responsibilities that no director can reach even minimum adequacy until he has achieved a high degree of mastery in this area. The fundamental principles of blocking will be discussed in Chapter 6; Chapter 7 describes the procedure to be followed in designing the blocking for a particular show.

Blocking serves four functions, three of which are similar to those served by scenery, and the fourth of which is closely related.

Expressing the Setting

The movement of the actors is dependent on the arrangement of the functional elements of the set, on the location of doors and windows, fireplaces, bookcases, and furniture. Usually information about such arrangement is so clearly provided by the set itself that the audience is unaware of the similar information provided by the blocking. Occasionally, however, shows are presented on a bare stage, and the location of the imaginary set elements is expressed only by the actors' movements. In one play, a fireplace was located on

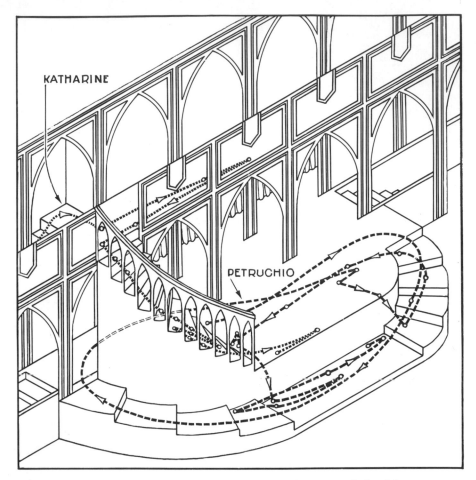

KATHARINE

PETRUCHIO

Figure 10a. Blocking as expressive of mood. This drawing and the following one reproduce the blocking designs prepared by one director for a production of *The Taming of the Shrew;* the section of the play shown is the wooing scene, in which Katharine and Petruchio meet for the first time.

   The pattern of movement clearly expresses the vivacity and high spirits of the scene, especially in Petruchio's leap from the platform at stage left down onto the step, and his run up the steps at stage right and around behind the tall stairs. The pattern of movement is unmistakably comic, and is inconceivable for a tragedy.

   Figure 10b (facing page). The pattern of movement for the last half of the scene is as clearly comic and high-spirited as that shown in the previous drawing. The wide swings from level to level, and the parallel movements of Gremio and Tranio are obviously expressive of comedy or farce, and would be entirely unsuited to serious drama.

the curtain line, at the center of the down-stage edge of the acting area. No actual fireplace was provided, but as actors moved to it and held out their hands for warmth, or crouched in front of it, pulling their coats closer around them, the fireplace became almost visible to the audience, and its position clear. In one production of Thornton Wilder's *Our Town,* the actor playing the druggist got a round of applause each evening when he had finished preparing two imaginary ice cream sodas, flipping back the lids of a nonexistent counter, and dipping down into invisible containers of ice cream with an imaginary scoop. Even when conventional scenery is provided, it becomes meaningful only as the actors display their use of it. How they are arranged on stage, the paths through which they move, where they stop, and what they do in the various areas of the stage all contribute to the audience's awareness of the setting and at the very least reinforce and make significant the information that the set designer has provided about the locale of the play.

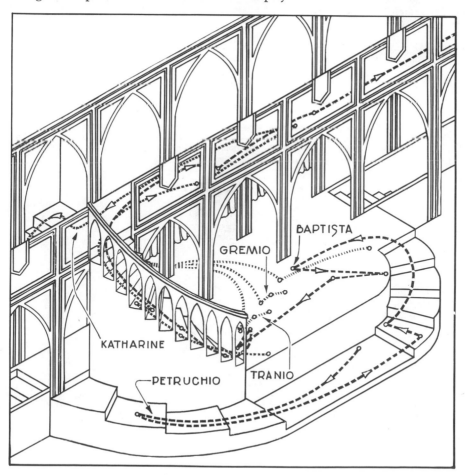

Figure 10c. The solemnity and ceremonial feeling of this scene from *The Lark* are effectively expressed by the careful spacing of the actors in a single plane, suggestive of figures in a stained-glass window. [Photograph by Douglas R. Hux]

Figure 10d. The director has made especially skillful use of an unusual set to express the harmony and triumph of Malcolm's army after the defeat of Macbeth. [Directed by Harold Tedford; photograph by Douglas R. Hux]

Expressing Mood

Blocking also contributes strongly to the expression of mood—that is, to the expression of all of the emotions portrayed by the actors. The movements of the actors are a more powerful factor here than their static arrangements, but even when they are standing or sitting motionless on stage the way they are arranged can help significantly in communicating their emotional relationships. In a trial scene, the separation of the defendant from the jury, the judge, and the lawyers, can help express his emotional isolation. In the famous scene in *Cyrano de Bergerac* in which Christian courts Roxane under Cyrano's guidance, her unattainability is emphasized by her position above them on the balcony, and Cyrano's feeling that his own love for her must be hidden is expressed by his position in the shadow under the balcony. In Act V of Shakespeare's *Antony and Cleopatra,* the placement of Cleopatra at the top of her monument, high above Caesar and his soldiers, emphasizes her regality, and increases the irony of the speeches in which she pretends submissiveness to him. Even when the set does not provide varying levels, the arrangement of the actors can be emotionally significant. In one scene in *Hedda Gabler,* Hedda and Ejlert sit side by side on a sofa at one side of the stage, carrying on an intimate and somewhat indiscreet conversation in low tones; Hedda's husband can be seen by the audience through the door leading to an adjoining room, sitting at a table in conversation with a neighbor; the furtiveness of Hedda's behavior, and her husband's lack of suspicion, are graphically expressed by the way the actors are arranged. Ibsen is especially skillful in the communicative use of blocking; several clear examples are provided by his play *Ghosts.*

Actors' movements are even more expressive of emotion. The degree of effort expressed by a movement is important in communicating the intensity of a scene. Since audiences tend to empathize with actors, the muscular tension displayed by the actors is significant. Fast movements require more effort than slow; a leisurely stroll obviously suggests different emotions from a headlong dash across the stage. Moving to a higher level involves more effort than moving horizontally, moving to a lower level suggests less effort. The expenditure of energy required to climb to a higher level also depends on the dimensions of the supporting surfaces. Occasionally slanted surfaces are provided by the set (ramps); more often, the support for the actors is in the form of a flight of stairs, even though the essential structure may be disguised by special shaping or surfacing, for example to suggest rock ledges. The shorter the risers of such steps the easier they are to climb, and as treads are made deeper they somewhat decrease the apparent effort of actors walking up the stairs. In the home, stair treads are usually eight to ten inches deep, and risers vary from seven to nine inches. To assist actors in using them gracefully, that is with a minimum of visible effort, stairs for the stage are more often made with six-inch risers and twelve-inch treads. In one production of Plautus's *Rope*, a major scenic element was a cliff that started at the center of the stage and extended left across the stage and out of sight. The visible end of the cliff was built in the form of steps, shaped to suggest ledges of rocks, with risers of eighteen inches. The obvious effort required to climb from the stage floor to the top of the cliff

Figure 10e. The combination of contradictory elements—formality, farce, absurdity, and ceremony—is suggested by the stylized arrangement of the actors, including the detail that the central character is almost hiding his face behind the diploma that has just been presented to him. The play is Moliere's *The Imaginary Invalid.* [Photograph by Dorothy Welker]

Figure 10f. The fun of a birthday party is suggested by the arrangement of the actors in this scene from the children's play *Winnie-the-Pooh.* [Photograph by Norm Burlingame]

was especially helpful to the two heroines in the first scene, when they had to indicate that they were exhausted from having been shipwrecked.

The horizontal shape of a movement functions similarly. In ordinary life people tend to move in gentle curves rather than in straight lines, and when buildings, trees, furniture, or other people are present, they tend to choose curving paths that take them through the centers of the open spaces. This subconscious preference for curves is often demonstrated in parks or college campuses; if paved walks are designed in straight lines, especially if they are arranged at right angles, pedestrians often cut unauthorized curving paths from building to building. Although straight paths are geometrically shorter, the inherent preference for curves makes curved movement on stage seem easier, more relaxed, and more natural. Straight-line movement is chosen in ordinary life when speed is important or when the movement is controlled by strong purpose; straight paths of movement on stage also suggest determination, energy, and purpose.

A long movement across the stage can be designed as a single line, straight or curved, or it can be made up of a series of separate straight lines or curves. A broken path suggests indecisiveness, agitation, conflict of purpose, and fear. Intense anger may also be expressed by a broken path, apparently because the violence of the emotion blinds the character to the purpose of the movement, which becomes aimless, not because of indifference but because his attention is focused on his own emotion rather than on purposive action.

An actor can also make a short movement in isolation, that is, one that is not joined with others to take him to a distant part of the stage. Such move-

Figure 10g. In this scene from *Oedipus at Colonus,* Polyneices' isolation and desperation are expressed by the arrangement of the actors, as well as the sympathetic but skeptical attitudes of the townspeople. [Photograph by Norm Burlingame]

ments are most often used to punctuate a speech, and can express emotion by their speed, abruptness, and direction.

The direction of stage movement can be measured by its relation to the audience, and by its relation to the positions of other actors or scenic elements, including furniture. The strongest path of movement is directly toward the audience, the weakest directly away from the audience. Movements directly toward the audience are rarely used in the theater; they are limited almost entirely to the first few steps taken by an actor after entering by a door in the center of the back wall when the wall is parallel with the front edge of the stage. Movements directly away from the audience are almost never used; not only are they excessively weak, but an actor making such a movement seems to have removed himself from the play. Even if an actor must exit through a door situated as described, the blocking is nearly always designed so that he is close to the door, and to one side of it, just before his exit, so that the exit itself takes the form of a curved path leading through the door and off stage, rather than a straight path with the actor moving directly away from the audience.

Figure 10h. The complicated emotions of *Waiting for Godot* are suggested by the arrangement of the actors—the tragedy, comedy, absurdity, and farcical elements all appear in this segment of the blocking design. [Photograph by the Austin-Everest Studio]

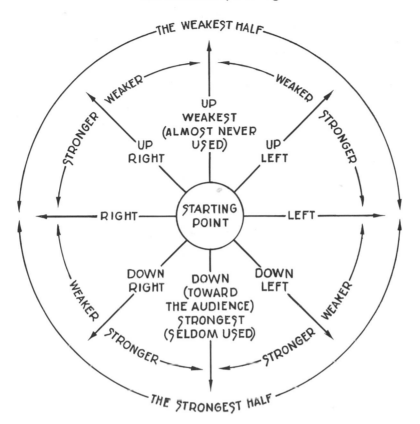

Figure 11. The direction of stage movements. The angles of actors' movements are described in terms of eight compass points, the three pointing toward the audience being the strongest.

Stage movements can therefore be most conveniently thought of in relation to three directions: straight across the stage, displaying a profile view to the audience, and left or right at an angle of 45° to the edge of the stage, moving toward the audience. It is not intended to imply that other angles of movement are impractical; rather, these directions serve as guidelines by means of which the other angles can be effectively described or imagined.

As movements toward the audience shift from the 45° angle toward right angles with the front edge of the stage, they become progressively stronger. As they shift upward, toward a path parallel with the front edge of the stage, they become steadily weaker. A further shift would turn the actors more and more away from the audience. When it is desired to turn the attention of the audience toward an actor, he is usually given a movement from the stronger group. Returning to a position farther back on the stage requires moving in one of the weaker directions; it is consequently inserted when the emotions the actor is expressing are less intense. Often, speeches involving uncertainty or confusion can be used to work the actor back up stage. Occasionally it is possible to move an actor up stage when the primary attention is turned to another actor; for example, when one actor enters at the back of the stage it is often natural for the other actors to turn toward him; taking a few steps toward the entering actor will enable another actor or actors to move up stage without distracting attention from the person who has just entered. From their new positions they can make stronger movements toward the audience on succeeding speeches. Moments of general and confused movement can also be used to shift into fresh and stronger positions actors who must dominate the remainder of the scene.

The relation of an actor's movements to the other actors on stage is important in expressing their emotional relationships. Movement toward another actor suggests affection and intimacy if it is relaxed and moderate in speed, diffidence and fear if it is slow and uncompleted, and aggressiveness (anger or a desire to dominate) if it is done quickly and ends with the two actors somewhat closer together than the ordinary conversational distance. Similar attitudes toward scenic elements can be expressed by movement, although such opportunities are rare in drama: a hesitant approach to a closet in which it is feared a murderer is hiding, shrinking back from a window, or leaning far out to wave at someone offstage.

Negative movements, motivated not by a desire to get toward someone or something but rather by the desire to get farther away, of course indicate the opposite of the emotions discussed. A circling movement, which on stage would usually trace not more than a third or half of a complete circle, suggests conflicting interest and fear, or attraction and repulsion.

A final factor in the effective significance of movement is height. Just as in a static arrangement of actors, movement above the stage floor, even if it does not involve a change in level, seems stronger than the same movement at stage level; thus a moving actor on a platform tends to dominate actors on the stage floor, and the higher the platform the more strength it provides.

THE ESTHETIC EFFECT OF BLOCKING

The most generally neglected aspect of blocking is its esthetic effect, and yet a blocking design can provide interest and even beauty, in addition to its service to the other elements of production, an effect which is important even though the audience may not be consciously aware of it.

Esthetics requires that the pattern of movement and the arrangement of the actors be both varied and unified. Fortunately, the requirements of the action of the play are likely to provide satisfactory variety of movement automatically, especially if the director is careful to use the resources of stage and

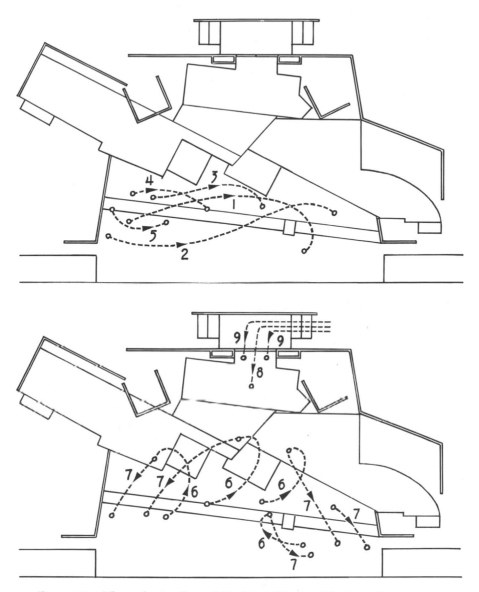

Figure 12a. The esthetic effect of blocking. The two blocking diagrams trace the movements of the chorus during a brief passage in Sophocles' *King Oedipus.* The numbers indicate the sequence of movements.

In the top diagram, members of the chorus start in a random clustered arrangement and move one at a time to a more open arrangement surrounding the altar. In the bottom diagram, they move simultaneously into a semi-elliptical pattern around the choral leader and then break into two groups at the down-left and down-right corners of the stage in preparation for the entrance of Oedipus (8) and his two guards (9). The entire pattern, accompanied by a choral chant, approaches dance and produces a clear esthetic effect while supporting the tension and uneasiness of the lines.

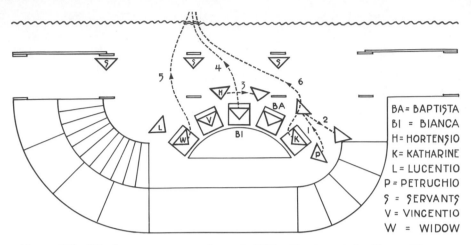

BA = BAPTISTA
BI = BIANCA
H = HORTENSIO
K = KATHARINE
L = LUCENTIO
P = PETRUCHIO
S = SERVANTS
V = VINCENTIO
W = WIDOW

Figure 12b. The banquet scene at the end of *The Taming of the Shrew.* The formality and ceremonial quality of the scene are expressed by a nearly symmetrical arrangement of the actors, with movements designed to form a clear pattern.

Figure 12c. The arrangement of the actors in this scene from *The Lark* echoes the verticals of the set, creating a stark and somewhat static but satisfying pattern. [Photograph by Douglas R. Hux]

Figure 12d (facing page). The excitement and lyricism of *Dark of the Moon* are effectively expressed by the arrangement of the actors, which in this case reaches the pitch of dance. [Directed by Doris Pardington]

Figure 12e (above). The division of the actors into groups of three establishes a strong pattern, and their assymetrical arrangement produces subtle balance. Variety and emphasis are achieved by spacing the trio of actors in the downcenter area irregularly, with one lying on an improvised bench. [*A Funny Thing Happened on the Way to the Forum;* directed by Harold Tedford; choreography by Duncan Noble; photograph by Douglas R. Hux]

setting to the fullest. If the script is emotionally or thematically unified, the types of movement chosen for the actors will reflect the same unity, so that blocking design which is based on a good script has a necessary esthetic quality, especially if the set has been well designed. Nevertheless, attention to the esthetic pattern of the blocking will often result in minor adjustments that may create an impression of polish that would otherwise be absent.

Unity can be provided easily by a symmetrical arrangement of actors, or by planning symmetrical movements. Such arrangements are rare outside the theater, however, except on ceremonial occasions, so that on stage they seem

Figure 13a. Balancing the stage picture. This scene from *We Bombed in New Haven* provides an especially strong illustration of the techniques by which one actor can be used to balance a group. The visual strength of the officer is increased by his raised position, by the lighter color of his costume, by his use of a white folder as a hand property, by his erect posture, with a forward angle, and by lighting him slightly more brightly than the other actors. As a result he not only dominates the center soldier, whose gesture is actually more vigorous, but easily balances the group of seated soldiers, whose positions are visually weakened by the use of technical and postural effects that are the opposite of those illustrated by the officer. [Photograph by Douglas R. Hux]

Figure 13b. These scenes from *The Importance of Being Earnest* illustrate nearly symmetrical balance in an artificial and somewhat formal farce. Nevertheless, the small deviations from symmetry are significant. In the top picture, Lady Bracknell's posture, gesture, and use of her costume enlarge her portion of the stage picture so as to balance the two actors on the loveseat, who are crowded together. In the bottom picture, the arrangement is less symmetrical, and Algernon's gesture strengthens his position so that the four actors at stage left balance the three actors in the right half of the stage. [Photographs by the Austin-Everest Studio]

artificial and contrived; furthermore, symmetry suggests a lack of tension. Most often drama aims at an impression of naturalness and excitement, so that symmetrical arrangements should generally be avoided. They are part of the director's resources, however, and can sometimes be used with great effect. When the two sets of twin brothers finally recognize each other at the end of Shakespeare's *Comedy of Errors,* for example, the falling-in-place of the pieces of the plot might be emphasized by blocking them symmetrically. In this case, the artificiality and lightheartedness of the play harmonize with a symmetrical arrangement of the actors.

Unity of the stage picture requires that the left and right halves balance each other. Such balance is automatically guaranteed in a symmetrical arrange-

Figure 13c. This scene from *Macbeth* illustrates an extremely unusual and effective handling of stage balance. The focus of attention is on the king, although he is stretched out on the floor of the ramp and has his back to the audience. The group of actors at up-stage left, who might be expected to dominate the picture, are clustered in a random arrangement that reduces their individual visual strength, and the figures of Lady Macbeth and the ghost of Banquo are strengthened by their separation, by their position on a raised platform, and by the gold stools provided for them. The result is that the two groups maintain an even balance, and the focus of attention is on the king, who acts as a point of fulcrum between them. [Photograph by Douglas R. Hux]

ment around the center line. However, actors can also be placed asymmetrically on stage so as to create an impression of balance. The key factor is the degree to which the actors on the two sides of the stage attract the attention of the audience. Since the attention is usually concentrated on a single actor at any given moment, the stage arrangement will be theoretically unbalanced unless the focal actor happens to be standing on the center line; however, the attention usually remains on one actor only briefly, and then snaps to a second, a third, and back to the first. The impression of balance comes from the use of the stage for an extended section of the play rather than depending on an isolated moment. All of the sources of strength affect balance; thus an actor placed high on a balcony at one side of a stage, addressing a mob standing below, might well have greater psychological weight—that is, attract the audience's attention more strongly—than all of the other actors.

The type of movement used by the actors also has esthetic implications. Broken straight-line paths and directness and speed of movement create quite a different esthetic impression from slow, graceful, gently curving movement.

Expressive movement, especially if it is patterned, becomes dance. It is excessive to suggest that a good blocking design should reach the pitch of dance and should provide a pattern interesting enough to hold the attention of the audience even in the absence of the dialog. Such movement, like too aggressive background music, would distract attention from the more important elements of the play. So long as it is unobtrusive, however, blocking can strengthen and support the esthetic effect of the production as a whole, and it is too valuable a resource to be neglected by the director.

CONTROLLING ATTENTION

Of the three functions of blocking that have been discussed, the expression of emotion is by far the most important. Still more important, however, is its effect on the control of the audience's attention.

As was indicated in the preceding chapter, the design of the scenery, lighting, and costumes all assist in controlling the attention of the audience; other production elements, such as makeup and properties, may also help in some degree. But blocking is perhaps the strongest force, followed next by the closely related elements of business and gesture.

Actors are more likely to be noticed by the audience if they are placed in certain areas of the stage; such areas are called "strong." If the stage floor is imagined as divided into three strips, running from the edge of the stage to the back wall, the center strip is stronger than the other two. If it is divided into three strips running from side to side, parallel with the front edge of the stage, the back third of the stage is the weakest of the three areas. Combining both divisions produces nine areas, of which the center is the strongest. The

Figure 14a. The arrangement of actors as a factor in controlling attention. The isolation of Erronius and Hysterium focuses attention on them, and the grouping of the three actors at stage left reduces their individual strength; both effects are reinforced by the concentration of light on the central figures. [*A Funny Thing Happened on the Way to the Forum;* photograph by Douglas R. Hux]

Figure 14b. The grouping of the actors clearly focuses the audience's attention on the executioner and Simon, in this scene from the children's play *Simon Big-Ears.* The balance is maintained by a number of subtle devices, which will repay study; for example, the methods by which the actors at the extreme edges of the picture are made less obtrusive, the grouping of the women at stage left so as to form a unit, and the balancing of the light-colored section of wall just behind the king by the apron of the cook at stage right. [Photograph by Norm Burlingame]

area immediately in front of it is as strong, or perhaps even stronger, but it cannot be used so frequently, and consequently is less important to the director.

Movement is one of the most powerful factors in attracting attention. If only one of a group of actors is moving, an audience will turn its attention toward him; only a very strong combination of other factors would compete with the superior attractiveness of the movement alone. If more than one actor is moving, the audience will tend to watch the actor who is moving most vigorously and through the largest space. One of the reasons that it is so disastrous for a dog to trot accidentally on stage during a performance is that his movements are so distracting. When actors in the past have attempted to "steal scenes," that is, to attract attention to themselves when it should have been turned to some other actor, the method they have used has most often been the exploitation of movement; the distracting actor might yawn, polish his nails, fan himself, pick up a book and leaf through it, or engage in exaggerated physical reactions to the other's speech. (Such behavior of course tends to lead to a swift end to the careers of actors who engage in it.) So important is the factor of movement that it has resulted in the construction of two rules: (for the actor) never move while another actor is speaking; and (for the director)

Figure 14c. The triangular arrangement, with Miles Gloriosus at the apex of the triangle, focuses attention on him, in spite of distracting elements. [*A Funny Thing Happened on the Way to the Forum;* photograph by Douglas R. Hux]

Figure 15a. The use of movement in controlling attention. Although both actors are in motion, Joan moves with greater vigor and occupies more space visually, as well as being more brightly lit; the result is a clear emphasis on her rather than on her brother. [*The Lark*; photograph by Douglas R. Hux]

plan at least some small movement for every speech. Such rules are subject to numerous exceptions in actual production, but they are sound guides in the vast majority of instances.

As an illustrative example of the second rule, for one production of *The Taming of the Shrew*, the director's blocking diagrams showed 1047 separate movements. Many movements were omitted from the diagrams, especially those involving large groups of actors, although they were described in written notes. The entire script contained 816 speeches, so that counting only the movements shown in the diagrams, 128 movements were planned for each 100 speeches. In addition, hundreds of small movements, gestures, and items of business were supplied by the actors or worked out during rehearsals.

The rule against one actor's moving during another's speech is suspended most frequently when the actors are engaged in simultaneous and related movements; thus, when a pair of actors are strolling side by side across the stage,

> *There be of them that will themselves laugh, to set on some quantity of barren spectators to laugh too, though in the meantime some necessary question of the play be then to be considered; that's villainous, and shows a most pitiful ambition in the fool that uses it.*
>
>   SHAKESPEARE

engaged in conversation, both continue to move, even though only one is speaking. Also, when one actor crosses to shake hands with another who is entering, the two movements form a unit, although they are in opposite directions. The fundamental principle underlying the rule, of course, is that no movement must be allowed to distract the audience's attention from the necessary focal point; the rule itself may be violated freely so long as the principle is observed.

Figure 15b. The expressive tension and the expansive movement of the standing actor provide so much visual strength that the three actors relaxed on the floor are likely to go unnoticed. [*We Bombed in New Haven*; photograph by Douglas R. Hux]

Figure 15c. Although several actors are moving, the greater vigor of Miles Gloriosus' action, as well as his central position and his isolation from other actors and contrast with the background, make his position stronger than that of any other actor. [*A Funny Thing Happened on the Way to the Forum*; photograph by Douglas R. Hux]

Figure 15d. The graceful simultaneous movements of the Geminae, the size of their gestures, and the use of waving fans and swirling costumes focus attention on them. [*A Funny Thing Happened on the Way to the Forum*; photograph by Douglas R. Hux]

Speech itself is a strong attention-attractor, and when it is combined with even so slight a movement as a turn of the head or a small gesture, it is often sufficient to direct the audience's attention. This is especially fortunate, since with rare exceptions the story at each moment is carried forward by the actor who is speaking.

Specific applications of these principles, as well as some additional factors in controlling attention, are discussed in the next chapter.

6/The Principles of Blocking

Blocking is so close to the center of theatrical technique that it cannot be designed effectively without an understanding of some of the most fundamental aspects of theater art. Since the purpose of blocking is to display the actors to the audience in meaningful patterns of arrangement and movement, blocking design must be preceded by a clear definition of the relationship which it is hoped will be set up between the actors and the audience. The possible relationships vary over a wide range, and each period of theatrical history tends to be characterized by a preference for a particular one of the available relationships, or at most for a narrow range. The relationships between actors and audience were very different in ancient Greece, ancient Rome, the middle ages, Renaissance England, and the seventeenth-century restoration period.

The identification of the relationship that the director hopes the actors and the play will establish with the audience is a necessary preliminary to his preparation of the blocking design. The arrangement of the actors, the angles at which they are placed, their patterns of movement—all depend on the director's conception of the preferred relation between the audience and the drama. In one play, he might hope that they would be so caught up in the action that they would feel they were an intimate part of it; in another, he might prefer that they sit as uninvolved observers and judges; in a third, he might hope that the actors could address the audience directly, in a kind of actor-spectator dialog, each acknowledging the presence of the other; again, he might see the play as a spectacle to be displayed. Although obviously individual plays might be better suited to one or another of the various treatments, many plays provide a wide range of possibilities. In any case, the director must define the audience-actor relationship before he can develop an effective blocking plan.

Empathy in Audience Response

To analyze all of the possible relations between actors and audience would require far more space than is available here. The key factor seems to be "esthetic distance," a useful concept but one which is difficult to define. It is related to the term "empathy," which means vicarious sharing of another person's experiences. It is possible to observe other people's activities without becoming emotionally involved, or without even sharing their point of view intellectually. At the opposite extreme, it is possible to share other people's experiences so fully in imagination that we are not only pleased or unhappy, with them, but may even show physical symptoms that match theirs: our muscles may tense as we watch others lift heavy weights, we may nod our heads as they do.

Between the two extremes is a wide range of empathy. Farce tends not to arouse much empathy; comedy, somewhat more; romantic drama usually produces strong empathy; and Aristotle identified the empathic effect of tragedy as one of its major strengths. The degree of empathy depends not only on the type of play but also on the attitudes of the audience, individually and as a group. In the last half of the nineteenth century, the popular melodramas aroused strong empathy in the audience; today, viewers are likely to feel almost no empathy while watching them, with the result that what were originally intended as romantic tragedies are now viewed as farces. Eighteenth-century audiences empathized strongly with the title character of *The Tragical History of George Barnwell,* and with his master, and hardly at all with the villainous Millwood; today the pattern of empathy has nearly reversed, and audiences are far more likely to empathize with Millwood, and to regard Thorowgood as a pompous Babbitt and George himself as something of a fool; the result is that the whole character of the play has changed.

We tend to empathize most readily with characters who are somewhat like ourselves; presumably the pattern of empathy of an Elizabethan Jew watching a performance of *The Merchant of Venice* would have been different from that of the Christian members of the audience.

The empathic range of twentieth-century drama seems broader than for almost any other period; exceptional plays can be cited at both extremes of the range, and at all points in between. Bertolt Brecht instructed his actors to attempt to prevent the audience from empathizing with the characters: he demanded an effect of "distancing" or "alienation." At the other extreme, Thornton Wilder's *Our Town* depends more on arousing extreme empathy than on any

other production element. Although modern plays cover the entire range, they
do not do so evenly; by far the great majority of contemporary plays aim at
producing strong empathy, and one of the characteristics of avant-garde productions is the attempt to involve the audience with the actors even more fully
than has been done in the past.

The various members of an audience do not empathize equally with the
characters. Rather than attempting to control the precise degree of involvement
of each member of the audience, the director's purpose in empathic drama is to
make each viewer feel that he is a part of the cast. If a party is in progress on
stage, it is hoped that he will feel that he is a guest at the party; if a scene
takes place in a living room, it is hoped that each member of the audience will
feel that he is sitting in the living room with the cast, as fully involved as each
character even if he has no lines of dialog to speak.

This involvement in the action of the play is of course imaginary; it is
contradicted by obvious facts. The viewer is not sitting on stage, he is placed
in what is almost a separate room. Even in a theater with the stage thrust out
into the audience, the actors and members of the audience are nearly always
placed in clearly defined and separate areas. The viewer is not surrounded by
the actors, he is surrounded by the other members of the audience. He does not
watch the actors (for instance in a living-room set) from the same distance as
if he were in an actual living room; instead, he is much farther away, perhaps
on the average about forty feet.

Where empathy is desired, all of the arts of the theater are exploited to
disguise those facts, to distract the viewer's attention from the presence of the
rest of the audience and the excessive distance between him and the action on
stage. For example, the dimming of the lights in the audience area and the
brilliant lighting of the actors tend to suppress the viewer's awareness of the rest
of the audience and to concentrate his attention on the stage.

PROJECTION

Besides concealing factors that are out of harmony with the empathic
effect, all of the elements of production are especially adjusted to match as
far as possible the experience which a viewer would have if he were actually on
stage, an observant even if silent member of the cast. Much of this adjustment
is identified by the term "projection," and some examples have already been
described, in scenery, costumes, and makeup. Projection is intended to compensate for the distortions and diminutions caused by the fact that the viewers are
seated farther from the stage than it is hoped they will empathically feel. The
production elements are especially designed to create at forty feet the same
effects as similar elements would produce outside the theater at normal viewing
distance. In an actual living room, the floral motifs in a wallpaper design might

be easily recognizable; the same design might appear simply as a textured blur from forty feet away. The set designer, then, would replan the pattern, enlarging the motifs and increasing their contrast and clarity of outline, so that the effect from forty feet away matched that of ordinary wallpaper at the more familiar viewing distance. In the same way, straight makeup is intended to make the actor look, at theatrical distance, exactly as he would look in ordinary life, at normal conversational distance. All aspects of production must be altered in this way, that is, they must be projected: costumes, makeup, properties, scenery, sound effects, blocking, gesture, and speech. Each element must be especially designed for the theater, and will deviate distinctly from matching elements in ordinary life outside the theater, although in realistic empathic drama the intention is that the experience provided for the audience will duplicate that of ordinary life; in other words, it is hoped that the diminution and distortion resulting from the special conditions of viewing in the theater will be precisely compensated by the projection adjustments.

Realism is only a background. It cannot form an artistic motive for a play that is to be a work of art.

OSCAR WILDE

It should be emphasized that what has been said applies only to the technique of a particular type of drama, which aims at illusion. Even in such plays, the impression of reality can only be a technical device chosen to serve a more important purpose. Every work of art involves a selection, rearrangement, and interpretation of the experiences of life. The production of empathy and the simulation of familiar experience are only two of the various techniques that can be employed to serve higher goals, but since they are so frequently specified or implied by playwrights, the ability to handle them is a necessary part of every director's skill.

Stage sets which represent rooms most often are designed in the form of a five-sided box, made up of the stage floor, a ceiling, and three walls. If the production is successful in making the viewer feel that he is sitting in the room as a member of the cast, the fourth wall will be placed immediately behind him. In the real room, the fourth wall would be invisible, and of course it exists in the theater only in imagination. The visual field for a person sitting in his chair in an ordinary room, with his back to the center of one wall, is very different from the appearance the same room would display if one wall were removed and the viewer were moved back to normal audience distance. Viewed from forty feet away, such a room would lose much of its three-dimensionality, and would seem shallower; the back wall would occupy a much larger part of the visible area, and the floor, ceiling, and side walls would become pro-

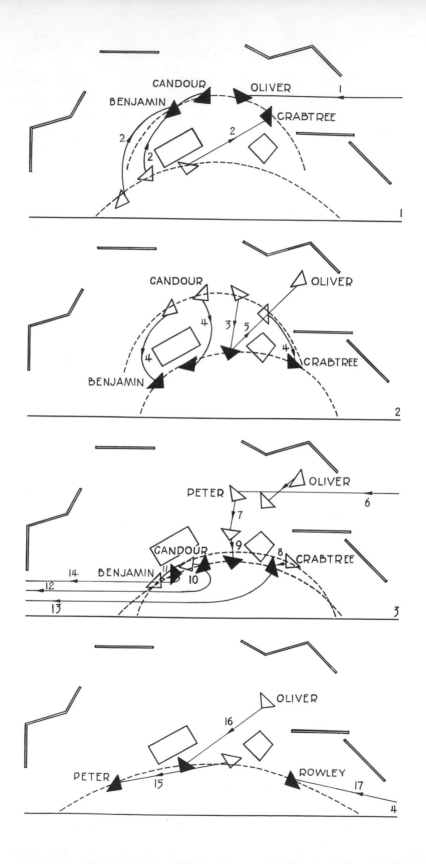

portionately smaller; in addition, the dimensions of all elements in the room would be apparently reduced, and some of them would become invisible or change their character (the floral pattern reduced to a texture, and furniture seeming more delicate and fragile). It is standard practice to compensate for such changes, in scenic design. A glance at a collection of ground plans for stage sets will demonstrate that walls are hardly ever placed at right angles; instead, the side walls are spread apart at the front; in addition, the walls are made much higher than is customary outside the theater. Such spreading and enlargement counteract some of the perspective alterations. The effect for the audience is to increase the percentage of the visual field occupied by the side walls, so as to match more closely the pattern of ordinary experience, to compensate for the apparent shrinking in height as the viewing distance is shifted from the familiar to the theatrical, and to somewhat enlarge the visual area occupied by the ceiling. With a single exception, all of the elements in the scenery are altered in this way; the exception is the height of chair seats, which must remain standard for the actors to use them without looking grotesque. Although such adjustment is clearest in interior scenes, it operates even when no straight lines appear in the set: the design of an outdoor scene, with trees and hills, involves the same kind of rearrangement, enlargement, and spreading.

The physical enlargement of the actors themselves was customary in the ancient Greek theater; it is used so infrequently and so minimally in the modern

Figure 16a (facing page). The elliptical arrangement of actors. The use of a partial ellipse as a basis for blocking design is a somewhat artificial device, so it is shown most clearly in a somewhat artificial and stylized play. The drawings reproduce the director's blocking plans for one production of Sheridan's *The School for Scandal*.

It has been rumored that Sir Peter has been seriously wounded in a duel; Sir Benjamin, Mrs. Candour, and Crabtree descend on his house to learn the details. In the top drawing, they are assembled at the down-right edge of the stage, at one end of an imaginary ellipse. Sir Oliver enters up left, and they rush to surround him, forming a second partial ellipse upstage. (In each drawing, the initial positions are indicated by open triangles, the second positions by black triangles; the numbers indicate the sequence of movements.)

In the second diagram, Sir Oliver in disgust walks out of the group to a downstage position, but they follow him, setting up a third ellipse. As Oliver hears Sir Peter approaching, he crosses up left to greet him. Sir Peter crosses to above Sir Oliver's previous position; Sir Oliver, who is not involved in the few following speeches, remains up left outside the group. Sir Peter makes two short crosses downstage, and the others crowd around him, forming a fourth ellipse. Peter angrily orders them out of his house, and they leave one at a time, each one hurling back a parting insult.

In the bottom drawing, Sir Peter crosses down-right after them, and Sir Oliver crosses toward him. Rowley then enters from down left, to introduce the next scene, the three actors being arranged at the front of the stage along a very open partial ellipse.

theater that it is negligible. Other methods of projection, however, are exploited as fully as possible. Their use in costuming and makeup has already been mentioned, and the techniques of vocal projection will be discussed in a later chapter. Here we are concerned with projective techniques involving actors' arrangement and movement.

The Basic Arrangement of Actors

A group of people in an ordinary living room could take up their positions in any conceivable arrangement; however, there is a strong tendency for them to

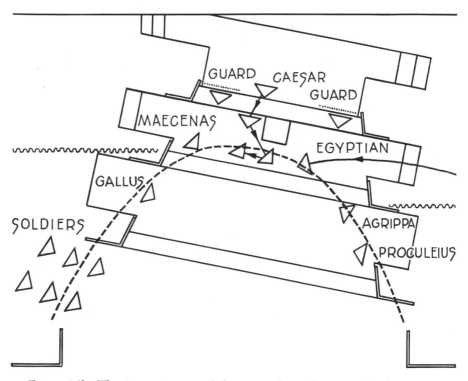

Figure 16b. The impressiveness of this scene from *Antony and Cleopatra* is emphasized by the arrangement of the actors along a narrow half-ellipse with the long diameter extending out into the audience. At the opening of the scene, the upper center of the ellipse is vacant. It is partially filled by the entrance of the Egyptian, who stops at a point on the ellipse, and is finally completed by Caesar's short crosses down-stage. Two points are of special interest. The down-right end of the elliptical arc is defined not by a single actor but by files of soldiers extending off-stage, who function visually as a group. Although the audience is unlikely to be consciously aware of the elliptical arrangement, Caesar's completion of the pattern produces a feeling of inevitability and rightness. (The two guards are placed outside the ellipse because they are not active in the scene, and function visually almost like scenic elements.)

sit or stand in an approximately elliptical pattern, facing the center of the room. One member of such a group of five or six people, sitting with his back to the center of one of the long walls, would see the others arranged in an arc. In the theater, the ellipse must be extended out into the auditorium, passing behind each seat (or, more simply, behind the last row); only the small section that extends into the stage space is available for the actors' use. On the stage, as in ordinary life, actual arrangements are varied, but the open arc is a kind of basic pattern from which the variations are derived.

One focus of the imaginary ellipse lies far out in the audience, perhaps two-thirds of the way toward the back wall of the auditorium; the other is a short distance in front of the stage; the basic arrangement of the actors turns them toward this nearest focus. Inexperienced actors often arrange themselves as they would in a real living room, pointing toward the center of the stage rather than out into the audience. Since all theatrical elements are psychologically audience-centered, and most of them physically audience-centered, the experience of working through a single play is usually enough to readjust actors' thinking in favor of the open-arc arrangement, pointed toward the audience; explaining the two patterns to the actors, however, may speed up their adoption of the correct one, and will help clarify the blocking design for them.

In blocking a play, the director usually must work at different points in the action with different numbers of actors, varying from one alone on the stage up to the full cast. Classic dramas tend to require larger casts than contemporary plays, which, partly for reasons of economy, are written for fewer characters. With a single actor, the problem of emphasis is automatically solved, since nothing is likely to distract the audience's attention from him. Further, great variety of movement is easy to achieve, since a single actor can use the entire stage, even the weakest areas, without losing command of the audience.

With two actors, the avoidance of symmetrical arrangements becomes of some concern, and unless adequate action has been provided by the script, the director must invent business and movements to prevent the play from sinking to a static conversation in which the two actors sit motionless on opposite sides of the stage for long periods.

TRIANGULAR ARRANGEMENTS OF ACTORS

Many directors find it convenient to think of their blocking designs primarily in terms of three actors. Like the open-arc arrangement, this is a point of departure rather than a restriction. However, many three-character scenes occur in plays, and even if more actors are present on stage, often only three will be intensely involved in the action being carried forward.

Three actors can be arranged essentially in only two ways, in a straight line or in a triangle. The straight-line arrangement generally seems artificial and static, and is consequently usually to be avoided. Symmetrical triangular ar-

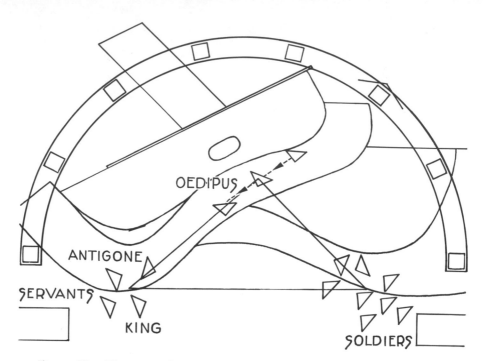

Figure 17a. The triangular arrangement of actors. In this scene from *Oedipus at Colonus,* the two down-stage corners of the basic triangle are defined by groups of actors, four at the right and eight at stage left. Oedipus is placed at the apex of the triangle, and attention is focused on him because most of the other characters are turned toward him, he is on a higher level, and in this brief segment of the play only he moves.

Figure 17b. In this scene from *Blood Wedding,* the down-stage corners of the basic triangle are defined by pairs of actors, the apex by a trio, and one actress is placed outside the triangle at slightly right of up-center. [Photograph by Dorothy Welker]

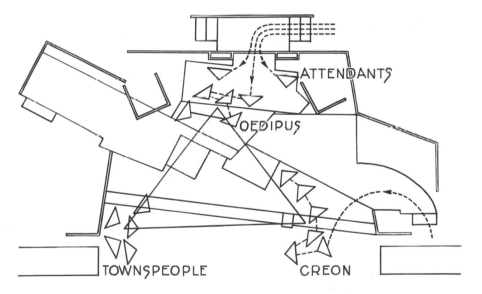

ATTENDANTS

OEDIPUS

TOWNSPEOPLE   CREON

Figure 17c. In this scene from *King Oedipus,* the stage-right corner of the triangle is defined by a small group of townspeople who have no crosses during this section of the play. The other two corners of the triangle are marked by Creon and Oedipus, both of whom move during the scene, subtly shifting the visual focus and the shape of the triangle. (As in FIGURE 16b, the two attendants are placed outside the basic pattern, since they are not functionally active in the scene.)

Figure 17d (facing page). This pattern is unusual in that the focus of attention is on the actor at the up-left corner of the triangle, and the actor at center is supposed to be unaware of what is going on. [*A Funny Thing Happened on the Way to the Forum;* photograph by Douglas R. Hux]

Figure 17e. The focus of attention is on Hysterium, at the up-stage apex of the triangle. The arrangement is unusual in that the other characters are placed so as to mark two full sides of the triangle, rather than simply defining the corners. [*A Funny Thing Happened on the Way to the Forum;* photograph by Douglas R. Hux]

rangements, with the dominant actor standing at stage center, and the other two actors down left and down right of him, have the same characteristics.

The most effective arrangement of three actors, then, is an asymmetrical triangle, with the dominant actor isolated. As the focus of attention shifts to a second actor, a short movement will not only call attention to him, but can be used to alter the shape of the triangular arrangement. Since an infinite number of triangular shapes are possible, continued variety of arrangement can be achieved, although the triangularity of all of them will provide a unifying similarity. More than three actors can be fitted into the triangular pattern; two actors placed close together may mark one corner, with a third and fourth actor placed at the remaining corners.

SPACING

Besides its influence on the general arrangement of actors, the fact that the typical spectator views the stage from a greater distance than for a similar scene outside the theater also affects the spacing of the actors. One member of a group of people seated in a living room sees the other people spread out over a wide area, occupying an angle of well over 90°; in the theater, a large part of the field of vision is taken up by the auditorium itself, and the angle filled by the stage may be less than 45°. The result is that in ordinary life each person is usually seen isolated, with a distinct space separating him from the people on his left and right, but if exactly the same arrangement is transferred to the stage the space seems to shrink, and the actors are apparently moved closer together. In addition, the actors must be placed so that they are visible from each seat in the auditorium. As a result, blocking must be planned to provide clear space around each actor, much larger than in similar scenes in ordinary life.

This recommendation is not intended to suggest that actors may never stand close together; in fact, spacing can be used effectively to express many subtle variations in relationship. Each culture is characterized by spatial customs and preferences, which are actually the largest examples of the varying gestural dialects. Especially important is the distance at which it is customary to carry on conversation, which varies greatly from culture to culture, being small in some South American countries and large in England, with the United States in between. Deviations from the familiar conversational distance are often interpreted emotionally. If Alistair Buckingham maintains a greater distance in conversation than Dick Jones is accustomed to, he is likely to be seen as aloof

Figure 17f (facing page). Two actors, brightly lit and dressed in light-colored clothes, stand at the focus of attention at the apex of the triangle; the downstage points are defined by a single actor (stage right) and a pair of actors (stage left). [*The School for Scandal;* photograph by Dorothy Welker]

Figure 18a (facing page). Effective spacing. The six actresses are effectively arranged so as to form a group and still contribute individually to the stage picture. The center of the group is slightly to the left of the stage so that it is balanced by the single figure of Pseudolus, placed down-right. [*A Funny Thing Happened on the Way to the Forum*; photograph by Douglas R. Hux]

Figure 18b. Effective spacing. The actors in this scene from *A Thurber Carnival* are arranged in pairs, yet each is spaced so that he is clearly visible and makes an individual contribution to the stage picture. [Photograph by Norm Burlingame]

Figure 18c (facing page). Effective spacing. The pyramidal arrangement of the actors is especially interesting. [*We Bombed in New Haven*; photograph by Douglas R. Hux]

Figure 18d. Effective spacing. The spacing of intimate scenes so as to suggest closeness and still maintain visibility is difficult; both effects are well achieved in this proposal scene from *The Importance of Being Earnest.* [Photograph by the Austin-Everest Studio]

and unfriendly; on the other hand, if José Seville moves closer than expected, he may be judged as pushy or aggressive; often such interpretations are made without any awareness of their basis.

These examples are crude, but variations in the distance between actors can be used with great subtlety to express minute differences in the relationships between characters on stage. The communication of intimacy, aggressiveness, dislike, affection, and many other emotions can be greatly assisted by the skillful use of spacing. However, the normal spacing on stage, the basic distance that serves as a measure of the variations, is much greater in the theater than outside it.

As a basic rule, then, actors should be blocked so that there is always

Figure 18e. Effective spacing. The massing of the actors is planned so that emphasis and visibility are maintained. [*A Funny Thing Happened on the Way to the Forum;* photograph by Douglas R. Hux]

Figure 18f. Effective spacing. The use of the varying levels provided by the large ramp is especially important in the effective arrangement of the actors. [*Macbeth;* photograph by Douglas R. Hux]

Figure 18g. Ineffective spacing. The blocking obscures three of the four actors in this scene at the close of *The Bald Soprano.* [Directed by Stancil Campbell]

Figure 18h. Ineffective spacing. The actors who should receive the focus of attention are the two at the back of the stage. Neither is effectively visible, although one is facing directly down-stage and the other is making an expansive gesture. [*We Bombed in New Haven;* photograph by Douglas R. Hux]

clear space between them; even when they are brought closer together to express intimacy or affection, usually the positions should be held only until the relationship has been clearly communicated, and then a motivation should be found for the actors' returning to the normal distance.

Just as spacing customs vary geographically, they also vary from period to period. In many of the premodern periods, the normal distance was greater than is now common. A moment's thought will make it obvious that the close spacing that might be acceptable for plays like *A Streetcar Named Desire* would be quite unsuited to Greek tragedy, Elizabethan drama, or Restoration comedy.

Providing for theatrical spacing is one of the director's concerns in blocking; its maintenance is a responsibility of the actors, and is discussed in the next chapter in connection with dressing the stage.

Figure 18i. Ineffective spacing. There is so much wrong with the blocking in this scene from *A Funny Thing Happened on the Way to the Forum* that it almost looks as though it were especially posed to illustrate what not to do. The scene is totally lacking in focus; one actor has his back turned directly toward the audience; Pseudolus is peering dreamily into the audience, apparently unaware of the other characters. All three of the soldiers at the back are partially hidden; the one at stage right seems to be berating the center one for standing in the wrong place, the one in center seems to be angrily demanding that the actors in front of him move out of the way, and the soldier at the left is staring off-stage as if looking for assistance in finding his place. Senex, at stage right, looks belligerently at Pseudolus as if about to order him off stage, and Miles Gloriosus glares at the general mess in outrage, as if he were about to demand a wholesale execution. [Photograph by Douglas R. Hux]

The Arrangement of Groups

Often a large number of actors join together in a crowd, rather than being seen individually. Such a group usually functions almost like a single actor, so that the principle of spacing applies to the group as a whole but not to the individual actors who compose it; for example, the scenes in *Antony and Cleopatra* in which Caesar addresses his soldiers are best thought of as made up of two elements, the soldiers as a group constituting one, and Caesar the other.

Regular arrangements of people in groups occasionally occur in ordinary life, as for example when a number of people cue up at a ticket window. In the last act of *Our Town,* actors representing the people of Grover's Corners who have died are seated on chairs arranged in the regular pattern of graves in a cemetery. Most often, however, people in groups are arranged irregularly, like the guests in the *Rubaiyat,* described in Fitzgerald's phrase as "star-scattered on the grass." At the same time, esthetic unity requires that such a group have a central focus.

The most important consideration in producing the effect of randomness is that elements of the arrangement should not be repeated. Thus, the actors should not be evenly spaced at identical intervals; they should not face in exactly the same direction; their spacing from front to back of the stage area should be uneven; they should not be allowed to cluster in subgroups of the same size; actors of the same height should not stand side by side. Usually groupings can be arranged effectively by allowing the actors to take whatever positions they like; then the director should study the arrangement for accidental repetitions; these can be adjusted by asking individual actors to move to new positions, to vary the directions toward which they face, or to exchange positions with other actors; usually only a few small adjustments will produce the effect desired.

Occasionally it will be desirable to focus the attention of all of the members of a group in the same direction, for example to represent the unity of purpose or attention produced by an exciting oration. The less unified the emotion of the group, the more varied their arrangement should be. At the beginning of Antony's harangue to the mob in *Julius Caesar,* for instance, the crowd should create an impression of confusion; at the end of the speech, their unified acceptance of his persuasion should be expressed by turning each member of the crowd toward the speaker.

Even when it seems desirable to avoid uniformity of arrangement, it is important that nothing lead the audience's attention away from the desired focus; a member of the crowd who stood looking off stage, for example, would distract at least some of the members of the audience. The solution to this problem is to select a few of the actors and instruct each one to turn toward another actor who is himself looking at the speaker; if a member of the audience then glances at one of the actors who is turned away from the speaker, he is most likely to follow the line of sight to the second actor, and then from him to the speaker; from the standpoint of the audience, then, the focus of the stage picture is still uniformly on the speaker, either directly or indirectly, although the intended impression of variety is created.

Making Crowds Seem Larger

Almost never does a director have as many actors available for crowd scenes as logic would require; not only may his supply of actors be limited, but the stage itself will not provide enough space to display, for example, an entire army. He must consequently design his arrangements in crowd scenes to make the groups look larger than they are.

Twenty actors spaced loosely so as to fill half the stage from the front edge to the back wall will create an impression of a much larger crowd than if they are huddled together in a thin line along the front edge of the acting area. However, gaps that enable the audience to look through the group to the back wall emphasize that the space is not actually filled; in checking the arrangement of a crowd of actors, the director should especially watch for such openings and fill them in by moving a few of the actors. A further device, and one that is much more convincing than it might seem, is to arrange the actors so that the group extends off stage and out of sight of the audience. If they are represented as listening to a speech, the speaker can assist in the illusion by directing his performance to the members of the crowd at the edge of the stage; since it is customary for a speaker to point his remarks to the center of the audience, the viewers will subconsciously picture the crowd as extending off stage with at least as many additional members as are visibly present. In using this device, it is important that the actors not be arranged so that the group fades off, getting smaller toward the side of the stage; if anything, it should do just the opposite, so that the audience will assume that the invisible section of the crowd is even larger than those present on stage.

In filling out a crowd, it is helpful to search the script for actors who are not present but who can be added to the group; even actors playing fairly important roles can be used effectively in groups if their entrance and positions are planned so that they are well covered by crowd members down stage of them; if they can be further disguised by alterations in costume, sometimes as simple as donning a hat and coat for the crowd scene, no one in the audience may identify them.

The Duke of Saxe-Meiningen, who is usually credited with having initiated the development of the position of director in the modern theater, was especially famous for his handling of crowd scenes. Although such groups must often function as a unit, it is important to remember that crowds are made up of individual human beings; each actor should be encouraged to work out a full characterization, and the older concept of crowds as made up of static "spear-carriers," shouting nonsense syllables like "Rhubarb, rhubarb!" or "Walla-walla!" when they were called on to ad lib responses, should be avoided. .

DESIGNING MOVEMENT

In designing blocking, and in teaching it to actors, it is almost inevitable that the director describe it in terms of a series of static pictures, with the actors assuming one arrangement, and then moving to the next. Such a description, however, is almost the opposite of the fact, and it is important that both director and actor recognize its artificiality; although any particular actor may be standing still more often than he is moving, some movement is occurring at almost every moment of the play, and the attention of the audience will almost always be directed toward the movement. Rather than being a series of still pictures, with transitional movements, a play is a constant pattern of focal movement, with what would otherwise be distracting elements held in suspense; there is more stillness than movement in a play, but it is the movement that counts; the motionless elements are background.

One rule of theater movement is somewhat different from ordinary life: actors normally cross in front of other actors rather than behind them. That rule depends on two considerations. One is the artificiality of stage arrangements. Because the stage is usually larger than the real-life scenes that are depicted on it, there is often more space behind furniture than would appear in ordinary rooms. Furthermore, the projective spreading of the entire scene tends to flatten out the central space, which in a normal room is much closer to a circle. The result of those factors is that beginning actors often interpret a cross in terms of the position of another actor, whereas in an ordinary room they would focus on the open space through which they were moving. On stage they sub-consciously say "I am walking in front of Lady Bracknell"; outside the theater they would say "I am walking across the room." The result of this difference in interpretation is that many actors at first automatically circle around above other actors rather than crossing firmly in front of them.

The second reason for the rule, and a far more important one, is the fact that the audience in the vast majority of cases will be following the actor who is moving. Since he is nearly always the actor who is speaking (in harmony with the rule that no actor should move during another actor's speech), and since he is consequently carrying the story of the play forward at the moment, it is important that the audience's focus on him not be interrupted. If he makes his cross by walking behind another actor who is standing, he is hidden as he passes, and the sight-line of the audience, moving with him, is interrupted by the other actor. Even if the actor being crossed is seated, the moving actor is partially hidden, and often the angle at which the audience sees him may be weaker than that at which they see the seated actor, with an ambiguity of focus.

Like all such rules, exceptions may be made provided the purposes of the production are achieved: rules may be broken, but not principles. The underlying principle is that the attention of the audience must be focused at the point that is essential to the play. A minor character, crossing simply to reach an exit, may well be blocked behind other characters. Even when the crossing actor is vital to the play at the moment, if his speech and action are directly related to a seated character it may be better to have him circle around behind the other actor; so long as he maintains his focus of attention on the seated actor, he will be more visible to the audience than if he had followed the usual rule. And finally, in cases where a character would move behind another in real life, especially if his action is of minimal significance, it is often preferable to follow the same pattern on stage. A butler serving tea to the duchess would cross behind her rather than in front; on the other hand, a butler bringing in an expected telegram on a tray, if the telegram was important to the play, should be blocked into a stronger position.

The Shape of Movements

As has been pointed out, outside the theater people tend to move through the centers of open spaces, and to prefer curved paths. Such movements should also be considered normal on stage; an actor who must walk between two other actors would normally cross halfway between them; if he passes between a sofa and a table on his way from the fireplace to the door, he would usually make his cross halfway between the two pieces of furniture, shaping the entire movement as a long curve. Strong purpose tends to straighten out the paths of movement, which then cut directly through open spaces by the shortest route, whether it lies through their centers or not. Intense emotion—hysterical fear, extreme joy—may carry this shift so far that the actor will actually bump into furniture or other actors, in a headlong rush toward or away from someone or something.

The Strength of Positions

The relative positions of two actors on stage are vitally important in expressing their emotional relationships. The differences in strength of the stage areas have already been discussed. Even more important is the relative distance from the front edge of the stage. If two actors carry on a conversation in a scene, they usually turn toward each other. If they are equidistant from the front edge of the stage, the audience then sees them in profile. Since this is the

Figure 19a. Actors' angles as a factor in the strength of their positions. Pseudolus, standing on the steps, is placed at the strong down-right angle; Hero and Philia, seated on the steps, are turned at a weak angle, right and slightly up; the result is that Pseudolus clearly dominates the picture. [*A Funny Thing Happened on the Way to the Forum;* photograph by Douglas R. Hux]

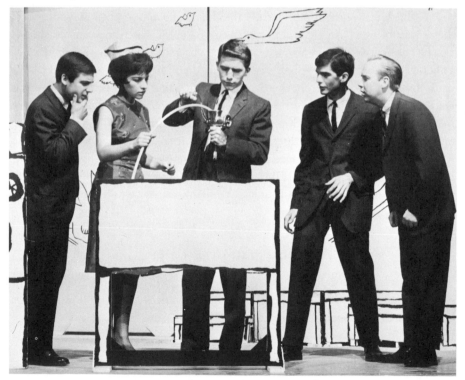

weakest of the generally acceptable positions, it is customary to ask them to turn artificially slightly more toward the audience (this technique is called "cheating"). If one actor is somewhat farther from the front edge of the stage than the other, turning toward each other will result in one actor's facing at least partially away from the audience, and the upstage actor's facing the audience more directly. The up-stage actor is thus in a stronger position.

Figure 19b. Although the face of the actress is lower than two of the actors, the greater strength provided by her frontal position enables her to dominate all five of the actors in this scene from *Rhinoceros*. [Photograph by Norm Burlingame]

Figure 19c (facing page). Matching the angles of the actors with the diagram in *Figure 11* will demonstrate why the center actor is most strongly emphasized. [*A Thurber Carnival;* photograph by Norm Burlingame]

Figure 19d. This scene from *A View from the Bridge* is especially interesting because the dominance of the figure standing at stage right depends entirely on the strength of his angle. Although other actors are more brightly lit, occupy more space, and form a tableau which has strong inherent interest, all of their angles are weaker, and the eye, after a brief study of the picture, comes to rest on the narrator, facing directly front. [Directed by Tracy Davis; photograph by Dorothy Welker]

"Upstaging" is another of the devices used in the past by actors who were attempting to steal a scene. One of the most painfully hilarious experiences for a director is watching two determined actors attempt to upstage each other throughout a scene, working toward the back wall in a kind of seesaw movement.

The farther apart the two actors are, left and right, the smaller the effect of their upstage-downstage positions. Since actors' positions are equally strong only when they are level with each other (that is, the same distance from the front of the stage), they nearly always differ in strength. That is often an advantage, of course, and it is one of the main techniques for throwing the focus of attention on one of a pair of actors. Seldom can such focus be maintained for very long, however; in a typical two-person scene, the attention of the audience is intended to snap alternately from one actor to another. If one actor clearly dominates a scene he should be given a stronger position than the other, so that other devices will need to be used for attracting the audience's attention for a smaller part of the scene or to reinforce the actor in the weaker position. Especially important is an adjustment in his angle. Although people usually face each other in conversation, they do not always do so, and they seldom stare fixedly at each other without occasionally turning away. On stage, the actor in the weaker position can strengthen it by taking advantage of every opportunity to turn more directly toward the audience. Such turns must be motivated, but often motives can be found in the speech itself, and sometimes they can be interpolated. An actor can turn away from the other as if to express impatience at something that has been said; he can pause for a moment in his speech, turn and take a step, perhaps taking hold of the back of a nearby chair, as if hesitating in an attempt to find a word or to decide what to say. A particularly vivid narration can be used as the motivation for turning more fully toward the audience, the actor pretending to visualize what he is describing. Almost any negative emotion—grief, embarrassment, guilt, irritation—can be used to motivate a turn.

These devices must be used if it is impractical for the actor to move from his position on the stage. Unless his speech is very short, it will often be possible to specify a cross that will move him up level, or even upstage of the other actor. The actor originally upstage can often be blocked also so that some movement toward the end of his speech takes him farther downstage to a position where only a slight cross will move the second actor into a dominant position.

Figure 19e. In spite of several factors that tend to strengthen Joan's position (for example, her lighter clothing), the fact that her angle is distinctly weaker than that of her fellow actor enables him easily to dominate this moment in *The Lark*. [Photograph by Douglas R. Hux]

Figure 19f. Sir Harry Bumper's raised position, his greater bulk, and his expansive gesture all contribute to his visual strength, but the decisive factor is the fact that both of the other characters are placed at much weaker angles. [*The School for Scandal;* photograph by Dorothy Welker]

Increasing the strength of the actor's position is especially important at the beginning of a speech, since it is necessary to attract the audience's attention from the other actor; once he has caught it, they are not likely to turn away so long as he continues speaking. The turn to the stronger angle does not have to be maintained for a long period if to do so would be awkward; if the actor can introduce two or three such turns into a speech of moderate length, he is likely to retain the attention of the audience, and they are likely to feel that they have an adequate view of him, whereas if the speech were entirely delivered with the face angled upstage they might feel that they could not follow it.

Fairly frequently it is necessary for actors to walk across the stage side by side while engaged in conversation. If one is placed directly above the other, he will be largely hidden. Visibility can be improved by placing the taller actor upstage, having him walk slightly ahead of the downstage actor, and angling their path as sharply as possible toward the audience; even a slight angle improves the appearance considerably. Such a walk can be interrupted; the actors can pause at a key point in the dialog. Especially if the speech is delivered by the upstage actor, pausing and moving forward slightly, with a small turn in the direction of the downstage actor, will open up the speaker to the audience; the walk can then be resumed when the point has been made.

It is standard practice for actors to execute turns on stage so as to make use of the strongest angles; usually, turning in one direction will display the actor's back to the audience for a much longer period of time than a turn in the opposite direction; in almost every instance, the "open" turn, in which the actor faces the audience for the greatest length of time, is to be preferred.

The basic principle that the actor should be displayed to the audience also affects smaller movements and adjustments of position. Thus an actor who is not facing the audience directly normally stands with his upstage foot slightly advanced, providing a more open position. Kneeling on the downstage knee gives a clearer view of the outline of the body, and is standard.

Synchronizing Speech and Movement

A constant problem in blocking is adjusting the movements to the space available. Occasionally a cross may take more time than the speech that accompanies it; most often, that occurs with an actor's last speech before an exit. The most effective solution to this problem is to reblock the actor's previous movements so that he can start the exit cross from a point closer to the door; sometimes, however, that is impossible—the previous speech, for instance, might require that he be talking into the telephone. A skilled actor can stretch a speech by as much as a hundred percent. The cross can be started first, and the speech delayed until a third of the cross is completed; the speech can be examined for points at which pauses can be motivated, and the speech broken at these points, while the movement continues without interruption; it may thus be possible to extend the speech so that it is finished at the same time that the actor reaches the exit.

This method does not shorten the amount of movement made in silence; rather it redistributes it, dividing it into sections each of which is shorter than if the speech were given without a pause, and shifting the major period of silence to before the speech rather than after it. This shift is more important than it might seem. Usually it would be expected that the audience would turn their attention to the actor at the beginning of his speech, and then at the end focus on the next speaker. If the movement is started in silence, in itself it is likely to attract the attention of the audience; if the speech is started simultaneously with the movement, however, with the silent section of the cross following it, the attention of the audience will remain on the moving actor beyond the point at which it should be shifted to the next speaker. If the second actor begins his speech at the conclusion of the first actor's speech, the audience is provided with conflicting instructions, and may be uncertain whether to watch the first actor completing his exit in silence, or the second, who is talking. Placing the silent section of the cross ahead of the speech prevents such ambiguity, and ensures that the audience will turn their attention to the correct actor at each moment.

EXPANDING THE AVAILABLE SPACE

Much commoner is the problem of having too little space for necessary movements. If two actors are involved in a quarrel, and the speech of one expresses a climactic pattern of aggressiveness or intensity, it might seem desirable to punctuate his speech by having him move toward the other actor in, say, three separate crosses. It is very likely that they might be standing so close together at the beginning of the speech that even a single movement would use up the distance between them. Again, the ideal solution to this problem is to reblock the preceding passage so as to provide more space between the two actors at the beginning of the speech; often, however, that may not be possible. The next best solution is to look for points in the speech where movement away from the second actor can be motivated. Perhaps the speaker can express momentary disgust by turning away; if so, the turn can be amplified by the addition of a step or two, thus providing more space for crosses during the rest of the speech. A sharp turn back to confront the other actor will have almost the same force as a movement toward him, and if it is reinforced with even a single short step, it will function as effectively as a longer cross. It may also be possible to find points at which the silent actor can motivate moving away from the speaker, turning away from him or shrinking back. This solution is less desirable because it violates the rule that no actor should move during another actor's speech. If the movement is clearly responsive to the speech, however, it may not distract the attention, and often will provide significantly more space for the speaker's crosses. And finally, an actor can be trained to make the most of each cross, so that it seems larger than it actually is. In the main, crosses are intended to communicate information to the audience about the emotional relationships between characters, in the case cited, to suggest increasing anger and dominance. A movement by the speaker toward the other actor of perhaps three feet might communicate most easily, but a movement of a single step can be made to function almost as well if it is done crisply and with definition, if the actor leans forward to emphasize his aggressiveness, and if he adds an appropriate gesture. The problem of making small movements serve when longer movements would be more suitable is especially severe with a very small stage, but it appears in almost every play no matter what the size of the stage.

ARRANGING SEATED ACTORS

Special problems involve the positions of actors sitting on chairs and sofas. Two actors sitting side by side on a sofa are ideally visible to the audience only if the sofa is parallel with the front edge of the stage; however, since that throws the actors into the face-front position, which makes it difficult for them to avoid acknowledging the presence of the audience, sofas are nearly always placed at some angle to the edge of the stage. The result is that the actor on the upstage end of the sofa is partly hidden by the other actor, and the down-stage actor is placed in a weak position requiring him to turn upstage toward the other.

In blocking actors in this position, the first consideration is to place the dominant actor and the one with the most lines upstage. If the upstage position can be assigned to the taller actor, visibility is still further improved. It may even be possible for him to sit on the arm of the sofa, so that his face is raised. Moving the actors as far apart on the sofa as possible will slightly improve their visibility. A greater improvement can be achieved by instructing the downstage actor to lean back, and the upstage actor to sit forward on the edge of the seat.

Finally, motivation can often be found in the lines or may be especially

Figure 20a. Arranging seated actors. This moment in the blocking design for *The Lark* illustrates an unusual and imaginative solution to the arrangement of four seated actors on a multilevel set. Each is individually visible; they form a well composed group; and each actor is placed so that he receives exactly the degree of emphasis required by the script, with Joan in the strongest position and the monk in the weakest at stage left. [Photograph by Douglas Hux]

Figure 20b. Intimacy is expressed by the closeness of the actors, but visibility is maintained by seating them on two levels, with the taller on the floor. [*Rhinoceros;* photograph by Norm Burlingame]

invented which will make it possible for the upstage actor to stand up and take a step or two into a position that will turn him at a stronger angle toward the audience. Similar motivations are more difficult to devise for the downstage actor, but they are worth considering. If an end table is placed by the downstage arm of the sofa, it may be possible for the actor to drop a sheaf of papers on it to which he can turn at significant moments, so as to open his position more fully to the audience. Even locating an ash tray there will make it possible for him to motivate an occasional turn that will improve his visibility.

A severe problem arises whenever actors must be shown seated at a table

Figure 21a (facing page). Arranging actors at table. Five solutions to the difficult table problem are shown. Since the orientation of the table is critical, in each case the center line and the edge of the stage are shown by dashed lines, and an arrow points from the direction of the center of the audience.

The *Antony and Cleopatra* set is shown in perspective in *Figure 32b*. In this drawing, the solid triangles indicate seated actors, the open triangles represent standing actors. The principal actors are seated in chairs arranged in a semicircle around the up-stage side of a square table.

The *J.B.* table is set on a circular platform. It was used for a family dinner, with the mother at stage right and the father in the center chair (see also *Figure 21c*).

The other diagrams illustrate the slanting of the tables and the angling of the chairs to provide maximum visibility and variations in the strength of the actors' positions.

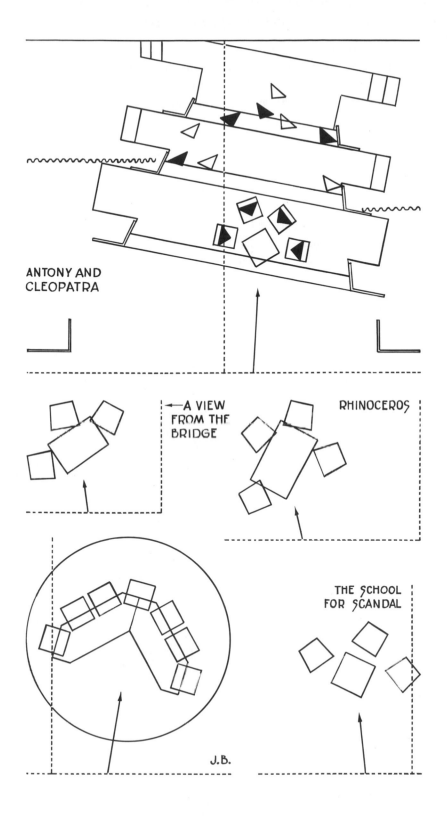

ANTONY AND
CLEOPATRA

←A VIEW
FROM THE
BRIDGE

RHINOCEROS

THE SCHOOL
FOR SCANDAL

J.B.

to eat. Only two cases of this kind are easy to handle: a single actor, eating alone, and actors shown at the speakers' table at a banquet. The diners at a speakers' table outside the theater are customarily arranged to provide maximum visibility; one side is left free, and turned toward the other diners, who constitute the audience; because this is an essentially theatrical arrangement, it can be copied precisely on stage.

The normal positions for two people eating at a table is facing each other. If a square table is placed on stage parallel with the front edge of the stage, and the two actors sit at the left and right sides, the audience sees them both in profile, that is at an angle of 90°, the largest angle at which actors can function effectively. If the table is slanted, the position of the upstage actor is greatly improved, but the other position is so weakened as to be unacceptable. Perhaps the best arrangement is to point one corner of the table toward the audience, and place the actors at the two adjacent upstage sides. Since this is a less common arrangement outside the theater, it may seem distractingly un-

Figure 21b. In this case, the table is placed parallel with the edge of the stage, and actors seated in profile at the ends, an unusual position. Variety and emphasis are provided by blocking the actress standing behind the table. [*Rhinoceros;* photograph by Norm Burlingame]

Figure 21c. Two solutions to the dinner scene in *J.B.* [Photographs by Norm Burlingame (top) and Harold Tedford (bottom)]

natural to the audience. Anything that will disguise its artificiality is an improvement. If chairs are placed at the downstage edges of the table, it may be possible to load them with magazines, packages, or clothing, as an explanation of why they are not used. Another device is to place a teacart along one of the downstage edges, with perhaps a toaster and condiment set on it. If the actors are intimate, emphasizing their emotional closeness can help provide an explanation for their sitting together; the side-by-side arrangement might be acceptable for a honeymoon couple, even without other explanatory devices.

Placing three actors at a table is still more difficult, and placing four or more presents almost insoluble problems. The table can be lengthened and slightly angled. If the actor who is least important in the scene is put in the weak position at the downstage end, the scene will be least damaged. Chairs can be turned toward the audience to improve the actors' positions, rather than being set parallel with the edges of the table.

If four actors are placed around the table, it is difficult to avoid the downstage edge, which is most nearly parallel with the audience. This position is not only impossibly weak, but the actor so placed will block the view of the actor opposite him. Some cheating is possible: moving the upstage chair slightly

Figure 21d. An inventive and unusual solution to the problem for the banquet scene in *Macbeth*. The table cloth is spread on the floor of the ramp, and the guests are seated beside it; Macbeth and Lady Macbeth are placed on a platform at stage right, and attendants hover in the background. The major effect of this arrangement is to weaken the positions of the dinner guests, so that Macbeth can more easily dominate the scene. [Photograph by Douglas R. Hux]

toward the down-stage end of the table, and moving the downstage chair in the opposite direction. Placing the tallest actor upstage and the shortest opposite him will also improve visibility.

Eating, like everything else in drama, is intended to be communicative; the arrangement and business of the actors is designed to say to the audience "See, we have sat down to have breakfast." The communication can be made very quickly; crossing to the table, sitting down, passing the food in themselves express the fact, especially as supplemented by the information in the dialog. Almost never is the act of eating carried out in full; an actor may take a symbolic bite or two, but very little food is actually consumed; not only is stage food almost always unpalatable, it is very difficult to speak effectively with food in the mouth, and it is nearly impossible to synchronize chewing and swallowing with the speeches. Even more importantly, watching others eat is one of life's least interesting occupations, and after the initial fact has been communicated to the audience, completion of the meal makes no further contribution to the play (unless, of course, the audience knows that the dessert has been poisoned, and is waiting in suspense for one of the actors to take his first bite of it and drop dead on the floor). Even a hurried lunch requires perhaps twenty minutes in actual life; a moment's reflection will demonstrate that the full time is almost never provided in plays.

Once the meal has started, the director can search for reasons that will enable the actors to leave the table. If an actor must deliver an important speech, and he is sitting in a weak position at the table, it may be possible to have him get up on a preceding speech and cross to a nearby table or even exit into the kitchen to get the coffeepot; his return to the table can then be timed so that he is able to stop halfway back, in a strong position, for his key line. He may walk around the table refilling the other actors' cups while delivering the speech; in this case he would cross upstage of the table, so that he would be turned toward the audience throughout the action. Ingenuity will suggest many such pieces of business to strengthen the positions of the actors at different moments in the scene. The actor sitting at the weak end of the table may even drop his napkin on the downstage side of his chair, enabling him to turn toward the audience to pick it up as he delivers an important line. The speeches should provide emotional motivations for strengthening movements. If an argument is in progress, one actor might rise and lean across the table, shaking his fist at another actor, thus attracting attention to his speech and making himself momentarily more visible. The second actor might react to the attack by rising from the table, tossing his napkin down, and crossing to sit in a chair at some distance. If his new position is carefully chosen, the actors remaining at the table might then be able to turn in their chairs toward him so as to improve the positions of all of them.

And finally, the meal can be concluded quickly, either simply by pretending that it is finished, or by devising a motivation for interrupting it. All of the actors remaining at the table when the first one leaves might get up and move to new positions expressing their emotional relationships with him, one walking over to pat his shoulder, another moving to the opposite side of the stage to suggest irritation, a third standing in the center of the open space, indecisively turning from the pair of actors to the isolated one as if uncertain which to respond to.

PATTERNS OF STAGE ARCHITECTURE

The discussion thus far has dealt with the proscenium stage, where actors and audience are placed in essentially separate rooms with a dividing wall in which an opening is cut. Through this the audience can watch the actors perform on an elevated platform, as through a picture frame. If all productions throughout the nation were counted, probably more than half would be found

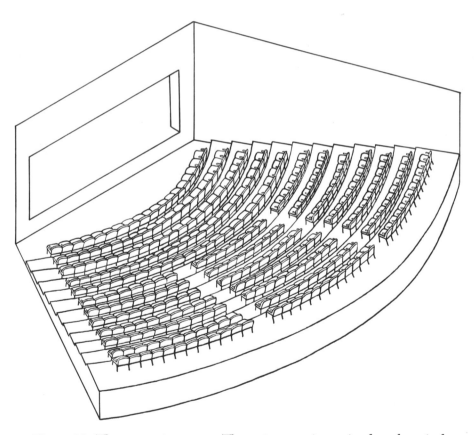

Figure 22. The proscenium stage. The acting area is restricted to the raised stage, visible through the rectangular opening in the proscenium wall.

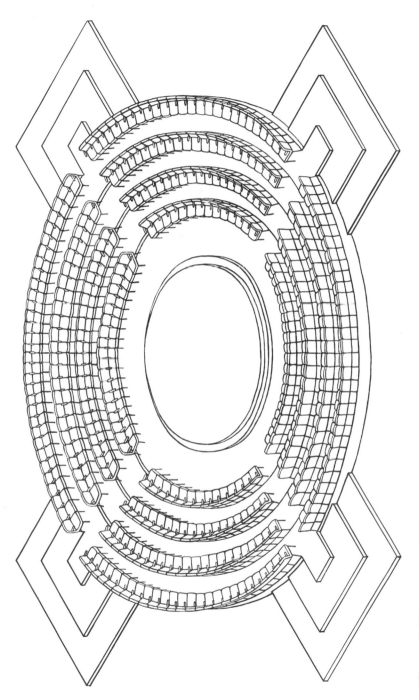

Figure 23. The arena stage. The acting area is entirely surrounded by the audience; it is raised for improved visibility and definition. Entrances are made by means of the four aisles through which the audience also enters the theater.

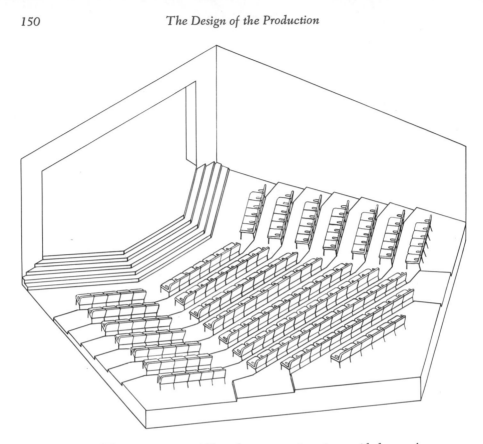

Figure 24. The apron stage. Although a proscenium is provided, a major section of the stage extends out in front of it toward the audience and can be used by the actors as an important part of the acting area.

to make use of such an arrangement, and it seems desirable for the student to focus first on mastering the problems and techniques adapted to it.

Other actor-audience relationships are possible, however, and for the last third of a century much of the most interesting, adventurous, and imaginative work has been done in theaters which differ in varying degrees from the proscenium arrangement. Most of the fine theater plants built on college campuses in recent years provide for a range of relationships between actors and audience, and many colleges that have not undertaken massive building programs have developed auxiliary theaters of the new type to supplement their proscenium stages.

So varied are the different architectural patterns that have been devised that it is impossible to discuss each one in a basic text. They are alike in that each moves the audience closer to the actors. At one extreme, the acting area is shifted out into the center of the audience, whose seats are arranged facing the actors approximately in an open circle only a few rows deep (arena or central staging), and the proscenium wall is dispensed with altogether. At the other extreme, the major acting area remains behind the proscenium, but the space in front of the act curtain is enlarged both in size and importance (apron stage), and the actors move freely throughout the entire stage space.

Both types of arrangement are in current use, but still more common is an architectural design lying between the two extremes, in which the stage is pushed well forward into the audience (thrust stage), but spectators sit on only three sides of it. The thrust stage typically stands against a wall that may serve as a neutral background or that may be especially decorated to suit the play.

All three types of stages are distinguished from the proscenium stage, which is enclosed on three sides, by being more open to the audience. Of the three, the arena stage is most open, and the apron stage least, but all are included in the term "open stages."

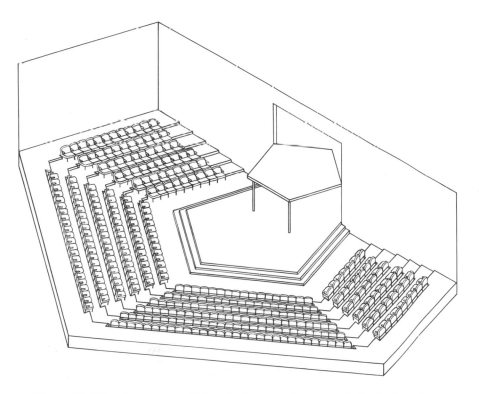

Figure 25. The thrust stage. Although the stage floor extends back through an opening cut in the wall, the opening is used only for entrances and exits; all acting takes place in the area in front of the wall. In this theater, a canopy extends over part of the stage, providing a second, raised acting area; actors can reach this level by two flights of stairs, placed behind the backing wall but not visible in this drawing.

The important aspects of the new staging are not its physical characteristics but the alterations it produces in the emotional and esthetic relationship between actors and viewers. If the thrust stage is high, as it apparently was in the Elizabethan theater, the actors tower over the audience, and the spectators, at least in the front rows, must look up at them. The result is an apparent physical and psychological expansion of the actors, which increases their apparent force and dominance. A study of Elizabethan drama will demonstrate how fully Marlowe, Shakespeare, and lesser playwrights exploited this quality.

In most contemporary theaters, the thrust stage is kept low, and often it is blended with the auditorium by steps running entirely around it. Actors then play almost level with the spectators, and the relationship acquires a high degree of intimacy and directness.

The arena, apron, and thrust stages require major technical adjustments by all theater artists, including actors and directors, the apron stage the least since it is most like the proscenium theater, the arena stage the greatest. Traditional stage divisions become meaningless; especially in the arena theater, there is no upstage or downstage, left or right. Even with the thrust stage, where the familiar divisions might conceivably be marked on the stage floor, the identification of strong and weak areas loses most of its value.

A major fact for both actor and director is the reduction in viewing distance in most open-stage theaters; voice and gesture need not be projected as far as in a proscenium theater of the same seating capacity; facial expression becomes more legible and more significant, and much greater subtlety is possible.

Sight lines are very much more complicated for open stages; no longer is it possible to select two or three key seats by which all arrangements can be checked. To some extent actors are more visible, but as the audience is wrapped farther around the stage, each actor tends to blot out vision for a small section of the audience, and in the arena theater even a single actor alone on stage has his back turned toward a fourth or fifth of the audience at each moment. Stairs and platforms are useful in raising individual actors above others so as to increase their visibility, but the scenic units themselves must be kept low enough that they will not cut off the vision for any of the spectators. The result of these factors is that blocking for the open stage regularly specifies more movement than on the proscenium stage, and the weaker areas where minor actors can be placed during a scene are reduced in size. Movement must also include more turns than with conventional staging.

Furniture must be kept low so as not to cut off sight lines, and in the absence of flats comes to serve more fully as focal points for organizing the action. Behind the proscenium, furniture tends to be arranged in a half-circle around the walls of the set, pointing forward. On an open stage, furniture more often is placed toward the center of the stage space, pointing outward toward the audience; blocking then tends toward a radial arrangement, away from the center. In other words, proscenium blocking is to some extent centripetal, open-stage blocking is centrifugal.

The proscenium wall acts as a psychological barrier between viewer and actor, enclosing the play within a picture frame and weakening the impression of depth, so that the stage picture is psychologically flattened in the direction of a single plane. The physical separation of audience and actors weakens the viewers' feeling of involvement and participation in the action of the play, so that their attitude becomes that of detached observers rather than sharers in the experiences portrayed. Counteracting this effect so as to produce empathic involvement on the part of the audience is one of the major concerns of all theater artists who must work on a proscenium stage—set designers, costumers, and property and makeup crews, as well as directors and actors.

The open stage, by de-emphasizing or dispensing with the proscenium wall, and by thrusting the actor out into the audience, replaces the picture-frame appearance of the proscenium stage with a sculpturesque effect, with actors viewed in the round, from all sides, and the third dimension displayed and emphasized rather than suppressed. The blending of the stage and auditorium areas by steps or ramps makes it possible to move actors out beyond the stage itself, so that the audience instead of simply surrounding the action is surrounded and interpenetrated by it. At the least, a play might open with a procession of actors through the audience, and the aisles can be used for entrances and exits. These areas are even usable as part of the acting space, although problems of visibility most often would require that the focus of attention remain on the stage itself.

The Brutus-Antony scenes after the death of Caesar in Shakespeare's play may be given as a suggestive example. At the end of Brutus's address to the mob, the director might choose to have them move up the aisles of the theater, in all directions (at least three, with a thrust stage). As Brutus exclaims "My countrymen,—" one of the plebeians at the back of the auditorium calls out "Peace, silence! Brutus speaks!," and another replies from the other side of the audience, "Peace, ho!" Brutus requests that they remain ("Let me depart alone") and allow Antony to give his funeral speech. As he exits up the center aisle, the voices of the plebeians are heard from all over the theater, shouting to each other, so that the audience seems to be surrounded by the scene. While Antony delivers his speech standing behind the coffin in the center of the stage, the plebeians listen from their positions in the aisle running around the wall outside the seating area, with a few of them in the aisles leading to the stage, kept back far enough not to interfere with sight lines. At the end of the speech, they swarm back on stage and bear the body out triumphantly through the audience.

The greater complexity of sight lines and problems of scene shifting which have not yet been fully solved for the open stage tend to free the director from some of the restrictions of traditional scenery, since the stage space is more fully available to him, but they also deprive him of some of the special assistance that scenery provides on the proscenium stage. Varying levels function more powerfully on the open stage, but cannot be used so freely as behind a proscenium; box sets become nearly impossible, and only minimal use can be made of walls or large architectural units. Opportunities for spectacle are at least as great as with the proscenium theater, although the methods that can be used are different. Hand properties become more important, and colorful banners, lanterns, and billowing smoke can be used spectacularly, especially if they are imaginatively lighted.

As might be expected, some plays are better suited to the open stage than others. Plays emphasizing physical movement, varied emotion, and a direct and intimate esthetic feeling are especially effective. Plays that are sharply localized and that seem to require a restricted setting are less well suited. Probably Sartres' *The Flies* would be especially effective on the open stage; his *No Exit*, which pictures the characters as caught in a narrow trap, would be more suited to proscenium production. Other examples of plays especially fitted to the open stage are Ibsen's *Peer Gynt*, all of Greek, Roman, and Elizabethan drama, Wilder's *Our Town*, and MacLeish's *J. B.* Examples of plays less suited are Ibsen's *Hedda Gabler* and *Ghosts*, Barrie's *Peter Pan*, Wilde's *The Importance of Being Earnest*, Shaw's *Major Barbara*, Williams's *The Glass Menagerie* and *A Streetcar Named Desire*, and Albee's *Who's Afraid of Virginia Woolf?*

A survey of the long sweep of theater history will demonstrate that for the greater part of its extent some form of open stage has been standard; even if only great masterpieces were listed, more of them are better suited to the open than to the proscenium stage. However, many of the finest plays of the last few centuries were especially written to be played behind a proscenium. For that reason, producing organizations with a policy of presenting a wide variety of types of plays have tended in recent decades to build flexible facilities, which could be adapted for either style of presentation. Sometimes these depend on massive elevator forestages or other mechanical devices; sometimes they involve the construction of paired proscenium and open-stage theaters, with technical facilities shared to reduce cost.

The open stage is now firmly established as a permanent part of contemporary theatrical resources. There has not yet been time to develop a definitive theory or set of techniques in using the new arrangement; problems remain to be solved, and its special advantages and resources have not yet been fully exploited.

Although each architectural arrangement requires the development of techniques that bypass its special restrictions and exploit its advantages, the fundamental principles of directing are equally applicable to all. Basically, the director's responsibility is to identify vividly and precisely the experience he hopes to create for the audience, including the relation between actor and viewer, and then to find the technical means by which actors and staff can produce that experience.

The Blocking Design as a Whole

The discussion so far has dealt primarily with individual positions and crosses, or isolated moments in the play. The blocking of a play has additional significance when considered as a total pattern. It should display variety in types of movement, in the use of stage areas, and in the speed and shape of crosses (straight or curved, long or short, simple or complex). The selection of arrangements and movements should, however, display an underlying unity which is expressive of the style and mood of the play as a whole. The character of a play cannot always be guessed from a series of blocking diagrams, but such guesses are accurate more often than might be expected. Often an experienced director, given blocking diagrams from various plays, would be able to distinguish a tragedy, a romantic comedy, a musical, or a farce, from the patterns of movement alone, if they have been well designed. Blocking should provide for the necessary action of the play, focus the attention of the audience at each moment on the actor or point on stage that is significant in carrying the action forward, and assist the actors in expressing their emotional relationships. It should express the pattern of mood that appears in the script and should constitute a meaningful pattern of esthetic interest in itself.

7/The Design of Blocking

Expressing the general mood and esthetic effect of a play through blocking requires that the director have identified them clearly. That should have been achieved through his four preliminary readings of the script. Adjusting the blocking to the momentary actions and emotions of the play requires a specific analysis of each point of the script—at least each individual speech, and for longer speeches each section of the speeches—which is much more concentrated than the general reading of the script that the director has already done.

The action requirements are easy to identify from the script, and the focus of attention that should be produced for the audience is usually immediately evident, since they are nearly always intended to watch the actor who is speaking. The most difficult blocking problem is fitting the positions and movements of the actors to the emotions they express and indicating their emotional relationships. The vocal treatment of a line—which words are emphasized, where pauses are introduced—must also be precisely matched by the blocking design.

The general impressions the director has received from his script readings must be extended to the most specific level—the meaning of each sentence, each phrase, even sometimes a single word. This analysis can be done simultaneously with the design of the blocking or it may be done first, but since the blocking depends on it, it cannot be delayed until after the blocking has been completed. Whether the director chooses to explore the interpretation and reading of the individual lines before he attacks the design of the blocking or whether he does both simultaneously is a matter of individual preference; even experienced and skilled directors differ. Beginning directors may find it easier to handle the two steps separately. Certainly, the study of the meaning and emotion of the script should be carried almost to the level of individual sentences before the blocking is done. If the director is at all in doubt about whether he has mastered it fully enough to begin blocking, he should restudy it until he is clearly ready to begin work at the most specific level.

Many beginning directors, however, and probably most experienced directors find that it is more effective to carry on their final detailed analysis of interpretation at the same time as they prepare their blocking designs. The decisions involved in blocking force an uninterrupted concentration of attention on the director. Even with the best intentions, he is likely to skip over passages and to miss important meanings if he is studying the play only for its meaning and emotion.

The whole question of how elaborately a director should plan his production in advance of the first rehearsal is one on which there is great difference of opinion and wide divergence of practice among successful directors. Some of the factors affecting this question will be taken up in later chapters. At this point, it is recommended that the beginning director prepare fully detailed plans. If he later concludes that his designs are unnecessarily elaborate, little harm will have been done; on the other hand, if he should discover in the middle of rehearsals that he has failed to make essential decisions, the result might well be chaos and a disastrous waste of rehearsal time.

Stage movements can be most conveniently thought of in two groups: those involving a change in location (walking from one side of the stage to the other, mounting a flight of stairs), and those which the actor executes without moving to a new location (standing up or sitting down, turning in a different direction). Movements of the first type can be shown clearly on diagrams; those of the second are usually not diagrammed, but are simply described in written notes. In addition, actors will engage in movements that are essentially extensions of gesture and that involve the body still less: an actor may reach for a cigarette lighter, open a book and take out a letter, rearrange the objects on a table beside him. Such small meaningful actions are called "business," a term that is not precisely definable, but which means small communicative movement. At one side, business merges with gesture; on the other, it fades into stage movement proper. Occasionally, instructions for business are prepared by the director, and most scripts include some business specifications. Most business, however, is developed by the actors themselves, and it becomes of concern to the director only because he must evaluate it or use his own ingenuity to suggest additional business when the actors' imagination is inadequate. Business hardly ever appears on blocking diagrams unless it involves movement to a new position on the stage.

THE USE OF ABBREVIATIONS

Movements across the stage are technically referred to as "crosses." However, the term is used for movements of all sizes that result in a geographical alteration of the actor's position on stage. Thus a movement of a single step would be included in the term, even though it is much shorter than one that would take the actor all the way across the stage. Since every play requires the preparation of hundreds of blocking directions, the more briefly they can be recorded the less time is needed for them. Actors are often asked to write their blocking directions in the margins of their scripts, and there is seldom space for full descriptions in ordinary language. Consequently, a number of abbreviations have been adopted that are both clear and brief. The word "cross" is represented by an X. "G X to stairs; B & F X to sofa" would be interpreted as "Gerald crosses to the stairs; Bill and Frank cross to the sofa"; the use of the initials of characters' names is a common method of abbreviating the notes.

Occasionally this may lead to confusion. If a cast included characters named Robert, Lloyd, Ulanov, David, Cynthia, and Xavier, the initials would be constantly mistaken for the identical abbreviations used to indicate crosses and stage areas. Large casts often contain different characters with matching initials (Gremio and Grumio, Baptista, Bianca, and Biondello in *The Taming of the Shrew*). In such cases, the director may find it more convenient to write the names out in full. Examples of stage directions given later in the chapter illustrate both methods.

STAGE GEOGRAPHY

The stage is divided into nine areas, each with a distinctive name and a traditional abbreviation. (Various patterns of division are used, some producing more than nine areas and some fewer, but the arrangement described here is perhaps the simplest and the most widely used. Which is chosen depends on the convenience and taste of the individual director, and to some extent on the shape of a particular set.)

Stage geography is concerned only with the acting area, that is, the section of the stage which is normally included within the walls of the set and which is available to the actors for their movements. The space to the left and right of the acting area is called the "wings," and that in front of the acting area is called the "apron."

The opening of the side walls at angles greater than 90° for purposes of visual projection and the improvement of sight lines results in the acting area's being shaped like a trapezoid rather than a rectangle, with the side edges symmetrical but not parallel, and the edge toward the audience longer than that at the back of the stage. The front edge of the acting area is usually thought of as connecting the back corners of the edges of the proscenium opening. The back edge of the acting area is parallel to but shorter than the front edge. If the stage is shallow, it may coincide with the back wall; on a deep stage, the entire stage area would not normally be included within the walls of the set. The back edge of the acting area would then fall at some distance in front of the back wall of the stage, perhaps fifteen feet from the front edge. The slanted side edges connect the ends of the back edge with the upstage corners of the proscenium opening (that is, with the ends of the line defining the front of the acting area).

Subdivisions of this area are made by dividing each of the four lines into thirds and connecting matching points of opposite edges with straight lines.

The center of the nine areas is called "center." Areas toward the audience are said to be "downstage," those at the back of the stage are said to be "up-

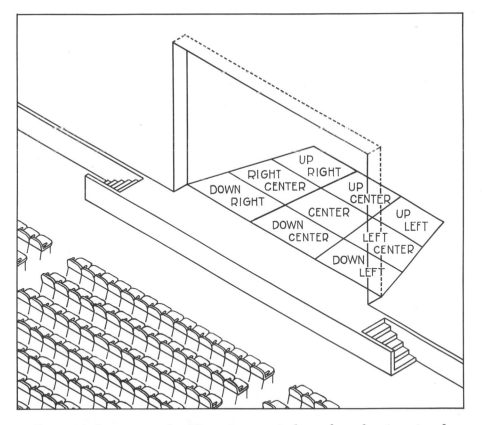

Figure 26. Stage geography. The acting area is shown from the viewpoint of the director (that is, from the audience), but its various subdivisions are traditionally named with reference to an actor standing at stage center facing the audience (his right is the director's left).

stage." If an actor stood in the center area, facing the audience, the area immediately in front of him would be called "down center," and the one immediately behind him "up center." The area to his right would be "right center," the corner area in front and to his right would be "down right," and the corner area behind and to the right would be "up right"; matching areas on the left would be named similarly.

The traditional abbreviations for these areas are as follows:

up center = UC
center = C
down center = DC
up right = UR
right center = RC
down right = DR
up left = UL
left center = LC
down left = DL

DIRECTIONAL TERMINOLOGY

The same terms, with the exception of "center," are also used directionally to describe positions and movements. Thus an actor might be asked to move down left two steps; the movement intended would follow a line starting at his feet and drawn at a 45° angle toward the audience and to the left. If he were standing in the up-center area, such a movement would probably take him to the left-center area rather than the down-left area, which might seem to be suggested by the instruction. This paradox is familiar outside the theater: it is possible to walk east for many blocks along West Main Street without reaching East Main; it is possible to drive south for a hundred miles in North Carolina without reaching South Carolina. Confusion of directions can be prevented by a careful use of the word "to"; an actor who is asked to cross "to down left" is expected to move to a position in the down-left area; an actor who is asked merely to cross "down left" is expected to move in the indicated direction; whether or not he stops in the down-left area depends on the length of the cross and the position from which he starts the movement.

The term "center" is not used directionally, because the position of the actor is always assumed as the center point, from which the other directions are defined.

The directional terms are also used with reference to other actors and to scenic elements. An actor might, for example, be instructed to stand "up left of the fireplace," or to "cross to down right" of another actor.

The terms "up" and "down" have also given rise to related expressions, especially "above," "below," and "level." All of them refer to the distance of actors or scenic elements from the front edge of the acting area; the left and

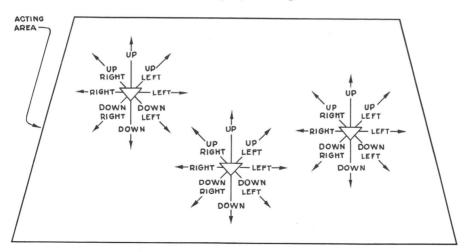

Figure 27. Directions on stage. The names of the stage areas are also used directionally in giving blocking instructions, except for "center." In this usage, center is assumed to be wherever a particular actor happens to be standing, and the directions refer to the angles of movement. The pattern is shown for three of the innumerable possible positions.

right relationships are not included in the use of these terms. Thus, an actor might be instructed to take up a position on one side of the stage "level with the upper corner of the fireplace," even though the fireplace is fixed to the wall on the other side of the stage. These terms are used most frequently in making minor adjustments in position; in revising crowd positions an actor might be asked to move to a spot "a little below" another actor. They are also frequently used to describe the location of a cross with reference to other actors or furniture: a butler might be instructed to "cross above the sofa," or a director might say to an actor who had crossed improperly, "No, I think it would be better if you would cross below John and Harriet."

All of the instructions assume that the actor is facing directly toward the audience. This may seem strange, since that is the one position actors least often assume. However, to state the directions in terms of each actor's actual position would result in chaotic complication. Beginning actors find this system of directions confusing at first; not only do they sometimes move right instead of left, but they may interpret the instructions with reference to the directions in which they are actually facing, rather than in terms of the theoretical position. The directions are so useful, however, that learning to interpret them correctly is an essential part of the actor's technical mastery. They should be clearly explained and demonstrated for beginning actors, and any misinterpretation of the directions should be immediately corrected. With concentration, even an inexperienced actor can usually master the system during the first two weeks of rehearsal, and can thereafter use it automatically.

It may have already been noticed that it is more troublesome for the director to use this method than for the actor. The descriptions at least average in conformity with the actor's positions, but they are exactly reversed for the director. As he sits in the auditorium, if he points toward the right side of the proscenium opening, he will be indicating the left side of the stage; stage right is on his left. In preparing his blocking instructions, the beginning director is likely to make many errors in left and right descriptions; he will find himself constantly instructing actors to move down right in terms of his own point of view, when the theatrical system requires the opposite instruction. The new director should make a determined effort to master this reversal in order to prevent confusion during rehearsals. He can expect it to occur more quickly with each succeeding play, although one experienced director reports that it always takes him about five rehearsals before he can say "right" automatically when he means "left"; furthermore, he says it takes him about a week after the play before he has his directions switched back again to conform to those of the world outside the theater.

Experience in blocking and directing will demonstrate that the geographical divisions of the stage, and the directional patterns, are not detailed enough for all of the blocking instructions that must be given to actors. Only nine areas and eight directions of movement are provided by this system. It would be possible to subdivide the stage into more areas and to invent terms for additional directions, but the efficiency gained by greater specificity would probably be more than offset by the loss due to the increasing complexity. It seems more effective to use the terms as given, but to supplement them with additional instructions when desired. Since the directional pattern can be centered at any point on the stage, it provides considerable flexibility; for instance, using the position of a table as center, an actor can be instructed to stand down right of it, no matter where the table is placed on the stage floor. Once a movement has been diagrammed, it can often be described simply in terms of the positions of other actors or scenic elements; thus, an actor might be instructed to move "a third of the way toward the floor lamp," or to a position "halfway between the desk and the stairs." The standard directions can also be adverbially modified, in instructions such as "cross to the upstage corner of the center area," or "cross left and a little down," or "face down right, a little more down than right."

The compression of the traditional abbreviations seems startling at first; instructions that would require several lines if written in ordinary English can often be recorded fully and clearly in a few symbols. Following are some examples taken from directors' scripts prepared for use in actual productions. The instructions are given in both theatrical symbols and standard English.

E X DL to 3′ DL of A	Enobarbus crosses down left to a position three feet down left of Antony.

E X DL ½ way to A2

O X R & a little D to the DS edge of P3, stopping 3′ from A; M X DL above O to the C of the DS edge of P3

O enters, X to within 3 or 4′ of love seat; M follows & stops 2 or 3′ to her L & about 1′ above her; V X a step toward O, bows; T & A X D slightly

Enobarbus crosses down left, half way to arch 2.

Octavius crosses right and a little down, to the downstage edge of platform 3, stopping three feet from Agrippa; Maecenas crosses down left above Octavius, to the center of the downstage edge of platform 3.

Olivia enters and crosses to within three or four feet of the love seat; Maria follows her, and stops two or three feet to her left and about a foot above her; Viola takes a step toward Olivia and bows; Sir Toby and Sir Andrew move down slightly.

THE DESCRIPTION OF POSITIONS FOR UNUSUAL SETS

The system which has been described was devised for box sets, placed behind prosceniums. If it is to be used effectively with other types of scenery and stages, it may be necessary to introduce modifications. Especially when the design of a set prescribes a ground plan that differs radically from the familiar trapezoid shape, it is often practical to dispense altogether with the traditional stage areas. One production of *The Taming of the Shrew* was played on a specially built forestage extending out beyond the permanent edge of the apron. The entire action of the play took place in front of the curtain line of the stage, so that none of the blocking made use of the traditional acting area. The set was made up of a series of platforms of various shapes and dimensions; one was eleven feet high (not counting its railing) and forty-six feet long. It was supported by a colonnade with a passageway extending under the high platform for twenty-four feet, leading to a short flight of stairs at each end. Straight and curved platforms three feet high were assembled to form a special forestage extending toward the audience, with two low curved stair units providing access from the three-foot platforms to a lower platform at the front. The high platform and the three-foot platforms were connected with a curving flight of stairs.

The familiar stage divisions were of no value with such a set. Instead, each platform and flight of stairs was assigned a code letter, and the individual steps of each flight of stairs were numbered. "B3" thus designated the third step of one flight of stairs. The set provided eight entrances, which were assigned code numbers, and each pillar in the colonnade was lettered.

All of these code letters and numbers were included in the ground plans, duplicated and distributed to the cast, and each was marked in chalk on the floor of the set before the first rehearsal. The director reported that he found this system of describing positions and movements somewhat more difficult to use than the familiar box-set method. Actors found it easy to follow, however, and it is possible that no other method of description would have pro-

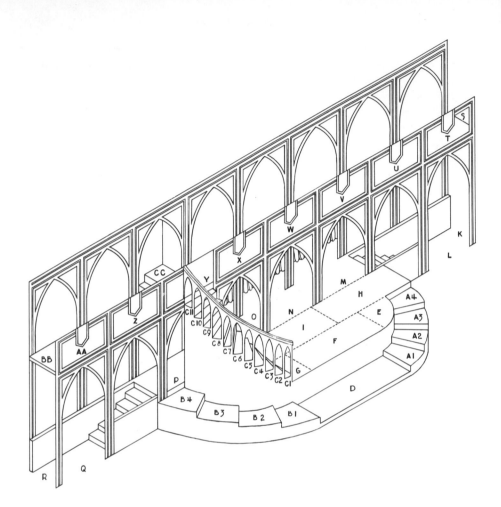

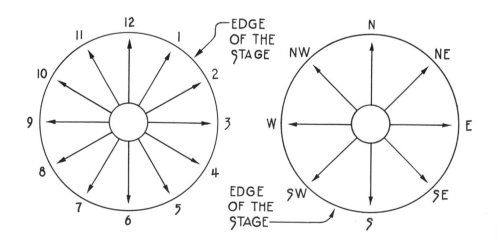

Figure 28 (*facing page*). Identifying positions for unusual sets. In this set for *The Taming of the Shrew,* traditional stage divisions were almost meaningless. Each flight of stairs was lettered, and each step numbered. Other letters were assigned to each entrance, each arch, and each area above an arch. The forestage was made up of five platforms. Although the joints between these platforms were hidden when the set was finished, the were visible during the early rehearsals, so each platform was given its own letter. These code letters were used in recording the blocking instructions, and were chalked on the stage floor to help the actors during the early blocking rehearsals.

vided more efficiency or clarity. Certainly the traditional system would have been almost unmanageable. Below is just one example of the directions prepared:

Petruchio enters R, followed by Grumio at a distance of 4′; Petruchio X below B to the center of D; he starts to speak at the DS corner of B2. Grumio X to the UR corner of D and leans against G.

(Because the scenic units were designated by letters, the names of the characters were spelled out in full, to reduce confusion. "U" indicates one of the entrances; "B" is a flight of stairs, and "B2" indicates the second step; "D" and "G" designate platforms.)

Recording the Directions

Each actor needs to write only his own blocking directions in his script, so that the margins usually provide enough space. The director, however, must record the entire blocking design. In order to get more space for his notes, it is common practice to tear two playbooks apart and paste the pages on larger sheets of paper, usually eight and a half by eleven inches. As an economy measure, a hole can be cut in each sheet larger than the area of printing but smaller than the outside edge of the pages of the playbook; the page on each side of the sheet can then be read. After the notes have been completed, the sheets can be fastened in ring notebooks, or otherwise loosely bound. It is important to choose a method of binding that will allow the pages to open flat. A director has his hands full, literally as well as figuratively, during rehearsals,

Figure 29 (*facing page*). Identifying positions in arena staging. When the audience surrounds the stage on all sides, the terms "left," "right," "up," and "down" become meaningless. Two methods of describing stage positions are shown. At the left, a point has been arbitrarily selected and numbered "12," and the circumference of the stage has been divided into twelve sections arranged like the face of a clock. In the pattern at the right, the points of the compass are used to divide the acting area into eight sections.

and a binding that tends to close the book as soon as it is laid down is a constant irritation.

It is customary to dictate the blocking instructions to the actors at the beginning of blocking rehearsals. At best, copying down the directions consumes precious time. Inevitably a good many of them are copied incorrectly, and straightening out the resulting confusion during rehearsals takes more time than anyone would believe who had not been through it. These difficulties can be avoided by typing the script on duplicator masters after the blocking has been worked out, and including all of the actors' instructions in the script itself; each actor can then be given a script with all of his directions included, in correct and unambiguous form. The time required for retyping the script and running off the copies may seem prohibitive, but in terms of man hours it is not so much greater than the familiar procedure as might be expected. Dictating the directions to the cast usually requires an entire evening, and correcting errors may well consume half of another rehearsal. Especially for a good-sized cast, the total time spent in this process by the actors and the director may be larger than the amount of time it takes to prepare special scripts. The reproduction of scripts is legally permissible for plays which are in the public domain (that is, most classic drama); it must not be used with plays covered by copyright, in order to avoid paying for enough copies for the cast and crews, and must not be done at all without the written permission of the copyright owner.

Movements are nearly always carried on simultaneously with the speeches. It is customary to insert the blocking direction into the script at the point at which the action is intended to begin. It is understood that the movement begins with the first word of the speech following the blocking direction and continues simultaneously with the speech until the movement is completed.

This is another of the readily breakable rules. It would be easy to supply dozens of examples of movements executed in silence, between speeches or during pauses in speeches. In the great majority of cases, however, the rule holds, so that the presumption of simultaneity saves a great deal of time, since it can be explained to inexperienced actors at the beginning of rehearsals and need not be repeated as a part of each individual direction. In the exceptional instance in which it is intended that speech be delayed until an action has been ccmpleted, the term "hold" may be used to indicate such a delay. For example, the actor might be instructed: "Knock on the door; hold line until the second-story window is opened"; or "Walk to the fireplace, pick up picture from mantel, look at it, then turn UR toward Herbert; hold line until turn." (Incidentally, the term "line" is used in the theater as synonymous with "speech," and does not refer to a line of print; only in verse drama does any confusion arise; there it may be desirable to reserve "line" for "line of verse" and use "speech" for each passage delivered by an actor without interruption.

Since the synchronization of movement and speech is so important, the point at which an action begins must be clearly marked in the enlarged margin of the director's master script. The clearest method of indicating the points in the speeches to which they apply is to draw a line from the beginning of the note to the matching point in the script. Such lines will be more visible and less ambiguous if they are not parallel with the lines of print but cut across them at an angle.

While the actors are still carrying their books, usually for almost two weeks of rehearsal, the director will frequently have occasion to ask them to look at a particular line in the script. This can be done much more quickly if the speeches are numbered identically in all scripts. Each speech should be numbered, no matter how short. It seems most convenient to number through the first scene or act, and then start again at the beginning of the next play division. If the scripts are duplicated, the numbering can be typed in when the masters are prepared; otherwise, the actors can be instructed to number the speeches in their own scripts outside rehearsal.

Using the Ground Plan

Planning the blocking requires that the director be able to visualize the various arrangements and movements of the actors on stage. It is a great help to have a perspective painting of the set to use as a guide, but an accurate ground plan of the set is absolutely necessary, with all the functional elements clearly marked, that is, those things which the actors will use and which affect their positions and movements.

Beginning directors are occasionally tempted to bypass the work of blocking by making use of the stage directions in the script. One director reports that although he has seen this tried several times it has never been acceptable. The script directions are of dubious and unidentifiable origin. They are most likely to be based on the playwright's rather hazy visualization of a possible set for the play or the inaccurate record of the blocking used in a professional production, scribbled down and inadequately revised by a harried assistant director during rehearsals. One director reported that when he attempted to follow script directions for one play early in his career ("Before I knew better"), he was stunned to discover that the set had been completely reversed between Acts I and II, with all entrances and furniture relocated, so that the directions as printed were chaotically confused.

In any case, even if the original blocking had been effective and accurately recorded, it would probably not be suited to the director's own stage and would have no relation to the scenery as planned by his own set designer. It does no harm for the director to read the directions as printed in the script, but the assumption should be that he will create his own blocking, and actors should be instructed to pay no attention to that recorded in the script.

Many directors like to arrange movable symbols on the ground plan to help visualize the positions of the actors. Buttons are especially effective; small buttons can be used for the women and larger ones for the men. If the buttons are of different colors, each one can be assigned to a different character in the play; choosing the brightest buttons for the major characters makes it easier to identify them.

The use of buttons makes it considerably easier to imagine the effect of the different arrangements. One of its special advantages is that it keeps the director from losing track of a character who is on stage but silent for a considerable period of time. It is disconcerting to block several pages and suddenly discover that a character has been left standing by the window when he should have exited early in the scene; having his symbolic button visibly on stage will prevent such an error.

One director who began his career with the button method reported that after blocking a few plays he found himself moving the actors across the ground plan in imagination, without bothering to move the buttons; after that he never bothered with them again. It seems likely that many directors might have the same experience. At first the physical symbols are a help, but with experience they become distractions rather than aids.

Preparing Diagrams

The recording of the blocking decisions in the form of abbreviated notes has been described. No written description of manageable size, however, can record an actor's movements and positions with sufficient clarity and precision. Many directors supplement their notes with drawings of the ground plan showing the placement and paths of the actors. How full such records should be can be determined only by the individual director. Some prefer to work from sketchy notations, others from diagrams showing every movement and position; most directors probably prepare records somewhere between the two extremes. It is suggested that the beginning director will find it more effective to record his blocking decisions as fully and clearly as possible, rather than trusting his memory. This is an entirely practical method, and the examples given in this book are taken from professionally directed plays, even though some professional directors choose other methods. Certainly this is the safest approach for the beginning director.

A duplicator master of the ground plan of the set is prepared, scaled to fit on an eight and a half by eleven sheet, and enough copies are then run off for recording the blocking designs. The number of copies needed will vary with the length and complexity of the play, the size of cast, and the style of blocking. One director who followed this method for a Shakespearean play used 189 copies of the ground plan, plus two for plotting the curtain calls. Two hundred copies should nearly always be ample, and usually fewer will be needed.

The director next takes a small card and draws on it an isosceles triangle, the base of which closely approximates the width of an actor's shoulders and the altitude of which matches the distance from the back of the shoulders to the tip of the nose (eighteen inches on the base and an altitude of ten inches) reduced to the scale of the ground plan. This triangle is cut out of the card with a razor blade and discarded.

The card and ground plans are used as follows. Taking one of the duplicated ground plans, the director writes "I:1," representing "Act I, Scene 1," in the lower left corner, and "1-" immediately below.

Let us suppose that the stage is bare at the opening of the curtain for the first scene of the first act, and that as it opens a telephone rings and a character named George enters by the door in the center of the right wall, walks left across the stage to a table on which the telephone is located, speaks into the phone, lays it down, walks to an archway in the back wall, calls "Hey, Jim, it's for you," and then crosses down right and sits on the right end of a sofa. Having identified this path of movement, the director notes the three points at which the actor stops crossing—when he stands beside the table to speak into the phone, when he stops in the arch to call to Jim, and when he sits on the sofa. Taking his card, the director places it on the ground plan so that the triangular hole is up right of the telephone table, with the apex of the triangle directed down left; he traces the outline of the triangle through the hole and writes the name of the character beside it. The triangle consequently provides an automatic spatial measurement: If it can be drawn in an

Figure 30a. A perspective drawing of the stage set used in the illustration of blocking given in the text. (See also *Figure 30b.*)

open space on the ground plan, there is enough space for an actor to stand in the same position. At the same time, the triangle indicates the direction in which the actor is turned.

The director then moves the card to a position just down left of the arch in the back wall, pointing up right, and traces the triangle again. The card is finally placed on the seat of the sofa, and retraced.

Laying the card aside, the director starts offstage and draws a line through

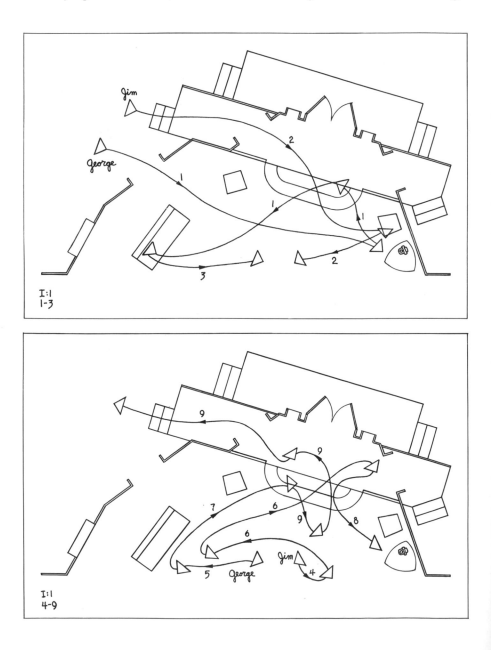

the door in the right wall across the stage to the first triangle; an arrowhead is added toward the middle of the line, and the figure "1" written above it, a second line is drawn to connect the first triangle to the one near the back wall, and a third is drawn down and around to the position on the sofa. An arrowhead is added to each line, and the figure "1" written beside it.

In this diagram, the triangles indicate the positions of the actor when he is not crossing; the lines indicate the paths of crosses; the arrowheads show the direction of the movement, and the figures indicate the number of the speech with which the action is synchronized.

The third line crosses the first, although they are both clearly legible. As Jim enters, and other positions and movements are recorded, the director watches to make sure that the diagram does not become too confused to follow easily. Let us suppose that the movements involved in the first three speeches of this plan can all be shown on the same copy of the ground plan without confusion, but that the positions for the fourth speech would make the diagram illegible. The director completes the notation in the lower corner of the diagram so that it reads "1–3," indicating the numbers of the speeches plotted on the sheet. He then takes a new copy of the ground plan, marks it "I:1" and "4–," and using his card redraws the last position of each actor who is on stage, writing the name of each beside the triangle. Further movements are traced as long as can be done legibly, the last positions are transferred to a new ground plan, and the recording of the blocking is continued. Usually several speeches can be blocked on a single copy; with a long speech involving complicated movement, it may be necessary to use two or three ground plans. In that case, the sequence of the diagrams can be indicated in the corner of the sheet by adding letters to the number of the speech; "6a," "6b," and "6c" would then indicate that three ground plans, in the order marked, were used to plot the movements for speech 6. Very occasionally, especially with movements which are intended to suggest confusion, it may seem desirable to ask the actors to ad lib their blocking; if an actor must pace during a speech, diagramming each cross and turn might be unnecessarily complicated: tracing the same paths would require several ground plans to record an essentially simple movement. In such cases, it may be more efficient to omit the movements altogether, although a note should be added at the bottom of the sheet indicating the omission: "Servants' movements in speech 18 not diagrammed"; or "Cecil's ad-libbed pacing not diagrammed."

When all of the blocking for the play has been recorded, the sheets should be bound so as to open flat. Such diagrams, in conjunction with the written instructions, constitute a very clear explanation of the design, which does not

Figure 30b (facing page). Blocking diagrams for the first nine speeches of a play, as described in the text.

depend on the memory of the director for interpretation. They are especially valuable as a guide to the assistant director, who can use them to follow the movements of the actors as soon as the blocking rehearsals are over, and who can point out any errors to the director as they develop. The director is thus freed from the necessity of constantly interpreting written directions and may turn his attention to further aspects of the production. If an error in the blocking design should develop during the blocking rehearsals, it can be traced, analyzed, and corrected much more easily by the use of the drawings than if the only record is the written directions inserted into the script.

As a final refinement, the director can retrace the blocking diagrams in color, using a pen with a plastic tip, and assigning a distinctive color to each character. If the hero's positions and movements are marked in green and the heroine's in red, for example, it will be easy to identify their positions at a glance.

IDENTIFYING CLIMACTIC SCENES

The director's major task is not the simple, even if laborious, writing down of directions and tracing diagrams, but making the decisions on which his records are based.

Before working out the blocking speech by speech, the director should glance through the script once more. He will already have noticed that the different passages vary in function and intensity. Early in the play, often in the opening scene, the playwright inserts information about what has happened before the rise of the curtain. Without such information the audience would find it difficult to recognize the full significance of the action presented in the play. Such background material is technically called "exposition." Often the first act of a three-act play presents a problem; the second act shows the characters working out a solution to it; and the third act depicts the results of their decisions. Since the play must develop enough momentum to carry across the interruption of the intermissions, playwrights usually try to increase the tension and interest throughout at least the last third of each act, rising to a climax just before the curtain falls. The last act does not present the same problem, but the effectiveness of the play as a whole requires not only that the last act produce a feeling of completeness, but also that it rise to its own climax, so that the play ends with a bang rather than fading off. The general pattern of interest of a play can then be thought of as a kind of mountain range, with the outline climbing to a peak toward the end of each act, slipping back slightly at the beginning of the next act, then climbing to a still higher peak.

Illustrations of this pattern could be cited by the thousands. On the other hand, many plays, among them great masterpieces, do not conform to it; in fact, one of the characteristics of masterpieces is that each tends to create its own pattern. Nevertheless, an examination of his script will demonstrate to the director that it has variations in interest and intensity, some passages that seem essentially preparatory, others that present climactic events which turn the play in unexpected directions, still others that display the outcome, explosive or quiet, of the lines of action preceding them. Before he can block effectively, the director must identify the overall structural pattern of his play, and particularly the moments of special significance and interest. If his blocking is to be successful, it must be adequate to these key scenes. And just as the playwright will have planned certain scenes as preparation for later, more important moments, much of the director's blocking must be guided by the requirements of the climactic scenes.

Having identified the key moments in the play and the relationship of the intervening passages to them, the director is ready to begin the actual work of blocking. He should turn to the first climactic moment in the play and try to fix in his mind its major blocking requirements. What character is of major significance in this scene? What is the relative importance of the other characters? What emotions are expressed in the scene; especially, what is the dominant mood? What actions take place: Does the effect of the scene, for instance, derive primarily from the sudden unexpected appearance of a character at an archway in the back wall, or a crucial telephone call, or the discovery of a gun lying under a chair?

It is not necessary that the precise blocking of the scene be worked out at this point, but the essential action and emotional requirements should be fixed clearly in mind.

BLOCKING THE OPENING SCENE

The preceding section of the play is then examined. Very much the same questions are asked of it, except that for each a major factor is the way in which the various elements relate to similar factors in the climactic scene, how the introductory scene prepares for and leads up to this first key moment.

The director then turns to the first few speeches in the play. He now has a clear picture of how they fit into the pattern of the preparatory section and ultimately lead to the first climax. At this point, he is ready to begin making specific decisions about the arrangement and movement of the actors.

In order to block effectively, it is necessary to create the total performance in imagination. The director must be able not only to see the actors move about the stage, but he must also be able to imagine their postures, their gestures, and the way they use their voices in reading the lines, their patterns of emphasis, their pauses. These elements are to be judged not for their own sake, but in terms of the experience they provide for the audience. In selecting from the various ways in which these factors might be handled, the director's guide is the action requirements of the play, the emotions which the characters feel, their relationships with each other, and the meanings of the lines.

This process of creating a total performance in imagination is difficult. It may be made easier to understand by following the thinking of one director in the planning of one speech of a play. This illustration is taken from the prompt script prepared for an actual production.

The play is Shakespeare's *Antony and Cleopatra*. The passage chosen for illustration is the first speech, thirteen lines long, requiring thirty-five seconds to deliver. Two characters, Philo and Demetrius, are on stage during the speech, which is delivered by Philo. Following is the entire first speech:

> Nay, but this dotage of our general's
> O'erflows the measure! Those his goodly eyes
> That o'er the files and musters of the war
> Have glowed like plated Mars, now bend, now turn
> The office and devotion of their view
> Upon a tawny front! His captain's heart,
> Which in the scuffles of great fights hath burst
> The buckles on his breast, reneges all temper,
> And is become the bellows and the fan
> To cool a gypsy's lust! Look where they come!
> Take but good note, and you shall see in him
> The triple pillar of the world transformed
> Into a strumpet's fool. Behold and see!

This speech is followed by the entrance of Cleopatra and Antony. Demetrius and Philo have no further dialog for two minutes and seven seconds, during which only Cleopatra and Antony speak, except for a single six-word sentence spoken by a messenger. At the end of this passage Antony and Cleopatra exit; Philo and Demetrius then engage in a brief conversation lasting seventeen seconds and exit to conclude the scene. The next scene begins with the entrance of a different group of characters.

The speeches in the first scene require two minutes and fifty-nine seconds; the blocking is likely to extend the time somewhat, but the speeches themselves can be diagrammed as shown in Figure 31.

Antony and Cleopatra are of course the major characters in the play, and a study of the scene as a whole indicates that their section of it provides the major

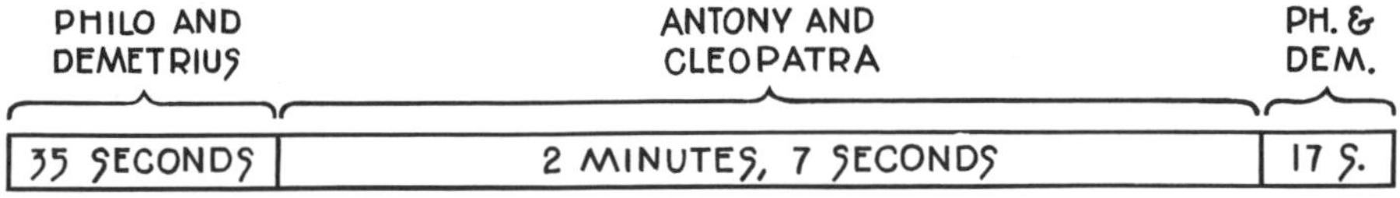

PHILO AND DEMETRIUS	ANTONY AND CLEOPATRA	PH. & DEM.
35 SECONDS	2 MINUTES, 7 SECONDS	17 S.

Figure 31. The structure of the first scene of *Antony and Cleopatra*.

interest of the scene. What is the purpose of the two sections during which Demetrius and Philo are alone on stage? The diagram given above suggests that
their speeches function somewhat like the picture frame, defining the edges of
the main section of the scene, which is dominated by Antony and Cleopatra.
The two bracketing passages contrast vividly in emotional tone with the central
section, heightening the playfulness of Antony and Cleopatra's scene, and producing an effect that is almost musical, Demetrius's first speech sounding a
harsh Roman theme, the Cleopatra passage answering with a light, bright
melody, and the final dialog repeating the Roman melody diminuendo.

A study of the central section of the scene also indicates that it begins and
ends at a high level; the first and last sentences are both short (ten and four
syllables respectively), and they both suggest a high-keyed delivery. The intervening material varies in intensity, but its level is fairly high. The underlying
mood of this passage is bright and rather light; the individual emotions expressed are varied—Cleopatra's teasing, burlesque impersonations of other people, and playfulness contrasting her pretense of anger and fear, which is carried
on as a kind of game. On Antony's part, the emotions include expansive high
spirits, some slight embarrassment in response to Cleopatra's teasing, and a
touch of real irritation with the messenger. This list of course does not exhaust
the scene, which is characterized by Shakespeare's fantastic variety.

The entrance of Antony and Cleopatra is a climactic moment. Not only
does it serve to introduce the two major characters of the play, but it is set at a
high, bright key, with an effect which in musical terms would be described as
"sforzando." A major function of Philo's opening speech is to prepare for this
entrance. He specifically indicates twice where Antony and Cleopatra are to
appear ("Look where they come!"; "Behold and see!"), and his entire speech is
concerned with them.

A summary of the director's analysis of this short scene preliminary to
blocking the specific speeches might be stated as follows: Cleopatra and Antony
must be given dominant positions throughout their section of the scene. Philo
and Demetrius must be blocked into strong positions when they are alone on
stage, but it must be possible to move them into weak positions before the
Antony and Cleopatra section, so that they will not distract the attention from
the major characters. The opening speech must focus the attention of the audience on the point on stage where Antony and Cleopatra will enter. Their entrance is the climactic point that should guide the blocking design of the opening speech.

The director's next step was to turn to the ground plan and perspective
painting of the set provided for him by the designer. This particular set was an
abstract arrangement of architectural forms, including eight different acting
levels, in the form of a flight of stairs which covered almost the entire stage.
The individual levels varied in depth from one to five feet, extending all the

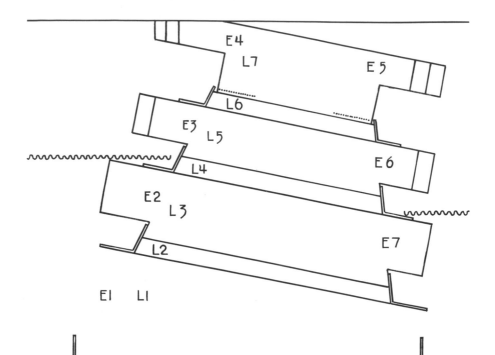

Figure 32a. Ground plan of a set for *Antony and Cleopatra*. (See also Figure 32b.)

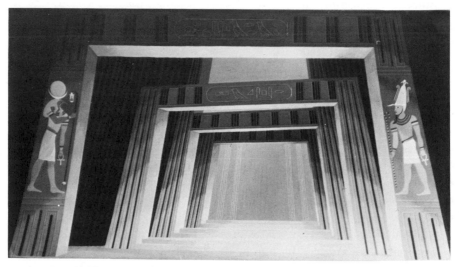

Figure 32b. The set for *Antony and Cleopatra*. (From David Welker, *Theatrical Set Design: The Basic Techniques* (Boston: Allyn and Bacon, Inc., 1959), p. ii. Used by permission.

way across the stage from left to right but turned at a slight angle to the front edge of the stage. The structure did not represent any particular place or building, but it was localized as Egyptian by including four massive sets of beams and pillars with characteristic Egyptian outline decorated with paintings of Egyptian gods and motifs related to ancient Egyptian architecture and jewelry. The beams and pillars were designed in what is called "forced perspective," producing the effect of greater depth than was actually provided by the stage.

Although the set did not represent any particular locale, the director decided to suggest localization by the directions from which actors entered. Entrances from Cleopatra's palace were planned to be made uniformly at the back of the stage from the left in order to give them greater strength, since actors entering at this point, between the pair of pillars farthest up stage, would be facing the audience at the strongest angle, would be standing on the highest step, and would be framed not only by the upstage pillars but by the set as a whole. The entire set, in fact, was designed to point toward this position.

The action of the opening speech, then, should direct the audience's attention as strongly as possible toward the upstage point where Antony and Cleopatra are to appear. In addition, Philo and Demetrius must be placed so that they can be quickly moved to a weak position, preferably an instant before the two main characters enter.

The set provided seven entrances (plus a hidden entrance used only in the last act). Four of these entrances were on stage right and three on the left. The entrances were placed at different levels, the downstage entrance on the right being at stage level, and the entrance farthest upstage at the level of the highest platform incorporated in the flight of stairs, with the other two entrances at intermediate levels. The three stage-left entrances matched the heights of the three upstage right entrances.

Since only Philo and Demetrius are on stage during the first speech, the entire set is available for their use. It would be possible to have them enter at the back of the stage, through the same opening where Antony and Cleopatra will appear. There are several reasons, however, why that entrance is undesirable. Keeping it open until the major characters appear strengthens their use of it: it seems to be waiting for their entrance. It can be approached from either the left or the right, but since Philo is not intimately associated with either Antony or Cleopatra and his opening speech consists of an attack on them, to have him enter from the same direction would indicate the wrong relationship; it would suggest that he was on their side, when in fact he is in opposition. An entrance from the right, opposite to the direction chosen for the palace, would correct that defect.

Tracing the entrance of the two characters from the right at the back of the stage, between the upstage pillars, suggests a further defect in the use of this area. The two actors, entering side by side, would be almost exactly equal in strength; but in the section of the play preceding the entrance of Antony and Cleopatra, Philo is strongly dominant. Demetrius has no speeches until after Antony and Cleopatra have come and gone, and during the entire scene he speaks only thirty-five words, as contrasted with Philo's hundred and twenty-six. Furthermore, Philo's mood is dominant throughout the scene. In the opening speech, to which Demetrius makes no reply, it is one of outraged anger, with tones of contempt and disgust. In the interests of clarity for the audience, that relationship should be expressed by the blocking, not contradicted, and the blocking should assist the actors in communicating their relationship to the audience, not make it more difficult for them.

The upstage entrance places Philo and Demetrius in the strongest position provided by the set. By the end of the speech they must have been moved to a weak position, the two weakest on this set being at the down-left and down-right corners of the stage. The upstage entrance is farther from those two positions than any other point on the stage. Consequently, if they must move from it to one of the downstage corners, they will have to cross the maximum distance on the set during the space of a single speech. While it would be possible for them to cover that distance in the thirty-five seconds available, almost the entire speech would have to be expended in motivating their crosses, a difficult task since there is nothing in the speech suggesting this kind of long, direct change in position. The movements that would be necessary simply to get them from one point on stage to another could be more effectively replaced by blocking that would have communicative rather than simply mechanical function—that would help them express the emotions required by the script.

On the basis of this reasoning, the director rejected the upstage entrance. The two remaining entrances at the left of the stage were rejected because they would bring the actors on from the direction of the palace. Having Philo and Demetrius enter from the right not only expresses their opposition to Antony and Cleopatra, but automatically turns them more directly toward the upstage entrance and makes the pattern of movement slightly more effective esthetically, the movement from the right being countered by the entrance of Antony and Cleopatra from the left a moment later, a more interesting pattern than parallel movements in the same direction.

The two center entrances on the right might be acceptable for Philo and Demetrius; certainly they would be far more satisfactory than the upstage entrance. However, testing all three of the remaining entrances on the right suggests that the most effective is the one farthest downstage.

Turning to the opening speech, the director next restudied it in order to identify its meaning and emotion as clearly as possible. Shakespeare has marked it to indicate that it is not the first speech in the conversation. The play opens in the middle of an argument, and Philo's speech is an answer to a remark which Demetrius has just finished but which we do not hear. Philo's first word is an explosive "No!" (actually "Nay," of course, in Elizabethan English). It is not difficult to reconstruct Demetrius's previous speech from Philo's answer and from the rest of the play.

Antony is the most admired citizen of Rome and the highest general of the army—the Eisenhower or MacArthur of Rome. He has been sent to Egypt in command of the army, has there met the fascinating Cleopatra, and has fallen so completely under her spell that he seems like a different person. The upright Roman hero, whose first concern has been his duty to Rome and whose second has been his own reputation, has taken to spending his days and nights in riotous partying and has neglected all of his responsibilities. During this scene he refuses even to listen to a message from Rome: "Speak not to us!" What makes his behavior still worse is that he has a respectable wife back in Rome, and both he and Cleopatra are long past the age when a foolish infatuation might have been understandable if not forgivable. By the standards of the time, in fact, they are an old man and an old woman, a point that is emphasized repeatedly throughout the play.

Antony is thus no longer himself. In Philo's embarrassed, pompous speech at the end of this scene he says, "Sir, sometimes when he is not Antony he comes too short of that great property which still should go with Antony." His behavior is the biggest current scandal in Rome, and the subject of fascinated gossip. His friends are horrified; his enemies are delighted.

Demetrius has come to Egypt to find out the truth for himself; it is so difficult for him to believe the stories he has been told that he protests to Philo that they must be exaggerations. There is nothing wrong with a Roman general's relaxing at the end of a day's work, attending a party now and then, he says. But Antony's behavior, Philo replies, goes far beyond the bounds of acceptability (and it is at this point that the play opens). He is not simply a tired Roman general who relaxes from business with an occasional banquet. This great hero, who once was one of the three strongest men on whose shoulders the entire government rested, has been turned into a contemptible playboy: "Take but good note, and you shall see in him the triple pillar of the world transformed into a strumpet's fool!"

It would have been possible, in this production of the play, to show Philo and Demetrius already on stage when the curtain opens. However, if Philo's opening sentence was to be heard it would have been necessary for him to wait in silence until the curtain was at least half open before he began to speak, which would have destroyed the impression that Shakespeare was careful to create that the play began in the middle of a conversation. Philo's first word must follow Demetrius's previous remark without a pause, and even if we do not hear Demetrius's speech it is important that Philo burst out immediately, without a preceding moment of silence. Furthermore, it would be much more difficult for the actor playing Philo to speak at the necessary level of intensity if he were required to start the speech without moving; and even if a movement were planned from one point on stage to another, it would be difficult to design one that could be excuted with the same degree of directness and intensity as an entrance. In the original Elizabethan production, the theater provided no front curtain, so that Philo's entrance would necessarily have been visible; he could not be shown already on stage at the opening of the play. For all of those reasons, the decision to have the curtain open on a bare stage, with Philo entering as he spoke, was made by the director very early in his analysis of the scene.

For this production, a full musical score was especially composed, and performed by an orchestra under the composer's direction. As an integrated part of the production, accompanying music occasionally has some effect on the blocking, and it was decided that the music should be used by Philo as the cue for his entrance. It may be helpful to describe the pattern of the overture.

An underlying theme of the play is the contrast between the Roman and Egyptian cultures. The play is set mainly in Egypt, and the Egyptian mood constitutes the fundamental pattern. Against it are placed the more vigorous Roman elements. In his specifications for the music, the director suggested that the overture begin by establishing the Egyptian setting, then shift to a Roman style, rising emotionally to suggest anger and intensity, as a support for the beginning of Philo's speech. The direction, as actually written for the composer, is as follows:

The overture begins with an Egyptian theme, sensuous, mysterious, sweet, haunting. It ends with a Roman theme, brassy, prosaic, which finishes with a crescendo and crash at fortissimo level.

The instructions continue:

Starting toward the end of the crescendo, the curtain opens fast. Using the crash concluding the overture as his cue, Philo strides on stage by E1, followed by Demetrius. [Since this set did not follow the box-set pattern, entrances were identified by "E" followed by a number; this is the extreme down-right entrance.]

Two actors entering together at the side of the stage can be arranged in four different ways: (1) They may enter side by side, that is, one directly upstage of the other; (2) the second can walk directly behind the other; (3) they can be arranged so that a line drawn from one to the other forms an angle other than 90° with the front edge of the acting area, with the actor at the upstage end of the line entering first, or (4) the line can be slanted in the opposite direction so that the downstage actor enters first. Since the positions of the two actors can be reversed in each of these patterns, eight different arrangements are possible.

A glance at the diagrams will demonstrate that the first position is not effective. The upstage actor is nearly hidden by the downstage actor. Actors using the second arrangement, if they move slowly and quietly, would suggest stealth;

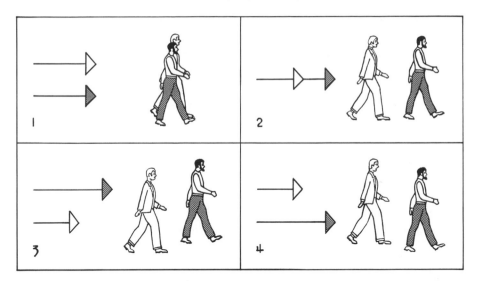

Figure 33. Alternative arrangements for two actors entering from the side of the stage.

if fast, such an entrance suggests that the second actor is pursuing the first. Either effect might be suited to some plays, but not to the one we are considering. The fourth position is an awkward one for our purposes. Although the upstage actor is revealed more fully than in the first position, sight of him will still be blocked for a significant strip of the audience, extending diagonally across the auditorium. The third position provides maximum visibility for all of the members of the audience.

In the third arrangement, the upstage actor is clearly in the stronger position. He is closer to the center of the stage as he enters; he enters first and so catches the attention immediately; and if he turns toward the other actor at the end of the cross, the angle at which he is facing is stronger than that of the other actor. The degree of difference between the effectiveness of the two positions would depend on the angle of the line joining them, but it would always favor the upstage actor. The conclusion, then, is that the third position should be used for this entrance, with Philo upstage. As he enters, he will be speaking with his back to Demetrius, which is normally an awkward arrangement. The violence of his lines, however, and the fact that his first sentence contradicts what Demetrius has just said, motivates his turning away; in fact this blocking pattern assists the actor in communicating the feeling of the line.

Only the first exclamatory sentence, however, can be spoken in this position. If the arrangement is not to seem unnatural, Philo must turn to face Demetrius at the beginning of his next sentence. Furthermore, the explosive effect of Philo's entrance is likely to have so totally caught the audience's attention that Demetrius's presence may hardly have been noticed. Although he has no

lines until the end of the scene, he must be included within the area of the audience's awareness in order to prevent the speech from seeming like a soliloquy.
Both of those requirements are satisfied by having Philo turn at the end of his
first sentence.

In diagramming the blocking, it is important to know how much space on
the stage each movement will occupy. The ability to estimate the length of
movements accurately depends on experience. When in doubt, however, a simple method of measuring is to walk through the cross, reciting the accompanying speech, and trying to move at the desired speed. In this case, the director
could stand just beyond the doorway of a room and stride through it and across
the floor while speaking the sentence. Experiment indicates that an actor crossing at the intended speed while speaking the sentence angrily would cover
about eleven feet, which on this set would take him just short of halfway across
the stage.

Demetrius must remain in a weaker position throughout the speech, so as
to maintain the focus of attention on Philo; also, since both must move to a
weak area of the stage at the end of the speech, it will be easier if Demetrius
can be blocked from the beginning close to his final position. However, it is important that he be seen by the audience as a partner in the opening conversation, even though he has no lines; consequently, he must be placed far enough
on stage to be associated visually with Philo rather than with nearby scenic elements. And finally, the major area of the stage must be kept free for Philo's
movements to assist him in expressing the emotions that are a part of his speech.

Balancing these various factors, the director decided to place Demetrius
halfway between the entrance and the point that Philo reached at the end of
his entrance cross. The description of this position was then added to the stage
directions. The second paragraph, in full, then read as follows:

Starting toward the end of the crescendo, the curtain opens fast. Using the crash
concluding the overture as his cue, Philo strides on stage by E1, followed by Demetrius. Philo starts speaking as soon as he is on stage. The entrance should be timed so
that he speaks the instant the music stops. He X to the C of L1. Demetrius stops halfway between E1 and Philo, slightly DS of Philo.

["X," "C," and "DS" are the standard abbreviations for "cross," "center," and
"down stage"; "L1" (level 1) indicates the stage floor itself; each step and platform
was designated by "L," followed by a distinctive number.]

Having made these decisions, the director then drew symbolic triangles on
a copy of the ground plan to indicate the positions of both actors at the end of
their entrance crosses. Lines were drawn from these triangles offstage to show
their paths of movement, and arrows and "1" added to express the direction of
the movement and the number of the speech during which it occurred.

On Philo's second sentence, it was decided that he should turn back toward

Demetrius. A simple turn would function here, but expanding it to a short cross makes it more visible and communicative; the direction as finally written said, "Philo turns back and X to slightly UL of Demetrius." This movement was then diagrammed on the ground plan.

The rest of the speech could logically be delivered from this position. Three considerations led the director to specify additional crosses. The most important was that it seemed that the intensity of Philo's feeling would be easier to express if he could move than if he had to deliver the speech from a stationary position. The second factor was that it seemed desirable to locate the position of the palace (offstage) as clearly as possible, preferably more than once. And the final consideration was that the sight lines in Philo's second position were less than ideal. Although he would be visible to the audience, he seemed uncomfortably close to Demetrius. Consequently, a movement was specified to be made beginning in the middle of his second sentence, starting with "now bend, now turn." The direction reads:

Philo X UL and stops with his L foot on L3 and his R foot on L2. He gestures toward Arch 4.

The passage chosen for this cross ends with a reference to Cleopatra, which supports his gesture up left toward the palace. His next sentence returns to the subject of Antony. At this point the blocking directs him to turn back toward Demetrius. This is not a cross: he remains at the same point on the stage, but strengthens his position by turning to face down right, and also swings the area of attention around to include Demetrius once more.

The next sentence is an exclamation: "Look where they come!" This could be motivated by having Philo pretend to see Cleopatra and Antony offstage, before they become visible to the audience. Their entrance could not itself be used as a cue for Philo's exclamation, because his speech continues for seven seconds beyond the exclamation. If the entrance of Antony and Cleopatra is placed before the exclamation, the audience's attention would be divided between the new characters and the speech, and at least one of the two elements would be ineffective. If Antony and Cleopatra continued to move throughout the remainder of Philo's speech, they would descend to a weaker position than the level at which they entered. If they avoided that descent by stopping at the entrance, they would have an unmotivated wait while Philo concluded his speech, which would be so out of character for Cleopatra that it would probably create the impression that the entrance had been made at the wrong time.

In order to provide a cue for Philo's exclamation that would be meaningful to the audience, the composer was asked to supply a fanfare, presumably sounded offstage to herald the approach of the queen. Taking this as his cue, Philo gestured again toward the up-left corner of the stage, simultaneously speaking his line "Look where they come!" He then continued his speech from the same position:

> Take but good note, and you shall see in him
> The triple pillar of the world transformed
> Into a strumpet's fool.

It is necessary to move both Philo and Demetrius to a weak stage position before the entrance of Cleopatra and Antony. It would have been possible to use the sentence just quoted for this purpose. However, to do so would have obscured the line, which is a fairly important one. Instead, the necessary crosses were delayed until after the sentence. However, only three words remain to cover them: "Behold and see!," providing only about a second of time. If Antony and Cleopatra appear at the cue "see," their entrance will be confused by the completion of the crosses of Demetrius and Philo; since this entrance is an especially important one, it should receive the greatest emphasis and the fullest attention.

In order to adjust to all of these considerations, the blocking design for this production amplified the minimal blocking requirements of the script. Before the entrance of the two principals, four minor characters are brought on stage and placed in a symmetrical arrangement, with an opening in the center. The result is to delay the entrance of Cleopatra and Antony, and to display an obviously incomplete pattern, the central element missing, to be supplied in a moment by the queen and the general. The result is a momentary increase in suspense. The symmetry of the arrangement creates a feeling of formality, the effect of all of these factors being that the entrance is given a processional quality which makes it seem especially significant. There is still some overlap between the final crosses of Demetrius and Philo and the entrance of the subordinate characters. This is advantageous rather than otherwise, however. The audience has been alerted to expect an entrance at the back of the stage, and they follow Philo as he moves down right to his final position; as he turns up left toward the upstage entrance, the audience follows the direction in which he is looking, and its attention also is turned toward the back entrance. The movements of the four minor actors as they take their positions up left assist in this shift in the direction of the audience's attention, and the overlapping of the two sets of movements, down right and up left, produces a feeling of simultaneous contrast, and an uninterrupted flow of movement from the area of the stage that has been of focal importance to the area that will serve as the focus during the next few speeches of the play.

The direction for Philo and Demetrius is as follows:

Philo X hastily to Demetrius, who moves DR, and both turn back to watch Antony and Cleopatra's entrance. (This movement is synchronized with Philo's last

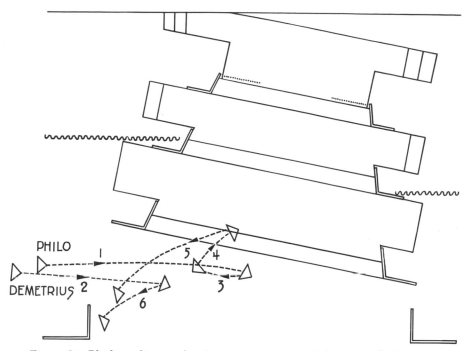

Figure 34. Blocking diagram for the opening speech of *Antony and Cleopatra*. (The numbers indicate the sequence of movements.)

three words, "Behold and see!," but will require more time than the speech; the action continues after the speech until it is completed.)

The entrances of the four minor characters are made in pairs, two women entering simultaneously, and then two men. The instructions prepared for them by the director are as follows:

Simultaneously (on cue "you shall see in him"):
> Woman 1 enters by E4 and stops at the DR corner of L7, centered behind the beaded screen.
> Woman 2 enters by E5 and stops at the DL corner of L7, centered behind the beaded screen.

Simultaneously (as soon as Women 1 and 2 are in position):
> Mardian enters by E4 carrying a large ceremonial fan, and X to the R end of L5.
> Alexas enters by E5 carrying a similar fan, and X to the L end of L5.

Beaded screens are mentioned in the directions for the women. They appeared in the open space between the two pillars farthest up stage, cutting of a quarter of the opening on each side. Special lights were placed to catch the beads, providing a glittering plane through which the audience could easily see, but which slightly de-emphasized actors standing behind it. The women were

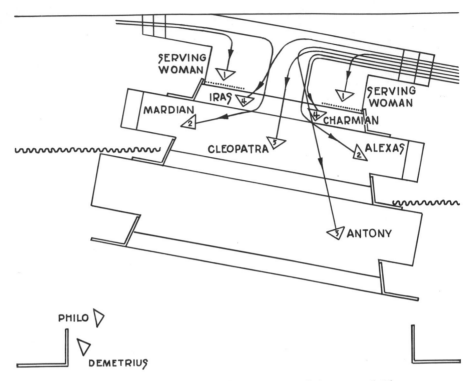

Figure 35. Blocking diagram for the first entrance of *Antony and Cleopatra.*

placed behind the screens to frame the opening, but also so that they would be slightly less visible, and would consequently not distract the attention from Cleopatra. The queen's costume was designed to help her catch the focus of attention, and included, for example, an ankle-length cape, royal purple on the outside, and lined with gold.

As soon as the four servants are in position, Antony and Cleopatra appear. In order to amplify their entrance and to make it more processional, they are accompanied by two additional servants. The instructions are as follows:

> Antony and Cleopatra enter by E5, Cleopatra R and slightly ahead of Antony. Cleopatra X to the C of L5. Antony X to the L end of L3, about a yard from the pillars. Iras and Charmian follow Antony and Cleopatra on, with Iras on the R, and stop on L6, one on each side of Cleopatra.

THE REASONS FOR ADVANCE PLANNING

Nontheater people who happen to pick up directors' plans frequently express surprise at the care with which they have been prepared. Even theater workers are often astonished on learning all that is involved in directing. A common response is, "Do you mean that all directors really plan their productions so carefully?"

The answer is no. An enormous range of technical methods appear in the work of directors. Even if the work of only the finest directors were studied, it would be found that the amount of prerehearsal planning and the detail and methods of recording the plans vary enormously. Some directors prefer to do less planning in advance and to leave larger areas of decision until the rehearsals are actually in progress. Such directors may have unusual skills, such as the ability to hold a large number of alternatives in their minds at once, and analyze and evaluate them, without being disturbed by the complex distractions of rehearsal. They may be able to carry through in five minutes during a rehearsal analyses and decisions that a less gifted director could work out only when he was sitting undistracted in his study, with perhaps an hour available for the work.

Other directors, however, avoid planning for less acceptable reasons, some because they are simply lazy and hope that problems will somehow solve themselves, others because they are indecisive and hope that the actors may be able to choose blocking patterns on their own. Perhaps the most understandable reason for omitting planning is that some directors have great difficulty visualizing the production. In the theater they can ask the actors to take up various positions on stage, and may be able to evaluate them very effectively, but it may be impossible for them to judge arrangements represented only by symbols drawn on ground plans, or buttons placed in various positions.

For most directors, precise preplanning has great advantages. The absence of distraction is of enormous importance. A related factor is the relaxation provided by not having to work under the pressure of time. A blocking decision which is made during rehearsal must be made very quickly—probably ten minutes is the maximum length of time that a cast can be asked to stand waiting while the director works out some problem. Even if the decisions can be made in that very short period, six such decisions would hold up the work for a full hour—a third of an evening's rehearsal. The number of separate decisions involved in blocking the single speech in the example described above should demonstrate the impracticality for most directors of trying to work out blocking without destroying large sections of the rehearsal time scheduled for other purposes.

The interlocking aspect of theater art has been mentioned; the blocking alone has some similarities to a jigsaw puzzle. Each piece—each position and movement—affects the design of all later positions and movements. All must fit together precisely if the design is to be effective. It is fairly easy to choose between two alternative positions or movements for an actor who is visibly on stage, but to make a sound decision, it is necessary to trace the effect of each alternative throughout all of the rest of the scene or act to whatever point the stage is cleared and a new blocking design can be begun. In such a simple matter as whether an actor is to sit in one chair or another, the immediate effect of each position may be quite clear; but a few speeches later the action of the play may require that another actor enter on stage right and make an indiscreet remark to the first actor, mistaking him for a third. One of the two positions might place the first actor with his back to the second, and consequently make the mistake credible, whereas the other might leave him facing the entrance, and make the later action impossible. Even more important, all of the movements that the actor makes after he sits down in the chair will start from different points, depending on which chair is chosen. Each will have a different relationship to the scenery and furniture and to the other actors on stage. The result is that shifting an actor's position only a couple of feet may produce a progressive alteration in all of his later movements, resulting in a totally different blocking arrangement. Since the positions of all of the actors must be precisely fitted together, even a slight shift in the position of a single actor will often require the complete reblocking of all the rest of the scene up to the fall of the curtain. One director, working with an unusually open stage, with two chairs as the only furniture, decided during rehearsal that the chairs would look more effective if each was moved eighteen inches. He reported that the result was chaos. The shifts in the positions of all of the actors, although in themselves small, so altered the spatial arrangements that, for example, when an actor was required to slip through an entrance door and take his position unobtrusively between two other actors in a group, the opening left for him had been moved just far enough to be unreachable, and the path from the door to the opening had been closed by an actor who had had to move back to make room for other actors who had been moved aside by the shift in position of the nearest chair. The director remarked, "If I had not seen it happen I wouldn't have believed it, but shifting those two chairs a foot and a half on an almost open stage made my blocking impossible." The chairs were eventually returned to their original positions, and the initial blocking design restored.

An additional advantage of careful planning is that it frees the director's attention during rehearsals for other things. Effective blocking requires such concentration and the handling of such a complexity of factors that few directors could give it adequate attention and have any left for other aspects of production. When blocking has been carefully planned and recorded both in script notes and detailed diagrams, an assistant director can follow it during rehearsal quite easily. The director is necessarily involved during the rehearsals when the actors first walk through their blocking patterns. They will not completely master the blocking at such rehearsals, however, and can be expected to make many mistakes during the following week, when their attention and that of the director has turned to the interpretation of the lines. If these mistakes are not caught and corrected at the instant they are made, they will repeat and multiply. If the director himself attempts to maintain a constant check on the blocking, he will have little attention left for the new tasks which should be the focus of the later rehearsals. By turning the blocking check over to the assistant director, he is able to free his mind of it except when a difficulty arises, and consequently to make much more efficient use of the valuable rehearsal time.

A final advantage of detailed preplanning is the feeling of confidence which results from knowing that blocking decisions have been made in full, under optimum conditions providing adequate time and freedom from distraction and pressure.

REPAIRING BREAKDOWNS IN BLOCKING

In order to illustrate the development of a blocking design, a single speech, the first one in the play, has been selected for analysis. The example, complex as it may seem, is in fact a very simple one. It lasts for scarcely more than half a minute, only two actors are present, and only one of them speaks. Furthermore, the action that follows it (the entrance of Antony and Cleopatra) is clearly localized, so that it was easy for the director to design the action of the opening speech so as to prepare for the next episode.

With more complicated scenes, the director cannot expect the work to go quite so smoothly. Even with the closest study of the script, sometimes the pattern of movement breaks down just when it should be strongest. Just when the hero must take the heroine's hand and lead her to her father, the director may discover that the hero is standing at one side of the stage with the heroine at the top of a flight of stairs on the other side, that the space between the two is filled with a dozen actors, and that even if he could lead her to her father, the father is standing in an upper corner of the stage, that he would be hidden by the two, and that their backs would necessarily be turned directly toward the audience. Extreme as this description sounds, a beginning director would be fortunate indeed if something like it did not occur at least once while he was planning his first play. Half a dozen such cul-de-sacs would not be unusual, and even an experienced director has to confront them frequently.

The only solution to such a problem is to go back and start again. Instead of starting at the beginning, however, it is better to start at the point the problem appears and trace the movements backward. Here the diagrams are invaluable; to work out such a problem from written instructions alone is almost impossible. The director will have a vivid picture of the blocking requirements in the problem scene: the hero and heroine must be within reachable distance from each other; characters who are not of major importance at the moment must be moved to weak positions, however important they have been in the preceding section of the play; and the father must be placed so that when hero and heroine approach him all three are emphatically visible. Tracing the blocking backward through the preceding transitional or preparatory passage will define the latest preceding key moment. The problem, then, is to plot the scene from that point to the key scene where the difficulty has arisen.

At what moment do the characters who obscure the scene lose their significance? Often the difficulty arises from having placed characters in strong positions when they were the focus of attention, and then simply having left them there after their function in the scene no longer justified their prominence. What motivation can be found or invented for their moving aside? If such movements cannot be done openly, can they be done unobtrusively at the same time as other movements so as to seem in response to the movements of the characters who occupy the focus of attention? Can a motivation be found for bringing the father into a stronger position during the preparatory scene, even though the audience's attention is on some other actor?

The director should not overlook minor characters. A butler whose only function is to stand waiting to help an actor on with his coat may have influenced the blocking without the director's realizing it. If the butler closes a path through which a major character might otherwise have moved, the director may not even have considered the possibility. Shifting him to a slightly different position, perhaps a foot or two upstage, or to the other side of the second actor, may provide space through which a major actor can move, resulting in a different pattern of movement for the entire cast.

One director had considerable difficulty with a late scene in *The Taming of the Shrew*. Old Vincentio, visiting in a strange town, is accused of being a criminal. Angry words follow, and Baptista calls out an officer to arrest him. The officer is an extremely minor character; he has no lines and does not even arrest Vincentio. Before he can, Vincentio's son and Baptista's daughter arrive from the church where they have just been secretly married. They confess and appeal to their fathers for forgiveness, and all are happily reunited.

On first study, the blocking broke down into the kind of chaos described. However the characters were arranged, Vincentio ended up stubbornly at stage center, without sufficient space for the lovers to squeeze between him and Baptista. Furthermore, the script requires that he not see his son immediately, and however the actors were placed, Lucentio came face to face with his father at the moment he entered.

Several agonizing reappraisals got nowhere until the director noticed the figure of the officer, who had been placed well out of the way up left to attract no further attention after his entrance. His presence suggested that he might supply a motivation for moving Vincentio out of the key position, thus opening it up for the lovers. Starting back with the officer's entrance, his movements were reblocked so that, instead of simply appearing on call, he actually took hold of Vincentio and dragged him protesting to stage left. As soon as it became clear that no immediate arrest was to be made, the officer was able to move back to his original unobtrusive position. A line of Vincentio's was found— " 'Tis thus that strangers may be haled and abused!"—that enabled him to turn down left, raising his hands in protest, so that he was facing away from the center of the stage when the two lovers crept in by a back entrance and into the strong positions between the fathers.

Every director could cite many such instances in his experience. Usually, tracing the movements back only a little way will make it possible to disentangle the problem. At the worst, it would be necessary to start again from the first page of the scene and develop a completely new pattern of movement.

It was indicated earlier in the chapter that effective blocking design must be based on a total visualization of the performance, including the interpretation of the lines and exactly how they are to be read by the actors. The *Antony and Cleopatra* example illustrated that fact several times: The positions and movements of Philo and Demetrius would have been completely different if the mood of the scene had varied, if, for instance, Philo had been in a mood of lighthearted playfulness. Furthermore, the patterns of positions and movements are expressive of, and synchronized with, the subjects the characters talk about, and even the way the lines are phrased. Although some directors prefer to record interpretative notes at the same time as they are preparing the blocking design, it seemed preferable to take up interpretation in connection with the administration of the interpretative rehearsals.

CURTAIN CALLS

It is customary to raise the curtain at the end of the last act of a play so that the cast can acknowledge the applause of the audience. Formerly the actors were arranged in a row just behind the curtain, which was then raised to reveal them in position. It is now commoner to open the curtain on the bare stage and have the actors enter and take their positions in the sight of the audience. Assembling the cast for the curtain call thus becomes a part of the visual pattern of the show and must be blocked like an additional scene.

The actors are usually brought on stage in the reverse order of their importance in the play, leaving an opening in the arrangement that is filled by the leading actor and actress. Usually actors who have been associated closely in the play are grouped together for the curtain call, especially each actor and actress who have been romantically paired in the play. Minor actors who have similar functions in the play may be brought on as a group. A dozen servants, for example, might be split into two groups of six and instructed to enter from opposite sides of the stage, joining in the center at the back or taking up their positions at left and right, leaving the major part of the stage open for the principals. The cast does not bow until all are on stage. The bow is begun by the leading actress, and the others take her bow as their cue. After the bow, the curtains are closed. If the audience continues to applaud, the curtains are opened again, the cast bows a second time, the curtains close, and the house lights are brought up as an indication that the performance is over.

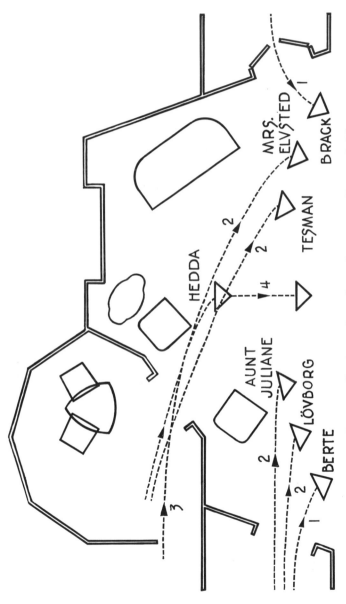

Figure 36*a*. Curtain calls. A simple traditional pattern is illustrated. The numbers indicate the sequence of crosses. At the rise of the curtain the stage is empty; then Brack and Berte enter simultaneously from opposite sides of the stage, then Lövborg and Aunt Juliane enter from down right and Tesman and Mrs. Elvsted from up right. Finally, Hedda Gabler enters from up right, stopping well above the other actors. Following their bow, the curtain closes. As it opens for the second call, Hedda crosses straight down, and the cast bows again.

Although the actors acknowledge the audience in the curtain call, it is more effective for them to maintain their characters. The single-row arrangement is still acceptable, but a more complex blocking is more interesting. It may even be possible to introduce a few amusing touches of business as the cast assembles. The second curtain call can show the actors in the same arrangement, or the director can work out different positions, which the actors can take during the few moments while the curtain is closed.

It is very important that the curtain be opened for the first call as quickly as possible. Actors should be instructed to run off stage at top speed as soon as they are hidden by the closing curtain, and to pop out of the entrances the instant it reopens, and cross smartly to their positions.

Audiences vaguely resent being denied a curtain call when they are applauding enthusiastically. Even worse, however, is to force them to continue to applaud by raising the curtain again and again after their enthusiasm has faded and they are ready to leave the theater. Judging when to close the curtain for the last time and bring up the house lights is the responsibility of the stage manager, and he should be instructed to err, if at all, by cutting off the calls too soon rather than extending them too long. It is best for the audience to feel that the cast actually deserved just one call more.

The director can count on one obligatory curtain call, and if the audience is reasonably responsive, he can assume two. It is probably best always to design blocking for two calls. If the audience genuinely demands more, the third and later calls can be handled as repetitions of the second, with the actors remaining in their places. Occasionally actors break and begin to exit after a second call, and are caught out of place when the curtain opens again. The effect is pleasant, however, rather than embarrassing. It suggests a becoming modesty on the part of the cast, and even if they are a little flustered, the fact that they had obviously not anticipated such an enthusiastic reception from the audience helps express their appreciation of it. Actors caught out of place should stop where they are, turn to the audience, and bow with the rest of the cast.

Curtain calls are rehearsed during the last week before opening, often following the technical rehearsal.

Of all the director's work, blocking is perhaps the most irksome, and one of the most frequently slighted. However, masterly blocking contributes to the confidence of both director and actors, and provides a solidity of foundation that supports all of the work of the actors during their weeks of rehearsal. A well-blocked play makes it easier for each actor to perform effectively; a poorly blocked play makes his work more difficult; an unblocked play makes it impossible. And once the director has carried through the detailed analysis that is necessary to blocking, he will have developed a total familiarity with the play which will make all the rest of his work easier and more effective.

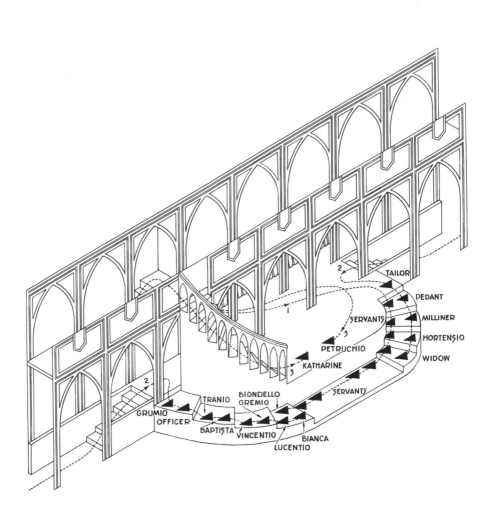

Figure 36b (above and on facing page). A complicated pattern
is illustrated. In this case, no front curtain is used. At the end
of the play, actors enter and take up the positions shown, with
Katharine and Petruchio entering last, and cuing the bow.
Katharine and Petruchio then exit at the back of the stage (as
shown in the second drawing), and the other actors move to
new positions. The two leading actors reenter on the upper level,
the cast bows again, and the actors exit. In these diagrams, the
positions at the end of the first curtain call are indicated by

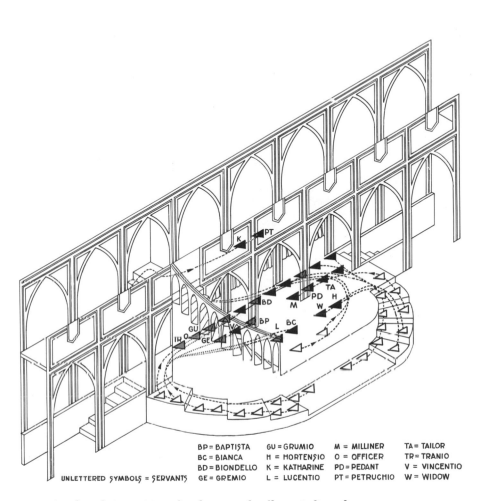

BP = BAPTISTA	GU = GRUMIO	M = MILLINER	TA = TAILOR
BC = BIANCA	H = HORTENSIO	O = OFFICER	TR = TRANIO
BD = BIONDELLO	K = KATHARINE	PD = PEDANT	V = VINCENTIO
UNLETTERED SYMBOLS = SERVANTS	GE = GREMIO	L = LUCENTIO	PT = PETRUCHIO	W = WIDOW

open triangles; their positions for the second call are indicated by triangles that have been filled in. Dotted lines and shaded triangles indicate paths and positions that would be hidden in this view. The isometric drawing used in these diagrams shows the set from a position radically different from that of the spectators; although some of the actors in the drawing are hidden by the scenery, all of them would be visible to most of the members of the audience, and all of the principal actors would be visible to the entire audience.

3

Casting and Rehearsal

8/Auditions and Casting

The selection of the actors for a play, and the assignment of their roles, is one of the director's most important duties, with a profound effect on the success of the production. It is also one of the most difficult and agonizing duties. This procedure is called "casting."

The Sources of Actors

Casting procedures vary greatly. Not only do directors differ in their methods, but the groups of actors from whom they select their casts are of many different types. In summer theaters, often a company is assembled for the season, and each play must be cast from this restricted group. The actors may be divided into two subgroups, principals and apprentices, with the provision, either expressly contractual or strongly presumed, that all major roles will be assigned to principals. Occasionally local residents may also be encouraged to audition, especially for small parts in large-cast shows. Repertory theaters follow essentially the same pattern. Some are associated with universities, whose students may also be included in the casts.

On Broadway, each cast is assembled uniquely, and disperses at the end of the run. If actors who have appeared together in one play become fellow members of another cast, that is to some extent accidental; there is no necessary continuity from one play to the next. The star system results in the major roles' being cast first, they almost never involve auditions, but are arranged in conference with the actors or their agents. Secondary roles are usually filled on the

199

basis of auditions from a group of actors recommended by agents. Open tryouts may also be announced, at which any actor may appear without an agent's recommendation.

In community theaters, auditions are usually open to all actors who are interested, and often are not even restricted to the community in which the theater is located. A cast may include actors from three or four nearby cities that are close enough that they can commute to the rehearsals and performances. Usually there is less continuity of cast than in repertory companies, but more than in professional productions. Most community theaters are organized around a fairly small group of dedicated and continuously active performers and technical workers who take part in nearly every production. A second group, perhaps two or three times as large, display continuing but sporadic interest; each member may try out for about one play out of three. Among those who audition are a third group who have not previously taken part in the plays. Some members of this group can be expected to move into one of the other two groups for later productions; others may never be seen again. Usually major roles are assigned to members of the first group, supporting roles to those of the second group, and the third group of actors are cast in walk-ons or small parts.

The educational theater displays a similar pattern, with some differences. Some attrition occurs in the community theater. A leading actor is transferred to a distant city and must withdraw from the theater; a leading actress finds that increasing family responsibilities prevent her from continuing to participate. In the educational theater, however, such attrition is much more extreme and remains very constant. Usually actors develop to the level of leading roles not earlier than the middle of their junior year in college, and each spring the strongest actors in the program are graduated. Without a continuing training program designed to raise supporting actors to the level of the major roles, a college theater would be destroyed in at least two years, and at most four.

Furthermore, the educational theater by definition has as one of its major purposes the training of its actors. A complete novice would be unacceptable in the professional theater and would be likely to be accepted with reluctance even in a semiprofessional summer theater; although he would undoubtedly be given a warm reception in most civic theaters, a more skilled actor would be preferred. Such an actor would be fully welcomed only in the educational theater, which is especially designed to receive him.

The apprentice system, which also operates to a lesser degree in the summer and community theaters, is standard in the educational theater. A new actor is usually restricted to a minor role, which gives him an opportunity to become acquainted with theatrical procedures, terminology, and traditions, without throwing on him the burden of carrying a major role. This also enables the director to assess his abilities without endangering the success of the production. If it should become evident that he needs an unusual amount of assistance, the fact that his part is short makes it likely that the director can find time for individual rehearsals and conferences. Similar assistance with a longer part might require more time than was available.

If the new actor decides to continue his work in the theater, he begins his next role from a much stronger position, having learned a great deal during his first play. In addition, the director will have become well acquainted with his work and can assess his potentialities more accurately. If he has handled his first part well, he will then be considered for a larger part. During a series of productions, the actor thus moves up, ultimately to the level of the leading roles. Of course, some actors cannot follow this path of development all the way. At some point in the climb, it may become evident that they have reached the limit of their ability, in which case, if they continue to take part in the program, they will be assigned further parts within the limits of their range. Some actors never rise above minor supporting roles. Some few may, during their four years in college, be usable only for walk-ons or very small speaking parts.

In the professional theater, the director is usually concerned only with the production he is working on at the moment. In community and college theaters, he more often is involved in the continuing program of the theater, and the strength of the organization in later months and years may be even more important than the immediate production. The director in the professional theater need not concern himself with the reactions to his handling of auditions of actors who will not be included in his cast. In community and college theaters, it is important that actors who might be needed in later productions be left with a favorable impression of the director and the theater program as a whole, even if they cannot be used in the present play. The director thus has important public relations responsibilities in handling auditions that go beyond simply avoiding rudeness or hurt feelings to the creation of a general atmosphere favorable to the theater program as a whole, even among the actors who cannot be included in the cast for the current show.

Since the continuance of community and educational theater programs depends on the steady attraction of new people, the critical area is at and just beyond the edge of the participating group. Here are the people who have either participated only minimally in the theater work, perhaps by minor work on a properties or makeup crew, and the people who have begun to feel a faint stirring of interest, sometimes as a result of having attended plays, or because a roommate or a friend has been involved in a recent production. Here are also the actors who feel a real desire to join in the work, but who are inhibited by timidity, by fear of an unfriendly reception, by a general uncertainty about their own ability, or by an awe of the more experienced workers.

This last group is especially important to the director. Many potentially fine actors display this initial conflict of timidity and interest. The stars of later productions are most likely to be found among this group.

MYTHS OF CASTING

The director will probably discover three attitudes or beliefs that are likely to appear in this peripheral group that are seriously destructive to the theater program and that are so widespread that they all appear more ofen than not in connection with civic and college theaters. One is the belief that the theater workers constitute a closed circle, a clique, originally formed in some inexplicable way, but having as its primary purpose the continued exclusion of outsiders. The second belief is that plays are actually cast in advance of tryouts, especially in the major roles, and that auditions are nothing but a gesture intended to conceal the fact that the decisions have already been made. The third destructive belief is that theater workers conform to a sharply defined and unusual personality pattern, and that it is an unpleasant one. Too often real interest is destroyed by the feeling "I wouldn't want to be associated with that crowd." This attitude is likely to be especially strong among men.

The clique theory is the easiest of the three to demolish. Only a little thought demonstrates very clearly that the health of a community theater requires the constant recruitment of new personnel, and the very existence of an educational theater depends on a constant inflow of new people. If the flow slackens for a single year, a major problem develops; and if it should stop for two years, a rebuilding would be necessary from the foundation up.

The second belief is slightly more understandable. In a healthy program, the leading actors are supported by a pyramidal foundation of less experienced developing actors, resting on a broad base of apprentices. Those at the top have the most extreme visibility; they stand at the center of the audience's attention for a larger part of each production. Growth occurs primarily at the least visible level, in the apprentice group. It is not surprising, then, that potential actors are likely to feel that major roles "always go to the same few actors," even though an analysis of the productions of a year or two is likely to demonstrate that that is not true.

Furthermore, there is a minute grain of truth in the precasting legend. An essential part of the director's preparation for auditions is to refresh his memory of the established actors who may choose to try out for the play. To make even tentative choices of actors for the play as a result of this analysis is dangerous; to make final decisions would be disastrous. The clearest argument against this belief is a statement of its implications, from the viewpoint of the director. Even people who make the precasting charge are likely to accept the fact that the director is anxious to produce the most effective performance of the play possible, if only to enhance his own reputation. In open tryouts, he can expect to audition actors who are new to him. Furthermore, familiar actors sometimes make surprising jumps in ability: an inhibited and rather pedestrian actor who has been developing slowly in a series of supporting parts may exhibit a sudden leap in his command of theater skills that places him well ahead of other actors who have previously displayed greater proficiency. If a director casts even a single part in advance of auditions and closes his mind during the tryouts with regard to the role, it will be impossible for him to take advantage of any actors with unexpected abilities, whether they are new to him or already familiar. The result is to weaken his production. Of course, if no better actor appears, he will cast one of the established performers. The legend, however, is that the already established actors are cast even when they are less effective than other actors who appear at tryouts. Obviously, a director who functioned in that way would be incompetent in the highest degree and would sabotage his own shows.

Far from operating with a closed mind, every director turns to each fresh actor who appears at a tryout with the unspoken but fervent hope that he is about to discover a new Noel Coward, Laurence Olivier, or Alfred Lunt, or a Lynn Fontanne or Helen Hayes. In fact, so anxious are most directors to find and encourage new talent that, far from underestimating and rejecting new actors, they are more likely to err by seeing more potential than actually exists. However firmly people seem to believe in the precasting myth, they can nearly always be persuaded to accept the fact that no director will intentionally weaken his own show.

The last belief, that the theater attracts unusual and unpleasant people, flamboyant show-offs and loudmouths, is also understandable, however false it may be. Theater people are very unusual in many ways; however, the personality too often ascribed to them is almost the opposite of the truth. Especially fine theater artists are far more likely to be quiet and unassuming people.

The concept of actors as wildly extroverted phonies is not restricted to ordinary people. Some of those who believe it are themselves wildly extroverted phonies, and they may be attracted to the theater in the hope of finding a suitable setting for themselves. In his anxiety to encourage maximum participation in the theater program, the director may welcome such people, hoping that experience will help them understand sound methods of artistry, and that they will develop the discipline without which effective acting or technical work is impossible. Fairly frequently that hoped-for transformation occurs, and they may become desirable members of the theater staff. If it does not occur, the actors are likely to be puzzled at being cast repeatedly in small parts or as walk-ons. They may conclude that the director is incompetent for failing to recognize their great abilities, or that he is prejudiced against them. Feeling that no opportunity for them exists under the circumstances, they may switch their attention to a different theater, with, they hope, a more perceptive and understanding director. If no alternative theater is available, they may choose to join the technical staff, where lack of discipline and sound method is even more immediately and objectively apparent. When they build a platform that collapses the first time an actor steps on it, or undertake to find half a dozen properties and fail to get a single one, the inadequacies of their methods of work become evident even to them. At that point, they are most likely to abandon the theater altogether, which is beneficial to the theater, although the director and technical supervisors are likely to be left with a nagging feeling that if they had found just exactly the right instructions, a good actor or staff member might have been carved out of apparently unpromising material.

The difficulty is that this process can take many months and a series of productions, and during this period the unsuitable actors or workers are likely to attract a degree of attention that is out of all proportion to their ability. In fact, inexperienced actors or casual visitors are likely hardly to notice the truly fine actors who are quietly going about their business, working so hard, and concentrating so intently on their tasks that they have no time or attention to expend on trying to impress those around them.

> *The artistic temperament is a disease that afflicts amateurs.*
> GILBERT KEITH CHESTERTON

Counteracting the common false impression of theater people is difficult. Few directors would want to exclude potential actors because of unpleasant mannerisms or flaws of personality. The director can do much by consistently indicating his standards of work and by expressing recognition of work well done. Apprentice actors especially can be guided by pointing out the effectiveness of the discipline, effort, and care displayed by actors who are following sound methods. An actor who is neglecting work on his role, who is acting the part of a "star" rather than acting his part in the play, can often have his attention directed back to his job by asking pertinent questions: "Are you sure you understand what that line means? How many other ways are there of saying it? Did you attempt to identify as many alternative ways of reading it as possible when you were studying the part outside the theater? If so, how many did you find? If the way you have just read the line is the best one you could devise, what was the next best, and what were the reasons that persuaded you to choose one rather than the other?" Similar questions can be asked of the actor's gestures, posture, timing. Without degenerating into a personal attack, they define and remind him of the work he is responsible for.

The too common prejudice against men's taking part in theater work is especially difficult to combat. It can be done most effectively by example, not only that of the director himself but also by the type of men who do appear in the plays. The director can do much to set the tone of the theater by demonstrating good theater practice in his own work, conducting rehearsals in as good-humored, businesslike, and efficient a way as possible. Even more important, however, is the persuasion of admired men in the community or on the campus to take part in the plays. If campus leaders, athletes, and well-liked men can be encouraged to perform in plays, provided they can be trained to act effectively, it is possible to create a tradition of masculine participation in a very short time. Even the development of a single especially admired student as a leading actor can be very influential with other students. It is not suggested that this is easy, but if a theater suffers from a general masculine boycott, as many do, it is worth more than whatever effort is necessary to re-verse the attitude. In the community theater, the same method can be used: If a respected banker, physician, mayor, or businessman can be interested in appearing in the plays and developed into a strikingly effective actor, a large group of actors will become available who might otherwise avoid participation in the program.

A director who has a continuing association with a particular theater is likely to be asked to address college and civic groups, and he will have num-erous conversations with members of the community who are not directly in-volved in theatrical production. Often people who are considering joining the theater group may attempt to judge how they will be received by engaging the director in conversation, if they are fearful, carefully avoiding any suggestion of their own possible participation. In all of these situations, the director can help keep the channels open for the movement of potential workers and artists into the theater group. When he discusses the theater, he should make a conscious attempt to picture it realistically, especially in order to counteract the myths mentioned, which tend to reduce or cut off the inflow of new talent. The most important persuasive factor, however, is the director's personality. If he is seen as a good-humored, businesslike, friendly person, with high standards of artistry, a person with whom apprentices will enjoy working and from whom they can learn, that impression will contribute greatly to the broadening participation of the community or campus and will be a major source of strength of the theater program as a whole.

Analyzing Casting Requirements

The director's preliminary study of the script has given him a thorough knowledge of the play, in general and in detail. His preparation for auditions involves not so much collecting new information as it does isolating and organ-izing from all that he has discovered the material that must serve him as a guide in selecting the cast.

The first step in his preparation consists of copying the names of the char-acters in three lists. One will include those parts that must be cast by women; the second, the parts that require men; the third those that could be cast either by men or women. This last group should probably be divided into two or three parts, indicating those characters who can be most effectively cast with men, or who are specified as male by the script, those where women are to be preferred, and those where either sex seems equally acceptable; this last group would usually include characters identified as "townspeople" or "guests."

Within each list, the characters should be arranged in the order of their difficulty of casting. There will be some correlation between that arrangement and one indicating their relative importance in the play, although the two lists would seldom show the characters in exactly the same order. Sometimes supporting roles require more acting ability than the leading parts.

The name of the man's part that seems most difficult to cast should be placed at the top of a fresh sheet of paper, and below it should be listed the characteristics that an actor must have to play it successfully. What is wanted is not a description of the character in the play, but a description of the type of actor needed for the role, including especially those skills or qualities of personality that not all of the actors can be expected to have.

Since the peculiar requirements for various parts differ greatly, no general pattern can be described. A few examples may illustrate the kind of items that the director needs to identify. Sir Harry Bumper, in Sheridan's *The School for Scandal,* must sing a song. Since this occurs during a drinking party, and Bumper is not represented in the play as having any special singing ability, it is not necessary that the actor playing the part have a voice of concert or operatic quality. However, the song is fairly long, it must sustain the interest of the audience, and to be effective it must be performed with clarity and spirit; casting an actor who was tone-deaf in the part, or who would feel very uncomfortable singing alone, would ruin the scene.

Often if a character must play a musical instrument, his performance can be faked, and the instrument actually played offstage by a musician. Occasionally, however, such handling would weaken the play significantly; Nicky in Noel Coward's *The Vortex* must be able to play the piano, for example. If an actor must dance or fence in a performance, he must either already possess the necessary skills, or be able to learn them before the date of the performance.

The deaf mute in *The Madwoman of Chaillot* communicates by gestures that are probably most effective if they are designed midway between the ordinary hand symbols and dance. An actor for this part must have considerable muscular control and must be able to learn a fairly complicated pattern of movements easily.

If an actor must speak in dialect, it is important to find one who has already mastered the dialect, or who will not be prevented from learning it either by emotional inhibitions or by an inability to hear the variant pronunciations.

Fairly often the physical appearance of the actor must meet special requirements for a part. In Plautus's *Menaechmi,* two characters represent identical twins who look so much alike that they are mistaken for each other by people who know them well. Costuming and makeup can do a great deal to change the appearance of the actors who play the two parts, but obviously they must be close to the same height, and one cannot be fat if the other is thin. Few actors are fat enough to play Falstaff in Shakespeare's *The Merry Wives of Windsor* without additional padding and makeup designed to make them look larger; but there is a limit to the degree to which such devices can be used to change an actor's appearance, and the part can be played much more convincingly by an actor who is at least plump. Occasionally the appearance of a character has been fixed by tradition, which must be taken into account in casting. Hamlet is always played by an actor who is thin, sometimes to the point of emaciation, although in the script his mother describes him as "fat," and in fact says he is so overweight that he cannot exercise without getting out of breath. Lady Macbeth is always played by an imposingly large woman, although there is a good deal of evidence in the script to suggest that she was small. Certainly, her reference to her "little hand," and Macbeth's pet name for her, "chuck," seem out of harmony with the Amazonian appearance of most actresses who have played the part.

In the educational theater, the ages of the characters can seldom be matched by those of the actors, although a wider range is usually available in community and professional theaters. Fortunately, makeup and acting techniques can alter the apparent age of actors remarkably. Helen Hayes's portrayal of Queen Victoria at various ages in a single evening is famous; and in one play, *I Know My Love,* Alfred Lunt and Lynn Fontanne represented the characters they were playing over a span of fifty years.

Various roles require that the actors display physical attractiveness in different degrees, ranging from the repulsiveness of the villain in *The Drunkard* to the beauty of Roxane in *Cyrano de Bergerac.* It may well be that directors tend to overemphasize this factor in casting. They are likely to realize the ease with which actors can be made to seem less attractive than they actually are, but they may be unaware of how much their appearance can be improved. Makeup, hair styling, and costuming can produce a startling improvement in an actress's appearance. A weak chin can be made more prominent, a large nose apparently reduced in size, and wrinkles or bags under the eyes concealed. Actors' appearance on stage, especially under theatrical lights, is very different from their appearance in everyday life. It is not unusual for a very ordinary looking actress to seem a striking beauty on stage, even with straight makeup. The major factor, however, is one that is too often neglected. The part of a beauty is a role, like any other part, and the use of the right acting techniques can transform the impression an actress makes on the audience. If she acts like a great beauty, the audience will see her as one, whatever her ordinary appearance is. The history of the theater provides many instances of such magic performances. Mae West played the role of a glamorous beauty throughout her career with such brilliantly virtuoso technique that to anyone who has seen her on stage it must seem not only *lèse majesté* but a patent absurdity to point out that in actuality she was a short, dumpy, distinctly overweight woman. Sarah Bernhardt, especially by the standards of her time, was frankly ugly, yet she mastered the role of beauty so successfully that audiences (both on stage and off) saw her as the most beautiful woman of her day. One acquaintance said that he had never been able to determine what she actually looked like, because her performance as a great beauty was so dazzling even offstage.

Of course, the necessity of training an actress to create an impression of beauty throws an extra burden on both the actress and the director. Certainly, physical appearance is a factor in casting, although it is frequently given undue weight.

In addition to these fairly clear-cut requirements, each major character in a play has his own personality, which the actor who plays the role must be able to communicate to the audience. Often a particular voice quality or pitch level, a special physical appearance, or a particular set of mannerisms seems best suited to a part, even if the script does not specifically state them. A short, slight actor with a high-pitched voice would seem unsuited to the part of Macbeth, although the play contains no description of the character. Elwood Dowd, in Mary Chase's *Harvey,* must display a gentle, relaxed, somewhat wistful personality.

Especially important is the impression of force or weakness that the characters are intended to exhibit. Birdie in *The Little Foxes* has withdrawn into a frightened seclusion; Laura in *The Glass Menagerie* has taken refuge among her collection of statues; both are weak characters who can be played more easily by actresses who do not look too athletic or sound too forceful. Tallulah Bankhead, for example, who had great success in the part of Regina in *The Little Foxes,* would have been miscast as Birdie. The parts of Martha and Honey in *Who's Afraid of Virginia Woolf?* require actresses who can display aggressiveness and its opposite. An actress whose personality and appearance were suited to one would be greatly handicapped in playing the other.

It is probably better for the director to record on his pretryout sheets only the clearer and more readily identifiable requirements of each part, trusting to his memory for the general personality and physical appearance needed. A separate sheet should be prepared for each character for whom such analysis is relevant. The requirements of minor roles often are much less stringent, so that almost any appearance or personality would be acceptable. There are few requirements, for instance, for the telegraph messenger in Thornton Wilder's *The Skin of Our Teeth,* and bit parts and walk-ons can often be of any shape or size. It is not necessary to prepare a list of specifications for such roles.

If the director suspects that he may have to select his cast from an inadequate number of volunteers, it is helpful for him to examine the script to see whether doubling is possible, or, failing that, whether the speeches of two characters can be assigned to a single actor. As a less desirable solution, he may even attempt to identify parts that can be cut from the play. For an actor to play two parts, it is of course necessary that the characters never appear on stage at the same time. If their appearances are widely separated in the play, there will be less chance of the audience's noticing that the same actor is playing both roles, and there must be enough time between the first character's exit and the last character's entrance to enable the actor to change costume and to alter his makeup.

Selecting Audition Passages

Having finished his analysis of the individual characters, the director selects a series of passages from the play that actors can be asked to read at the tryouts, one group of passages for the men and another for the women.

It is very difficult to evaluate the reading of more than one actor at a time. In choosing the tryout passages, the director should look for long speeches, or for scenes in which one character is almost exclusively the center of interest. During the actual tryout, it is preferable to have an assistant read the "feeder" lines for the actor who is being tried out, so that each actor will be matched by the same reader, and so that it will be easier to concentrate on the actor alone.

The passages should illustrate the range of each part, so that if varied moods or skills are necessary, the director will be able to check them.

No one can be expected to act at a tryout; consequently, it is not necessary to include selections from each role. However, actors tend to assume that they are being considered only for the characters whose speeches they are asked to read, so that it is desirable that the passages be taken from the speeches of at least all the major characters.

When the selections have been made, they should be marked in three or four copies of the script. If the play is in the public domain it is much more convenient to have the passages duplicated, so that each actor can be given a set and need not waste time in leafing through the playbook.

Scheduling Auditions

Almost every director develops individual tryout methods; none so far devised is completely effective, and no particular pattern can be generally recommended. Each director must experiment in an attempt to find the methods most congenial to him.

Auditions should be scheduled during a period when most of the potential actors can be expected to be free of conflicting obligations. Usually they are held in the evening, in the Monday to Thursday period, in order to avoid weekend engagements. Students may be enrolled in evening classes, so that it is desirable to schedule two evening sessions, one on Tuesday or Thursday, and the other on Monday or Wednesday. Since classes generally are scheduled for Tuesday-Thursday or Monday-Wednesday-Friday, it is important to include one evening from each sequence. Of course an actor might have all of his week nights filled with classes or other activities, but in that case it would usually be impossible for him to attend the rehearsals, and so excluding him from the tryouts is no handicap. For community theaters, it is often customary to hold tryouts on Sunday afternoons, instead of or in addition to the evening sessions.

Some directors prefer that actors schedule their appointments, and provide a sheet with the tryout periods divided into segments that actors can reserve by signing their names beside the times. Other directors invite actors to attend the tryouts at any time during the scheduled period. Prescheduling increases the efficiency of the auditions and avoids having a group of actors appear at the same time and have to wait while they are tried out one at a time. Signing the sheet, however, suggests that a rigid commitment has been made, and many fine actors have been discovered when they dropped in during an audition period without appointments, hoping to assure themselves that they would not be embarrassed by the experience and not having quite decided whether they would try out or not. A little encouragement by the director and some remark such as "Since you're here you might as well read" will often persuade them to take part, when if they had been required to commit themselves by signing a schedule, they might have refused to audition. It might be supposed that a reluctant actor would make an undesirable cast member; exactly the opposite is very often the case. Many of the finest actors show great apprehension and reluctance in taking part in their first audition.

Some directors feel that they can cast as effectively on the basis of a single reading as after hearing the actors a second time. Other directors prefer to hold a second or even a third audition, after they have had time to analyze the notes they have taken during the first session. If the three-session method is followed, the director's study of his first-session notes consists primarily of weeding out the obvious impossibles. Following the second reading, he then completes his cast selection as nearly as possible. The third audition is used to check his decisions, to refresh his memory of the actors, to enable him to decide which of two similar actors should be assigned to which of two similar roles, and to enable him to judge the cast as a group. In particular, similarities and contrasts of appearance, voice, and personality can be more easily checked in the final call.

Probably the two-session schedule is commonest. The second call then matches the last session of the three-part pattern. To cast from a single reading requires that the director have analyzed the auditions very carefully, and that he have an excellent memory. It is especially difficult if many of the actors who appear are unfamiliar to him. The recall enables him to test any decisions he has made and to announce the cast with greater assurance. The three-session method is the easiest to use, but takes what is often an unnecessary amount of time. By keeping the actors in continued suspense, it may create an undesirable degree of tension. All three patterns, however, are workable, and all are used by experienced and skillful directors.

It is especially important that all actors who might be interested in trying out for parts in the play know about the auditions well in advance. Posters, newspaper stories, announcements at meetings, can all be used to publicize the tryouts. Word of mouth should not be neglected. People who are already active in the theater program should be asked to remind potential actors of the auditions, and the director himself can mention them as widely as possible.

Directors also differ in how fully they prefer actors to be acquainted with the play in advance of tryouts. Some directors make scripts available to actors a week or two before the auditions and urge them to study the play; others prefer that the actors see the script for the first time when they appear for their tryouts.

An actor's reading from a familiar script is much easier to judge than if he sees it for the first time when it is handed to him at the tryout. On the other hand, when the director must choose between two actors for the same part, one of whom has read at sight and the other has studied the play exhaustively in advance, he must discount the differences in reading that are due only to the differences in familiarity with the play, since by the end of the rehearsal period either would have become fully acquainted with the script. When scripts are made available in advance, the actors who audition are likely to vary widely between the two extremes of pretryout preparation; these variations must be identified by the director and discounted in making his decisions.

Asking actors to study the script in advance of tryouts thus provides advantages and disadvantages, and each director must decide which set outweighs the other for him. A beginning director will probably find it easier to evaluate the tryout readings if all of the actors are equally familiar with the play—and in practice that means that scripts should not be distributed in advance. With growing experience, he may decide that the other method is more effective for him.

PUBLIC-RELATIONS ASPECTS OF AUDITIONS

Aside from their immediate purpose of assisting the director in assembling a cast, auditions are an extremely important part of the public-relations program of a theater. For many of the actors who appear, the audition will be their first contact with the theater, and their experience may determine whether they will try out for a later production, or take part in technical work, or decide not to participate in the theater at all.

A very brief reading, perhaps as short as half a sentence, sometimes demonstrates clearly that an actor is not suited to a particular role, either because he lacks ability, or because his voice or appearance is inharmonious with the part, or because a previous actor is clearly preferable. To be cut off early in the reading is devastatingly embarrassing for an actor. Furthermore, even though the director feels sure that an actor cannot play certain parts, refusing to give him an opportunity to read for them is certain to convince the actor that he has not been given a fair chance. Every actor, then, should be asked to read sections of at least each major or strong supporting role, and he should be allowed to finish each selection. This is especially important for the actors who the director feels will probably not be included in the cast.

The treatment of the actors during the tryout should go beyond simple politeness, it should be warm and gracious. In effect the director is a host, and each actor should be made to feel that he is a welcome guest. Actors should be greeted individually as they are called, and it is desirable to hold a brief conversation with each. Even though the topics discussed may not be directly concerned with the play, such a conversation gives the director an opportunity to identify the actor's ordinary speech style. Some actors adopt an artificial "performance" style for tryout readings that may be much less effective than their normal speech. Hearing a sample of both helps the director identify an actor who may be able to speak very well, but who reads badly during the audition itself.

During the reading, it is important that the director demonstrate that he is listening and watching closely. He should feel perfectly free to jot down notes, but yawning, staring at the ceiling, or carrying on whispered conversations with others will convince the actor that he is being treated unfairly, even though the director might actually be able to evaluate his audition very accurately while carrying on the other activities.

After each reading, the actor should be thanked for his interest, and the method of announcing the casting decisions should be explained to him. A complimentary word or two is also in order. Even a very bad reader usually displays some variation in the quality of his reading. If the director can find nothing that he can honestly praise in the audition, he can resort to the comment, "I thought your best reading was in the third passage, especially toward the end." Such a remark seems friendly and is likely to be treasured by the actor, even though it does not involve any falsification on the part of the director.

Anything which suggests that the director has reached a decision about casting is disastrous. Not only does it persuade the actor that he has not been auditioned fairly, but it reinforces the damaging myth that plays are regularly cast in advance of tryouts. The closest a director should come in commenting on the actors who have been auditioned is some remark such as "I have been surprised at what a fine group of readers have been coming in for the tryouts." If actors inquire about their own chances of getting parts, it is far safer to give them an underestimate. Referring to the number of actors who have tried out and emphasizing the fact that many of them have performed well is much more desirable than saying "Well, you have read the lead part as well as anyone who has shown up so far." If the actors are prepared for not being cast, their disappointment will be less bitter if they do not appear on the list; and their pleasure at being selected, if they are included, is not reduced.

Auditioning is a disturbing experience at best, even for experienced actors; it may be terrifying for novices. Everything possible should be done to put them at ease. If the director has assistants at the tryout, they should not be lined up in a row, so that the actors feel they are facing a judge and jury.

It is not necessary to hold tryouts in a theater, and actors may feel more at ease in a smaller room. However, the glamor of the theater can be felt even under tryout conditions, and probably most actors would prefer to audition

Figure 37. Auditioning actors. Donald Wolfe makes suggestions to Sam Cardea, while his assistant, Linda Edwards, waits to read feeder lines. Mrs. Rupert Bagby assists the director, and other actors wait their turns. The stage has been especially prepared for the audition; a table and chairs have been provided, and the audition area has been lit so as to reduce the feeling of emptiness. The director sits close to the stage in an attempt to create an atmosphere of conversational ease. [Photograph by Dorothy Welker]

there. Being able to see them actually on stage makes it easier for the director to visualize their appearance in the play. The atmosphere of a bare stage is not conducive to relaxation, especially if the actor is alone on it, blinded by spotlights and peering out into a darkened auditorium. It is better to provide a little furniture, at least two or three chairs and a table, and the assistant who will read cue lines for the actors should appear on stage with them. Work lights, which cast a uniform wash across the entire stage, emphasize its emptiness; a few spotlights, well dimmed and pointed toward the center area, create a more intimate and less frightening atmosphere. The auditorium lights should be dimmed, but not so much that the actors have difficulty seeing the director; instructions shouted out of a darkened void by an invisible director are not reassuring. Actors who are waiting to read should be seated in the house, behind the director, and preferably irregularly rather than in a solid mass or a single row.

TRYOUT SHEETS

Some of the information that the director may find helpful can be recorded most efficiently by the actors themselves. It is customary to prepare tryout sheets and ask each actor to fill one out before he reads. Some items may be of great importance for one play and of no importance for another, for example, an actor's ability to sing or dance. One essential item of information is the actor's age. Only a brave director would ask an actress to state her age, but in the educational theater the information can be acquired indirectly by asking each actor to identify his year in school. Height and weight are also useful to know and seldom offend on a questionnaire, although occasionally an actor or actress may leave one of the items blank. Hair coloring has little significance for the play, since it is always possible to tint the hair to suit the part. However, it will help the director recall an actor's appearance after the tryouts, when he is trying to select the cast, so it is a useful item to include.

Occasionally it may be important to notify an actor of a second tryout session or a change in rehearsal schedule. The sheets should include a blank for the actor's phone number and address.

Tryout sheets always ask for a report of the actor's previous experience in the theater. This item is a somewhat unfortunate one. It suggests that casting is closed to beginning actors, and the information provided is of much less value than might be expected. Only if the director has worked with an actor himself or has seen him in performance can he evaluate his past work. The mere fact that he has played one part or another indicates very little about his ability or even his range as an actor. Furthermore, if an actor has adopted or been trained in unsatisfactory techniques, the longer he has practiced them the worse. Of course, if his training and thinking have been sound, experience is an asset. In spite of the ambiguity and uninterpretability of an experi-ence record, it still seems desirable to include it on the sheet.

It is important to find out in advance of casting any prior commitments that would interfere with the actor's work on the play. The question can be raised in conversation, or each actor may be asked to answer it in writing on the sheet. In all types of amateur production, actors can be expected to be able

---

Actor's Name

Phone Number   Address

Height   Weight   Sex   Hair Color   Year in School

Can you sing? specify well or average.   Specify training, if any.

List musical instruments you can play, and indicate well or fairly well, etc.; specify training, if any; continue on the back of the sheet if necessary.

Can you dance? specify type (ballet, ballroom, waltz, etc.), and well or average.

On the chart at the right, cross out any periods when it would usually be difficult for you to rehearse.

P. M.	Sun	Mon	Tue	Wed	Thur	Fri	Sat
1–3:30							
3:30–6							
7–10							

If you have done any of the types of work listed below, write the number of plays on which you have worked, for each item.

____ director	____ set shifting	____ makeup
____ assistant director	____ lighting	____ sound
____ stage manager	____ stage properties	____ ushering
____ set designer	____ hand properties	____ publicity
____ set construction	____ costumes	____ box-office

List the parts you have played, in chronological order; continue on the back of the sheet if necessary.

Role	Play	Theater	Year

Figure 38. A typical tryout sheet.

to devote only a minority of their time to the play, and they may have legitimate obligations that hamper their work. If a student must attend an evening class on Tuesday and Thursday of each week, for example, it is important that the director be aware of that fact before he makes his cast selections. For several reasons, great effort should be made to work out cast assignments and scheduling so that such actors are not automatically excluded from participation. Often rehearsals can be scheduled so that on the evenings when a particular actor cannot attend, scenes in which he does not appear can be rehearsed. Usually, if a director makes a sincere effort to work out such conflicts, the actor will be willing to make some adjustments in his other obligations. For instance, if the rehearsal schedule is planned so that the actor can attend his evening class during the first three weeks, both he and the instructor are most likely to agree to his being absent from class during the final critical week of rehearsal and performance.

ACTORS' RESTRICTIONS ON CASTING

Some actors are strongly opposed to certain types of parts, or to specific roles in a play. For them to refuse an assignment to one of these parts creates embarrassing difficulties. The actor who is substituted after the cast has been announced inevitably feels that he has been insulted by not having been the first choice. If the actor accepts the role that he does not want, his morale, and that of the cast as a whole, is likely to suffer. It is therefore desirable to ask each actor before he reads whether there are specific roles or groups of roles that he would prefer not to be considered for.

When actors reject parts, they usually indicate either that they do not want major roles or that they do not want small parts. The actor who does not want to play large parts usually has a good reason for his decision. He may have heavy commitments outside the theater that do not leave him enough time to master a long part; or he may feel that he has not reached a level of proficiency that would enable him to carry a heavy part. The first reason is unarguable. It is possible that the actor's evaluation of his ability may be unduly modest, and if the director feels that he is ready for a major role, discussing the matter may lead the actor to change his mind. Actors often have a very acute and accurate evaluation of their own abilities, however, and when their reluctance to assume a demanding part seems to be based on a thoughtful assessment rather than simply on timidity, the director would do well to consider it carefully.

Actors who refuse any parts except leads should almost without exception not be cast in any parts at all. The implication that only starring roles are important in the theater suggests a failure to understand dramatic art and theatrical procedures. The rejection of any part except a lead also implies an arrogant feeling on the part of the actor that his abilities are so great they would be wasted in any but the most important roles. Theoretical grounds (which will be discussed in a later chapter) make it likely that only actors of very low ability evaluate themselves in that way, and experience supports the theoretical presumption. Out of every thousand actors who indicate that only the major roles will do them justice, at least nine hundred and ninety-nine are at the very bottom of the range of effectiveness. Not only are they not usable in major roles, but their ineptness is so great that even if they should accept a part requiring only that they enter, pick up a book from a table, and exit again, they would perform so badly as to attract unfavorable comments from the least critical members of the audience.

These actors must be auditioned with great care, at length, and with the closest attention, so that at least they cannot attack the director for having failed to audition them (they will, of course, attack his judgment for not having recognized their great abilities). Since it would be disastrous to include them in the cast by accident, especially in an important role, it is vital that they be identified before they are auditioned.

Especially if the director has worked with an actor before and is convinced of the soundness of the actor's judgment, it is sometimes desirable to ask him what parts he feels he is best suited for. Actors with good sense often have a very accurate concept of what roles fit them best. The director must make his final decisions on the basis of his own judgment, but the opinions of a sensible actor are often a helpful guide.

Recording Evaluations During Auditions

If the notes the director makes during auditions are to have any value, they must be clear, frank, and accurate; he has no time to soften his evaluations or to state them with inoffensive indirectness. It is important that an actor not read the director's comments about himself or other actors, yet to obviously conceal the notes from the actors would be almost worse, since each would assume that what had been written about him was unbearably unfavorable. Each director should develop a set of symbols that will be clear to him but unintelligible to anyone else. For instance, if he likes to use traditional grades to evaluate actors' performance at auditions (A+, A, A−, B+, B, etc.), he might substitute numbers from 1 to 13. The significance of the numbers can be remembered more easily if they are interpreted by groups; thus, 1–3 could be used for actors who would perform a part outstandingly well, 4–6 for actors who would perform well, 7–9 for actors who could be used but who would be barely adequate, 10–12 for actors who should be cast only in case of desperate need, and 13 (representing a grade of F) for actors who are unusable for a particular role under any circumstances. If the director finds himself writing a few comments frequently, he might work out similar symbols, perhaps acronyms, to represent the familiar notes. The numerical system can also be added to written notes to conceal their meaning; for instance, instead of writing "very bad voice quality," the director might jot down "quality 12" or "q 12."

Besides the tryout form that the actor fills out before he reads, it is desirable to have duplicated cast lists, one set with the women's roles, another with the men's, with the characters arranged in the order of difficulty of casting, the most difficult roles being placed first. A different sheet should be used for each actor who auditions, identified by writing his name at the top. As he reads, the director should evaluate his suitability for the character who appears first on the list and should record his decision by writing the appropriate code number beside the character's name. He should then turn his attention to the next character listed and jot down his judgment of the actor's effectiveness for that part. This should be continued name by name until he has recorded an evaluation of the actor in terms of each character of the same sex in the play. Additional notes can be recorded in the space below the list.

One of the most distressing experiences for the director is to discover after tryouts, when he is attempting to choose the cast, that he has similar ratings for two or more actors, but that he cannot remember them. As actors audition who are strangers to him, he should watch for details of appearance, voice, or personality which will assist his memory, and jot them down on the evaluation sheets. Often, they will be details of clothing—one actress wore a dress with large flowers on it; another brought a red parasol with her; an actor had an unusually broad tie, or wore half-glasses.

Evaluating Audition Performances

Recording the decisions is easy enough; the difficult task is the evaluation itself. The fundamental problem is that auditioning requires something approaching extrasensory perception—it is an act of precognition. The essential question is not what an actor does at the tryout but what he will do after a month's rehearsals. So far, no test or method of evaluation has been devised that will make such a prediction with any assurance of accuracy. Essentially, the director must listen and watch as intently as possible, must collect all of the hard information he can get, and then must fill out the gaps on the basis of intuition and hunch.

The process is made more difficult by the fact that actors' performances at tryouts are often very different from their performances in the play itself. Some actors sight-read with great skill; others mispronounce words, stumble through simple sentences, and read with little expression. Yet there is very little correlation between skill in sight-reading and ability to act. Some of those who sight-read well may prove to be very fine actors, but others may be completely ineffective. Of those who sound so bad when they sight-read, some may be inept and untrainable actors, while others may have star potential.

In collecting what information he can, it is best for the director to examine one aspect of the actor's work at a time. Perhaps the most important is his language sense, his feeling for words. Can he make simple sense out of the script? Stumbling may be due to the fact that the meaning of long and complicated sentences is not evident to him at a glance. After he has read through a passage once, the director can ask him to go back and reread some of the shorter and more obvious sentences. Can he identify the key word in the sentence and point it by giving it major emphasis? Following are some examples from Shakespeare which illustrate the type of sentence that might be used to test the actor:

> Is this the man?
> Show him your hand!
> Hush! Here comes Antony!
> What's your pleasure, sir?
> Though I am mad, I will not bite him.
> Come on; there is sixpence for you. Let's have a song!
> Here comes the little villain!

Such sentences are so clear that reading them so as to express their meaning is a kind of minimal test of language sense. If the actor handles them effectively, he can be asked to read more difficult sentences.

At least throughout the first three-fourths of the month's rehearsals, the actor will be experimenting with different ways of reading lines. The ability to speak the same line in various ways is consequently essential to his work. This can be tested in the audition by asking him to repeat some of the sentences with altered emphasis. If he first said "Is *this* the man?," he can be asked to reread it with major emphasis on the last word. "Show him your *hand!*" can be altered to "*Show* him your hand," "Show *him* your hand," and "Show him *your* hand." The ability to control the pattern of emphasis in a phrase or sentence is basic to acting. If an actor cannot change his pattern, his first reading of a line cannot be improved in any great degree. Actors vary greatly in this ability; some can do it with ease; others find it impossible.

Vocally, an actor's resources consist almost entirely of pitch, time, and loudness. In mechanical terms, the improvement of a reading consists of making fine adjustments in the use of those three vocal elements. The actor's control of them can be tested by asking him to read a sentence at a higher pitch, and then at a lower pitch; more loudly and more quietly; faster and more slowly. Even more important, however, is his ability to alter these qualities in a single word or syllable. He might be asked to vary the word "bite" in the sentence "Though I am mad, I will not bite him," stretching the vowel as far as possible, snapping it out as quickly as possible, raising and lowering the pitch, and altering the loudness, in each instance repeating the rest of the sentence without variation. If an actor has desirable flexibility and control, he will be able to do these essentially meaningless exercises in tryout.

The actor's muscular control is also important, and it can be tested in somewhat the same way. He can be asked to sit relaxed on the arm of a chair, slouching against the back, to sit up alertly, to walk quickly across the stage, to walk as slowly as possible. It is helpful to ask him to assume a posture and movements different from those he has displayed during the early part of the tryout, to determine whether he can adapt his body to express the personality of a character different from his own.

Finally, the director needs to know about some of the actor's own personality traits, which are vitally important to his effectiveness in the theater, even though they are especially difficult to determine during the audition. Theatrical production is a group activity, involving dozens of people. Docility is not a particularly valuable characteristic for an actor, but cooperativeness is absolutely essential. If a single member of a cast sees his relationship to the other actors as competitive, especially if he feels that his strength is increased by their weakness, he can create chaos in rehearsal and performance. Any hints the director can get about the actor's understanding and full acceptance of the cooperative method are of great value. The best source of such information is the experience of having worked with him in other plays; next best is having attended a play in which he appeared. His general behavior during the auditions, the tone of his conversation, and the relationship he assumes with the director's assistant all provide at least faint clues to his cooperativeness. (It should be re-emphasized that the critical quality here is cooperativeness, not subservience. "Cooperating" means "working together," and it is so essential to theatrical production that all theater artists must display it, the director perhaps more than any other.)

A second characteristic is what might be called the actor's empathability—his ability to empathize with others. Not only is this of value in working effectively with the rest of the theater staff, but one of the actor's major activities is carrying out a detailed emphatic analysis of the part he is to perform. If he cannot look at the action of the play from the viewpoint of his character, it is impossible for him to act the part; and the ability to take someone else's point of view is exactly what "empathy" means. To a lesser extent, but still significantly, the actor also needs to empathize with the audience, in imagination during rehearsals and on the basis of their responses during performance. A person who cannot empathize cannot act, any more than a paralyzed person in an iron lung could play Tarzan.

The actor's whole attitude toward the theater is significant, but nearly impossible to identify in tryouts. However, an actor who sees the theater only as a means for personal display is severely handicapped. A desire for success, for audience approval, for the admiration of his fellow actors, is not in itself a defect; in fact, it would be difficult to find an actor or even to imagine one who did not feel such a desire. The defect consists in the absence of any other concern. If the actor places this desire first in his scheme of theatrical values and has no other interest in the theater, he is largely unsuited for performance.

A final factor is of great importance, and also extremely complicated: the actor's pattern of inhibitions. Timidity, shyness, and inhibition are so constant a part of actors' personalities as to be almost universal. Furthermore, this inhibitory pattern seems to be positively correlated with acting ability: actors with the greatest potential seem to display these characteristics in the greatest degree. They tend to be assets, then, rather than liabilities, with one exception. Fine actors seem to differ from nonactors who may display the same degree of inhibition in the fact that the actors dislike their inhibitions and are determined to overcome them. Much of the intensity that actors bring to their work seems to come from the energy needed to fight their shyness.

The critical factor from the viewpoint of a director, then, is not so much an actor's degree of inhibition, but whether or not he wants to overcome it. If his habitual response to challenge is self-protective, if he regularly adopts an avoidance response to difficult situations, he cannot function effectively as an actor. If, on the other hand, he is determined to overcome his inhibitions, and to learn to perform impressively rather than hiding in the hope that he will not be noticed, the inhibitions themselves may prove to be an energizing asset. When an actor responds to the challenge of rehearsal by reinforcing and attempting to protect his inhibitions from the suggestions of the director, both the actor and the director fail, and effective acting cannot take place. When the actor works with the director to overcome inhibition and replace it with impressive performance, the result is nearly always gratifying, and may astonish the director, the audience, and the actor himself.

This factor is so important that it should be discussed openly with the actor whenever the director is uncertain about the actor's attitudes. If necessary, the conversation can be carried on privately in a room offstage. Experience suggests that most actors are not embarrassed by such a discussion. The fact that the director's concern is practical, and that he accepts shyness and inhibition as a normal part of an actor's makeup, is more likely to put the actor at ease than otherwise: he is delighted to find that someone else understands how he feels. One director's experience may illustrate how this problem can be handled.

Polly Macratia had worked under the direction of Les Bonicus in one play during her junior year in college. She had had a moderate supporting role, and had performed very badly, displaying such extreme inhibition that it was not only impossible for her to alter the reading of a line, it was actually difficult for her to move from one stage area to another.

Auditions for the first play the following year were scheduled through two days. Five minutes before the end of the audition period on the last day, Polly appeared uncertainly in the door. On being asked if she would like to try out for the play, she replied that she had been trying to get up enough courage to volunteer. Bonicus invited her to sit down and read.

He was in a state of some distress at this point in the tryouts. A flood of actors and actresses had appeared who were well suited to all of the parts in the play except one, but the play was of the type called a "vehicle"—a one-woman show, and the one unfilled part was that of the major actress.

He listened to Polly in astonishment. Her reading was free, varied, easy, and meaningful. He tried her on passage after passage and could find no evidence of the paralyzing inhibitions that had made it impossible for her to act the preceding year.

When he had completed the audition, he leaned back in his chair and discussed the situation with her frankly. He reminded her of her difficulties the year before. He told her that not only had she read the lead role better than any other actress, but that her reading was superb, whereas no one else who had tried out was even minimally acceptable. "The problem is this," he finally said. "If you can read like this during rehearsals and performance, we'll get a show that will knock every member of the audience out of his seat. But if this is an accident, and all your inhibitions come falling back during the first week of rehearsals, then we will not be able to get a performance that is even adequate. I am sure that you and I, working together, can fight this problem and win, but if you start fighting me in an attempt to hide behind your inhibitions, we will both lose."

He then asked Polly for her most careful prediction of what would happen if she took the role. She thought the question over carefully before she answered, "I really think the problem won't overwhelm me again. I am determined to fight it this time, instead of the play and you, and I would predict that I can do it."

The story has a happy ending. Once at the beginning of the second week of rehearsals Bonicus sensed empathically that the old rigidity and inhibition were returning. For the rest of the rehearsal he ignored all of the actors except Polly and worked with her with the greatest intensity to fight back the dangerous pattern. It never appeared again, except for a moment here and there, and when it did Polly was able to overcome it by herself.

Rehearsals were extremely hard work. Bonicus reported that few actors in his experience had shown such dedication and concentration. Polly rehearsed the smallest gestures, the minutest vocal inflections, again and again, going to the theater afternoons to work by herself. In one scene she slipped off her shoe and wiggled her toes; this simple business was rehearsed something like forty times.

The first climax came one night, when the entire cast burst out into applause for her at the end of a scene. But the big climax came on opening night, when the audience went wild at her performance.

Polly went on to appear in further plays, with Bonicus and other directors, and she was the acknowledged star of the college theater throughout her senior year. (Incidentally, she accepted a bit part in one succeeding play, with a single short scene—a further indication of her stature as an actress.) After graduating, she enrolled in graduate school to continue her study of the theater.

This anecdote illustrates a number of points.

1. In spite of the director's difficulty with the actress the preceding year (she was almost totally undirectable), their relationship had remained one of

mutual respect. Not only had he understood, sympathized, and empathized with her problems as an actress, but their work had been carried on without hysterics or recriminations, which, if they had occurred, would have lost her permanently to the theater program.

2. Her improvement had been sudden and extreme; she had, in fact, leaped from being a nonactress to an actress. The director never inquired what had produced this effect. It might have been due to a significant experience over the summer, or simply maturation, or an extended thinking through of her own values and abilities that led to a decision to launch an aggressive attack on her inhibitions.

3. The relationship of respect and friendliness made it possible for the director to discuss the problem with her frankly and without offense.

4. Her good judgment led her to treat the questions seriously and to answer them thoughtfully. She was asked "What do you predict will happen?" and she answered that question, not "What do you hope will happen?"

5. Relying on her judgment and honesty, the director accepted her analysis without further question.

6. When the problem reappeared in rehearsal, he came to her assistance with all of the force and technique at his command. She instantly recognized his direction as helpful, not antagonistic, and added her own effort to it.

7. The other members of the cast understood and empathized with Polly's work. They were pleased rather than envious when she succeeded, and they applauded her performance when she achieved brilliance—but not before. This point alone illustrates the whole concept of theatrical cooperation. The entire cast saw Polly's success as their own, since all shared the same goal, the achievement of the best possible performance.

8. The inhibitions themselves supplied energy and force to the performance.

9. Great acting depends on the intensest kind of work, and the perfectionist application of the highest standards.

And finally, the story helps explain why actors over and over again voluntarily endure the drudgery and occasional agony, the blood, toil, tears and sweat typical of theatrical work. The personal feeling of growth and the consciousness of a hard-won success are among the most gratifying of experiences.

SELECTING THE CAST

At the end of auditions, the director has a series of notes, an impression of the attitudes of each actor, and some memory of the appearance and voice of each one.

The first step in working over his material is to separate the sheets of notes into two piles, by sex. He will have two sheets for each actor, one filled out by the actor himself, the other a sheet with the list of the cast members of the matching sex, on which the director has jotted down his impressions of the actor during the reading. These should be separated, since he will work primarily with the cast lists.

Since the supply of men is likely to be smaller than the supply of women, it is usually best to start with the men's roles, first the one that he has selected as most difficult to cast. Each sheet contains a record of the director's judgment of the suitability of the actor for this part. Assuming that the suggested code has been used, the sheets marked "13" (unusable for the role under any circumstances) should be pulled out and laid aside. The other sheets should then be arranged in numerical order, so that the actors who are best suited to the part appear together at the top of the pile. It is of course preferable that the actor with the highest rating be cast for this part, but that is not always possible. Suppose for example that four actors have been given high ratings for the part most difficult to cast, as follows:

Art O'Trogus 1
Perry Plectomenus 2
Phil O'Comasium 2
Simon Senex 3

Suppose that Art O'Trogus has also been rated 3 for the part which has been judged second most difficult to cast, and that no other actor has been given a rating for this part higher than 10 (usable only in case of desperate need). If Art is cast in the top role, the second part will have to be filled by an actor who is unsuited for it. On the other hand, if Perry or Phil is cast in the top role, the second role can be assigned to Art, whose rating indicates that he will play it "outstandingly well," even though his rating for the first role is still higher. The director may well decide that the play will be strengthened by assigning Art to the second part and giving the most difficult part to an actor who is slightly less suited to it.

This example is a simplified illustration of the kind of juggling that must be done with the total list of parts in the play. Casting each role with the actor who has been given the highest rating for the part will usually leave some parts uncast, or will force the casting of some actors in roles to which they are only minimally suited. The various assignments must be balanced and fitted together to produce the strongest possible ensemble, even though individual actors are sometimes assigned to parts other than those which they could handle most easily.

It is not uncommon to audition an actor who may be able to perform very well in a particular type of role, but whose range is severely limited. For example, an actor may be extremely effective as an ironic comic, but totally unsuited to a serious part. Suppose that such a role appears in the play being cast, and that three actors have been given high ratings for it, as follows:

Simon Senex 2
Stephen Ancilla 2
Cal Idorus 3

Either Simon or Stephen will be slightly more effective in the role; suppose however that Cal has received ratings of 11, 12, or 13 for every other part in the play (essentially unusable), whereas the other two actors have been assigned high ratings for several parts. If Cal is not cast in this role, he cannot be used at all; Simon or Stephen can be fitted into the cast at several points. Especially if an inadequate number of actors have tried out, it may be necessary to cast Cal, even though two other actors have higher ratings, in order to fill all of the men's parts acceptably.

It will be seen that this method may be unfair to the versatile actor who can play many roles. His assignment may be due less to his real abilities than to the vacancies that are left after more restricted actors have been fitted into the few parts which they can play. It is important for the director to avoid that as much as possible. Not only is it unfair to penalize an actor for breadth of ability, but casting him in a minor part simply because no one else can play it well is likely to discourage him or make him feel resentful, and may weaken the drama program by leading him to decide not to try out for later plays. The director should make every effort to assign an especially skilled and versatile actor to a part that will challenge him and enable him to use his ability as fully as possible, even if another actor must be cast in a part to which he is not well suited.

If that cannot be done without seriously weakening the cast, it may be possible to explain the reasons for the casting to the more accomplished actor so that he will understand that the assignment does not indicate a low estimate of his ability. The messenger who appears at the end of *King Oedipus* to report the suicide of Jocasta and Oedipus's self-mutilation has only a single scene, in essence only one long speech. This speech, however, is vitally important to the play, and may be the most difficult. It occurs at the climax of the action and prepares for the dramatic re-entrance of Oedipus, with the blood streaming down from his blinded eyes. The speech is narrative, and the actor, with almost no assistance from the rest of the cast, must match the intensity of the preceding scene and build it toward the entrance of the king. The playwright has provided so little help that only a very skilled actor can deliver the speech effectively, and if interest sags at this point the play as a whole is severely damaged. It is quite possible that only one actor would be found during auditions for this play who could handle the part acceptably. If, as is likely, he might have been well suited to longer and more interesting parts, it may be necessary to reject him for those parts, for which other actors are available, in order to give him this small but crucial role that only he can play. The actor is likely to accept an explanation of the reasons for his assignment to this apparently small part. However, it is important that he not be given similar treatment in play after play. The explanation will probably be acceptable only once, and certainly in the following play the director should make an extreme effort to cast the actor in a part that fully matches his ability.

When a tentative cast has been worked out, the director should attempt to visualize it as a whole, and to evaluate the interrelationships among the actors. At the simplest level, it is desirable that an actor not be very much shorter than an actress with whom he is romantically paired in the play, if the romance is to be taken seriously by the audience. There is some slight advantage in having close relatives resemble each other in appearance. There should be variety and contrast among the actors as a group, in appearance, voice, and personality. The two leading women's roles should not usually be played by actresses with similar low-pitched voices; the hero and the villain should usually contrast physically and vocally.

Other factors should be considered that have implications extending beyond the immediate production. In particular, the casting should contribute to the continuing strength of the drama program as a whole.

Especially in the educational theater, it is vitally important that each cast include a number of new actors to provide training that will prepare them for the leading roles when the current most accomplished actors have been graduated. Probably the director should aim at filling about a fourth of the cast with new actors. He should expect that half the roles will be played by actors who have appeared in one or two previous plays presented by the same organization, and that the remaining fourth should be actors who are thoroughly trained and experienced, and of proved ability. The larger the cast the easier it is to match this formula, but in few plays can it be followed precisely. As a kind of ideal measure, however, it is useful in testing the variety of experience represented in a proposed cast.

The apprentice system presumes that actors' experience and ability both operate as a ceiling on the importance of parts that are assigned to them. New actors should always be given small and less critical roles. With each succeeding play, more and more impotant roles are opened to them, until they reach the limit of their ability. Some actors continue to grow in skill, and may be expected to move into major roles; others stop at some lower step on the ladder.

This pattern, too, is one that can seldom be followed precisely. Many other factors are involved in casting, but the apprentice system should be included among the things considered. It is especially dangerous to omit the first step. An actor should be given a strong supporting role in his first play at the theater only after very careful thought. To cast a new actor in a leading role is to invite disaster, even though the disaster may not always occur. Working with an actor on even a very small speaking part will give the director much more information about him than can be collected during an audition, and in later plays, if the actor's work justifies it, he can be advanced faster up the ladder of responsibility than might usually be the case, although, even then, jumping over steps should be done only with great care.

It has already been pointed out that the general belief that casting is done on the basis of the "star system" damages a theater program. Major roles are necessarily assigned to the actors who have the most experience and who have developed the greatest skill. The pernicious aspect of the star tradition is the belief that the circle of leading actors is closed and that major roles are cast from this group without regard to any other factors—that a single star actress and actor are automatically cast as leads in every play, whether they are suited to the parts or not.

It is desirable that casting demonstrate emphatically that the star system is not applied in that way. The steady movement of actors from walk-ons through small speaking parts, to supporting roles of various sizes, and then into the major parts, should be maintained as fully as possible. Ideally, each play should introduce at least one actor in his first major role.

The experience and ability of actors should operate as a ceiling on the importance of the parts available to them, not as a floor. In a healthy theater, it is accepted that an actor may play a leading role in one production, a strong supporting role in a second, a walk-on in a third, and a leading role in the fourth. That practice is not followed in the professional theater in America, where for a star to appear in a subordinate role is often interpreted as an indication of failure. In European theaters, the performance of parts on a variety of levels by an established star is far more commonly accepted. Even in the American professional theater, major actors fairly frequently accept parts in off-Broadway or regional theaters that they could not afford to play in fully professional productions, in order to broaden their range and to provide them with more varied and interesting acting experiences. In one noteworthy instance, Alfred Lunt, perhaps the most distinguished actor on the American stage, accepted a walk-on part with the Metropolitan Opera Company—and was given rave reviews.

Destroying the star system in a particular theater is a difficult and delicate job. An actor who has established himself as exceptionally skillful should not be given an uninteresting or unsuitable role simply to demonstrate that actors must play roles of different sizes. The director should instead study the parts with the greatest care in an attempt to fit them as closely as possible to the skills of the available actors, and should assign actors roles that they can handle with the greatest effectiveness, whatever the size of the parts. An actor who had demon-

strated great skill in wistful comedy by his performance of the leading role in
Harvey might well be cast in the demanding but relatively minor part of Feste
in *Twelfth Night,* or even as Grumio in *The Taming of the Shrew.*

TYPECASTING

One difficult question appears as a constant troublesome problem in all casting. Should actors be chosen for parts that match their real personalities, or
should they be given parts very different from themselves: in other words, what
about typecasting?

There is no fully acceptable answer to that question. If an actor has demonstrated a special ability to handle a certain type of role, casting him repeatedly
in similar parts can increase the effectiveness of the productions, and can reduce
the director's work, since the actor will require much less attention during rehearsals. On the other hand, the repetition of a performance already mastered,
with minute variations, provides the actor with little opportunity for growth. In
the professional theater, typecasting is standard; it must usually be done in the
community theater. Since a major function of the college theater is to enable actors to broaden their areas of mastery, typecasting tends to prevent the program
from achieving its educational goals. Probably the best solution for the college
director is to try to assign parts so that each actor will be able to use his present
skills fully, but so that he must extend his mastery into new areas. Such extension is almost inevitable if the theater program includes plays of varied quality
and kind; especially in great drama, characters tend to be individual rather than
established types. The educational value of acting depends to some extent on
the pattern of emphasis: if the actor is encouraged to extend his style in order to
express the full potentialities of the character he is playing, he will grow in
skill. If, instead, he is allowed or encouraged to reduce and reshape the character
as written to fit the performance personality which he has already mastered, not
only will he learn nothing new, but the play itself will be made less effective.

One aspect of typecasting that is extremely important is the exploitation
of actors' defects, especially if they are used as sources of humor. The assignment of an actor who stammers, or who is seriously overweight, or who has effeminate mannerisms, to a part in which such characteristics must be emphasized by rehearsal, and subjected to ridicule, is a serious breach of ethics. No
play can be defended that damages an actor's self-respect, or that provokes ridicule of him as a person. Occasionally an actor may volunteer for such a part. In
one instance, an exceptionally plump actress asked to be allowed to play a part
in which the character's gluttony was made the subject of a number of jokes.
The director agreed to the assignment, and the actress gave an excellent performance, accepting the appropriateness of the jokes with good humor. Even
when an actor volunteers for such a part, however, the director should assign it

to him only after careful thought has convinced him that it will have no harmful effect on the actor as a person.

The effect of living with a role for a month should always be considered in
casting, if there seems the slightest chance that an actor might be damaged by
the experience. Probably only a well-adjusted actress should be cast in such a
role as Martha in *Who's Afraid of Virginia Woolf?* Few actors should be asked
to re-enact tragic experiences of their own on the stage; an actor whose mother
was in fact a drug addict should not be asked to play the part of one of the sons
in *A Long Day's Journey into Night.* Even though actors are encouraged to attack their work with some objectivity, the repetition over a period of some
weeks of an experience that has caused them pain or disturbance outside the
theater can have a devastating effect on them. It is, of course, possible that getting such a part might help them in their adjustment by enabling them to handle it safely in a context different from their own. This is dangerous, however,
and in almost every case in which the director is aware of such a problem, he
should avoid casting the actor in the sensitive role. It is hoped that every actor
will be in some degree a better and more capable person as the result of having
taken part in a play; certainly, he should never be left worse.

A final concern involves the use of actors who are well suited to parts except for some distinctive inharmonious characteristic. This may be a foreign or
regional accent unsuited to the play or markedly different from the speech of
the rest of the cast; it may be a notable physical feature, such as a pronounced
limp. The problem is most likely to occur in considering actors of a different
race from those represented in the script.

Casting policies in the past, especially with regard to black actors, have involved curious contradictions. The racial line was readily crossed in one direction, and was considered to be almost impassable in the other direction. Thus,
white actors were frequently cast in black roles, so much so that makeup manu-
facturers regularly stocked makeup especially designed to enable white actors to
appear as blacks; the reverse, however, with very few exceptions, never occurred. Obviously, the degree to which the appearance of an actor needed to be
altered in order for him to play a character from a different race was identical,
whether the alteration was from white to black or black to white.

Within very recent years, attitudes have changed radically. It is now much
more realistic, and actors are generally cast on the basis of ability and suitability
to the roles, leaving it to the makeup and costume crews to adjust their appearance to fit the parts. Audiences are extremely receptive and suggestible, and recent experience has demonstrated that they are equally ready to accept a white
Laurence Olivier made up to look like a black for the part of Othello, a black
actor playing the part, or an oriental appearing as Benjamin Franklin.

Even an actor whose appearance is not altered will often be readily accepted by an audience, especially if the play is not extremely realistic. A black

actor who appeared as Sir Harry Bumper in one production of *The School for Scandal* particularly requested that he not be made up to look white. In one scene he sang a drinking song that included a reference to a "nut-brown maid," and he explained that he wanted to try to get a laugh on the line. The director agreed, the actor performed with high good humor, and the audience shared the joke with obvious enjoyment. Of course, the director's decision might have been different with a play that was less artificial and more solemn.

The cultures and traditions of minority groups, in so far as they differ from the general culture of the nation, are a rich source of strength for the theater. They are immediately evident in such plays as *The Fiddler on the Roof, Green Pastures, A View from the Bridge,* and other plays dealing with special ethnic groups. But the contributions of individual actors and other artists from such groups have been so great as to seem out of all proportion to their numbers. If the work even of only Jews and blacks were removed from the entertainment world, the American theater would be weakened to the point of collapse.

The time has long passed when blacks were restricted to playing butlers and maids, with the career of an outstanding actor being limited to Othello and Emperor Jones, and of Jews to Shylock. To far too great an extent, however, educational and community theaters have lagged behind in their handling of actors from minority groups. This is an area in which the educational theater in particular should lead the professional theater, not follow it.

Dialects and physical handicaps can also easily be overemphasized. Variations in speech and physique occur as part of ordinary experience. Often much can be done to alter speech patterns during a month's rehearsals. And an audience is likely to forget a physical handicap, provided the acting performance is a good one. In fact, if they notice it at all, it is more likely to enhance their appreciation of a performance, rather than detract from it. In one theater production, the director was asked by a speech correctionist especially to consider an actor with a stammer. He was cast in a small part, as a butler, but one calling for real acting, and providing him with enough lines to present a distinct challenge. He not only handled the part well, but he was able to master his stammer for the performances. The speech correctionist made a special point of expressing his appreciation, and for the actor himself it was a personal triumph of great value. In another theater, one of the leading actresses wore corrective shoes and walked with a distinct limp. The fact that all of the characters she played obviously limped seemed not to bother the audiences at all, and the director and her fellow actors quickly became unaware of it.

If there is any theater with an oversupply of talented actors, it has not yet been located. It would be a serious blunder for a director to cut himself off from a major source of talent because of a mistaken belief that minor characteristics of potentially fine actors were in fact significant problems.

At some point in the casting procedure, but most often toward the end, when the director is concerned with the smallest parts, he is likely to find two or more actors who seem exactly equal in their suitability to a particular role. A choice can be made in this case either at random, essentially by flipping a coin, or the director can search for small differences that would normally hardly be considered at all. Of two evenly matched actors, for example, the director might prefer to cast one who had auditioned for a series of plays without getting a part, rather than one who had appeared at the tryouts for the first time. An actor who had displayed continuing interest in the theater program by working as a member of the technical staffs for a number of shows might be preferred to someone who had taken no part. An experienced actor who had apparently reached the limit of his possibilities for growth might be rejected in favor of a less experienced actor who seemed to have greater potentialities, and who might be expected to contribute more to the theater in future productions.

DOUBLE CASTING AND UNDERSTUDIES

Where it seems impossible to select between two actors for important roles, directors sometimes double cast, that is they assign both actors to the same role and schedule each one to play half the performances, usually alternating between the two. Double casting has several advantages. It makes it possible to involve more actors in the program, which may be important in small-cast shows; it provides automatic understudies for the roles, so that in case of sickness a second actor is fully trained to take over; and if the runs are very long it makes less demand on the actors' time. There are several disadvantages. The major part of the cast must adjust to two different actors on alternate evenings. Seldom are both actors equally effective, and casting both invites unfortunate comparisons. Additional rehearsals must be scheduled, probably a few involving the entire cast and others with the individual actors, to make up for the fact that each one can take part in only half of the rehearsals. For these reasons, directors usually avoid double casting. If a role is double cast, each actor should be asked to attend all rehearsals, so that he can benefit from the director's work with the other actor. If the part is not too demanding, it may be desirable to cast each actor also in the same minor role, so that each is on stage at every rehearsal; both parts can then be alternated.

Every director dreads the midnight telephone call informing him that an actor has just been taken to the hospital for an appendectomy and cannot appear in the play. Ideally every part should be understudied, that is, a second actor should have memorized the lines and attended rehearsals so that he is ready to replace the regular actor in case of emergency. In the college and community theater that is simply not possible. The sacrifice of time required for preparing a role when there is little likelihood that the actor will get to perform it is too great to ask of a nonprofessional actor.

The handling of an emergency dropout from a cast depends on the amount of notice given the director. The best replacement is an actor who already has a minor role in the play, since he will be familiar with the play as a whole, and will have absorbed a good deal of information about the vacant role. His part can then be recast with an outside actor.

An actor unacquainted with the play needs a minimum of three days to memorize a major role. Usually it is better to find a skilled actor who did not try out for the play, rather than to try to use one of those who was rejected as unsuited. Very little can be done to rehearse the actor except for working out the basic blocking; most of his time must be given to memorizing the lines. Obviously, finding an actor who is a quick study is of great importance.

The director should go through the playbook carefully in an attempt to identify all of the moments when it is possible for the actor to use his script on stage. For instance, if he stands beside a fireplace in one scene, it may be possible to tear out pages of the script and paste them on the top of the mantel, out of sight of the audience. Others can be put on a table, perhaps behind a bowl of flowers. If the actor sits on a sofa during the play, a magazine might be left on the coffee table beside him, which he can leaf through, with pages of the script pasted to the sheets of the magazine. Of course the actor cannot read all of his lines from the script while on stage, but having crucial scenes at hand will enable him to glance down if he goes blank on a particular line and will, at the very least, give him greater confidence. Even if performances are regularly run without a prompter, a special prompter should be provided for an actor who has stepped in in an emergency.

If the replacement must be made with still shorter notice, it is better to send the actor on stage with a complete script in his hand, instructing him to use it as unobtrusively as possible, but without trying to hide it. The stage manager or the assistant director can be asked to fill in, or an actor with a small part can double. In one production of *Antony and Cleopatra,* the director was informed five minutes before curtain time that one of the actors had been injured earlier in the day and was in the hospital. His part was that of the countryman who brought the snakes to Cleopatra at the end of the play. He appeared only in the last scene and his lines totaled less than two minutes; however, he had eight speeches, involving as many cues, and rather complicated blocking. Lepidus does not appear on stage during the last half of the play, and the actor playing that part was asked to double as the countryman. He was instructed to tear the pages with his new speeches out of the playbook, to fold them up into a thin strip, and to take them with him so that he could read from them if necessary. He spent the time while he was off stage memorizing the lines, and was able to play the scene without having to refer to his script a single time.

Actors typically rise to an emergency and may even seem to enjoy the challcngc. Some have performed amazing feats of memory within even a shorter period than three days. An announcement of a substitution should always be made, either by a duplicated slip inserted in the programs or orally from the stage before the performance begins. Audiences are understanding and sympathetic in crises and will readily accept a performance even when a script is openly displayed, if they understand the reason.

CASTING CONSULTATIONS

Because casting nearly always involves great uncertainty, it is desirable to ask another theater artist to review the decisions. An associated director is best; a technical director or other staff member whose judgment is respected can serve almost equally well. The cast list should be presented to the adviser, as well as the sheets for actors who have been rejected. Typically, he will question some of the assignments. These should then be discussed in detail, exploring again the reasons for including or rejecting the actors whose assignment has been questioned. This consultation is especially valuable with regard to actors who are new to the casting director but who have worked in the past under the direction of the consultant.

ANNOUNCING THE CAST

Any final changes that seem desirable after the conference should be made. The cast list is then typed up in final form for posting. It is preferable to arrange the actors' names alphabetically to avoid implications about the relative importance of the parts. Instructions for picking up scripts, as well as the date and place of the first meeting or rehearsal, can be added in a note at the bottom of the sheet. Actors should be asked to initial the list, so that it can be checked to make sure each one has learned about his being included.

Some directors like to include a word of appreciation to the actors who tried out but who did not receive parts, and perhaps invite them to join in the technical work for the play.

FILING PERMANENT RECORDS

It is useful to have the tryout sheets on file. The actors can be included in a mailing list used to publicize tryouts for later plays. In future casting, the director may find it helpful to check his evaluations of actors at previous tryouts. When more than one director is associated with the theater, he can check his judgments of actors by referring to the sheets filled out during earlier auditions by other directors.

There is also some value in preparing a folder for each actor who has been cast. After the performance, the director should record his evaluation of the actor, and particularly note any conclusions or experiences that might be helpful to the directors of later shows, whether they are favorable or unfavorable. Typical comments might read as follows:

A slow study. [That is, takes more time than usual to memorize his lines.]
Difficulty with pitch control.
Excellent projection of voice and personality.
Gives strong support to other actors who appear with him.
Tends not to understand directions.
Outstanding ability as a dancer.

9/The Rehearsal Schedule

The preparation of a rehearsal schedule is so important that a cast and director who could achieve a brilliant production with the aid of an excellent schedule might be unable to rise above the level of mediocrity with a bad one.

The actors should be informed of the time and place of the first rehearsal when they come to check the announcement of the cast. If the full schedule has been prepared and duplicated at that time, copies can be distributed along with the scripts. However it is equally effective to hand them out at the beginning of the first rehearsal; delay beyond that time weakens the production.

One of the important effects of a well-planned schedule, distributed at the beginning of the work on the play, is the impression that it creates on the actors. It demonstrates, even before the first rehearsal has actually begun, that the work will be handled with efficiency, clarity of organization, and careful attention both to its larger aspects and its individual details, and those qualities are likely to be imitated immediately by the actors. A badly planned schedule, or no schedule at all, suggests disorganized improvisation, and the actors are equally likely to display the same qualities in their own work from the start.

The schedule, expressly or by clear implication, includes a series of deadlines showing the times at which different aspects of the work must be completed. Actors who are given only a general instruction to memorize their parts as quickly as possible will delay their work until the opening performance; when the schedule indicates that scripts are not to be used on stage after a specific rehearsal, they are far more likely to meet the earlier deadline. At the very least, the schedule reminds an actor who falls behind in his work. If he has neglected his analysis of the fundamental interpretation of his role, the schedule will indicate clearly to him exactly how far behind he is, and will remind him that he must spend additional time in order to catch up with the rest of the cast. The deadlines are also a useful reminder to the director, so that he is able to check on the progress of the work at any point and to discover immediately if the preparation for the play falls behind schedule, so that he can handle problems the instant they arise, rather than waiting till a week before opening night and discovering that two or three weeks' work must somehow be done in a few days.

A well-planned schedule enables the director to use the time with maximum efficiency and may make it possible to reduce the number of evenings that actors playing minor roles must give to rehearsals. The schedule also helps the director handle the various aspects of the work in the most effective order, rather than at random as they happen to come to his attention, and makes it much less likely that some particular task will be forgotten.

The period available for rehearsals stretches from the announcement of the cast to the rise of the curtain on opening night. Usually the dates of performance are set by the administrative board of the theater; most often the dates for an entire season are chosen near the end of the preceding season. The director can control the length of the time available for rehearsals somewhat by his choice of tryout dates, although sometimes other events, such as holidays and the dates of the previous production, may limit his choice. Whatever the length of the period available for rehearsals, the universal experience is that it is too short. One experienced university theater director remarked that however much time was spent on any play he always felt the cast and staff needed one more week.

As with all of the aspects of their work, directors differ in the order in which they take up the various tasks that must be handled in rehearsal and in the amount of time spent on each. The number of hours that must be assigned to similar parts of the work also varies greatly from play to play. Rehearsing the blocking for Bolt's *A Man for All Seasons* or Shakespeare's *A Midsummer Night's Dream* requires many times as long as for *Harvey* or *Blithe Spirit*; even a single scene of Ibsen's *Peer Gynt* might take as long to block as an entire act of his *Ghosts*. It is consequently impossible to describe a rehearsal schedule that will fit all plays or all directors. Experiment and experience will enable the student director to develop the pattern that is most congenial for him, and to adjust it to the requirements of the individual plays with which he works.

The Order of Work

It is convenient to think of the work of rehearsals as falling into seven divisions. The actors must learn the blocking pattern that has been designed for the play. They must achieve a full and accurate understanding of the characters they represent, and the meaning of the lines. They must discover the vocal and physical techniques by which those meanings can be communicated to the audience. They must learn to relate the various characters to each other, to blend the performance into a unified whole. They must polish the production and fix or stabilize their performances, so that they can be repeated at a uniform level of maximum effectiveness.

They must also acquire an understanding of the general pattern of the play —its tone, its moods, and its esthetic organization. Probably there is more variation in the handling of this part of the work than any other. Some directors devote many rehearsals to it; others provide no rehearsals specifically designated for considering this aspect of the play, but handle it throughout the entire rehearsal period or simultaneously with the study of the interpretation of lines and characters. The length of time that must be spent on this part of the work also varies enormously from play to play. A director might well decide that not even half a rehearsal need be especially scheduled for discussing the overall tone of *Arsenic and Old Lace* or *The Merry Wives of Windsor;* several rehearsals might be needed for discussing the same aspect of *Hamlet* or Chekhov's *The Cherry Orchard.*

THE NUMBER OF REHEARSALS

How many rehearsals are needed for a particular production depends on the skill and experience of both director and actors, and on the difficulty of the play. One of the clear differences between the professional and nonprofessional theaters is that much more rehearsal time is available for professional productions, nearly always twice as much and more often many times as much. Summer theaters usually spend less rehearsal time than educational and community theaters; often only a week is available for the rehearsals, although each may extend through an entire morning and afternoon, so that the difference is not so great as it might seem. In addition, the actors are usually free of other responsibilities, and often roles are alternated in size, so that an actor who has a long part in the play being currently shown is given a smaller part in the play being rehearsed for presentation the following week.

Rehearsals for college and community theater productions must usually be held in the evening because of the actors' conflicting business or class commitments during the day. The total rehearsal period is probably most often set at a month, during which somewhat more than twenty rehearsals are scheduled. If the rehearsal period must be interrupted, for instance because of a vacation, from one to three additional rehearsals must be scheduled to compensate for the loss of momentum produced by the interruption. Twenty rehearsals are inadequate for a fairly easy full-length play (as the director mentioned above said, "We always need another week"). A more difficult play requires more rehearsals.

One director scheduled thirty rehearsals for *Antony and Cleopatra* and twenty-seven for *The Taming of the Shrew;* the same director produced Tom Taylor's *Our American Cousin* in twenty rehearsals. These times were inadequate for all three plays, but they give some indication of the relative amount of time needed for productions of varying degrees of difficulty.

The regular rehearsals can be supplemented by special rehearsals with individual actors, or small groups of two or three. Such rehearsals involve fewer conflicts with outside commitments than those that require the attendance of the entire cast, so that they are usually held during the day, or occasionally on weekends. Actors who need additional work, either because their parts are unusually demanding or because of individual difficulties, are usually eager for the extra help. Such rehearsals make heavy demands on the director's time, when he is likely to have the fewest hours to spare, but it is often possible to produce striking improvement in the performance of key actors in private rehearsals, when the director's full attention can be focused on their work, and when the actors may feel less inhibited than in the presence of the rest of the cast. Such improvement, when carried back to the general rehearsals, may result in a significant advance for the cast as a whole.

Most directors use the first rehearsal as an orientation period. The cast members are introduced individually, since usually some of them have not met each other. The rehearsal schedules are distributed and discussed, and rehearsal policies and methods of procedure are described. The actors read through the play, either sitting in chairs on stage, arranged in a semicircle, or in the auditorium. Some directors prefer to hold the first meeting outside the theater proper, if the theater has an adequate green room, that is an ideal location; if not, the session can be held in a large office, in a fraternity lounge, or in the director's home. ("The green room" is the traditional name for an all-purpose lounge and conference room—one of the most important and most used facilities in the theater.) Sometimes refreshments are served in order to help create an atmosphere of ease and informality. Following the reading, actors are invited to make comments or ask questions, and then the broader aspects of the play are discussed. All of this makes a very full evening, and if the play is especially difficult or significant it may be desirable to schedule a second rehearsal or even more for a continued exploration of its general interpretation.

There are obviously great advantages to this method of beginning work on the play. Some of the actors may have worked together previously; some may already be close friends; others are likely to feel like strangers and outsiders. At the end of a session of the type described, a group feeling is almost certain to have been developed, and an atmosphere of friendliness and ease created that may carry through the entire month's work on the play. The meeting gives the director an opportunity to establish an effective relationship with the cast, something that is more difficult under the conditions of work on stage.

As might be expected, however, such a session also has disadvantages, the most important one being the expenditure of a full evening in achieving effects that might have been produced automatically during the time spent in other activities. If the actors have been urged to read the play through before the first meeting, they may have become better acquainted with it than is possible from hearing it read aloud at sight. Furthermore, actors' sight-reading of the script is typically so ineffective that new actors may be dismayed rather than encouraged, and even an experienced director may curse the fate that led him into the theater. Some directors, then, especially with relatively simple plays, dispense with the script-reading get-acquainted session altogether, and begin immediately with blocking rehearsals, taking only a very few minutes at the start of the first rehearsal to discuss procedures and policies.

It is necessary for actors to walk through their blocking patterns twice in order for them to fix the basic positions and movements in their minds. This rehearsal will be reinforced by their independent study and by their continued practice in blocking after they have turned their attention to other aspects of the performance. A single walk-through, however, is likely to leave them with only the vaguest memory of the blocking. It is more effective for the repetition to be immediate; for instance, it is better to go through the first-act blocking twice at the first rehearsal, and the second act twice at the second rehearsal, than to run through both acts the first night and repeat them the second. Usually, in a three-act play, one evening will be needed for each act.

The actors will have read through the entire play twice during the blocking rehearsals (in addition to having studied their own lines outside the theater), and so will have acquired a basic familiarity with the plot and tone of the play. The next group of rehearsals is devoted to an analysis of the interpretation of the lines, with regard to their simple meaning, their relation to the play as a whole, and their accompanying emotions. Probably two rehearsals should be assigned to each act. Unlike the blocking rehearsals, the work of interpretation is facilitated by scheduling an interval between the two evenings spent on a single act. It is best to schedule the interpretative work on the first act for the first and fourth rehearsals in this group of six, devoting the second and fifth to Act II, and the third and sixth to Act III. Not only is the interpretation of each act enriched and facilitated by the work on the intervening acts, but such spacing also gives the actor more time to study the interpretations between rehearsals, and to absorb and integrate it. This same pattern is usually best for later groups of rehearsals, up to the point in the schedule where the entire play is performed each evening.

The director and cast then turn their attention to the problem of finding techniques that will communicate the meaning and emotions of the play to the audience. Two rehearsals will usually be needed for each act in this group.

So far, the attention of each actor has been focused almost exclusively on his own role; but the individual performances must be blended into a unified whole. The director can hope to achieve such coordination in two rehearsals, but the entire play should be performed each evening. Each previous rehearsal typically involves only a single act; beginning with the blending step, the entire play is run through at each rehearsal.

It can be expected that fine adjustments will still need to be made in the performance. While actors are struggling to remember blocking positions, to work out interpretations, and to experiment with alternative techniques, it will probably be impossible to identify the details of performance that are important in producing an effect of smoothness and polish. Once the previous problems have been taken care of, the director and the actors turn their attention to these final adjustments. Two rehearsals are generally adequate for polishing the production.

One of the differences between amateur and professional acting is the greater variability of amateur performance. A professional is able to repeat a reading with little variation; an amateur may read a line brilliantly one night and much less effectively the next. To some extent the difference is due to the shorter experience of the amateur actor; a larger factor, however, is the much greater number of hours of rehearsal which are available in the professional theater. The ability to sustain and repeat a performance is very important to the effectiveness of the production, so that as many rehearsals as possible should be scheduled for fixing or stabilizing the performance pattern that has been developed. It is presumed that experimentation has been completed by the beginning of this group of rehearsals and that the actors' concern is to repeat their performances enough times to guarantee that they will not deviate significantly from the pattern they have spent three weeks or more in preparing. Probably four rehearsals should be scheduled for this stabilizing process.

The director's work in this group of rehearsals is still important, but less critical than previously. One of the rehearsals is selected for checking the work of the technical staff—lighting, sound, properties, costumes, and makeup. During this rehearsal the director intentionally ignores the actors and gives his attention exclusively to the technical aspects of the production. The technical rehearsal should not be the last one, since if technical problems are found the staff must be given whatever time is necessary to solve them. Usually the rehearsal selected is the one scheduled for the last Monday before opening night, assuming that the play opens on Friday or Saturday.

The schedule described specifies twenty-three rehearsals, assuming that the initial orientation is omitted and that blocking begins at the first rehearsal. Altering the schedule to suit special circumstances or the needs of a particular script consists primarily of extending individual groups of rehearsals. For instance, if the director feels that the interpretation of the lines is especially difficult, he might schedule three interpretation rehearsals for each act, thus increasing the total number of rehearsals to twenty-six. Much less often will it be possible to shorten any of the sections.

The names given to the various groups of rehearsals do not mean that only the aspect of the work mentioned is considered during a particular group; rather they indicate the focus of attention. The work, in fact, is cumulative. Only three rehearsals are included in this schedule for blocking, but the blocking is not removed from the production when the actors' attention turns to interpretation. The actors continue to move through the blocking patterns they have studied, steadily learning them more and more thoroughly, even though their major attention is on a new aspect of the work. It will be seen, in fact, that each new area of concern depends on all of the decisions made previously.

SCHEDULING SCENES BY CHARACTERS

The schedule discussed assumes that the sections of the play are rehearsed in the same order in which they appear in the script. That is the most common, but not the universal practice. It is much easier for the director if the play can be handled in this way, but it may require an unnecessary expenditure of time for individual actors, especially those with minor roles. A butler, for example, might appear at the beginning and end of Act I, but be off stage throughout most of the act. If he is included only in the first act, he would be required to attend five rehearsals during the period when a full evening was spent on each act, although it might be possible to handle all of the rehearsals of his scenes in an hour or an hour and a half.

Scheduling the different sections of a play out of sequence so as to use the actors' time more efficiently is a difficult and troublesome job, and may sometimes prove impossible. If significant savings can be made, however, it is often worth attempting. Such special scheduling requires an analysis of the periods in the play during which each actor is on stage.

Premodern plays are often divided into short scenes, each involving a special group of characters. Even if such units are not marked in the scripts, an examination of almost any play will demonstrate that each act contains a number of points of natural division, often with different groups of characters appearing in the passage immediately preceding the dividing point and the one immediately following. Even though such divisions are not separated by closing the curtain, they can be numbered as scenes for purposes of analysis. Following are the divisions of the first act of Giraudoux's *The Madwoman of Chaillot*.

1. A conversation between the Baron and the President, sitting at a table on the sidewalk in front of a cafe in Paris.

THE LENGTH AND DISTRIBUTION OF PARTS IN THE TAMING OF THE SHREW

Acts	I		II	III		IV					V		
Scenes	1	2	1	1	2	1	2	3	4	5	1	2	
Baptista	22		63		31				19		10	10	155
Bianca	4		16	31	1		4				2	4	62
Biondello	5	2	12		31		7		19		15	4	95
Curtis						20							20
Gremio	21	37	45		32						10	2	147
Grumio		41			1	75		33				0	150
Hortensio	22	75	33	28			25	9		7		8	207
Katharine	12		44		28	3		43		21	4	49	204
Lucentio	88	6	13	25	6		4		10		13	22	187
Milliner								1					1
Officer											0		0
Pedant							12		20		9		41
Petruchio		75	155		58	69		82		37	16	55	547
Servant 1			0	3	0	1		0		0	0	0	4
Servant 2				0	0	1		0		0	0	0	1
Servant 3				0	0	1		0		0	0	0	1
Servant 4					0	2		0		0	0	0	2
Servant 5					0	1		0		0	0	0	1
Servant 6					0			0		0	0	0	0
Tailor								13					13
Tranio	60	32	47		41		62		25		10	4	281
Vincentio										8	30	2	40
Widow												7	7
Totals	234	268	428	81	229	173	114	181	93	73	119	167	2166

2. The Broker joins them and reports on the sale of stock.
3. The Prospector moves to their table and discusses his search for oil.
4. The Policeman brings in Pierre, whom he has rescued from an attempt to drown himself.
5. Countess Aurelia attempts to persuade Pierre that life is worth living.
6. Pierre and the Ragpicker explain the attempts of evil men to take over control of Paris.
7. The Countess sets in motion a plan to foil their attempt.
8. Irma talks about her experiences in a soliloquy.

When the divisions have been identified and numbered, a list should be made of all the characters who appear in each scene. It is important to distinguish between actors who speak and those who are present but have no lines; walk-ons can be marked by writing "O" in the proper spaces; characters with speeches can be marked with a check, or the number of speeches each has can be written in. A somewhat more accurate indication can be provided by writing not the number of speeches but the total number of lines of print occupied by each person's speeches.

On page 242 is a chart prepared for a production of *The Taming of the Shrew*. In this case, the figures indicate the lines of verse rather than the number of speeches. The play was somewhat adapted, so that the counts do not exactly match the standard script.

The chart explains graphically the pattern of scenes in which any particular character is involved. Often three or four characters will appear together in a number of scenes scattered throughout the play. If these scenes can be grouped in a single rehearsal, it will not be necessary to ask the actors to wait while intervening scenes are worked on. In *The Taming of the Shrew*, Baptista appears in six of the twelve scenes; in only one case does he take part in two successive scenes, and one pair of scenes have three scenes between them during which he does not appear.

Even if the scenes in which minor actors appear cannot be isolated and grouped in a few rehearsals, it is often possible to excuse them from as many as half of the sessions in which their scenes are worked on without damaging the performance of the actors with the larger parts. The saving in time for the minor actors may be very great, and such scheduling may make it possible for actors to take part who would otherwise be lost to the theater. However, the director should avoid scheduling the rehearsals so that any actor is absent from the theater for many evenings in succession. It is important that each one not lose touch with the play and not come to feel that he is excluded from the group.

Even if it should prove impossible to increase rehearsal efficiency by scheduling scenes out of sequence, the chart provides useful information to the director. If the rows of figures are totaled, the size of each part is indicated, which is helpful in setting up the schedule of memorization deadlines. If the columns are totaled, the length of each scene is expressed. If the acts of a three-act play are approximately equal in length, it is usually best to plan to cover a single act at each of the early rehearsals. However, if the acts vary greatly in size, if, for instance, the second act is much longer than the first, it may be desirable to add the first or second scenes to the first-act rehearsals, so that the amounts of work that must be done at each rehearsal are more evenly balanced.

The actors must carry their scripts during the blocking rehearsals, and they are more a help than a handicap during the interpretation rehearsals. However, actors with very short parts may be encouraged to drop scripts as soon as blocking has been finished, and the memorization schedule for the other actors should be worked out carefully, with the longest parts appearing last on the list. Including the deadlines in the rehearsal schedule gives each actor notice of his responsibility for memorizing and makes it impossible for him to plead misunderstanding.

Following is a fairly typical schedule worked out for a college production of a play of moderate difficulty.

REHEARSAL SCHEDULE FOR NOEL COWARD'S *BLITHE SPIRIT*

Blocking Rehearsals

1. Friday, September 25, 7:00 P.M. Act I, Scenes 1 and 2.
   Technical: Platforms to be used in the set are to be in place on stage.
       The ground plan of other scenic units is to be marked on the floor.
       Rehearsal furniture is to be provided.
   Actors: Between rehearsals work on the memorization of cues, lines, and
       blocking.
2. Monday, September 28, 7:00 P.M. Act II, Scenes 1, 2, and 3.
3. Tuesday, September 29, 7:00 P.M. Act III, Scenes 1 and 2.
   Actors: Between rehearsals work on the interpretation of lines and charac-
       ters.

Interpretation Rehearsals

4. Wednesday, September 30, 7:00 P.M. Act I, Scenes 1 and 2.
   Memorization deadline for Edith.
5. Thursday, October 1, 7:00 P.M. Act II, Scenes 1 and 2.
6. Friday, October 2, 7:00 P.M. Act II, Scene 3, and Act III, Scene 1.
   Memorization deadline for Dr. and Mrs. Bradman.
7. Monday, October 5, 7:00 P.M. Act III, Scene 2, and Act 1, Scene 1.

8. Tuesday, October 6, 7:00 P.M. Act I, Scene 2.
   Memorization deadline for Elvira.

9. Wednesday, October 7, 7:00 P.M. Act II, Scenes 1 and 2.
   Memorization deadline for Madame Arcati.

10. Thursday, October 8, 7:00 P.M. Act II, Scene 3, and Act III, Scenes 1 and 2.
    Actors: Between rehearsals work on the development of vocal and physical techniques.

Acting Techniques

11. Friday, October 9, 7:00 P.M. Act I, Scenes 1 and 2.
    Technical: Rehearsal properties are to be supplied for this and the following rehearsals, through October 22.

12. Monday, October 12, 7:00 P.M. Act II, Scenes 1, 2, and 3.
    Memorization deadline for Ruth.

13. Tuesday, October 13, 7:00 P.M. Act III, Scenes 1 and 2.

14. Wednesday, October 14, 7:00 P.M. Act I, Scenes 1 and 2.
    Memorization deadline for Charles.
    The director's comments will be given only between scenes.

15. Thursday, October 15, 7:00 P.M. Act II, Scenes 1, 2, and 3.

16. Friday, October 16, 7:00 P.M. Act III, Scenes 1 and 2.

Rehearsals for Blending

17. Monday, October 19, 7:00 P.M. The entire play.
    The director's comments will be given only between acts.
    Technical: Deadline for the completion of all functional elements of the set, including flats with doors.

18. Tuesday, October 20, 7:00 P.M. The entire play.

Rehearsals for Polishing and Projection

19. Wednesday, October 21, 7:00 P.M. The entire play.
    The director's comments will be given only at the beginning and end of the rehearsal.
    Technical: Deadline for the completion of the set.
        The supernatural effects are to be provided for this and all following rehearsals.

20. Thursday, October 22, 7:00 P.M. The entire play.
    The makeup schedule for rehearsal 21 will be announced by the chief of the makeup crew.

The Technical Rehearsal

21. Friday, October 23, 8:00 P.M. The entire play.
    Makeup and costume parade on stage at 7:45 P.M.

Deadline for the completion of all technical work; all crews will operate as for performance.

The director's comments will be given only on technical work; the rehearsal may be interrupted for conferences with the technical crews.

Actors should report any technical difficulties to the director.

In case of emergency, an additional rehearsal may be scheduled for Saturday or Sunday, October 24 or 25.

Stabilizing Rehearsals

22. Monday, October 26, 7:30 P.M. The entire play.
    The director's comments will be given only after the last act.
    Technical: Omit makeup; all other technical crews will operate as for performance.

23. Tuesday, October 27, 7:30 P.M. The entire play.
    The director's comments will be given only after the last act.
    Technical: Omit makeup; all other technical crews will operate as for performance.

24. Wednesday, October 28, 7:30 P.M. The entire play.
    The director's comments will be given only after the last act.
    Technical: Omit makeup; all other technical crews will operate as for performance.
    The makeup schedule for rehearsal 25 will be announced by the chief of the makeup crew.

25. Thursday, October 28, 7:45 P.M. The entire play.
    The director's comments will be given only after the last act.
    Technical: All technical crews, including makeup, will operate as for performance.

Performances

Friday, October 30, 8:15 P.M.; opening night
Saturday, October 31, 8:15 P.M.
Monday, November 2, 8:15 P.M.
Tuesday, November 3, 8:15 P.M.
Wednesday, November 4, 8:15 P.M.
Thursday, November 5, 8:15 P.M.
Friday, November 6, 8:15 P.M.
Sunday, November 8, 3:30 P.M.

Photographs of the cast will be taken immediately following the play.
Supper will be served to the cast and crews in the green room at 6:30.

Strike (All Technical Crews)

Monday, November 9, 7:00 P.M.

All of the director's preparatory work should be completed by the time of the first rehearsal. It is the least interesting part of his work, but with it behind him he is free to devote his entire attention to his most important task, the training of the actors. The familiarity with the play that results from careful analysis, as well as the knowledge that the work has been planned with maximum care and thoroughness, enables him to proceed without distraction and with relaxed assurance.

10/Rehearsal Policies and Procedures

The work of rehearsals will proceed more efficiently if a few general policies are adopted. When a director joins an established theater, it is wise for him to inquire about the familiar conduct of rehearsals, and to adopt as many as possible of the established methods. When a new theater program is being developed, the creation of a set of policies is an essential part of the director's responsibilities.

A great deal of friction can be avoided by making sure that each member of the cast understands the rehearsal policies clearly. Often they are discussed briefly at the first meeting of the cast; they may be incorporated in a handbook describing the organization and work of the theater as a whole. Probably the ideal method of handling the policy problem is to develop a general familiarity with them so that they become a tradition. As actors join the group, they will learn the procedures from the more experienced actors, and the policies will become self-perpetuating.

Directors vary greatly in their rehearsal policies, so much so that equally effective directors sometimes seem to operate with diametrically opposed policies. No single pattern can be recommended as necessarily right; each director must choose the one that works best for him by experimenting with the various alternatives. All rehearsal policies have the same purpose: the achievement of the best possible production of the play with the greatest efficiency. A director's policy decisions are sound if they enable him and his cast to make the best possible use of the rehearsal time, if they reduce friction to a minimum, if they create an atmosphere of ease and hard work.

Some directors choose quite restrictive guide rules for rehearsals; others operate very freely. Actors will usually accept even rigid policies if it is clear

248

that they are motivated by a desire to make the work as effective as possible; they are likely to resent policies that are apparently adopted only out of a love for rules. If a director is uncertain as to whether a policy will improve the conduct of rehearsals or not, it is probably better for him not to adopt it. He should assume that actors will display dedication and hard work without the necessity of providing a rule designed to force their concentration.

OPEN AND CLOSED REHEARSALS

One of the decisions that must be made is whether rehearsals are to be "open" or "closed," that is, whether visitors are to be allowed or rigidly excluded. Bernard Shaw, in "The Art of Rehearsal," takes the extreme position that no visitor should ever be permitted at an actual rehearsal under any circumstances. (A visitor is defined as a person who is not involved in the production of the play; even the most rigid exclusion does not apply to costume, set, properties, or other staff members.)

The major argument for closed rehearsals is that visitors distract and inhibit actors. It may seem strange that an actor who will eventually perform before hundreds of people should be hampered at rehearsal by the presence of a single outsider sitting quietly in the back row. However, at least half of the rehearsals involve trial-and-error experimentation. The actor may speak a line in twenty different ways, finally rejecting all but one, which is then incorporated in the performance. A casual observer of rehearsals is thus most likely to see the actor at his worst, whereas the audience will be shown only the readings and business selected as best. Even with excellent actors, some of the alternatives tried will be so bad as to be absurd. The director and the other members of the cast, being familiar with the experimental aspect of the work, can be expected to understand that every actor will occasionally make a fool of himself, but the brief visitor may misinterpret what he sees. Every director who conducts open rehearsals will frequently see fine actors freeze up as someone wanders into the theater, and their work lose almost all of its effectiveness until the visitor has left. The necessity of adjusting comments and analyses to the possible responses of a stranger in the theater also inhibits the director. He can work effectively only if he is free to comment frankly on an actor's work. To make unfavorable criticisms in the presence of a stranger, or even of a friend who is not involved in the production of the play, is a breach of etiquette, and may cause enough embarrassment to prevent the actor's benefiting from the comments; to attempt to soften the criticisms or state them indirectly may make them meaningless.

The most disturbing visitor is one who drops in for only a few minutes. If he attends a series of rehearsals, he will quickly become familiar with theatrical methods of work and will be able to interpret what he sees and hears correctly. Usually, if an outsider asked permission to attend all of the rehearsals of a play, in order to study directorial or production methods, he would be welcomed even in a theater with a rigid closed-rehearsal policy.

Some excellent directors do follow the open policy, however. One university director reports that visitors at rehearsals tend to return for performances, most often with a friend, so that the open policy builds his audiences. Other advantages could be cited, although they are less clear-cut and more difficult to describe than the disadvantages. If the director himself is not distracted or constrained by the presence of a visitor, and if the actors are able to work freely, then there may be no objection to open rehearsals, but the decision to admit visitors should be made with great care. If there is any doubt about their effect on the work, it should be resolved by excluding them; in this case it is better to err in the direction of rigidity than permissiveness.

ATTENDANCE

It has already been recommended that an extreme effort be made to use actors' time as efficiently as possible. They should not be required to spend long hours waiting at rehearsals while other actors perform, if that can be avoided, and an effort should be made to adjust the rehearsal schedule to genuine outside commitments.

Actors should be expected to respond to such consideration, however, by attending rehearsals promptly and faithfully. The work should start exactly at the time it has been scheduled, and it should be made clear that casual tardiness is a serious offense. Especially in the educational theater, actors are likely to carry their attitudes toward tardiness from the classroom into the theater, even though what may be a minor lapse in a course is a major interference in rehearsal. A student who is ten minutes late to a class has damaged only himself; the work of the class will have gone on without him. If he delays the start of a rehearsal by ten minutes, he has wasted the time of the entire cast as well as the director; with a cast of six, he has destroyed the equivalent of a full man-hour of work; with a cast of twelve, he has shortened the work by two man-hours.

Since actors tend to copy the standards and procedures displayed by the director, it is important that he hold himself to standards of promptness at least as rigid as those which the actors are expected to meet. If he is unavoidably late to a rehearsal, even by a single minute, he should give the cast a full explanation before the rehearsal starts. No rehearsal should be held up for an absent actor. It should start exactly at the scheduled time, with the assistant director reading the missing actor's lines, and the director should refuse to repeat the section of the play that the tardy actor has missed unless he can demonstrate that his lateness was unavoidable.

On the other hand, to ask an actor to be present at the beginning of a rehearsal when he does not appear on stage until late in the act being worked on is unreasonable. The enforcement of promptness can be made more acceptable if each actor is required to appear only at the time he is needed. If the rehearsal begins at 7:00, and the actor can reasonably asume that his first entrance will not occur before 8:30, then he should be considered to be on time if he appears then. Furthermore, since the amount of time spent in rehearsing a scene varies greatly, an actor should not be reprimanded if he appears at a reasonable time, even though the rehearsal has actually reached his scene earlier. The same policy should apply to periods when the actor is offstage within a rehearsal. If his only scenes in an act occur at the beginning and end, he should be free to use the intervening time as he likes, to study or even to leave the theater, provided he returns by the time when a reasonable estimate would suggest he would be needed. Often it is possible by special arrangement to permit an actor to leave the auditorium to study in the lobby or a nearby room, with the assistant director assuming responsibility for notifying him shortly before his next entrance.

Occasionally members of the technical staff may request that the director allow them to work with actors while they are offstage. This is most likely to involve measuring actors for costumes, although property, makeup, or other crews may make similar requests. An actor whose entrance is delayed for such reasons should not be considered tardy, since he is working on an authorized assignment for the play. If desired, the assistant director can undertake to warn such actors in time for them to get on stage.

Each director must decide what reasons he will accept for absence from rehearsal. In the professional theater, only serious illness or reasons that are beyond the control of the actor are acceptable. In civic and college theaters it will be necessary for the director to approve somewhat more reasons for absence, because the actors have other commitments that must necessarily take precedence over the drama work. Most directors would agree that studying for a crucial examination would justify missing an early rehearsal. That does not mean that a cast must be excused en masse during midterm examinations; no excuse should be accepted unless the actor clearly demonstrates that it is impossible for him to attend, or that attending would seriously jeopardize his work outside the theater.

It is a great handicap not to have a complete cast during the blocking rehearsals, and absences are even more serious during the last quarter or third of the rehearsal period. The intervening rehearsals are less damaged if an actor must miss one, and often an individual rehearsal can be scheduled to make up for what has been missed.

It should be standard policy that an actor who must miss a rehearsal inform the director as early as possible, so that he can replan the work so as to use the time efficiently. The report should be made in writing and should explain the reason for the absence. The director may prefer that the report be sent to the assistant director, who can then pass it on. Even if an emergency develops that prevents giving notice ahead of time, the actor should make a phone call or send a messenger if at all possible. If a message is not received, the director should assume that it could not be sent, but the actor should be required to supply a satisfactory explanation at the next rehearsal. If no such explanation is made, the attendance and tardiness policy should be explained again, with a warning of possible removal from the cast.

The suggested policy, then, is that great effort be made to adjust the work to the individual needs and commitments of the actors, but that in return they be expected to hold themselves to rigid standards of attendance and promptness. Such a policy is self-perpetuating, and once it has been established, new actors absorb it from the veterans. A tradition of laxness also tends to continue, and once it has become accepted is very difficult to break. Not only does it affect the amount of time available for rehearsal and the efficiency with which the time is used, but it is influential in establishing the general atmosphere of work in the theater. Actors and members of the technical staff are more likely to do all of their work thoroughly and on time if a high standard of efficiency has been established in the rehearsal attendance policy.

REHEARSAL CONDUCT

The conduct of actors and staff members at rehearsals is also important to the effectiveness of the work. Some directors forbid any conversations at rehearsals except those concerned with the work of the play. Undoubtedly that policy makes acting and directing easier and promotes concentration. Since most actors will spend a great deal of time offstage during rehearsals, however, the necessity for maintaining complete silence produces considerable tension, and makes periods of waiting much more irksome. Conversations carried on by groups standing or sitting between the director and the stage tend to be extremely distracting; if the actors are located behind the director their conversations are much easier to ignore. The best rule, then, seems to be that actors should be permitted to carry on quiet conversations farther back in the theater than the row where the director is sitting, and preferably well toward the back wall, but that they not be allowed to speak if they are between the director and the stage.

Conversations backstage are extremely audible to those on stage and are distracting even to the director; actors often are not aware of that fact and may disturb a rehearsal without realizing it. Essential backstage conversations among actors or members of the technical staff are acceptable, although they should be carried on as quietly as possible. All other backstage conversations should be forbidden.

Inexperienced actors often assume that the director is free for consultation when he is sitting quietly while the actors are performing. This is a natural feeling, but completely wrong. The director is typically working hardest when he is watching and listening to the actors. When a director is approached at such moments, he should either ask the actor to wait until later or the rehearsal should be stopped until the conference is finished. It is best to explain this policy at the first rehearsal. Since emergencies may arise that make it impossible for a conversation to be delayed until a natural break in the rehearsal, it may be desirable to adopt the policy that the actor confer with the assistant director in such a case, who can then interrupt the director, or ask the actor to wait, depending on the importance of the problem. Visitors who attempt to interrupt the director's analysis of the actors' work should be told politely but firmly that they must wait—unless, of course, the theater is on fire.

THE DIVISION OF WORK

An easy working relationship should be developed and maintained between actors and the director. The actors should feel completely free of constraint in their conversations with the director, and they should be confident that no legitimate comment or question will be met with ridicule or criticism. If there is the slightest doubt of the propriety of a remark made by an actor, the doubt should be resolved by the assumption that it is a proper one.

Some topics, however, are not the legitimate concern of the actor and should not be discussed during rehearsal. An actor who feels that he must confer with the director about such things should do so in private. Perhaps the most excusable disruptive behavior is that of the actor who is genuinely trying to be helpful by making suggestions with regard to aspects of production that lie outside his own area of responsibility. The actor who points out that a picture on the wall of the set is crooked, who provides unauthorized assistance with the prompting, who kindly reports to the director that one of the cast members is not projecting adequately, who attempts to help the director by clarifying his comments to other actors, most often is actually trying to improve the production. Such interference, however, may be seriously disruptive, and at best is irritating. It should be explained to such an actor that theatrical procedures require a clear division of work, and that efficiency is not promoted when he attempts to do other people's work for them. The most serious of these violations of good practice consists of attempting to give clandestine directorial advice to fellow actors. The direction must be carefully adjusted to each performer, and each instruction must be fitted into the total pattern of the play. Those requirements can be met only if all of the direction is handled by a single person. Such an explanation is usually enough to stop officious misguided assistance, even if it does not convince the actor; continued experience will make its soundness clear to him.

These examples suggest the basis for distinguishing between topics that are legitimate for discussion by the actor and those that are not. Director and actor, each has his own functions and responsibilities. It is as impossible, and as destructive, for an actor to attempt to do the director's work as it is for the director to attempt to act each part in the play himself. Any question or comment by an actor that is related even indirectly to his own assignment is legitimate; interference with the director's responsibilities is illegitimate.

This division of labor carries no implications of personal superiority for either director or actor. Inevitably actors must frequently follow the director's instructions. His authority, however, is organizational, not personal. It is not unheard of for the director of one play to appear in another play directed by one of the actors in the first. With people who are thoroughly familiar with theater practice, such a reversal of positions produces not the slightest friction or difficulty. Each understands his own responsibilities and each carries out his own assignment, either as actor or director.

Even illegitimate questions or comments should normally be treated with courtesy, especially if they are offered by apprentice actors who have not yet learned theatrical methods. Probably the best response to such a suggestion is to ask the actor to wait until the next break in the rehearsal. The lines of responsibility can then be explained, and it can be made clear why the comment was out of order. For an experienced actor to attempt repeatedly to operate in areas that are the director's exclusive responsibility is an extreme breach of theatrical etiquette, may damage a production seriously, and would at the very least justify his exclusion from later plays.

The Use of Scripts

Some aspects of the work can best be done while the actors still have their scripts in their hands. Blocking rehearsals must be done with scripts, and working out the interpretation of the lines can be done better before the memorization has been completed. If the lines are memorized before their meanings are fully understood, readings will have become fixed that do not express them accurately. These must then be destroyed and replaced with more effective ones, and the necessity for unlearning the unacceptable methods of reading uses up rehearsal time that could better be spent on other things.

As soon as the interpretation of the lines has been basically completed, however, the rehearsal work is greatly impeded by the actors' continuing to carry their scripts on stage. Not only will their eyes be on the playbooks rather than on their fellow actors, but simple business like holding a coffee cup or shaking hands is difficult, and more important factors such as timing and the development of an ensemble style are seriously impeded. Actors should therefore be held rigidly to the memorization deadlines. When an actor is scheduled to appear on stage without his playbook, he should be required to leave it behind. There is no objection to an actor's keeping a book in the offstage area for consultation before an entrance, but any actor who carries a script with him on stage after the deadline has arrived, whether he uses it or not, should have it taken physically from him. In fact, the rehearsal should be stopped instantly when a forbidden playbook appears, and the assistant director should be sent up on stage to confiscate it. The interruption is valuable in making the enforcement of the policy visibly emphatic. If the actor protests that he cannot get through the scene without the script, he should be assured that he will be prompted as fully as necessary, even if the prompter must supply him with each line a phrase at a time—and that should then be done.

As in almost all of his relationships with actors, the director's enforcement of the drop-script rule should be clear and firm, but not punitive or unfriendly. Actors are likely to have less feeling of security than other people, and they are almost certain not to have become fully secure in their lines by the time they must surrender their scripts. It should be possible for the director to sympathize fully with their distress. The reason for the policy should have been made clear: that the remaining work will be severely hampered by scripts, a fact that even the most fearful actor is likely to recognize. If the actor is actually not ready to work without his script because he has neglected his study, then the necessity for constant prompting will painfully demonstrate that fact, and it is one of the strongest motivations for catching up with his work. Few actors who have gone through the agony of a rehearsal with every speech supplied by the prompter phrase by phrase ever show up at another rehearsal without their lines fully memorized. Of course, if an actor has been prevented from studying his lines by a serious illness or by other factors not subject to his control, his memorization schedule should be revised, and he should be given a later deadline. Preferably this should be done in advance of the deadline for dropping the script.

Constant prompting is as agonizing for the director as for the actor, not only because he empathizes with the actor's feelings, but because it involves repeated interruption of the flow of the rehearsal. The director should resist the temptation to suspend the memorization schedule and allow the actor to continue using his book, however faithfully he promises to complete his memorization by the following rehearsal. He is most unlikely to keep such a promise, and every other actor is certain to be late with his own memorization and to demand the same indulgence. Even if the work of one rehearsal is largely destroyed by adhering to the first deadline, it is better to sacrifice it than to weaken all of the rehearsals for the next two weeks.

PROMPTING

Prompting is one of the most difficult simple tasks in the theater. A good prompter makes rehearsals much more efficient, a bad prompter causes irritation and great loss of time. It is perfectly possible to run performances without a prompter. If cast members know they will not be prompted, experience indicates that they learn their lines. If they assume prompting, they at least subconsciously hold themselves to less rigid standards of memorization. If a prompter is used in performance, it is much better for him to serve at all rehearsals starting with the first at which one or more actors are required to perform without scripts. If performances are given without a prompter, the assistant director can prompt during rehearsals. He is needed to follow the blocking during the interpretation rehearsals, but he may be able to give his full attention to prompting during the rehearsals in which the actors experiment with techniques without seriously interfering with his other responsibilities. He is needed in later rehearsals to write down the director's instructions, but by that time prompting should be necessary only very occasionally.

If a prompter is to be used during the performances, he should sit in his position backstage for at least the last few rehearsals devoted to fixing and stabilizing the performances. At all other rehearsals (and at the last rehearsals, if prompting is dispensed with during performances), the prompter should sit out front, in the first or second row. Such prompting should be done full voice. Ideally, the prompter should read only when the actor has forgotten his line and should give the actor only the minimum section of the speech that he needs in order to continue. It is especially irritating to an actor to have a dramatic pause ruined by the prompter's shouting out the beginning of the next speech, when the actor has not forgotten it. These ideals are easier to state than to achieve in actual practice. As the actor develops his pattern of timing, the prompter should attempt to learn it, so that he knows when a pause is intended and when it is due to an inability to remember the speech. A good prompter should learn to empathize with the actors so that he can sense their struggles to remember speeches and can supply them with the shortest possible wait. Sitting out in front enables him to watch them more easily and to adjust to accidental variations in timing. If an actor should knock his coat off a chair and stoop to replace it, the prompter would then recognize the reason for the delay and would not intrude with an unnecessary prompt.

Even the best prompter finds it impossible to tell at what point in the line an actor's memory will begin to function again. The actor can indicate that best simply by beginning to speak the line as soon as it is clear, at which moment the prompter stops reading. Actors should be firmly warned against arguing or carrying on other unnecessary conversations with the prompter. Shouting "Line!" or commenting "I hadn't forgotten—I was pausing on purpose," or "That's enough—I've got it now" is disruptive to the rehearsal as a whole and involves a loss of characterization that few actors can restore immediately. Actors can hardly be blamed for such comments if the prompter functions badly, but the director should attempt to train him well and to suppress comments on the prompting by the actors.

Prompters are often unaware of their importance in rehearsal work. All good actors are sensitive to the speech of others and are likely to imitate the level of tension and meaning of speeches to which they must respond. Especially in the early rehearsals, a series of stumbling, uninflected, low-keyed prompts may steadily reduce the level of the actors' performances. A prompter cannot be expected to act the various roles, but he should read even a short phrase as meaningfully as possible, matching the timing and volume of the actors' speeches, to avoid making the rehearsals sag. In fact, since his voice comes from offstage, he should if anything speak with more vigor and clarity of enunciation than the actors themselves.

Besides filling in when actors have forgotten their lines, the prompter must occasionally interrupt to correct a misreading. What errors should be corrected and which allowed to pass without comment cannot be identified with precision, and different directors would make different rulings. Since the actors must recognize the cue for each speech, even a small error in a cue should be corrected from the beginning. Usually cues consist of the last phrase of the preceding speech; thus, if an actor's speech ends with the sentence "I'll see to it at once," and he misreads it "I'll see to it immediately," the prompter should correct him, since the actor who says the next speech might fail to recognize the altered cue. Similar errors within a speech should probably be let pass without comment, assuming that the actor will correct them during his study of his lines outside rehearsal. Of course an error that seriously affects the rehearsal should be corrected, for instance, if a large passage is skipped or if an actor replaces his line with a similar one from a different scene, thus jumping the cast into the wrong section of the play.

The prompter can also help by reading the entire speeches of actors who are absent. If the assistant director is not prompting, it may be better to ask him to fill in. If possible, it is preferable for the reader to work on stage and walk through the blocking as he reads the lines, but unless he can approximate the missing actor's positions fairly accurately it may be better for him to read from out front.

Actors are occasionally moved to assist in the prompting. This interference in the responsibilities of another member of the staff is as unacceptable, although not so disastrous, as an actor's attempting to do the work of the director, and should be firmly discouraged. Especially if no prompting is to be done during performances, it is important that the cast go through the last week of rehearsals without a prompter. Unofficial prompting during these rehearsals can have serious results by concealing the points at which memorization has been inadequate. If an actor cannot get through a scene on his own, the speeches that cause him difficulty must be identified for further work. If a breakdown is to occur, it should be during a rehearsal, not in performance. It is not difficult to understand the impulse that leads an actor to whisper a forgotten line to another in rehearsal, but it should be equally easy for the actor to understand that he is making it less rather than more likely that the performance will go smoothly.

THE ASSISTANT DIRECTOR

The work assigned to the assistant depends on the director's needs and methods. Some assistants are sensitive to the work being done and can anticipate the director's needs. If he is jotting down notes and comes to his last sheet of paper, he will discover that the assistant director has a new set of blank sheets ready for him. The assistant will turn house lights on and off as needed without special instructions. When the director needs a stand on which to spread out his notes while discussing them with the cast, he will find that his assistant has already moved one into the right position. Such an assistant is a jewel of great price, and not typical, although not so rare as to be astonishing.

The assistant can help distribute rehearsal schedules, scripts, and similar materials; he can see that a supply of pencils is available for the inevitable percentage of the cast who forget to bring them; he can warn actors who have stepped outside the theater, just before they are needed on stage; and he can handle many conferences with actors and technical people that do not require the director's attention. For instance, he can answer such questions as "What page are they on now?" and "Do you have any idea how long it will be till we get to my scene?" If the rehearsals are recorded, the assistant can set up the equipment at the beginning of each rehearsal, change tapes as needed, and store them at the end. The assistant should reach the theater a few minutes before the cast is scheduled to arrive, turn on the lights, and set the rehearsal furniture in place if it has been moved since the previous session; he also turns off the lights at the end of the rehearsal period.

After the rehearsals specifically devoted to blocking, he follows the script and the blocking diagrams and informs the director whenever errors occur. The director may delegate the correction of such errors to his assistant, so that in this respect he assumes a true directorial function. If the director finds it impossible to attend a rehearsal, the assistant can substitute for him, even though he will be unable to give the actors new instructions.

In the later rehearsals, after prompting has stopped, the assistant usually sits beside the director in the auditorium and jots down notes dictated to him by the director during the rehearsal. If the assistant is not serving as prompter, he may begin such note-taking much earlier in the series of rehearsals.

THE STAGE MANAGER

The work of the director and his assistant is essentially finished by the end of the last rehearsal; both may prefer to join the audience during the performances. Backstage efficiency requires that a few of the directorial functions be continued. Someone must check to make sure that all the actors have arrived at the theater and are ready to go on stage when they are needed; decisions about curtain time must be made and passed on to the light and sound crews; and one person must be invested with authority for handling unforeseeable emergencies. The stage manager is the staff member who carries out these functions.

Usually he will have little to do besides routine checking to make sure that the cast and technical staff are operating smoothly, but his authority is vitally important in time of crisis. If an actor should fall and injure himself backstage and be unable to go on, if a costume or property should have been lost, the fact that one person has been assigned responsibility for deciding how the problem should be handled ensures maximum efficiency and prevents the difficulty from growing to chaotic proportions. Sometimes the assistant director is also asked to serve as stage manager; more often someone else assumes the position. Since it is important that he be well acquainted with the show, he will need to attend the last ten or twelve rehearsals, and he should take over his duties beginning with the technical rehearsal.

DIRECTORIAL COMMENTS

The handling of the director's comments varies throughout the rehearsal period. During the blocking rehearsals, he can read the blocking directions to the actors as they move about the stage; more commonly each actor reads his own instructions out loud before making the crosses. Even so, the director is likely to be constantly involved in the procedure, correcting errors and making fine adjustments in the actors' positions.

The interpretation rehearsals also require constant participation on the part of the director. Each line is worked over individually, various interpretations are discussed, and different readings tried and analyzed. Since each act will be rehearsed at least twice in this group of rehearsals, it seems most effective for the director to work with the actors sentence by sentence during the first run-through, making comments during the second interpretation rehearsal for the act only at natural breaks in the action. The divisions may be very short, perhaps half a page, although they will not be uniform in length. If the development of interpretation has not proceeded far enough to justify running the rehearsal even in these short sections, then probably the sentence-by-sentence work should be continued and an additional rehearsal scheduled for the short-scene treatment.

The group of rehearsals in which the actors experiment in order to discover the techniques that will communicate the meaning and emotions of the lines to the audience should be conducted in essentially the same way. They may be worked over in short sections, or even speech by speech. In the second of the two rehearsals in this group given to a particular act, the actors should be allowed to continue without interruption longer than previously, in sections not much shorter than a page of the script. The longer these sections can be made the better, although there is no value in withholding assistance from actors who need it just to preserve an arbitrary formula.

With the start of the blending rehearsals, the director should no longer break into any structural unit of the play. If it is written in clearly marked scenes, like Noel Coward's *Blithe Spirit,* where the three acts are divided into seven scenes, the director is free to assemble the cast for comments at the breaks. No scene should be interrupted, however, that will be played continuously during the performance.

During the polishing rehearsals, comments should be given only where intermissions will occur in actual performance. During the fixing rehearsals, comments should be made only at the beginning or end of a rehearsal. Usually it is preferable to assemble the cast in the front rows of the auditorium at the end of the last act for an analysis of their work. If a rehearsal has lasted unusually late it is sometimes better to dismiss them and reserve the comments for the period just before the curtain rises at rehearsal the next evening.

The rule that late rehearsals should not be interrupted has one exception, the technical rehearsal, during which the work of the various crews is checked. Some technical problems may be reserved for the intermission breaks (if a property is put on the wrong table, for example). In other cases, solving them requires interrupting the rehearsal and perhaps running over a passage again. For instance, if the sound crew has difficulty in timing music or sound effects during one of the scenes it may be preferable to ask the actors to repeat it until the problems have been worked out. This rehearsal, however, is not part of the total pattern, but is inserted into it. The director does not analyze the actors' performances during this session and makes no comments on them.

The Length of Rehearsals

The length of rehearsals varies a great deal in different types of theaters, being longest in the commercial theater, and nearly as long in summer theaters. In civic and educational theaters, commentators are uniformly agreed that three hours is the ideal rehearsal length. It is very difficult to achieve clear progress during a shorter rehearsal, and fatigue appears very quickly during the fourth hour, with loss of energy, difficulty in concentration, weakening of memory, and failure in judgment. The reason professional actors can rehearse effectively for eight hours, whereas amateurs must stop at the end of three, is not so much the professionals' greater stamina as the fact that their entire energy during the day can be devoted to the rehearsal. The student, house-wife, or businessman who attends a community or college rehearsal has already put in a full day's work, so that the evening session stretches his day to ten or eleven hours, which may actually be longer rather than shorter than the professional actor's work day.

The director is more likely to feel the effects of an extended rehearsal than are the actors. Even a leading actor is unlikely to be on stage constantly throughout a rehearsal so that he has frequent rest periods, but the director must remain constantly alert during the entire evening. Even while an actor is on stage, the demands on his attention vary, so that while he must expend great energy he does not need to do so continuously, but can relax at least slightly while other actors are speaking. The director, on the other hand, must concentrate his attention on the play at the highest pitch of intensity throughout the entire rehearsal; he must analyze and evaluate and make decisions, all at great speed. Even with a three-hour rehearsal, it is often wise to insert two or three ten-minute breaks during which the director can rest, chat, and have a cup of coffee. When a director becomes overtired, not only does his judgment suffer but he is likely to find it impossible to keep his attention on the actors' performance; and while lapses of attention may not destroy the rehearsal, he is likely to miss essential points that should be worked on. It is embarrassing to be asked by an actor "Did I do that speech any better this time?" and have to confess "I'm sorry, but my mind went blank for a moment and I didn't hear it."

STANDARDS OF EFFORT

Even with rehearsals limited to three hours, actors can be expected to vary from evening to evening in the effectiveness of their work. Not only are actors probably inherently subject to greater swings in efficiency than other people, but experiences not related to the theater may affect their work: an incipient cold, a lovers' quarrel, "pulling an all-nighter" before a major examination, or getting a report card with six A's or an unexpected three-hundred-dollar check from home. A director should be prepared for apparently inexplicable changes in actors' effectiveness during a month's rehearsals. A sudden sag may be due to some outside factor, and often can best be handled not by increasing pressure on the actor but by reducing it. Certainly, if the director suspects that an actor may not be feeling well, he should ask him; and if the actor is overtired or disturbed by some event outside the theater, it is often best to suggest that he not force himself to great effort that evening. In that case, the director can concentrate on working with the other actors.

With such exceptions, every actor should be expected to do the best he can at each rehearsal. Occasionally a performer will ostentatiously "walk through" a rehearsal, displaying the fact that he is not trying. Intense effort is absolutely necessary for advancement in acting. If an actor does not feel that he has stretched himself a little farther than he could go during a rehearsal, it is extremely likely that he has achieved almost nothing during the session. In order to adapt himself to his role, to master new ways of moving and speaking, each actor must push his voice and his body out into patterns of use that are new to him. Ultimately it is hoped that constant practice will make them seem easy and automatic, but progress at least up to the polishing rehearsals is necessarily accompanied by a feeling of strain. If an actor feels relaxed and at ease, feels no sense of unusual effort, throughout an early rehearsal, then he is reperforming his part as Cyrano (or whatever his last role was), or, even worse, he is simply being himself on stage, and is consequently not acting at all.

Such an actor fails to develop his own role, but what is far more important, he weakens the performance of every other actor in the cast. Actors' sensitivity to others leads them to copy each other's methods of work. Experienced actors will recognize the problem and can be expected to supply extra effort to overcome the influence of the example provided by the careless performer; but it is improper for them to have to make such an effort, and their attention is distracted to some degree from their own performance. Furthermore, each speech is typically a response to the previous speech. If an actor must express surprise or anger, the previous speaker must usually have provided him with the stimulus for the emotion, against which he can throw his own line: each line is expected to motivate the next one. All the members of a cast tend, therefore, to improve throughout rehearsals as a group, and at something of the same rate: they pull themselves up by each other's bootstraps. When one actor achieves a strikingly effective reading of a particular line, the actor who replies to it finds his own reading improved and made easier, and the improvement extends to the third actor who speaks. The increase in momentum from such an improvement will often be visible even in later acts. A performer who consciously and intentionally does the least he can get by with, who fails to motivate the other speakers' lines, who drags down the rest of the cast rather than sharing in lifting the weight of the play as a whole, is guilty of one of the most extreme and inexcusable violations of theatrical etiquette.

A somewhat more difficult problem is the actor who performs ineffectively and who may seem not to be trying when he is actually struggling to do his best. If an actor is cast in a part that he cannot handle, even with the intensest effort, that is extremely unfortunate, but the only person who can properly be blamed is the director himself for having made an error in casting. There may be some justification for the director's being irritated with himself, although no director is infallible and every director makes errors in casting occasionally; but there is no justification whatever for his being irritated in the slightest with the actor, assuming that he is actually doing his best.

This problem is not limited to performers who have little potential as actors. Especially in the educational theater, beginning actors of great ability may work ineffectively simply because they have not yet learned efficient methods, or have not gained control of their voices and bodies. Even more experienced actors may be so greatly inhibited by fear—simple stage fright, or fear of a demanding role, especially if it is their first lead part—that they may be unable to function. In a recent production, one actress playing her first lead was so terrified by her climactic speech, the most important speech in the play, that she could not force herself to go straight through it during one of the middle rehearsals, and repeated passages and insisted on stopping to rethink what she was doing so frequently that she stretched the three-minute speech to twenty minutes. After the rehearsal she thanked the director for not having expressed his impatience with her. "But I never felt any impatience," he replied. "You were trying as hard as you could try, weren't you? I would certainly be unreasonable if I got impatient with an actor who was doing his absolute best. I must say I suffered, but I was with you all the way, and I knew you would make it."

In the same production, one actor had a very strong supporting role that he did not handle well. The director worked with him intensively for three weeks, assuming, since he had never directed the actor before, that he was doing his best to master the part. One evening the actor casually remarked that he had not yet begun to work on the play. He had not started to memorize his lines, had not analyzed them for characterization, and had not worked out their meaning or emotions. He was replaced in the cast the next day, on the grounds that an actor who would not do his best was unusable. Incidentally, the other actors were so appalled at this admission of negligence that the director was criticized, not for dropping him from the cast but for waiting twenty-four hours to do it.

A bricklayer who was hired to build a wall and spent his hours of work sitting on the pile of bricks reading comic books could hardly expect to be paid or retained. An actor who does the best he can must be helped as fully as possible; one who intentionally does much less than his best should have the requirements of his assignment explained to him, and then, if he indicates he does not choose to carry them out, should be expelled from the play.

The failure of an actor to carry his share of the performance is serious enough, but the attempt by a performer to make himself look better by damaging the work of other cast members is inexcusable. The classic devices used to achieve such an effect are upstaging other actors, to force them to weaken their positions by turning away from the audience, and stealing the attention from them by introducing irrelevant and distracting business. Even more sinister methods are sometimes used: giving fellow actors clandestine backstage advice on their performances, actually designed to weaken them; attempting to demoralize them or increase their stage fright. Such behavior fails to achieve its purpose. The result is not to enhance the offender's performance but to sabotage the play as a whole, in which case he suffers along with the rest of the cast. Fortunately this most serious offense is extremely rare, but if it should occur, it must be dealt with instantly and with the greatest firmness. Such a performer should never be considered for any later play unless he is able to provide overwhelming evidence of reform.

Anything that disrupts the work of rehearsals should be corrected, whether it is absence, tardiness, loud conversation, or playing the piano. It is very important, however, to distinguish between intentional and accidental or thoughtless disruption. A group of actors clustered around the piano singing while waiting for the rest of the cast to arrive may continue past the time set for beginning the rehearsal, not because they intend to disrupt it but simply because they fail to watch the clock. It should be the assistant director's responsibility to remind actors a moment or two before the rehearsal is scheduled to start, either by speaking to them or by striking a bell.

During the rehearsal, the director must not mistake high spirits for negligence. Especially when actors have been working intensely at the top of their range of effort, they may break into apparently disruptive horseplay. If the director stops a scene to make comments to one of the actors, the other members of the cast may almost instantaneously begin playing games of pantomime, pretended fist fights, or start humming and dancing at the back of the stage. Even while a scene is in progress, some slip of the tongue or error in business may be picked up by the cast as a whole, and the rest of the scene turned into a hilarious burlesque of itself. The tape recording of one rehearsal of a Shakespearean play startles everyone who listens to it when the entire cast suddenly begin making enthusiastic Tarzan calls.

Such episodes may lay waste to the director's immediate comments and may seem to send the play crashing in a tangled mass across the stage. They can be suppressed by sufficient firmness and condemnatory violence on the part of the director. These interruptions, however, may be beneficial rather than harmful. They are most likely to occur with a cast that has been stretching itself to the breaking point; casual and careless actors seldom indulge in such antics. They may well be a valuable indication to the director that it is time for a brief rehearsal break. He may himself be as badly in need of a respite as the cast, perhaps without having realized it. It is usually better for the director to relax and enjoy the fun, and call time out for general coffee. If his dignity will stand it, he might join in with a Tarzan yell or two himself. The inexperienced director is likely to feel that he has lost all control of the rehearsal at such a moment, but a little experience will demonstrate that more may be accomplished at rehearsals when actors feel unconstrained and easy than if an artificial and rigid uniformity of behavior is enforced.

A general failure to pay attention at rehearsals, to stretch toward a greater and greater mastery of their roles, is inexcusable in actors, and should be attacked by the director with all the force and persuasiveness he can command; but a cast that has been working at top level for more than an hour has earned a few minutes relief, and the director should grant it, not as an indulgence but as a real contribution to the total efficiency of the rehearsal. Nor will the director's authority or the actors' respect for him have been in any way reduced; if anything, they will be increased by his understanding of their response to the work of rehearsal.

4

Training the Actors

11/Using the Body

The director's work with the actors requires a larger share of his time than any other single task. It is also the most varied, interesting, difficult, and rewarding of his activities.

If the director and actor are to function effectively, each must understand his own responsibilities clearly, and must carry them out to the best of his ability. Each must avoid attempting to work in areas which are assigned to the other. Activities of director and actor are so closely fitted together that it is difficult to trace the dividing line between them, and productions are sometimes weakened because actors attempt to handle work for which the director is responsible and neglect parts of their own assignment because they are unaware of them.

THE RELATIONSHIP BETWEEN THE WORK OF ACTORS AND DIRECTOR

Clarifying the two areas may be assisted by an analogy. A familiar amusement for children makes use of sheets of paper with a series of dots scattered across the surface; when straight lines are drawn from dot to dot in the right order a picture develops; it is possible to complete it by coloring in the areas with crayon.

The work of the playwright is analogous to that of the designer of such a picture. He supplies a very large number of specific points, which are recorded in the playscript. The most detailed script, however, has many gaps in it, which must be filled in before the picture is complete.

The director's first task is to identify the position of each part of the picture that the playwright has given. He then completes the outline by

269

filling in the missing lines, so as to trace the connections between the various points. His contribution to the picture is extensive, but the finished outline must incorporate all the data that the playwright has supplied. In addition, he selects the general color scheme to be used in finishing the picture.

The actor is concerned only with one of the characters shown in the picture, the one which he will represent in the finished production. Taking the outline provided by the director, he analyzes the script in order to identify all the points that lie within the outline of his character. He carefully places these inside that outline, and then draws in the lines that show the connections between the various points. Finally, the picture of his character is rounded and finished by coloring it in harmony with the scheme specified by the director.

All of this work is difficult, and different people vary greatly in their ability to handle it, with resulting variations in the completed production. Some actors and directors are much more perceptive than others. One director reading a script may be able to identify three times as many specific items of information as a less sensitive, less intelligent, or less experienced director. The various points are not clearly marked, as they are in the child's dot-drawing. Many will be indicated by a single phrase in a long speech and might easily be missed; some may even consist of the use of one word rather than another; for example, the fact that Cleopatra never uses the word "wife" is of considerable significance. Furthermore, the points are not numbered, so that only a close analysis will reveal which are related and should be joined by an added line. Cleopatra's awkward avoidance of the word "wife" in the first scene of Shakespeare's play is matched by her use of the word "husband" in the last scene. The use and the avoidance are significantly connected, and if an actress is to say either line effectively she must have discovered this connection and practiced to express it. It must be included in her picture of Cleopatra.

> *Many plays—certainly mine—are like blank checks. The actors and directors put their own signatures on them.*
>
> THORNTON WILDER

Both director and actor must add greatly to the data supplied by the playwright. Using a slightly different figure, the script can be thought of as the blueprint for a building, the performance being the finished structure; although the shape of the completed building is dependent on the blueprint, they are very different in appearance. In fact, far more than half of what the audience sees and hears is supplied by the director and actors. The script is hardly even an outline of the production; it becomes complete only when it has been fully drawn by the director, and colored, rounded, and embodied by the actors. All that they add, however, must be in harmony with the playwright's specifications. The effectiveness of the final production is thus very largely dependent on the richness of imagination of the director and actors, and its harmony (or unity) depends to a great extent on their esthetic taste.

Bernard Shaw has said that at the first rehearsal the director should know more about each character than the actor who plays it; at the last rehearsal the actor should know much more about his character than the director. The picture analogy explains why that is true.

The relation of director and actor to stage movement is also clarified by this analogy. Since the blocking pattern expresses the relationships among the characters in the play and involves the picture as a whole, it is the responsibility of the director to design it. Business and gesture involve only the individual actor, so that developing them is primarily his responsibility rather than the director's.

Since the clear definition of the directorial function hardly more than a hundred years ago, the organizational position of the director has become so generally accepted that beginning actors often understand subservience to the director as constituting their total responsibility. As one actor said, "When the director tells you to jump, you jump, and ask which direction on the way up." The picture of the actor as an unresisting puppet who moves only when the director pulls the strings is unrealistic and tends to weaken productions to which it is applied. Not only does a director not have time to make the actors' decisions for them, but their perceptiveness, imagination, and varied points of view are important sources of strength for a production, which are lost to it if the actors sedulously inhibit them. If any actor has not filled in his role with more detail and color than the director has been able to supply—if he does not know more about his part than the director—by the beginning of the third week of rehearsals, then he has not done his job.

The responsibilities of the actor are so great, the amount of analysis and the number of decisions he must make are so staggering, that few things are more frightening to a director than the display by an actor of an attitude of subservience and passivity. No director wants to be addressed by an actor in the terms of the old hymn:

> Have thine own way;
> Thou art the potter, I am the clay;
> Mold me and make me after thy will,
> Here I am waiting yielded and still.

A passive actor is no actor at all—at best he is an awkward puppet. The job of the actor requires the most vigorous activity, an attitude of aggressiveness, and the application of the highest analytical intelligence, emotional sensitivity, and inventiveness.

Dictating the Blocking Instructions

Blocking is studied early in the rehearsal period. If the blocking instructions have been typed into the script, the cast can go on stage immediately and start rehearsal. If the instructions do not appear in the script, they must be dictated to the cast. All of the instructions needed for the current rehearsal should be dictated before they begin their walk-through. The cast should be assembled in the front rows of the auditorium, and the instructions read off, either by the director or his assistant. Each actor need write down only those instructions involving him, so that much of the time it will be possible to read at great speed. While an actor is copying the instructions for one speech, those for the next speech can be dictated to the second actor. When one character dominates a scene, the intervening speeches may be too short for the actor to complete his notes, and it will be necessary to wait until he has finished before going on to his next speech.

It is important that each instruction be copied accurately, and that the point in the dialog at which each action is to begin be clearly marked. It is best to identify the cue point first; the actor should then be instructed to draw a line from this point in the script to the margin and write in the blocking direction. The traditional abbreviations should be explained before the dictation begins, and the necessity for copying the directions exactly as read should be emphasized.

Rehearsing the Blocking

When the blocking has been recorded, the actors should go on stage and rehearse it.

All scenic elements that affect the blocking should be supplied for this rehearsal, or at least be marked on the floor. Preparing the stage for the first blocking rehearsal is the responsibility of the technical director. Masking tape or chalk lines can be used to show the position of walls and entrances, as well as any parts of the scenery that actors must use, such as windows or fireplaces. If they are only decorative, if, for example, actors do not look out of windows or place objects on the mantel, they may be omitted. The heights of any levels above the stage floor should be marked. Furniture should be supplied that approximates the size and shape of the pieces to be used in the performance. It is customary to represent davenports by armless chairs set side by side.

It is an enormous advantage to have stairs and platforms already in place. Actors may be able to pantomime stepping up on a low platform, and to imagine small variations in level, but it is very difficult for them to simulate walking up a flight of stairs represented only by an outline on the floor of the stage. Especially if a very high platform appears in the set, which actors must walk both on and under, blocking is almost impossible without the full structure.

Even with minor changes in level, actors will find it difficult to synchronize their movements properly with the speeches. An actor who has rehearsed a cross requiring five steps on the stage floor may find it disconcerting, when the levels are supplied, to discover that he must take seven steps. Not only is the movement changed, but the phrasing of the speech often must be revised. From the director's point of view, it is difficult to evaluate a blocking design intended to show the actors at different heights when they are all actually at stage level.

It is customary for scenery to be supplied only during the last week of rehearsals. There seems no compelling reason why it cannot be completed before the first rehearsal; the only real change would be rescheduling the work of design and construction; the tradition of building a set during the month of rehearsals has few inherent advantages.

Of course, if the theater is also used for performances in music or public speaking (a most unsatisfactory arrangement), it may not be possible to erect the scenery before the rehearsals begin. In the professional theater, for reasons of economy, all but the last few rehearsals are held off stage, usually in a different building. This practice is such a severe handicap to cast and director that it should be followed only in case of dire necessity. Unfortunately it is sometimes impossible to rehearse on stage even in community or college productions, but such theaters lack adequate facilities, and such makeshift procedures should be tolerated only until the theater plant can be improved to meet minimum standards. If a substitute room must be used for rehearsal, it is extremely important that it be large enough to mark the outline of the full set with masking tape. Actors cannot memorize blocking effectively if the rehearsal space is smaller than the actual set, and synchronizing blocking and speeches correctly is impossible. Shifting from a small rehearsal room to the full stage results in a number of problems, which require at least two extra rehearsals to solve.

Some directors prefer to have the actors skip through the lines, reading only the blocking cues. Little time is saved by skipping, and a full reading increases the actors' acquaintance with the lines and is necessary for the synchronization of movements and speeches. For the first time through, it is desirable for the actors to stand still and read each blocking instruction out loud, and then continue with the speech as they move. It is nearly impossible for actors to follow the instructions while they read them, and having them read out loud makes it possible to check the accuracy with which they have been copied.

It is impossible to state blocking directions with absolute precision. If an actor is instructed to "X 3 steps DL" (cross three steps down left), his final position may vary as much as a foot or two, depending on the length of his stride. Sometimes such variation may not be significant, but at other times a cross a little longer or shorter than was planned may leave him in an awkward position with regard to a piece of furniture, or may result in his partially covering another actor, so that an adjustment is necessary. The rehearsal should also be used to check the director's decisions. Some details of his design are almost certain to appear different when he sees them on stage from what he had imagined. He can therefore expect to need to make constant adjustments, in order to correct his own errors, to refine directions, and to assist actors who are not yet familiar with stage geography.

It is easiest to direct this rehearsal if the director stands on the auditorium floor, just in front of the stage. His script and blocking diagrams can be laid on the stage for easy reference. It is a great help for the assistant director to stand beside him and follow the script and diagrams, turning the pages as needed. Since he will be asked to assume responsibility for checking the blocking at an early rehearsal, this gives him an opportunity to become familiar with the blocking designs.

The actor's first responsibility with regard to blocking is to record the pattern accurately and then memorize it. Since it is primarily learned kinesthetically, his study of it is done mainly on stage during rehearsals. The blocking rehearsals enable him to concentrate his full attention on his movements and positions during two rehearsals of each act. That is not enough to fix the pattern completely in his mind, but although his attention is turned to the interpretation of the lines during the next six rehearsals, the assistant director checks the blocking throughout each run-through, and corrects any errors as they appear, so that the actors' practice of the blocking continues until it has been fully learned.

Motivating Blocking

The actor is also responsible for working the blocking into the total pattern of his character as he develops it. He does that primarily by devising a motivation for each blocking direction. If the movements have been well planned, they will synchronize naturally with the speeches and will assist the actor in expressing the meaning and emotions indicated by his lines. If one of his speeches requires that he display a delayed reaction to the preceding remark, the director might block the line so that he walks away from the previous speaker for a step or two, stops as he realizes what has been said, and then turns back toward the first actor to respond. In a quarrel scene, the blocking pattern might provide a number of points at which the dominant actor can step forward toward the person he is quarreling with, to emphasize the aggressiveness of his lines. Careful study of the blocking instructions will thus reveal a clear motivation for most of the movements. It will be seen that they assist in expressing the lines, and if the actor walks through the movements, or even vividly imagines them, as he studies his lines, he will memorize both together. Instead of requiring additional study time, the blocking will actually speed up his memorization of the lines themselves.

Sometimes the blocking created for a part will seem awkward and unnatural to the actor. This may be an indication that the movements have been badly designed, although that is likely to be exceptional. The critical question, of course, is not whether the movements are natural to the actor but whether they are natural to the character he is representing. For an actor to object to strutting about the stage and engaging in swordfights on the grounds that he himself would not behave in that way is absurd if he is playing the part of Cyrano. If careful analysis leads the actor to feel that his blocking is unsuited to the character, then the problem should be discussed with the director. Of course, if the actor is simply incapable of making a particular movement, it will be necessary to alter it, whether it is suited to the character or not. An unusual example is an actor who received a head injury in a sports event during the period of work on a play. At one point the blocking design specified that two actresses should catch his arms and whirl him around several times, but his accident had left him dizzy, and he could not maintain his balance during the whirling scene, so that the blocking at this point was redesigned for his benefit.

It is very common for actors to have difficulty adjusting blocking to speeches because the movements specified seem excessive in number or speed. In this case it is most likely that the speeches involve more tension and excitement than the actor realizes. When the director's blocking seems to require a higher degree of activity than the speeches support, the actor should restudy the lines very carefully to make sure that he has not missed levels of meaning and emotion that, when fully expressed, will match the intensity of the movement.

This kind of analysis should take care of nearly all the blocking specifications; however, there will be a few that cannot be easily motivated by the obvious implications of the lines. In preparing the blocking designs, the director is concerned not simply with the meaning of each role, but with the play as a whole, and particularly with the experience provided for the audience. When an actor is dominant in a scene, the director will place him in a strong position. If he has a subordinate role in the following scene, it will be necessary to move him to a weaker position and to strengthen the position of the newly dominant actor. If an important character is to come bursting through an entrance and run to the fireplace, then a path must be cleared for him before the cue for his entrance. The blocking for each play must satisfy hundreds of such requirements, which regularly involve movements of actors that do not spring automatically from their own lines. Since such movements are more difficult to manage, the director will hold them to a minimum, but even so, every actor can be expected to find a sizable number included in his blocking instructions.

These movements, too, must be motivated if they are to seem natural to the audience. Finding reasons for his character to move in such cases tests the actor's ingenuity. Essentially, he must add a new line to his dot picture in an area that the playwright has left open. The solutions to this problem cannot be described in terms of a principle or pattern, but a few illustrations can be given. If an actor must cross three or four feet down right on a speech that does not clearly motivate such a change in position, the actor might insert a sharp break in the middle of a phrase or clause and cross slowly as if struggling for a word, then at the end of the cross turn back and finish the line. If the line is accompanied by an emotion of moderate strength, it may be possible for him to intensify the emotion, perhaps starting a speech or two earlier, and build to a pitch that will enable him to suggest that his movement is a restless response to the strength of his emotion. If his cross takes him toward a table or a fireplace, he might look for a moment earlier in the scene when he was close to the spot to lay his pipe on the table or mantel; then when he must make the artificial cross, he can walk over and pick up the pipe, supplying a visible motivation. If the cross takes him closer to another actor, it may be possible for him to direct the last part of his line to him, or to turn to him as if to check his response. If all else fails, he may be able to lengthen other movements so as to get close to his final position in advance, so that only a single step is needed for the last cross.

It is the actor's responsibility to work out a clear motivation for each of his blocking instructions. If he is unable to devise an effective motivation even after concentrated analysis, he should make a note of the problem and ask the director for help at the next rehearsal. If the actors have done their work well, it will be necessary for the director to resolve only a few blocking difficulties. Obviously, if the actors do not meet their responsibilities, but rely on the director to supply most or all of their blocking motivations, he will have time for nothing else. In this, as in most aspects of his work, the actor must function actively and aggressively: the actor who waits passively to be prodded is simply not doing his job.

If an actor fails to handle the motivation of his blocking adequately, either through negligence or because of inexperience, it is helpful to assign him to write down a clear statement of his character's reason for each cross specified for him in one scene. This exercise forces him to make firm decisions and provides a record that the director can analyze with him in an attempt to discover the source of his difficulty. Probably it is better to carry on the analysis in an individual conference during the day, rather than taking rehearsal time for it. Usually one such session will give the actor a clear enough understanding of the process of motivating movements so that he will be able to handle the rest of the play satisfactorily without further help.

MAKING MOVEMENT COMMUNICATIVE

The development of motivations for movements and the memorization of the blocking are only two of three steps which must be taken in handling the body on stage. The third consists of learning to perform the positions on stage. Even a bedridden invalid could carry out the first two steps, but they become part of the play only when they are physically displayed by the actor to the audience.

The purpose of a theatrical performance is to provide an experience for the audience—intellectual, emotional, esthetic, or sensory—all at once, or in any combination. That intended experience is the criterion by which all technical questions must be tested, and this principle has several corollaries. One is that all that exists in a play is what the audience can see or hear: if they can neither see it nor hear it, it does not exist—is not part of the play. If an actor clenches his fist to express anger, the gesture is part of the play only if the audience can see it; if it is hidden by his body, it does not exist in the play. A movement which the audience cannot guess the meaning of has no meaning for them; if it is intended to communicate an idea, then the idea simply does not exist in the play.

This principle is so obvious that beginning actors often overlook it. An actor in one production who was asked by the director to portray more intense anger replied, "But I'm feeling just as angry as I know how." Feeling an emotion is not enough; it must be displayed to the audience.

In ordinary life, movement is nearly always purposeful. Most often we cross a room to look out a window, to adjust a crooked picture, to pick up the newspaper, or to answer the telephone. Some movements depend on inner motivations that do not involve present external objects: the pacing of an expectant father in the hospital corridor; getting up and sitting down, picking up a magazine and tossing it down, while waiting for the dentist, or an appointment with the boss, or a conference with the high school principal; strolling along a street for the simple pleasure of enjoying the summer air. In other cases, the motivations may be weak or conflicting, so that the movements are erratic or difficult to interpret.

But it is not enough for the actor to have found or devised an acceptable motive for a cross; if it is to function in the play it must be communicated to the audience. It is not enough for the actress playing Hedda Gabler to hide Lövborg's manuscript when she hears someone coming in through the front hall; she must display to the audience the fact that she is hiding it. Her movements must be planned so that they say to the audience, "Look: I have this manuscript in my hand, and I am anxious that no one know about it. Someone is coming in the hall, and I am frightened that he might see me holding the manuscript. I must find a place to hide it very quickly. Look: I am hiding it behind the sofa! Now I am hurrying back to the fireplace and trying to assume a carelessly negligent air so that whoever is coming in will not suspect that something important has been going on." The stage direction reads: "Hedda X L to sofa, hides manuscript on floor behind upstage end of sofa, X back to L end of fireplace." The difference between the work of the director and the actor is vividly illustrated by that small example. The director plans the path of movement and records it in the stage direction; the actor must determine why the character makes the movement, what it is designed to indicate, and then must find physical techniques which will express its meaning (intellectual and emotional) so clearly that no member of the audience will miss it. Actors who complain that a director's blocking has left them no decisions to make on their own do not understand acting.

Theater movement, then, like most movements in life, is motivated. It differs from ordinary life in that it must be clear, communicative, and visible to the entire audience. In order to provide those characteristics, a number of helpful hints to directors and actors have been developed. Any rule is subordinate to the purposes it serves, and although these rules assist, in the majority of instances, in producing the effect that is desired, directors should feel free to suspend them whenever an exception seems preferable. Since they apply so frequently, however, a good deal of time can be saved if they are taught to actors during rehearsals. They will then take care of most situations, and only the exceptional cases need be discussed.

Every movement should be sharply defined; a movement should begin sharply, be carried on vividly, and end definitely. If an actor who is standing by a bookcase is instructed to walk to the center of the stage, he should not ooze into the movement and then fade it out at the end. When he is standing still he should be standing completely still. He should take his first step firmly and crisply, should continue without hesitation to stage center, and should stop without slowing down. Even the smallest cross, in which the actor takes a single step and then brings his second foot up beside the other, should be done with crispness and clarity. Sometimes of course an actor is asked to communicate indecision or reluctance, and may need to creep forward with slow steps; even such a cross should be made with clear definition. When a broad movement is made up of two or three distinguishable elements, when, for instance, an actor walks toward a window, glances out, and then turns back to comment on what he has seen, the separate parts of the action should be distinctly marked. The actor should make his cross: then glance out: and then turn back, as three distinguishable actions. When a walk ends with a turn, the two actions should not be so faded together as to be indistinguishable.

These examples assume that the various movements are intended to be noticed by the audience, and that they are intended to be meaningful and communicative. If it is hoped that the audience will not notice a movement or part of a movement, then the rule would not apply. Occasionally, for instance, an actor may be instructed to walk and turn, not as an expressive gesture intended to communicate an emotion to the audience, but simply to take up a more effective position for a later speech. In that case, the two actions should be smoothly and unobtrusively integrated. In other words, blending tends to prevent the audience from noticing movements. If that is the purpose, then it should be used; but if a movement is intended to communicate something important to the play, then it must be marked for them.

The director's test for actors' use of their bodies on stage is to determine what purpose their postures, gestures, business, or crosses are intended to serve, and then to watch to see whether the desired effect is actually produced. If an actress slips along the back wall of the set and peers eagerly through a slit in the curtain to watch a fascinating family quarrel taking place next door, the director should check to make sure that her movements are visible to the audience—that everyone can see her hand as she pulls the curtains open an inch, and that her posture and the direction in which she is looking express her prying interest in her neighbors as clearly as possible. If they do not, or if he believes that the business could be made more effective, he should suggest alternative techniques.

BLOCKING RULES

In real life people almost never walk backward or sideways; beginning actors do it constantly in the theater. Especially after they have just learned to direct their playing toward the audience, they may maintain a frontal position rigidly. Watching a novice actor sidle crablike halfway across the stage with his face turned directly front and apparently unconcerned with where he is going or what might lie in his path is an unnerving experience. For such actors, it is useful to state as a rule, "Always look where you are going; never back up; never walk sideways." Again, such a rule can be effectively suspended, perhaps dozens of times within a single play. These movements are appropriate whenever they would be so in ordinary life: an actor involved in a quarrel might well back up nervously as his opponent pushes toward him; an actor standing in front of a door might step to the side and open it as an actress approaches to exit. Such actions are so reasonable that they seldom become problems; the difficulty arises when actors move in ways that are unlikely in ordinary situations, and the rule is a useful one in helping them correct what is a strangely widespread tendency.

Most of the rules governing actors' movements are specific applications of the principle that the actor must be displayed to the audience as clearly as possible—that an open turn should be preferred to a closed, for example, and that an actor should gesture with his upstage hand when possible.

Suspending Movement

Since movement attracts attention so powerfully, it is a rule that no actor should move except the one who should be the focus of the audience's interest, that is in almost every case an actor should move only when he himself is speaking. (When an actor moves as he speaks, the movement is said to be "on his line.") Actors are regularly told to "freeze" when another actor is speaking. The principle is sound, but the verb suggests an ostentatious rigidity, when instead its purpose is to avoid attracting the attention of the audience. The actors' postures should be easy and natural. If a member of the audience should happen to glance at one of them, he should see nothing strange in the actor's appearance. Almost equally important in maintaining focus on the actor who is performing at the moment is for all of the other actors to turn their eyes toward him. Occasionally a character's relationship to the speaker may require him to turn away, but as a rule all of the actors on stage should watch the one who is important at the moment. Then, if the eyes of a member of the audience should stray to one of the silent actors, he is most likely to follow his gaze to the desired point of attention.

Figure 39a. Suspending movement. The four actors at the left freeze to focus attention on the actor at stage right, who is most important to the scene at the moment. [*A Thurber Carnival;* photograph by Norm Burlingame]

Figure 39b. The soldiers, Lycus, Pseudolus, and Hysterium stop moving so that the audience's attention will be caught by the gesture and speech of Miles Gloriosus. [*A Funny Thing Happened on the Way to the Forum;* photograph by Douglas R. Hux]

Figure 39c. This moment in the play is unusual in that the movement involves two actors, Gymnasia's swing of the hip, and Pseudolus's reaction of falling off his stool. The other actors stop their crosses and gestures, so as not to distract the audience. [*A Funny Thing Happened on the Way to the Forum;* photograph by Douglas R. Hux]

This suspension of activity except for the single actor who is carrying on the story of the play at the moment is one of the many artificialities of theater art, although even in ordinary life a speaker tends to be more mobile than a listener. An actor often feels awkward and conspicuous when he freezes. The director can support the rule with two suggestions: If the actor will try to assume a relaxed position suited to the character he will feel less constrained; and so long as he remains quiet, he will be unnoticed by anyone in the audience.

The Continuity of Speech

The communicative function of movement and business is real, but it is likely to operate below the level of full awareness; the major expression of ideas and emotions is provided by the speeches, the movements being supplementary. For that reason, few movements will sustain interest effectively enough to be presented alone; they can rarely be expected to carry the whole burden of the show, even for a brief moment. That fact is expressed in the rule that every movement must be made on a speech, not between speeches.

This rule is subject to constant violation. Every experienced director can remember dozens of instances in which a movement or piece of business carried out in absolute silence provided a climactic moment for a performance, rather than allowing the interest to sag as the rule would suggest. One critic identified as a high point in a production of Shaw's *Saint Joan* a brief moment when Joan entered after having been released from prison, walked silently to the center of the stage, and looked at a tree. Obviously only a very great actress could make that simple cross communicative enough to hold the attention, but it is easy to imagine that, with high skill, it could vividly express Joan's delight at getting out of her dungeon and being able to look at nature again.

One director blocked *The Taming of the Shrew* with continuous fast movement, almost all of it played on the lines, so that there was seldom a moment of silence. In the contest scene at the end of the play, however, when suspense had been built up to a high pitch over whether Katharine would appear at Petruchio's summons or not, the actors were instructed to perform a series of movements in total silence. As the messenger ran up the stairs to summon Katharine, the men stood waiting for her answer. When the silence had become unbearable, they all turned very slowly and looked up toward the top of the stairs, where either Katharine or the messenger would appear. They held this position for an additional long wait, while suspense continued to build. Finally, when the pause had been stretched almost to the breaking point, Katharine appeared in the entrance, moved slowly to the head of the stairs, curtsied gracefully to Petruchio, and said sweetly, "What is your will, sir, that you send for me?" He instructed her to go get the other two brides and she exited. Baptista, Vincentio, and Lucentio simultaneously sank stunned on their stools, at which point the audience burst into laughter. In this case, the effectiveness of the business and the response of the audience were dependent on the exceptionally long pause, interrupted only by the men's turning and Katharine's entrance. It is also worth noting that the pause was strongly emphasized by preceding it with a steady stream of sound and movement and by stretching it as far as possible.

However frequent such examples may be, they are always exceptional. Unless especially instructed to carry on a particular cross or piece of business in silence, actors should be trained to follow the basic rule that all movement must be done on the speeches.

SYNCHRONIZING MOVEMENT AND SPEECH

A major concern of the actor, starting with the technique rehearsals, is achieving a precise synchronization of blocking and lines. No movement should require a longer time than its accompanying line. If it did, the movement would have to be completed in silence or during the first part of the next actor's speech—both unacceptable. When an actor exits at the end of a line, he should be speaking the last word as he crosses the threshold, he should not have to make a three-foot cross in silence after the line has been completed. If it has been planned that an actor cross to a certain point on stage during the first half of a line, and then stop and turn in order to punctuate and emphasize the rest of the speech, it is important that he reach the position for his turn at exactly the right moment. The director must have considered synchronization problems throughout his work on the blocking and may have tested his plans by speaking critical lines as he walked through the movements. The greatest care, however, will not always produce an accurate matching. The actor may walk or speak at a different rate from the one the director has imagined. When blocking and speeches are not synchronized, the actor must adjust them until they match, or the blocking must be redesigned. Probably each solution is adopted in about half the cases that appear. Sometimes it is possible to compromise by making small adjustments in both the actor's timing and the blocking.

These problems should be solved as quickly as possible. Effective use of the blocking design, enriched by business and gesture invented by the actor, can assist him greatly in making the lines more expressive and meaningful; so long as blocking and lines are in conflict, little progress can be made.

CLARIFYING CONFUSED MOVEMENT

A peculiar fact appears in scenes involving extremely fast action—chase scenes, fist fights, high-spirited romping: If they are played at the same speed as similar actions outside the theater, they will seem hopelessly confused, chaotic, and meaningless to the audience, no matter how precisely they have been blocked. As a result, it may be stated as a rule that all extremely fast action must be played slowly. That is something of an overstatement. Such scenes are, of course, played faster than others in the production, but when they are timed properly, they are likely to appear slow to the actors. This rule is based on the principle that all actions must be clearly defined, not blurred or fused together, and that a series of actions must be presented in identifiable sequence. The test is to view the scene from the audience. If it is clear what is going on and the action does not seem slow, it is all right; if the action is confused and meaningless, the scene should be slowed slightly and each individual bit of business more sharply defined. Of course, if the effect desired is one of meaningless confusion the rule would not apply.

The Subliminal Communication of Visual Elements

Beginning actors sometimes express surprise at the minuteness of detail that a director asks them to control. They may be asked to make fine adjustments in posture or placement that they correctly feel the audience will not be aware of, and they may ask if such planning is not wasted. A very great number of elements in a production function below the threshold of awareness; but far from being negligible, their influence on the effectiveness of the production may be enormous. To some extent, their strength derives from the very fact that the audience is not consciously aware of them. An earlier chapter included a discussion of the influence on audience attention of shifts in lighting so subtle that the audience was not conscious of them, even though they responded to them. The listeners may not notice the background music supporting the mood of a love scene. They may not hear it begin, may not be aware of it during the scene, and may not notice when it fades out, and yet the effectiveness of the performance may be increased significantly by the music. It has been argued that one of the major subarts of the theater, set design, should regularly function below the level of consciousness, at least that the attention of the audience should never be focused on the scenery itself; yet the support that an outstanding set can give actors is undeniable.

The Visual Communication of Personality and Emotion

The impression created by an actor depends primarily on the larger effects, of which the audience can be expected to be aware, but the subliminal elements bulk very large in the total impression, accounting for nearly a third of it. Everyone has had the experience of walking into a crowded room, glancing across at some stranger, and receiving an immediate impression of his personality, perhaps even before such details as hair or skin coloring have been consciously identified. This flash impression may sometimes prove to be false, but often it may be perfectly correct. It is due to a number of clues responded to subliminally without being individually noted. Among these factors, the posture and the pattern of muscular tension and relaxation are very important, especially in suggesting general emotional patterns. When we see one stranger as an easy-going, good-humored person, and another as a tense, irritable, defensive person, we are usually interpreting subtle details of muscular tension.

It is part of familiar experience that immediate emotions can be recognized by their accompanying muscular patterns: a stormy frown, a broad smile, a hearty laugh, embarrassment, fear—all of these emotions may be apparent even through a closed window.

It is not so generally realized, however, that what might be called permanent emotions are also expressed muscularly. Not only does each person display a shifting sequence of temporary emotions, but he gradually evolves his own set of general attitudes toward life. He expects the worst of life, and believes the worst of others; or he looks forward optimistically to each day's experiences. He is fundamentally and permanently embarrassed, frightened, convinced of his own inadequacy; or he greets each person he sees with an intense aggressiveness. These emotional sets are of course only illustrative; each person has his own. Sometimes they may be concealed by a person who is skilled in acting; certainly they may be misread by the viewers. But more often they are matched by muscular patterns that become fixed and habitual with continued repetition. Temporary emotions are then expressed as an overlay on the surface of the basic patterns, or at most as brief interruptions, the muscles falling back to their regular positions as soon as the momentary laughter or surprise or pain has subsided.

Because nontheater people tend to respond to these muscular clues without consciously identifying them, they can be illustrated only by extreme examples.

Let us suppose that you are sitting in a college cafeteria with two or three friends, and that another friend, Denny Arckus, joins the group, carrying a cup of coffee. He sits down, picks up a spoon, and stirs his coffee. The mood is casual; the conversation is concerned with life's small tragedies (having been assigned an extra chapter to read in a history course) and life's small triumphs (having just received a five-dollar check from Aunt Phronesia). After twenty minutes, Denny gets up with some reluctance, remarking that he has to drive to the next town fifteen miles away to pick up some clothes for his roommate, who had bought them but had left them for alterations.

An hour later, the group having maintained itself, with some arrivals and departures, Denny reappears. He is white and shaking, so much so that he spills his coffee as he sets the cup down on the table. He picks up another spoon and stirs it, finally laying the spoon in the saucer to tell his story.

As he was driving through the streets of the nearby town, an elderly man suddenly fell forward from between two parked cars, directly into Denny's path, and although he was going well below the speed limit and slammed on his brakes instantly, the front wheels of his car passed over the man's body. Denny ran into the nearest house and frantically called a doctor and the police. The doctor, after a careful examination, certified that the man had had a severe heart attack, which was not unexpected, that it was probably the reason for his falling forward, and that it had been the cause of his death. The police, after questioning Denny and the neighbors who had seen the accident, were convinced he was not at fault, and released him without even a warning about his driving.

If this imaginary episode had actually occurred, you would have seen Denny on two occasions, an hour apart, when he was feeling very different emotions. It is easy to visualize the contrasting muscular patterns he would have displayed in the two situations. He would have been relaxed and easy on his first entrance. His walk to the table, the act of pulling back the chair, taking his seat, and setting down the cup of coffee would have been done with a minimum of tension; his facial muscles would most probably have been relaxed, perhaps with a smile of greeting; his eyes and his attention would have been turned toward the people who were already at the table.

Every aspect of his muscular pattern would have been different when he entered the second time. He would have been nervous and tense; his muscles would now be generally contracted, in many cases with opposing pairs both contracted, producing muscular rigidity and trembling. His attention would probably be much less sharply focused on those at the table, but rather still caught by the terrifying experience he had just gone through, so much so that he might fail to notice exactly who was at the table.

It is especially instructive to concentrate on one very small movement, which appeared in each of the two episodes: Denny's stirring his coffee. A moment's thought will make it clear that he would have stirred the coffee very differently the second time from the way he had stirred it the first: his arm and hand muscles would be much tenser, the speed at which he stirred would probably be different, and the stirring would almost certainly be less controlled, so that it would not be surprising if on his return he slopped a good deal of the coffee out into the saucer. A slow-motion movie of the two stirrings would almost certainly reveal that they differed recognizably in every detail.

To make it easier to visualize, an especially extreme example was chosen to illustrate the effect of emotion on the use of the muscles, but continued observation in a variety of everyday situations will demonstrate that the principle operates constantly. Not only does each person perform the simplest acts differently from other people, but the way he performs them is an expression of his emotions and experiences. The general style each person displays, in greeting a friend, opening a door, warming his hands at the fireplace, stirring a cup of coffee, and other actions more and less important, is

> *To the young beginner I would say, when you go upon the stage do not be full of yourself, but be full of your part. That is mistaking vanity for genius, and is the fault of many more than perhaps you are aware of. If actors' and actresses' minds be employed upon themselves, and not on the character they wish and aspire to perform, they never really get out of themselves. Many think they are studying their character when they are only studying themselves. Actors and actresses frequently come to me and say, "Have you any part that will fit me?" They never dream of saying, "Have you any part that I can fit? that I can expand myself or contract myself into, that I can put myself inside of: that I, as a Protean, can shape myself into, even alter my voice and everything that nature has given to me, and be what you have contrived? I do not want you to contrive like a tailor to fit me."*
>
> DION BOUCICAULT

affected by his general set of attitudes toward life. Variations in the way he does such things are due to his temporary moods and emotions.

In enacting a part on stage, it is necessary for the actor to determine his character's basic emotional pattern and its momentary surface variations, and then to find ways of using his body that are suited to and expressive of those emotional factors. An ideal impersonation of the character would involve a total alteration in the actor's own muscular pattern. In practice, many details are so small and subtle that the actor does not have time or ability to control them. He must, however, adjust to the larger and more visible aspects of his character's muscular patterns, moving steadily down the list so as to master the smallest and subtlest effects possible for him during the time he has to work on the play. To a considerable degree the quality of an actor's performance depends on the extent to which he is able to replace his own muscular patterns with those that are suited to the part he is playing.

This necessity is obvious even to an inexperienced actor, in its larger aspects. He will see at once that an actor playing Hamlet must stand, walk, and sit very differently from one playing Macbeth, Romeo, or Falstaff. To represent Theodore Roosevelt convincingly, gestures must be made fuller and more vigorous than for Franklin Roosevelt. An actor who appeared as Dwight Eisenhower in one play and Adolph Hitler in another would have to adopt a totally different pattern of posture, gesture, and muscular tension for the two roles; and both patterns would necessarily be very different from his own. An actor who altered his use of his body only in the large aspects suggested by these examples, however, would be presenting a caricature of his part rather than the desired fully rounded enactment. Usually an actor must start with the most obvious characteristics, but he should work steadily throughout the rehearsal period (and between rehearsals, in his private study) to refine his performance and carry his use of his body as far as possible in the direction of a total transformation. Although that is an unreachable ideal, the closer the actor comes to it the more effective his performance will be.

Of course, it is possible that the personality and emotional pattern of the character an actor represents might be very similar to his own. If the match is extremely close, the actor may be able to play the part with little adjustment. (This matching of actor to character is what is called typecasting.) Alexander Woollcott was the inspiration for the title role in *The Man Who Came to Dinner*. Although the picture of him in the play is not very flattering, Woollcott was delighted to find himself represented on stage, and got permission to play the part himself for a performance or two. To the extent that the fictional Sheridan Whiteside matched Woollcott himself, he could simply display his own familiar muscular patterns.

It might seem that typecasting would be an ideal practice, and the fact that it does save rehearsal and study time makes it common in theaters that operate with very tight schedules, especially civic and summer theaters. One of the many paradoxes of the theater, however, is that actors often find it hardest to play a character who is almost but not quite like themselves. In singing, one of the most difficult stunts is to sing just a tiny fraction out of tune (on purpose, that is—many singers do it without intending to); it is easy to jump from one note to another, but to sing minutely flat requires great skill. In the same way, it is much easier for an actor to assume a role which is very different from his own personality (like that of Squire Cribbs, the villain of *The Drunkard*) than it is for him to play one that is slightly but clearly different from himself.

Posture and Muscular Tonus

The preceding illustrations have emphasized gesture and movement. Perhaps even more important for the actor are the related factors of posture and general muscular tonus.

The varying patterns of tension that move the muscles and the parts of the body in expressing emotions and carrying on activities are overlaid on a basic tension level. This basic level varies, not only from person to person but from moment to moment. As emotion rises, the basic tension rises with it. It is high at exciting moments at a football game; it will shoot up instantly at a confrontation with a bear or rattlesnake in the woods. It is also associated with the general energy level; a person who is full of energy displays a higher tension than one who is exhausted or bored. This fundamental generalized level of tension is technically called "tonus."

Although it varies, it must be maintained within a certain range for ordinary activities to go on. If it drops too low it is no longer possible to continue standing, and the reason a fainting person slumps and falls to the floor is that loss of consciousness is accompanied by an extreme drop in tonus. On the other hand, if tonus is too high, effective functioning is also prevented. Work, gesturing, even breathing require both tension and relaxation, often alternately. If the general tension level is raised too high it may prove impossible to control the muscles that must be relaxed in order to make action possible; thus the sudden sight of a rattlesnake in the woods may raise the tonus so high that flight is impossible, and the person stands frozen in terror. A more common experience is the interference with performance resulting from extreme stage fright. The increase in tonus may raise the tension level of all the muscles in the body, including the diaphragm, so high that it is impossible to relax them sufficiently to draw in an adequate supply of air, and the performer feels breathless. Most of the other symptoms of stage fright—hand tremor, shaking knees, and a rise in vocal pitch—are also the result of high tonus.

As with gestures, each person has his own characteristic pattern of tonus, and it is important for the actor to replace his with that of the character he is representing. What may seem more surprising is that tonal patterns also vary from period to period and culture to culture: there are fashions in tonus. In the

Figure 40a. The physical expression of personality. Hugh Cary effectively portrays an excited boy in the children's play *Peter, Peter, Pumpkin Eater.* [Photograph by Austin-Everest Studio]

Figure 40b (left). Johnny Collins in *Twelfth Night.* [Directed by Harold Tedford]

Figure 40c. James Welker as the puritanical servant Malvolio in *Twelfth Night.*

Figure 40d (left). Caymichael Patten as Mrs. Candour in *The School for Scandal.* [Photograph by Dorothy Welker]

Figure 40e. Jeff Crawford and Rick McGaw as Estragon and Vladimir in *Waiting for Godot.* [Photograph by Austin Everest Studio]

Figure 40f. Eve Pruden beautifully expresses the discontent and haughtiness of Hedda Gabler by means of posture and facial expression. [Photograph by Dorothy Welker]

Figure 40g. Al Tweedy creates a period portrait of the handsome Judge Brack through stylized posture. [*Hedda Gabler;* photograph by Dorothy Welker]

Figure 40h. Linda Edwards sings her love song about her husband as Domina in *A Funny Thing Happened on the Way to the Forum.* [Photograph by Douglas R. Hux]

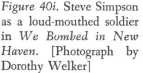

Figure 40i. Steve Simpson as a loud-mouthed soldier in *We Bombed in New Haven*. [Photograph by Dorothy Welker]

absence of motion picture records, it may be difficult to reconstruct the tonal patterns of another age, but paintings of the period offer clues, especially portraits, where characteristic postures are displayed. The current twentieth-century style sets the tonal level lower than most periods in the past. To some extent this century is characterized by the slouch, the slump, and the shuffle, by the chaise longue or the reclining chair, which may actually impose relaxation on the sitter. A man in shirtsleeves, slumped in an amorphous chair, with visual stimuli reduced by turning off the lights, watching the flickering colored images on television and further relaxed by the can of beer, which he holds symbolically in his hand when not drinking from it, might well be taken as a caricature of the tonal pattern of the century. Playscripts from other periods, as well as the record of paintings, the design of furniture, and the shape of clothing, indicate that in most of them the tonal level was much higher. It is nearly impossible to slouch in an Elizabethan chair; it was totally impossible for a warrior in armor; and even Elizabethan clothing imposed an alertness of posture on its wearers. When Mrs. Partridge, in *The Solid Gold Cadillac,* remarks that during her career as an actress she always hated to appear in Shakespeare's plays because no one ever got to sit down except the king, she is pointing out a fact that may be partly due to the special conditions of staging in the Elizabethan theater, but it is also related to the contemporary life style. Even when the kings sat, there is a good deal of evidence that they sat alert and erect.

Playwrights have made use of a great diversity of material, and even the modern slouch and slump have been effectively incorporated in some plays and productions. They seem less suited to drama, however, than a more vigorous use of the body. It is the aim of most plays to provide the most vivid experience possible for the audience, with maximum stimuli and high tension. The slouching so common offstage is seldom effective even for contemporary plays, and most actors in most roles will need to display a tonal pattern that suggests a good deal more alertness than the one they use most frequently in the classroom, the living room, the coffee shop, or on the street.

One postural detail has some significance for actors. The degree of aggressiveness or withdrawal is associated with the vertical angle of the body: Leaning forward makes an actor look aggressively dominant, leaning back produces the opposite effect. This can be easily demonstrated by having an actor move one of his feet toward the front and then assume two positions, the first with his weight on the forward foot, the second with his weight on the back foot; even if he makes no other change in gesture or facial expression the difference in apparent aggressiveness and vigor is startling.

Most of the principles governing stage movement are also applicable to posture. The actor's tonal level and muscular pattern should be clearly defined and displayed, and his posture should be carefully controlled so as to match the personality and emotions of the character who is being portrayed.

Avoiding Irrelevant Tension

The aim of providing the greatest possible tension and stimulation for an audience is a valid one, but it needs some qualification. If the tension is to function esthetically, it must be relevant to the purpose of the production. It must fit precisely into the unified pattern which controls the selection and arrangement of all of the production elements. It is very easy to supply an abundance of stimuli; the problem is to make the tension meaningful. Irrelevant tension is an irritation to the audience; esthetically meaningful tension is a source of interest, excitement, and enjoyment. The actor's handling of tension must consequently be double: he must try to identify all of the sources of tension implied by the script, and to add to them as much further tension as he can devise that will be expressive of the character and contributory to the central purpose of the play. Conversely, he must identify and carefully remove any tensions that appear in his performance that do not assist in producing the desired experience for the audience.

The precise adjustment of tension or effort to the requirements of a task creates an impression of gracefulness; irrelevant tension suggests awkwardness and strain. This can be demonstrated by a very simple test. Form the hand into a cup, with the fingers pointed up and slightly separated, and consciously focus on the degree of tension displayed; then place some small object in the hand, an orange or a teacup, without moving the fingers except to grip it lightly, and analyze again the impression of effort. The empty hand will be seen as excessively tense, and the minute something is placed in it, all tension will apparently disappear. The difference is not due to a real change in the level of tension, which may actually be slightly greater when an object is being supported, but to the fact that the force required to hold the fingers separated and curved seems excessive because it is meaningless, purposeless, and inexplicable when the hand is empty. When an object is being supported, the tension is explained, and seems easy and natural. The impression of awkwardness, then, depends not on the amount of tension displayed but on the amount of unnecessary, irrelevant, and meaningless tension.

Not all characters are intended to appear graceful on stage. Awkwardness is as legitimate an effect as any other, provided it fits the character, but the pattern of tension should always be adjusted to the experience that the play is designed to create for the audience. Tension that contributes to that experience should be raised to the highest level possible, and tension that does not contribute to it should be avoided.

Actors who have a little experience, and even some beginning actors, aware that their final performances should create the highest possible level of excitement and interest, may be greatly disturbed during early rehearsals by the feeling that their readings and the use of their bodies are unacceptably relaxed. They can be reassured by pointing out that the development of a pattern of tension is a major purpose of the rehearsals, that the esthetic structure must be built one part at a time, and will necessarily appear unfinished for at least a couple of weeks.

A more serious problem arises when such actors, in a desperate attempt to fill the void which distresses them, uncritically toss into the part any kind of tension, relevant or not. At the first or second rehearsal after the completion of blocking, they shout their lines, employ vocal tricks with pitch and time, and use extravagant gestures—none of these devices having any relevance to their roles, which they have only begun to analyze. This method of handling acting is very dangerous. At best, once the meaningful vocal patterns have been identified, and gestures, business, and movements have been devised that are adjusted to the lines, the actor must unlearn the habits he has been rehearsing in order to replace them with the correct ones, with a resulting loss of time that can be serious for any part except the shortest.

A much more important effect, however, is still more likely. The actor who is permitted to rehearse patterns of tension that are irrelevant to the play is likely to feel satisfied with them. Sensing that his performance must achieve a high

> *Oh, there be players that I have seen play, and heard others praise, and that highly, that, neither having the accent of Christians nor the gait of Christian, pagan, nor man, have so strutted and bellowed that I have thought some of Nature's journeymen had made men and not made them well, they imitated humanity so abominably.*
>
> SHAKESPEARE

level of excitement, he may conclude that it is acceptable simply because it has reached that level, and he will consequently fail to apply the test of relevance to it and to search for more meaningful techniques. This is so destructive to a production that the director should be constantly alert to the danger and should attack it the moment it appears, even during a blocking rehearsal, before the attention of the cast has been turned directly to the interpretation of the play. When an actor does not know what business or gestures are suited to a line, it is far safer for him to use none. Developing business should always be guided by a careful analysis of the meaning and emotions of the lines. It may be difficult to paint the proper picture on a blank canvas, but if the wrong picture has been painted in first there will probably not be time to scrape it off and replace it with the right one.

The necessity for visibility, not simply visibility of body but clarity in the use of the body, requires that gestures be larger and more sharply defined than matching examples in ordinary life; in other words, they must be projected. One aspect of such projection is expressed in the rule that each gesture should involve the entire body. The rigid application of that rule would produce unfortunate results, but as a guiding principle it is sound, and as a hint to certain actors it is invaluable. Some actors limit gestures to the smallest possible part of the body, turning the eyes but not the head, or turning the head but not the body; pointing with the finger rather than the hand or the full arm. Such an actor should be reminded that he must not simply gesture, he must communicate to the audience the fact that he is gesturing, must make each movement visible to every single viewer. Asking him to consciously make use of his entire body to support and emphasize each movement should quickly break through the inhibitory pattern, after which it should be possible for the actor to use his body effectively, making movements full and clear without overdoing them.

The actors cannot be expected to motivate or project their movements, gestures, and business during the blocking rehearsals, when they are concentrating on identifying and memorizing the movements. Their decisions with regard to motivating movement should be completed as early as possible, however, and by the end of the interpretation rehearsals the motivation and projection of blocking should be nearly completed. This contrasts with the work on vocal projection, which is usually delayed until a week before the play opens.

Figure 41a. Physical projection. Jodi Whittington communicates joy by an expansive gesture. [*The Lark;* photograph by Douglas R. Hux]

Figure 41b. Mimi Gass expresses the fashionable ennui of Lady Teazle in *The School for Scandal.* [Photograph by Dorothy Welker]

Figure 41c (facing page). Jodi Whittington displays a gesture so as to make it visible to the entire audience. [*The Lark;* photograph by Douglas R. Hux]

Figure 41d. Jeff Crawford uses his entire body to express both his desperation and his defiance of the world in *Rhinoceros*. [Photograph by Norm Burlingame]

Figure 41e (facing page). Steve Lewis integrates his posture, gesture, and facial expression and expands them so as to communicate clearly. [*A Funny Thing Happened on the Way to the Forum;* photograph by Douglas R. Hux]

Figure 41f. Wiley Jones's delight at the thought of freedom is expressed broadly; David Parsons reveals his amusement more subtly but with equal clarity. [*A Funny Thing Happened on the Way to the Forum;* photograph by Douglas R. Hux]

Figure 41g. The spirit of cameraderie and fun is projected with effective clarity by five soldiers in *We Bombed in New Haven.* [Photograph by Douglas R. Hux]

Figure 41h. Laurel Dane and Paul Wolf use posture and facial expression to communicate her amusement, haughtiness, and skepticism, and his extravagant pretense of humility in the wooing scene of *The Taming of the Shrew*. [Photograph by Dorothy Welker]

Figure 41i. Belina's total personality is revealed by Miss Caymichael Patten through posture, tonus, and facial expression [*The Imaginary Invalid;* photograph by Dorothy Welker]

Figure 41j. Tim Moyer and Linda Edwards illustrate an exaggerated degree of projection that would be unsuited to serious drama, but which is exactly right for the farcical conclusion of *A Funny Thing Happened on the Way to the Forum.* [Photograph by Douglas R. Hux]

Figure 41k. Ray Urbas and Mish Munz demonstrate expressive gestures projected so as to be effective to all the members of a large audience. [*Twelfth Night*]

Figure 41l (facing page). Physical projection. Each character in this scene from *Twelfth Night* illustrates effective physical projection; the actors have found techniques for making the attitudes, emotions, and personalities of their characters so clearly visible that no one in the audience could miss them.

DRESSING THE STAGE

In addition to his concern for his own role, a skilled and experienced actor remains constantly aware of his part in the stage picture as a whole. Every performance involves some blocking variations; crosses are never exactly the same length as in a previous rehearsal or performance, the angles at which actors are turned are never exactly the same from evening to evening. Often such deviations have no significance, but sometimes they will. If two actors cross toward each other and each one happens to move even six inches farther than usual, they may stop uncomfortably close together. Each actor should therefore constantly assess the total arrangement of the people on stage, and should readjust it whenever it seems ineffective. This process, which is called "dressing the stage," does not require conscious analysis; in fact, it functions best when actors have learned to do it automatically and instinctively. If they are made aware of the factor, most actors can very quickly develop a feeling for a well-arranged stage and learn to lengthen or shorten crosses, to amplify turns with a step or two, in order to keep the stage picture effective.

One particular type of adjustment is so common that it has been given a special name, "countering." When an actor crosses in front of another, the upstage actor is covered for an appreciable length of time, and unless the cross is fairly long it is likely to leave the two actors uncomfortably close together. It is standard procedure for the upstage actor to counter by moving a step in the opposite direction at the moment when the other passes in front of him. This not only shortens the time when he is covered but helps separate the two actors at the end of the cross. Since the action is almost entirely hidden by the downstage actor, it is unlikely to be noticed by the audience, and in any case it can usually be motivated by turning slightly toward the crossing actor, so that the focus of attention remains on the person who is making the major movement.

The only resources available to the actor are his voice and his body, and of the two, the voice is generally more important. However, the actor's use of his body, even if secondary, can contribute significantly to the effectiveness of a production, and it should be planned and rehearsed as carefully as any other performance element.

12/USING THE VOICE

The relative strength of sight and sound in the theater can be realized most easily by referring to productions in which each is used alone. The popularity and effectiveness of radio drama in the thirties and forties demonstrate clearly that the full range of emotion and ideas can be expressed with sound alone.

That it is possible to present a play intelligibly with sight alone is demonstrated by the silent movies. In nearly all of the early movies, however, the communication provided by the setting and the actors' bodies was felt inadequate, and at least brief passages of dialog were supplied by flashing printed sentences across the screen. The attitudes of listeners and viewers in these two cases were very different. The people who followed radio drama seldom had any feeling of incompleteness or constraint, whereas silent movies always carry an implication of difficulty overcome. When they are admired, it is as tours de force—there is always some feeling of special admiration at the virtuosity of actors who are able to communicate so much even without the voice. Sarah Bernhardt was able to continue to act with remarkable success even after she could no longer walk. If, instead, she had lost the power of speech, it seems impossible that she could have continued her career at anything like the same level.

Both elements contribute powerfully to the theater, and both should be exploited to the full, but the element of sound is clearly stronger. Drama is not a

> There can be no question that the legitimate drama is primarily an auditory art, and that the dialogue is its primary element.
> CLEANTH BROOKS AND ROBERT HEILMAN

> *Every dramaturgic practice that subordinates the words to any other medium has trivialized the drama.*
>
> ERIC BENTLEY
>
> *The subordination of the words to other theater arts is death to the drama.*
>
> ERIC BENTLEY

fabric of action decorated with an embroidery of speech; it is a structure fundamentally made up of speech, assisted and supplemented by the visual experience provided by watching the actions of the performers, and to a smaller extent by the other visible elements of production—lighting, scenery, costumes, make-up, and properties. The director can expect to spend more rehearsal time in working over the reading of the lines than in all other aspects of production.

THE ELEMENTS OF VOICE

Physicists provide the simplest analysis of voice in terms of two variables: time and loudness. Psychologically, however, we interpret voice as involving four factors: time (or rate), loudness, pitch, and tone quality. Each of these terms has synonyms; for example, physicists and musicians prefer the term "dynamics" to "loudness." The terms used here have been selected as the most familiar; the various synonyms seem equally accurate.

Each of the four elements of sound can be varied independently, or any pair, any three, or all four together. Variation in quality is the major method by which the stream of sound is shaped to form words, and such variations are prescribed within very narrow limits by the language itself: the distinctions between *big, beg, bog, bug,* and *bag* are due to differences in tone quality, as are the distinctions between apparently unrelated words such as *faction* and *water*. Besides such surface variations, each speaker displays a unique quality, which enables us to distinguish the voices of two friends both of whom speak the same words. This fundamental quality varies with emotion, age, and physical condition, but it is also genetically influenced, which is one of the reasons (but not the only one) why members of a family often sound very much alike. This quality is seldom varied significantly in public speaking or conversation. Actors sometimes attempt to alter their vocal quality to suggest the age of their characters, or other aspects such as strong emotion; variation in quality, for example, may be of assistance in expressing hysteria. In general, however, except for its obligatory use in articulating the different sounds in the language, quality is the least significant of the four psychologically identifiable vocal elements. The concern of the director, an overwhelming percentage of the time, is with the actors' use of time, loudness, and pitch.

The obligatory conventional patterns, which specify how a word is to be pronounced, also make some use of these three elements. Sometimes they are semantic, as in the two pronunciations of the word *desert* ("Soldiers who are stationed in the *des*ert seldom de*sert*"), where one of the syllables is spoken at a higher pitch than the other, the sound of the vowel is continued for a longer period of time, and it is spoken louder. The meaning of the word depends on which of the two syllables is selected. In the vast majority of cases, however, the distinctive characteristic of a word is determined primarily by the pattern of tone quality. The pitch-loudness-time pattern is equally fixed by convention, but is less significant. If it is altered, the listener notices that the word has been mispronounced by putting "the em*phas*is on the wrong syl*lab*le," but in most cases he would recognize the word nevertheless.

When the analysis of the use of the voice is extended beyond a single word to a phrase, a clause, or a full sentence, it is discovered that here, too, certain patterns are conventionally prescribed. Examples are the drop in pitch at the end of a declarative sentence, and the rise in pitch at the end of a question. These conventional patterns have never been adequately described. The attempts of linguistic scholars in recent decades to define them are undoubtedly valuable as a first step, but their formulations are still incomplete, not only in detail but in fundamental ways. The familiar folk formulations are no better. The rule cited above, for example, about the use of a rising or falling pitch at the ends of sentences, has some slight validity, but in fact a very large percentage of declarative sentences are not ended with a drop in pitch, and a large percentage of questions do not end with a pitch rise.

A complete and accurate statement of these conventional patterns will be of considerable value to directors and actors when it has been developed. Its absence, however, is not so great a handicap as might be expected. The obligatory patterns are so regularly displayed in normal speech that they are absorbed and applied subconsciously by almost every native speaker, and consequently do not cause trouble. They are of concern mainly when an actor must alter his dialect, either to adopt a foreign accent or to replace his native dialect with another that is felt to be more suited to the stage. The prescribed pitch-loudness-time patterns vary from language to language and dialect to dialect, functioning strongly in producing the special overall impression of the language. Such patterns are different, for example, in the British and American dialects. Because they operate subconsciously, and because they have never been fully described, they are difficult for actors to hear and reproduce, and in learning a foreign dialect (or indeed a foreign language) they are the single element that is least likely to be reproduced accurately.

The actor is left free, then, to make expressive use of these three vocal elements to the extent that they are not controlled by the specifications of the language.

The Purpose of Vocal Variation

In normal speech, the three elements are usually varied simultaneously and in the same direction, so that if the use of each in a particular conversational sentence is recorded graphically, the three lines are seen to have identical or very similar shapes. The function of such variation is to indicate to the listener the relative importance of the different words included in a statement. Since the assessment of such variations in importance depends on the speaker's own scheme of values, his interests, attitudes, and emotions, the pitch-time-loudness elements are the actor's major resource for the communication of emotion, and supplement the meanings of the words or lines of the script. The appropriate vocal pattern for a particular sentence or speech can thus be determined only after its emotional content or connotation has been fully realized. It is for this reason that actors' early readings in tryouts and blocking rehearsals are nearly always so appallingly inexpressive. It is impossible for them to use their vocal resources communicatively until they have developed a detailed and vivid understanding of what is to be communicated.

The operation of these factors is easiest to identify in extreme examples. In the wager scene at the end of *The Taming of the Shrew,* each new bridegroom sends a message to his wife asking her to come to him; the one whose wife appears most readily will win the wager. Lucentio sends the first message, only to be brought word that his wife is busy and cannot come. Petruchio makes fun of him for having been given such an answer, and Tranio replies, "Pray God, sir, your wife send you not a worse!" In this sentence, the most important word is clearly the last; it is the point of the entire sentence. Probably the least important word is the next to the last, *a;* it is included to satisfy a somewhat arbitrary grammatical rule, and carries so little meaning that it would be omitted altogether if the sentence were translated into some languages (for example, Latin). Even in English, it can be deleted without any significant change in meaning, although the line becomes slightly awkward. In this case, then, we have two words side by side, the first at the bottom of the range of importance, the second at the top of the range (within this sentence; of course the total range available extends beyond the small section included here). According to the pattern of normal speech, the word *worse* would be spoken at a higher pitch, more time would be given to it, and it would be spoken louder. *A* would display the opposite characteristics: it would be spoken at a low pitch, very quickly, and much less loudly. That statement is not precisely accurate as it stands; the vocal variations typically do not involve all of

the sounds in a word, but instead affect only the vowel, and in the ca
polysyllabic words, only the vowel in the syllable that takes the primary a
The reason for this restriction is both psychological and mechanical; the attention is primarily focused on the accented syllable, and many consonant sounds
cannot be lengthened without making them unrecognizable (*k, p, t, b, d,* and
others), and it is difficult to alter clearly either their loudness or pitch.

These variations are easy to hear and can be readily demonstrated mechanically by recording normal conversational speech on tape and analyzing it by the
use of electronic equipment. The pitch is the most difficult to determine mechanically, although the easiest to hear; loudness can be readily identified by the
use of a VU meter; and the length of time given to each vowel is especially easy
to measure. With a little experience an operator can learn to find and mark the
points on the tape where each vowel begins and ends, and their length can be
measured accurately within a very small fraction of a second by the use of a
finely divided ruler. It will be seen that a strongly emphasized vowel may
stretch many times as long as one that is low on the scale of emphasis.

Speech varies throughout the entire scale, however, not just at the two extremes. In a typical sentence, no two words are of precisely equal importance. In
most cases, one word can be selected as the key of the sentence, expressing the
idea that lies at the focus of the speaker's concern; a second word will be next in
importance, and so on down to the least important. When two words seem
equally important, it is usually at this lowest level. Articles, prepositions, conjunctions, and similar words whose primary function is syntactical rather than
meaningful, may seem so unimportant that it is impossible to distinguish between two of them. This assessment, however, is dependent on the values of
the individual speaker, and these words, too, may occasionally rise to major significance: "Are you *the* Spiro Agnew?" "I said throw it *in* the wastebasket, not
at it!"; "Let me *out!*"

Because the identification of the relative importance of the words in a sentence, like most aspects of language, is regularly done subconsciously, it is very
difficult to number the words in a written sentence in the order of their importance. The extremes are usually easy to find, but the words in the middle of the
range require very difficult and close analysis. Such conscious study is usually
not only time-consuming but impractical. It becomes necessary only when problems appear, when an actor has difficulty reading a line meaningfully, or selecting
among alternative readings. The most efficient attack on a line is to match the
psychological pattern of ordinary speech. The actor concentrates on developing
the most intense understanding of the meaning and emotion expressed by the
line, from the viewpoint of his character, and the selection of vocal techniques is
done automatically.

However, if the words in a sentence were ranked in the order of their significance to the speaker, analysis of an effective reading of the sentence would de-

monstrate a precise correlation of their rankings with the pitch-loudness-time factors. The accented vowel in the key word would be placed highest in the group on the three scales, and the least important words lowest. In good normal speech, these adjustments are made at great speed and with great precision. Even minute variations in importance are expressed clearly by small but accurately matched variations in pitch, loudness, and time.

The Range of Vocal Variation

It might seem that three variables would be inadequate to express all of the subtle shades of emotion that are actually communicated by the voice. No individual speaker can make use of the total conceivable vocal range. His pitch range is limited, extending for approximately two musical octaves. Speech can be made louder only up to a certain point; and in the theater, the lower limit of loudness is much more restricted than in ordinary life, since all theatrical speech must be held at a level that ensures audibility for the entire audience. Time is perhaps more widely variable, but still must operate within fairly narrow limits. Within these restricted ranges, however, a large number of variations are poossible, theoretically infinite. If all three factors are varied together, the range of possibilities is identical with the number of variations that can be controlled and sensed. In pitch, the standard chromatic scale of Western music arranges twenty-four different pitches within the range of two octaves; the voice is capable of sounding many times that number of distinguishable pitches within the same range, and the pitch levels available in practice number in the hundreds. If the three aspects of voice are varied independently rather than identically, the permutative possibilities become astronomical. Analysis thus supports familiar experience: the vocal range seems fully adequate to the expression of the totality of human emotion, of all kinds and degrees of intensity. The range of vocal effects is, in fact, so wide that even a single word such as *yes* can be spoken in at least dozens of ways, each one expressing a different shade of meaning and emotion. The number of distinguishably different readings possible for even a five-word sentence is thus incalculably enormous.

The Vocal Communication of Value and Emotion

The selection of one out of all of the possible ways to speak a sentence is determined by and expressive of the speaker's own emotional and valuational pattern. If the same sentence appears in the speeches of two characters in a play, the presumption is that each would speak it differently. Even if the same sentence is spoken by one actor at different points in a play, it is almost certain that the intervening events would have altered his character's attitudes enough to result in at least a slight difference between the two readings. There is thus no single correct way in which a sentence must be read, inherent in the words themselves;

rather, the reading is the result of the interaction of the meaning of the sentence with the speaker's scheme of values and emotions. That does not mean, however, that any reading is as effective as any other; quite the opposite. Presumably, if we could develop a total and accurate realization of a character's mental, valuation, and emotional pattern, we would discover that they would enforce the selection of only one particular reading of the sentence. This task is so difficult as to be unmanageable. It is seldom possible for any actor or director to absorb a character in a play so fully that the choice of a reading can be made with complete confidence. Often, in fact, the most skilled and careful theater artists disagree strongly about how a particular line should be read. Walter Kerr (*Thirty Plays Hath November*) argues persuasively that the character of Shylock has been generally misinterpreted in recent productions of the play, with the result that lines intended to be comic are read with dignity. In another essay, he makes a strong case for the belief that Chekhov's plays have been given the opposite treatment, that actors have read speeches solemnly that the playwright intended to be ironically comic. Whether a particular theater artist accepts or rejects those arguments, the important point is that the reading of the lines depends on the personalities of the characters who speak them, and if they have been misunderstood, the lines will be misread.

Expressing Character through Voice

In using his voice, then, the actor's first responsibility is to develop the fullest possible understanding of the character he is to represent. Achieving such an understanding begins with a careful, detailed, and systematic analysis of all of the information that the playwright has provided in the script. It ends with an act of intense empathy—the imaginative adoption of the attitudes, emotions, and values of the character. It is not necessary that an actor playing Cyrano have a grotesque nose—that can be readily supplied by the makeup crew; it is not even necessary that he himself have suffered embarrassment because of a physical defect; but he must be able to take Cyrano's place in imagination, to adopt his attitudes and emotions, and to respond to events as he would. And as with posture and gestures, he must be able to develop vocal patterns suited to Cyrano's personality and expressing his emotions.

Ideally, then, there is one correct way to read a particular sentence spoken in a specific situation by an individual character in a play, and it is the actor's responsibility to find that single best reading and practice until he can duplicate it with his own voice. As with posture, business, gesture, and blocking, the way the actor himself would be most likely to read a line is irrelevant. For him to object to a reading on the grounds that it was not natural to him would be theatrically irrational; the only significant objection that can be made to the way a line is read is that it is unsuited to the character the actor is portraying.

A detailed discussion of the reading of a line usually occurs only when an actor is having serious difficulty. Especially during the experimental rehearsals, it is assumed that an actor may try several alternative readings in order to identify the best one. Most of the readings will be less than ideally effective, but it is more efficient for the director to let them pass without comment, since the actor can be expected to work out the necessary improvements himself. When the actor is obviously in difficulty, when he asks for assistance, or when an ineffective reading is repeated several times without change, it is useful to stop for a discussion of the passage.

It is best to start such a discussion by asking the actor to explain the simple meaning of the problem sentence. The line may contain an ambiguity of which the director is unaware, or the actor may misinterpret one of the words; in either case, a correct reading is not possible until the mistake has been corrected. The actor who played Grumio in one production of *The Taming of the Shrew* misunderstood the word *stuff* in one of his speeches; in this context it meant *cloth*. Another actor interpreted *kite* as a child's toy, when in fact it meant a kind of bird, and *crab* as an animal, although it actually meant an apple. In another case, in a production of Plautus's *The Rope,* a line contained a simple ambiguity that the director had not recognized; the actor's reading was ineffective because he had identified the wrong one of the two possible meanings. A brief discussion cleared up the point, and the actor immediately supplied the correct reading.

Once it has been determined that the actor and director agree on the fundamental meaning of the line, the motivation and emotions accompanying it should be explored. The director can carry on this part of the discussion best by questions, asking the actor to describe the emotions he believes his character would feel at this point in the play. If his description of the emotional pattern seems inaccurate, the director should ask him to cite the specific evidence on which his conclusions are based, and to trace the analysis that led him from the evidence to the conclusions. If the actor's conclusions are incorrect, the reason is most often that he has missed some of the items of information provided by the playwright, often because relevant points may be scattered widely throughout the script. In *Antony and Cleopatra,* for example, Enobarbus is both attracted and repelled by the queen; at different points, he attacks and defends her with equal fervor. If any one such episode is viewed in isolation, it might seem to justify a quite false reading. Taken all together, they make it clear that she enchants him even when he is criticizing her, and angers him even when he speaks most favorably; only a reading that expresses this ambivalence will be entirely accurate.

If the actor has missed such items of evidence, then the director should point them out, if necessary turning to the specific lines in the play that have a bearing on the problem speech and examining them with the actor. If the director is unable to demonstrate such additional evidence or to find errors in the actor's reasoning or analysis, the best response is to withdraw his objection gracefully and instruct the actor to continue with his established reading. The director can, of course, use his administrative position to force a reading on the actor that he is unable to support by reasoning and analysis, but if neither of the readings is based on a study of the evidence presented in the script, the disagreement becomes simply a confrontation of whims: the director says "Well, I feel it this way; this way just seems better to me somehow," and the actor can properly counter with the same defense of his own reading. Sound reading is based on a careful study of the information provided by the script. There is no reason to suppose that the director's interpretation, based on whim or "feeling," is any better than that based on the actor's whim or feeling, and in that case, the actor is better left with a reading that seems most natural to him. The same considerations apply to the actor's reading. If he is unable to support it by the evidence of the script, then it should be clear that it has no defense, and if the director is able to point to lines that are relevant to his interpretation of the contested speech, even a few weak items of evidence should outweigh an interpretation by the actor based only on whim.

If discussion demonstrates that the actor's and director's analyses of the meaning and emotions of a line are in agreement, then the techniques chosen for expressing them should be examined. At this point, it is especially useful to have a tape recording of the actor's reading of the speech. The whole difficulty may be that the actor intended to use a different vocal pattern from the one he actually employed, and a single hearing may demonstrate that for him. Perhaps the first question to ask is "What is the most important word in the sentence?" If there is disagreement on this point, it can be resolved by testing the various words against the emotional pattern of the character that has already been identified in the discussion. Once agreement has been reached, the recording should be replayed to determine whether the key word has actually been given major emphasis. Usually this is enough to demonstrate what is wrong with the reading. The actor will be able to correct it quickly, and the rehearsal of the scene can continue. If more complex adjustment seems necessary, the analysis can be carried to other words as far down the scale of importance as is desirable.

Sometimes actors find it difficult to adjust their emphasis properly to lines even though they may understand the meaning and emotional implications of the speeches, when the character uses a verbal style that is very different from the actor's ordinary speech. Classic plays, plays of other countries, verse drama, and dialect plays are especially difficult. Often the problem is syntactical: the order of words in the speeches is different from the actor's natural speech. One technique that may help in such cases is to ask the actor to rephrase the speech, translating it into his own style, which will make it easier for him to identify the correct levels of emphasis. The corresponding words in the original speech should then be spoken with the same emphasis, even though they may appear in different order from the paraphrase.

False Emphasis

Perhaps the commonest simple error in reading is misidentifying the crucial word in a clause or sentence, so that the idea that should be given major emphasis is reduced to second place. Seldom are words at the lowest level of importance raised far above their natural level. This error, however, does occur with two types of words frequently enough that the director should be aware of the possibility.

The first group consists of two grammatical categories. Prepositions and conjunctions seldom lie at the focus of a speaker's attention. Their syntactical function is likely to be more important than their meaning; they are consequently among the least emphatic words in normal speech. Although few actors deviate from the familiar pattern in their ordinary conversation, some regularly give major emphasis to these words when they are reading from manuscript, and by the time they begin to rehearse from memory, the unnatural reading may have become so fixed that they continue to use it. Such errors should be corrected early, at least at the beginning of the interpretation rehearsals.

The absurdity of such a reading is immediately evident to everyone—except the actor who is addicted to it. Imagine, for example, a reading by an actress playing Palaestra in Plautus's *The Rope* giving major emphasis to the italicized words in the following speech: "I'll make it easy *for* you. There ought to be a little jewel box there *in* the trunk. I'll tell you everything that's *in* it *by* name; don't show me anything. If I tell you wrong, then I'll have told you *for* nothing; you can still keep *for* yourself whatever there is *in* there; *but* if I am right, then I beg you to return my things *to* me." It may seem incredible that any actress would be tempted to such a diametrically false reading; what is more astonishing is the tenacity with which actors who follow this pattern cling to it. Experience suggests that no argument will destroy their fondness for prepositions and conjunctions. However, a simple demonstration will provide unanswerable evidence that their readings are artificial, and with constant reminders they can usually be persuaded to correct it, even if they still feel that the director's instructions are wrong.

The demonstration is conducted as follows. While the tape recorder continues to run, the director engages the actor in an ordinary conversation, preferably on topics not related to the play; when a sample of several connected sentences has been recorded, the tape is rewound, and the actor is asked to listen to his own natural speech. Almost without exception he will have handled prepositions and conjunctions in the normal way; in fact they are likely to be so de-emphasized that he will have trouble identifying them as the recording is played. It is helpful to rewind the tape again and replay each phrase containing a preposition or conjunction in isolation. At least, this procedure will demonstrate that the actor is not following his own normal practice in the reading of his lines.

The other type of overemphasis is more understandable. The language includes a number of words that once served primarily to intensify statements—*quite, very, awfully, really, surely, certainly*, etc. Through long use, most of these words have lost their intensive force; sometimes they seem to weaken the statements into which they are inserted rather than make them stronger. Actors are often tempted to give major emphasis to this kind of words, which might be called "false intensives," with the result that the attention of the audience is directed toward some of the least meaningful words, and distracted from the key words. A simple test for a false intensive is to read the line without it. If essential meaning has been lost, or if the line is weakened, the word makes a real contribution to the significance of the statement; if the line seems equally strong and meaningful, the omitted word is almost certain to be of little importance, and should be de-emphasized.

The Vocal Pattern of Normal Speech

Most beginning actors, as well as other people not trained in speech, speak most effectively in ordinary conversation, less effectively from the platform, and least effectively when they are reading words previously written down, whether directly from the manuscript or from memory. This variation is not surprising, since it matches most people's experience. They will have engaged in conversation for thousands of times as many hours as they have spent in public speaking or manuscript reading. Even in conversation, however, speakers differ greatly in effectiveness in all aspects of speech, including the use of the voice. Some speak flatly and inexpressively; others use their vocal resources skillfully, and consequently are not only more interesting but communicate much more of their thinking and feeling. During the many thousands of hours of speaking in which almost everyone engages while growing up, each person tends to fix his individual pattern very firmly, until it becomes so familiar that he employs it without conscious thought. If the speaker uses what has been called the "normal" pattern, the adjustment to the requirements of the stage is fairly easy. In essence, the normal pattern is no pattern at all: the entire vocal range is used freely, in all three of its aspects, and emphasis is varied to correspond to the meanings and emotions that are expressed.

Abnormal Vocal Patterns

Probably the majority of speakers deviate from this norm; their use of one or more of the three vocal resources is restricted, and rather than adjusting their speech to the meaning and emotion, they may monotonously repeat a simple pattern, imposing it on whatever they have to say whether it fits or not.

Since the pattern of meaningful stage speech must be developed from what is to be expressed, and not externally imposed on it, training an actor who regularly uses a restricted pattern in his ordinary speech requires not simply analyzing the lines of his part, but destroying the nonstandard pattern that has become automatic for him as a result of years of practice. The difficulty of such a transformation depends on many factors, including the actor's ability to hear differences in speech, his ability to understand the reasons for preferring one pattern to another, and his vocal control. Most important of all are the intensity of his desire to improve his speech and his habitual flexibility or conservatism. An actor who is strongly motivated, who is willing to work with great concentration, and who is not temperamentally resistant to change can achieve astonishing improvement in his speech during the month or six weeks that he spends in studying and rehearsing a play.

THE PRIMER PATTERN

Many different nonstandard restricted patterns appear in ordinary speech, but three are so common that they are likely to show up in some degree in any sizable cast.

One of them, called the "primer pattern," is almost universal among children who are first learning to read. In this type of speech, all words are spoken at the same high level of emphasis, except for the last word in each sentence, which is sharply dropped, particularly in pitch but also in loudness and time. Each of the nonstandard patterns may appear in varying degrees; the primer pattern is heard less often in extreme form than as a tendency. To the extent that it operates, it flattens out distinctions among words, so that the great majority of words are not only given undue emphasis, but the most important ones are all at the same level, and the listener is given no help in identifying the key

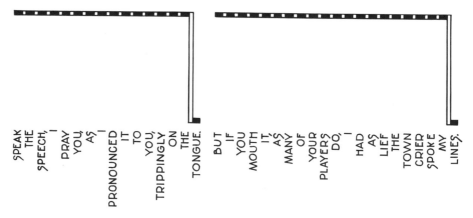

Figure 42. The primer pattern.

> *Old Peking Prompter Say:*
>
> *Two way not be understood—*
> *Neglect every syllable:*
> *Nothing stand out*
> *Nothing understood.*
> *Emphasize every syllable:*
> *Nothing stand out*
> *Nothing understood.*

word in a sentence or clause. The pattern may be varied by dropping the emphasis not only at periods but also at commas, semicolons, or other punctuation marks. Occasionally the speaker may habitually raise the pitch at the end of each sentence, rather than dropping it.

The Jack-and-Jill Pattern

A second pattern seems derived from the primer; it is called the "Jack-and-Jill pattern" because the speaker steadily rolls down a hill throughout each sentence. The first and last words in a sentence match the emphasis given them in the primer pattern, the first being placed at the highest level of emphasis and the last at the lowest. Instead of the intervening words' being spoken at the same high level as the first, as they are in the primer pattern, each is made slightly less emphatic than the word before it, so that a graph of such a sentence looks like a descending flight of stairs. For the first word of the next sentence, the speaker jumps back again to the highest level of emphasis, and repeats the pattern. If the changes in loudness, time, and pitch are large, the speaker sounds somewhat as if he were repetitiously singing the opening line

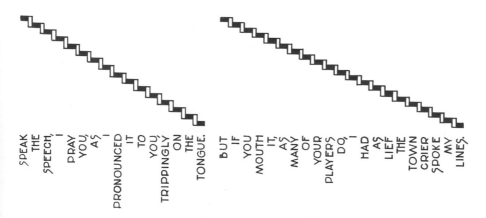

Figure 43. The Jack-and-Jill pattern.

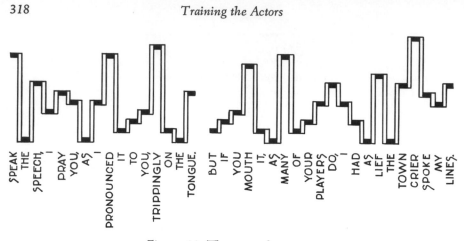

Figure 44. The normal pattern.

of "Joy to the World"; if the steps are very small, he may sound like an old spring-wind phonograph running down. This pattern is occasionally heard in extreme form; it too may be approximated in greater or less degree. Some speakers start the pattern over again with each punctuation mark, rather than extending it all the way to the period.

THE GLACIATED PATTERN

The third pattern is most like that of normal speech. In fact, it can be defined most easily in terms of the normal pattern. The arrangement of words in a sentence is determined primarily by grammatical and syntactical rules, not by the relative importance of the words. Consequently a graph of normal speech is

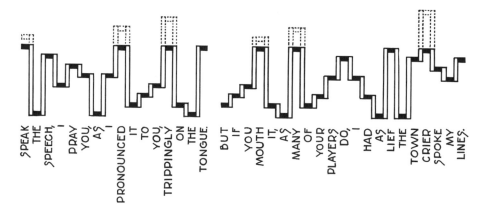

Figure 45. The glaciated pattern. (The dashed lines indicate the positions of the key words if the normal pattern had been used.)

characterized by an essential randomness. The key word may be followed or preceded by a word at the lowest level of emphasis; the three or four most important words in the sentence may be scattered or bunched, and they may be arranged in any sequence. A graph of such speech has been described as resembling a highly irregular mountain range, with hills and valleys of all sizes, although the different levels are joined by vertical lines rather than slopes, as they would be in an actual mountain range. If a glacier can be imagined as moving across this range, cutting off the tallest peaks all at the same level, and then melting, the pattern remaining would be exactly as it was originally except for the fact that all of the highest points would have been reduced to the same level; on the basis of this rather far-fetched analogy, this has been given the name "glaciated pattern."

It will be seen that when applied to speech this pattern produces more damage than might be expected from its general shape. Most of the words in a sentence of glaciated speech are spoken exactly as they would be in the normal pattern. However, the glaciated pattern damages communication at the most important point—on those highest levels of emphasis where the most important words appear; it fails to distinguish the relative importance of these words, and, for instance, hides the key word by pulling it down to the level of the words immediately below it in importance.

This is the most difficult of the nonstandard patterns to hear. It can be recognized most easily by running through a recorded sample two or three times, listening first to the variations below the highest level of emphasis: they will be seen to match the normal pattern closely. On the second hearing, an attempt should be made to ignore these lower levels of emphasis and concentrate on the top level by itself; the pitch is likely to be easier to identify than loudness or rate. Such speech, at the highest level, sounds like a single gong struck at irregular intervals.

MONOTONOUS SPEECH

It has been pointed out that loudness, time, and pitch can all be varied together or independently. It is not uncommon to find a speaker who varies two in almost normal fashion, but who handles the third monotonously. Some years ago there was a fashion among high school students to speak at a fast monorate, narrowing the rate range and fitting all speech into the unemphatic end of the scale. This faddish pattern became permanent for some people and was carried into adult life, even showing up occasionally on the stage. A slow monorate is also common: the less important words and syllables are given undue time, so that the rate is restricted to the upper (emphatic) section of the range.

Monopitch and monotony in loudness can also be heard frequently; in such speech all words are spoken at almost the same pitch, whether it is high, low, or somewhere in between, or speech is uniformly quiet or loud, with almost no variation.

Monotonous speech, of whatever type, significantly reduces the vocal resources available to the speaker. Helping an actor make a fuller use of a neglected element is facilitated by the use of a tape recorder, since a prerequisite to any change is for him to hear clearly how he is handling the problem factor. If his speech is monotonous in pitch, it should not be difficult to find a clause or

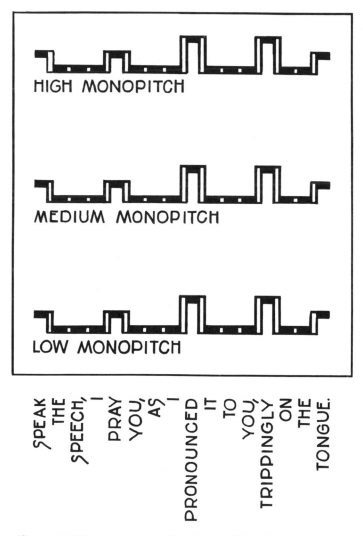

Figure 46. Monotonous speech. Monopitch has been diagramed, but monotonous rate and loudness could be illustrated by the same patterns.

sentence of considerable length in which every word is spoken at exactly the same pitch. Usually such an actor uses at least somewhat greater pitch variety in normal conversation, and an illustrative comparison with a recorded sample of his ordinary speech is especially informative; a comparison with varied speech of other actors may be almost as valuable. If each rehearsal is recorded, playing four or five performances of a single speech in sequence will give the actor a vivid picture of his progress or lack of progress in exploiting his pitch resource.

An exercise that is sometimes valuable works best with an actor who tends to rely almost exclusively on a single vocal element, perhaps using variations in loudness to an extreme degree but varying his pitch and rate minimally. The actor should be asked to abandon variety in loudness for one rehearsal, to attempt to speak all of his lines quietly; at the same time he should attempt to use as much pitch and rate variety as he can. He should try to communicate at least as fully as he has been doing with loudness. At the following rehearsal, he can restore variety in loudness to his performance, and will probably retain a significant percentage of the improvement in the use of pitch and rate that was achieved the previous evening.

Old Peking Prompter Say:

Good actor get meaning
  Where bad actor yell.
One good inflection
  Worth thousand decibel.

VOCAL PROJECTION

Like all aspects of theatrical production, voice must be projected. Every member of the audience must be able to hear every significant word. If the people in the last row of seats cannot hear, they would be fully justified in demanding their money back. At the same time, the fact of projection and the techniques by which it is achieved must be kept unobtrusive. When an actor and actress sit alone on a park bench in the center of the stage, with a street lamp throwing a pool of light over them as dusk falls, and engage in a quiet, intimate conversation, each member of the audience must feel that they are speaking exactly as they would in the matching circumstances outside the theater. The speech should seem so natural that it should never occur to the listener to wonder how he can hear it at a distance of fifty feet, even though it is audible to all of the hundreds of people seated in the auditorium. In order to achieve this effect, every aspect of speech must be altered for stage use; here as elsewhere in the theater nothing seems less realistic than the real and ordinary.

Work on projection is usually delayed until quite late in the series of rehearsals. It should be done not earlier than the blending rehearsals, and it is
even better to wait until the polishing rehearsals. The problems of learning
blocking, working out interpretations, and the development of techniques, require such concentration from the actor that asking him to work on his projection at the same time would interfere with the major assignments of the early
rehearsals and would seem to be an irritating interruption. When the basic pattern of performance has been developed, the actors can turn their attention to
projection as a natural part of the process of polishing the performance.

At the beginning of the first polishing rehearsal, they should be instructed
to include projection as one of the purposes of the rehearsal. The critical members of the audience will be those seated in the back row of the theater, since
if they are able to hear, all of the other listeners will also.

Within a narrow range, variations in projection are part of ordinary experience. If two friends are sitting in a booth at a restaurant, engaged in a quiet
conversation, they are most likely to speak so as to be heard comfortably at the
very small distance separating them, perhaps two feet. If two others join them,
they will instinctively enlarge their speech to adjust to the increase in the size
of the group. If the group is still further enlarged by the arrival of friends who
pull up chairs and arrange them in a semicircle at the end of the booth, the
speech will be projected still further, often without conscious intention. The
limit of projection in ordinary experience, however, is to an audience of twelve
or fifteen people. Projection across a greater distance than ten to fifteen feet
requires special techniques.

Inexperienced actors who have not been trained in theatrical projection
usually enlarge their speech to the limit of ordinary experience, but not beyond
it. At most their performances are likely to be effective for listeners seated in the
front row of the audience. It might be supposed that the effectiveness of vocal
projection would fade gradually, as the listener's distance increased. Instead,
the dividing line between the area within which an actor can be heard easily
and the area within which he is not projecting sufficiently is astonishingly precise and narrow. If an actor is projecting acceptably for the first row of seats, it
is quite possible that it will be difficult to follow what he says from the second
row. As the director works with the actors on projection, he will need to test
their performances frequently. This can best be done by standing close to the
stage on the auditorium floor while the rehearsal is in progress. If the actor is
clearly audible from that point, the director should move back to the first row of
seats and recheck; from there he should back up the aisle slowly, listening
carefully. If the actor's projection is not yet fully adequate, the director will be
able to identify the extent of the projection very clearly. He will find that when
he is standing beside one row of seats he can follow the dialog easily, but that
when he moves back one more row, or at most two, the speech becomes un-

intelligible. The difference is not so much in the absolute audibility as in the intensity of attention required to understand what is said. The director will find that so long as he is within the effective area, understanding the dialog is almost automatic, but that when he moves beyond its farthest edge he can follow what is said only by conscious effort.

REHEARSING FOR PROJECTION

As each actor practices the techniques of projection, the dividing line marking the far edge of the area within which he is projecting effectively can be expected to move steadily back from the edge of the stage. An inexperienced actor might, for example, be able to enlarge his projection in a single rehearsal to include the front quarter of the auditorium; at each later rehearsal he can be expected to push it farther and farther back, until he is able to make his speech intelligible throughout the entire audience. Actors differ in the ease with which they are able to master projection, and some will be able to extend their range much more quickly than others. Fully experienced actors may project throughout the entire theater as soon as they are asked to.

Inexperienced actors have great difficulty in judging projection, so the director must give them constant reports. If projection is a serious problem for one or more actors, it is desirable to schedule a special rehearsal devoted entirely to this aspect of performance. Such a rehearsal need not take very long and may be held following a regular rehearsal that has not run overtime.

It is best to work with one actor at a time, although the other actors may remain on stage and take part in the scene. The director should follow the testing procedure described above. He should take a position in the aisle well within the actor's area of effective projection. As the actor performs his lines, the director should back up the aisle to the cut-off point. Having explained the procedure in advance to the actor, when he reaches the limit of the effective area he should call out "Project!"; this can be done without stopping the scene or interrupting the speech. When the actor has responded with greater projection, the director should slowly move farther back in the aisle until the new critical distance is reached, and then should repeat his instruction. When the director has reached the back row, and the actor has increased his projection to cover the entire theater, the scene should be stopped and the actor asked to turn directly front and look at the position of the director, attempting to memorize the distance to the back row and the type of speech that provided adequate projection. The director can then turn to the second actor and repeat this procedure.

It is not necessary to rehearse a large section of the play in this way. The important thing is for the actor to achieve adequate projection and then fix in his mind the style of speech which was effective. Remembering this pattern is partly kinesthetic—he will have a sense of a particular degree of muscular effort necessary for full projection—and it is partly psychological. He must focus his attention on the distance to the back row, and on the necessity of communicating clearly to someone seated there. This should almost solve the problem, and it can be supplemented by a few shouts of "Project!" at the following rehearsal or two, until the actor is able to maintain full projection throughout the play.

Audibility is closely correlated with variations in the strength of actors' positions on stage, especially with the angles at which they are placed with reference to the front edge of the acting area. As an actor turns upstage, away from the audience, the audibility of his speech drops very sharply, much more than he is likely to realize. As an essential technical skill, every actor should be trained to adjust his projection to the angle of his position; and if he must speak an important line with his face turned partly or fully away from the audience, he must make an extreme increase in projection.

Such positions are uncommon, but they do occasionally occur. At the end of Act III of *Hedda Gabler,* Hedda takes the only copy of the manuscript of a book and destroys it by throwing it onto the fire in the fireplace a few sheets at a time, at the same time speaking with intense emotion bordering on hysteria. Since it is very difficult to simulate flames leaping up through burning paper, the fireplace for one production was built into the back wall, and the actress playing Hedda was instructed to hide the business with her body, thus necessarily turning away from the audience, with a considerable loss in the intelligibility of her speech. Blocking of that type is so unusual that not even an experienced actor can be expected to be able to judge the amount of projection needed, and must be tested and guided by the director.

As has been indicated, projection in the theater requires special techniques, not simply an exaggeration of those used in adapting to groups of the sizes that are commonly encountered in ordinary life. Outside the theater, when it is necessary to make speech heard at a distance, the usual practice is to increase it somewhat in pitch and greatly in loudness, that is, to yell. Neither of these methods is available to the actor in any important degree; the hero, sitting beside the heroine on a park bench at dusk, cannot yell a proposal of marriage in her ear without seeming ridiculous. Loudness must be increased somewhat, but it is safer to keep the increase too small than to risk making it too great. The single exception to this is the situation in which the actor must turn away from the audience; this position produces such an extreme loss in the volume of sound reaching the listener that the actor must compensate by speaking much louder. Pitch should not be raised at all; ideally it should remain at normal level, although it is often desirable to counteract actors' instinctive tendency to raise their average pitch in order to project by asking them instead to attempt to lower it.

Articulation

Projection requires two major vocal alterations; one involves articulation.

Most language sounds originate with the vocal chords, in the form of a neutral stream. This fundamental sound is then sent up into the mouth and nasal cavities, which alter it by absorbing certain frequencies and amplifying others. The nasal cavity can only be opened or closed, but the shape of the oral cavity can be changed and its reflective characteristics otherwise altered by variations in the pattern of muscular tension. Each different arrangement of the echo chambers changes the sound stream audibly. At least hundreds of distinctive sounds can be produced by the vocal mechanism. No language makes use of all of them; out of all the possible sounds, somewhat more than three dozen are selected for combination into the words that make up the language. Learning to speak these words involves experimentation with different oral positions, to identify the particular arrangement that will produce a particular sound. The various positions are practiced and memorized kinesthetically; continued use normally develops control of the speech muscles to an astonishing degree, and ultimately makes their operation almost automatic, so much so that it is not uncommon for people to talk even while unconscious.

Each sound in the language, then, depends on setting the vocal organs into a unique position, and the more distinctly different these positions are from each other, the clearer and more distinct the sounds will be. Moving the speech muscles from one position to another must be done at great speed, since each successive sound in a word requires a new position. If not enough energy is provided for the movements, they will be incomplete. The tip of the tongue may start upward toward the gums to pronounce the letter *l*, but may move so sluggishly that the movement is not completed in time, and the sound is altered or simply omitted. A major distinction between the sounds of *ah* and *aw*, as in *not* and *naught*, is that the jaws are opened moderately for the *aw* sound and widely for *ah*. If the muscles are too relaxed, and the mouth is opened a little too widely for *aw* and not quite enough for *ah*, the positions come closer together and may become identical, in which case the two sounds are indistinguishable.

The most useful device for unobtrusive vocal projection in the theater is making the sounds as unmistakably distinctive as possible; sharply articulated

> *Speak the speech, I pray you, as I pronounced it to you, trippingly on the tongue; but if you mouth it, as many of your players do, I had as lief the town crier spoke my lines.*
>
> SHAKESPEARE

speech is very much more audible than mushy or even normal speech, even without an increase in loudness or a raise in pitch. The most important suggestion that can be made to actors with regard to vocal projection, then, is to articulate with maximum clarity; indeed, as compared with ordinary living-room or sidewalk speech, they should *over*articulate.

The direction to overarticulate may be misinterpreted by actors, so that they substitute an incorrect sound for a correct one. For instance, the letter *t* is pronounced in ten different ways in English, two of which are illustrated in the word *title*. The selection of which particular pronunciation is to be used is determined by quite rigid rules, which are followed very precisely in normal speech, even though the speaker may have no conscious awareness of them. In the word *title*, for example, the first *t* sound is a "plosive," and never occurs at the end of a word, or between vowels within a word. One actor, when asked to sharpen his enunciation, did so by replacing the normal *t* sound in *Peter* with the plosive sound, in violation of the rule. The resulting pronunciation, which can perhaps be suggested by the spelling *pea turr,* was recognizable but clearly nonstandard, and was interpreted by the listener as affected. Improvement in articulation does not involve replacing a standard sound with one that is not standard, even if the nonstandard sound is believed to be clearer. Instead, it consists of sharpening the distinctions between the positions assumed by the vocal organs for all of the various sounds. For the speaker, this produces a greater feeling of tension in the vocal organs, and a considerable increase in the muscular energy expended. This tension should involve the oral muscles, not the muscles attacked to the vocal chords, and usually not the diaphragm; in other words, it should be felt in the mouth, not in the throat. Psychologically, the feeling is much the same as that which accompanies an improvement in posture and gesture: the speaker feels more alert, more active, and more in control of what he is doing. For the listener, the primary change should be an increased ease of understanding; as the speaker provides more effort, the listener should need to provide less. The change in pronunciation should not call attention to itself; if the listener is aware of any difference at all, he should notice only that he can understand more easily.

PROJECTION BY MEANS OF VOCAL VARIETY

The second major device for projection is an expanded use of variety in emphasis, which employs all three of the available resources, pitch, rate, and loudness. This does not contradict the suggestion that pitch be held at the same level, and loudness be increased only slightly. The average pitch of expanded stage speech should remain at the same level as the average pitch of the actor's normal speech outside the theater. He should attempt, however, to use his entire pitch range. An effective speaker might normally use perhaps an octave, located in the center of his total range, to indicate differences in the importance of the words he speaks. For the stage, the same number of pitch levels should be used, but they should be spread out across the speaker's full pitch range. The result is analogous to the sharpening of articulation. Each two distinctive pitch levels are spread farther apart, so that they are more clearly distinguishable. Once learned, this fuller exploitation of vocal resources is often retained outside the theater, and one of the clearest simple marks of the trained speaker is that he uses the entire range of his vocal resources, perhaps twice as wide a range of time, pitch, and loudness as an untrained speaker who has the same potential ranges and whose speech averages at the same point for the three factors. The wider use of the voice makes speech clearer and more attractive, without seeming artificial or affected, and usually without calling attention to the deviation from the commoner pattern of use.

Spreading speech over a broader area of the vocal range is quite different from altering the average pitch, rate, or loudness. Particularly with pitch, the actor should usually not be asked to change the average level at which he speaks. His average pitch should be accepted as given, and assumed to be the easiest and most natural for him. Occasionally an actor, intentionally or by accident, will have forced his speech into a section of his pitch range that is difficult for him to handle, even though continued practice may make the placement habitual. Especially during adolescence, some boys attempt to force their average pitch toward the bottom of their range, so as to sound more forceful or masculine. If it is suspected that an actor is speaking at a level that is not natural or easy for him, his total range should be determined. Starting at middle C on the piano, he should be asked to sing each note in the diatonic scale up to his highest note; starting again at C, he should then be asked to sing down to the bottom of his range. Listening to a recording of a few typical sentences from his performance should make it possible to identify the approximate position of his average pitch. Ideally it should be about a fourth or a third of the way up from the bottom of his range. This is a comfortable basic pitch, and provides adequate space for expressing the different degrees of importance in the upper two thirds of the scale. Since forcing the average pitch level to a position significantly higher or lower than this preferred one constitutes a misuse of the voice, it is appropriate to encourage the actor to move to his best level. This should be stated in terms that emphasize the advantages of the better position; that is, the director should not say "Well, I would like your voice better at this other pitch," but "You should try to use your voice as easily and naturally as possible; you are forcing it to a level that is unnatural for you, and you will find it takes much less effort if you move to this new level, and it will also become much easier to express what you have to communicate."

When actors are asked to expand their vocal range in a particular direction, they often respond by contracting it still further at the opposite end of the scale. For instance, an actor who is asked to make fuller use of the upper half of his pitch range may instead suppress the lower pitches, without making any change in the use of the higher pitches; the result is a slight shift upward in the average pitch (which is not desired), but no improvement in the use of pitch to emphasize the more important words. For that reason, it is better to direct the actor to expand at both ends of the scale. He should be instructed to move the words receiving the highest emphasis still farther up in his pitch range, and at the same time to drop the words at the lowest levels of emphasis still farther down in pitch. Since the function of variations in pitch, as well as in rate and loudness, is to differentiate between levels of importance in what is said, and since an actor who fails to use one end of his range adequately usually also avoids the other end, this is nearly always sound advice in itself, in addition to preventing the actor from simply cutting off still more of his range.

Especially if an actor's pitch range is somewhat higher than the norm, he may resist attempts to get him to use the higher pitches because of fear of sounding effeminate. In ordinary life the average pitch of women's speech is, of course, higher than men's; furthermore, women tend to use a wider vocal range than men. However, the impression of masculinity or femininity seems to depend much more on other factors, particularly on the use of different sets of inflectional or emphasis patterns; that is, if the speech of men and women were graphed, it seems probable that the outlines would differ in shape, aside from their differences in range and average pitch. This aspect of speech has not been adequately studied, so that the director must judge it intuitively. Certainly, the impression of effeminacy should almost always be carefully avoided. When the director senses it, he should attempt to correct it by altering the pattern of emphasis rather than by reducing the range, cutting off the top pitches, or forcing the actor's voice down to a level that is unnatural for him.

With pitch as with other aspects of the actor's speech, often his normal conversational speech is better than that which he uses on stage when reading from the script. One director remembers vividly an actress who, when urged to make more use of the upper section of her pitch range, shrieked, "But I *can't* raise my pitch; I never *could,* and it doesn't do any good to *try!*" Playing the recording of the remark, which on the emphatic words approached the pitch stratosphere, not only occasioned general laughter, but provided an unanswerable demonstration that the actress not only could use her pitch range effectively but did—when she was not reading from her script.

Probably the vocal resource beginning actors use least effectively is time or rate; it also seems neglected in ordinary conversational speech. If the vowel lengths in a recorded sample of especially skilled speech were measured, and those of an ordinary or ineffective speaker measured, it is probable that the range covered, that is the difference in length between the vowel in each sample held for the longest time and the vowel spoken most quickly, would be several times as great for the skilled speaker as for the other. As with pitch, the average rate is less significant than the amount of variety provided. The number of levels of importance that can be expressed by time depends on the number of different time-lengths used by the speaker. If he uses only twenty different durations for vowels, then he is able to express only twenty levels of importance so far as time is concerned. The range is less significant than the amount of variety provided, but it is important because, as the range is widened, it is possible to distinguish more easily between adjacent durations, and the broader range makes it possible to fit in additional steps. Most speakers seem to find it more difficult to sense variations in rate than in pitch or loudness. Continued experiment with speakers consciously trying to read a particular passage at different rates has revealed that they would often read at exactly the same speed each time, even though they were sure that the rate had varied. The director must consequently rely almost entirely on his own hearing in judging actors' handling of time, although an actor can often hear an extreme example of good or bad timing when it is analyzed for him and played from recording.

When rate monotony appears in actors' speech, it is most often produced by the avoidance of the upper end of the rate range, producing a fast monorate, or of the lower end, producing a slow monorate. Avoidance of both extremes is less common although it does occur, resulting in a monorate at the middle of the scale. Because it is difficult for the actor to hear or control his rate pattern, an actor who is asked to enlarge his range by speaking important words more slowly is most likely to respond by stretching all of his words, which slows down the average rate but leaves the speech equally monotonous. For this reason, such an instruction should nearly always be directed at the total range; the actor should be asked to stretch the range in both directions, making the most important words slower and the least important words faster, concentrating on the need for expressing greater distinctions between the levels of importance rather than simply on stretching the scale at one end.

Aside from the amount of time given to the various words, time is also important in phrasing. The uniformity with which words are spaced in the script seems to produce a matching uniformity in actors' speech. Old elocution books sometimes attempted to base phrasing instructions on punctuation, recommending a short pause for commas ("count *one* silently"), a slightly longer for colons and semicolons ("count *one-two*"), and a still longer for periods ("count *one-two-three*"). There is some correspondence between punctuation and the phrasing of normal speech, but the relation is so erratic and the correlation so low that attempting to make use of it is more a handicap than a help. Punctuation expresses grammatical structure; phrasing in speech should be psychological rather than grammatical. It should express the emotions, interests, and thinking of the speaker rather than the syntactical arrangement of his sentences.

Psychological Phrasing

In normal speech, the degree of attention given to individual words varies enormously. In most cases, each clause or sentence is pointed toward a key idea expressed in a single word. The path toward it is not reached by steady uniform steps; instead, each segment of the sentence typically contains a key word of its own, leading to the focal idea of the sentence, at a level of importance above most of the sentence but subordinate to the word of first importance. Psychologically, the attention is focused most sharply on the most important idea of the sentence, with the words next to it in importance being included in the area of sharp focus; the other words fall at the edge of the focal circle, and the speaker gives them little conscious attention. Speaking a sentence is psychologically analogous to the physical movement employed in playing hopscotch: the speaker leaps from one area to the next in a series of jumps in various directions that nevertheless move him toward a predetermined goal. This analogy implies that the key ideas are arranged in order of increasing importance. Actually, their order is strongly affected by syntactical rules, so that any arrangement is possible, although there is some tendency for the key idea to be placed close to the end of the sentence. This tendency toward a serial arrangement of ideas seems to be one of the marks distinguishing the style of speech from that of writing, although the differences have never been adequately studied, and in our present state of knowledge can only be guessed at.

In speech, then, each sentence tends to be divided into short sections, each with its own focal word, around which the subordinate words are arranged. In effective performance, the vocal resources are used to express these psychological units by marking each key word. In addition, the breaks between the units are indicated by the use of pitch and loudness, but especially by pauses between them. Marking these divisions is of great importance in clarity of communication. When a listener complains that he cannot "hear" an actor, it is seldom the case that the voice is actually inaudible; it is far more likely that the listener can hear but cannot understand. Often, simply telling the actor to "phrase it" will be enough to make the speech intelligible.

These psychological units to some extent correspond to grammatical or syntactical units, and in that case the reading may follow the punctuation. More often they will differ, so that words separated by commas in the script must be read in a single unit, and phrasal breaks must be spoken between words that in the script are printed without intervening punctuation. Sometimes an actor needs to express indecision, or distraction, or the inability to think of a word, by inserting perhaps even a long, sharp break into what is syntactically a smooth and unified phrase. Such a pause can also be used to suggest a character's desire to avoid speaking a particular word. An especially significant line in the first act of *Antony and Cleopatra* has already been mentioned. Antony has received a letter from Rome, which Cleopatra assumes has come from his wife, and she is about to ask him (translating the line into the comparatively flat modern English) "What does your wife say in her letter?" However, her jealousy of Fulvia, and other emotions too complex to describe here, leads her to avoid the word *wife,* and what she actually asks is, "What says the married woman?" It is important that the actress point out to the audience Cleopatra's avoidance of the obvious word. At least one way of reading it would be to insert a break, "What says—the married woman?," to suggest that the forbidden word was on the tip of her tongue, and that the effort to find a replacement for it produced a momentary interruption in the speech.

Incidentally, a close study of Shakespeare's better plays reveals that syntactical units are often extended across the joint between lines of verse, a phrase or clause beginning at the end of one line and finishing at the beginning of the next. Sometimes there seems no reason for the placement of the pause between lines that is necessary if the verse pattern is to be made clear; in a surprising number of cases, however, a close study of the passage will suggest that there is a psychological reason for a break at the end of a verse line, even though grammatically the phrase or clause flows without interruption. As she is about to commit suicide, for instance, Cleopatra says "Methinks I hear Antony call." This sentence is divided between two lines, the first ending with the word "hear." Syntactically, "Antony" is joined to the verb "hear" as its object. Reading the line with an interrupting pause at this point, however, may well be psychologically sounder and theatrically more expressive than following the syntactical pattern: "Methinks I hear—Antony call." The effect is a heightening of emotion, as if by a sudden catch of the breath, with a resulting emphasis on "Antony," which can be reinforced by the vocal treatment given the name. It is difficult at this point in time to determine Shakespeare's intentions, but what at first seem obtrusive and meaningless verse pauses so often provide valuable hints for more effective readings that it is at least possible that they are intended to guide the actor by means of a kind of spatial punctuation.

As was illustrated by that example, a pause tends to emphasize the word or phrase that follows it; the longer the pause, the stronger that effect, since it results from an increase in suspense during the break. A pause also has some slight effect in emphasizing the word which precedes it, since it is allowed to remain in the listener's mind for a longer period of time.

One of the special marks of an accomplished actor is his skillful use of pauses. Beginning actors must be instructed constantly to use more and longer pauses, so much so that "Phrase it!" is one of the director's commoner instructions.

It might seem that the use of pauses is a violation of the rule that there should never be a moment of silence in the theater. The principle that the rule is designed to serve, however, is that the experience of the audience should continue without a break. So long as the communication of emotions or ideas continues, silence is as acceptable as speech. If the audience interprets a pause as expressive of an emotion, the flow of the play will seem uninterrupted so long as the emotion can be credibly assumed to last, and so long as it seems to provide new and significant information for the audience. The more intense the emotion, the longer the pause can be stretched. Any pause will break if stretched too far, that is, it will fail to hold the attention of the audience beyond a certain limit. This break point is very easy to sense from a seat in the auditorium; it is much more difficult for the actors. Since actors tend to use pauses too infrequently and to weaken their effect by shortening them, it is often helpful to ask an actor to hold a pause in rehearsal beyond the break point—to stretch it so far that it will no longer sustain attention. If the actor cannot even then identify this point, the director can ask him to hold the pause indefinitely, can himself assess when the break point has been reached, and can indicate it by snapping his fingers or shouting "Now!" or "Break!" when it has been reached. It is often helpful for the director to demonstrate by reading the line himself and stretching the pause until it is just short of breaking; this is especially effective if the two readings can be compared on recording, and timed with a stopwatch or by counting. Recordings of performances by highly skilled actors can also be used to demonstrate the effective use of rate variety, as well as pauses, although it is better to use recordings of plays other than the one the cast is rehearsing. It is not suggested, of course, that all pauses should be held to the break point, but since actors tend to underuse this resource, it is a useful point of reference, and identifying the full length a particular pause can be held without losing the audience's attention will demonstrate the extent of time available for the actor's use.

CUES

In a few exceptional instances, pauses can be used effectively between speeches, but such moments are so rare that actors should be trained to deliver speeches regularly with no silence between them at all. The first phrase of one speech should follow the end of the preceding speech so precisely that the flow of sound is continuous.

Usually the last phrase of each speech is marked as a cue to the following speech, and memorized along with the line. Responding to a cue is not instantaneous, so that if the actor fixes on the last word of the preceding speech as his signal to start his own line, an unwanted pause will occur. Since the length of time it takes to respond varies, each actor should be instructed to experiment in rehearsal to identify the single word that will cue him to start his speech at exactly the right time. In *The Taming of the Shrew,* Grumio cries "Help, masters, help! My master is mad!," and Petruchio replies "Now, knock when

I bid you, sirrah villain!" If the actor playing Petruchio listens for the word *mad* as his cue, there is likely to be a sizable pause before he is able to start his own speech; a better choice is probably *master*; perhaps it will even be necessary to select the last *help* as the actual cue word. Experimenting in rehearsal will demonstrate which word provides the right timing. Petruchio's *now* should follow Grumio's *mad* as closely as *mad* follows *is*, but usually the speeches should not overlap.

The insertion of even a brief pause between each two speeches can lengthen a play measurably. Far more important is the fact that each such pause seems to the audience to break the continuity of the play, which then disintegrates into a slow and tedious series of fragments.

It will take several rehearsals for actors to learn to handle cues properly, and they can hardly work on it until they are fairly secure in their lines. They should begin to make progress as soon as they begin to rehearse without scripts, but the mastery of cuing is achieved primarily during the polishing rehearsals. It is difficult for actors to sense their handling of cues, and so the director must give them continuing reports. He should watch for lagging cues throughout the fixing rehearsals, although the presumption is that the actors will generally handle the timing effectively during the last week. Actors tend to copy each other's pacing, often without realizing it, so that if cuing is slow during the opening scene of a rehearsal it is wise to report it to the actors in order to avoid their carrying the error throughout the entire evening. The instruction for remedying slow cues is "Pick it up!" or "Pick up your cues!"

It is a common practice to time acts or scenes at the later rehearsals, preferably with a stopwatch; slow cues may lengthen a scene appreciably. Far more important than clock time, however, is psychological timing, whether a scene seems exciting and interesting to the audience or static and slow, and that is less dependent on the actual length of the scene than on the richness of the experience created for the audience. Certainly the idea that playing a scene in ten minutes is necessarily more effective than playing it in eleven is quite false. An increase in tempo that obscures meaning or makes it impossible for the audience to absorb what is offered them may seem tedious, and may even paradoxically make the scene seem slower than a performance that actually takes more time. Asking the assistant director to hold a stopwatch during a rehearsal may give the director information that will be useful in advising the actors, but he should always supplement it by his own empathic response to the scene, which should always take precedence over the mechanical report of the elapsed time.

VOICE QUALITY

Nothing has been said about voice quality, except in connection with articulation. For special reasons, extreme attention is given to voice quality in training singers, and it is often assumed that it is equally important in drama. A beautiful voice is of course an asset to an actor, as is a beautiful profile, but its effect is very small as compared with other elements. In fact, many of the most famous and successful actors have had voices of only ordinary quality, and a surprising number have had voices less pleasant than the average. The purpose of the voice in the theater is to express ideas and emotions; it is an instrument for communication, not an artifact to be displayed for its own beauty. Skilled actors differ from ordinary speakers in the extent to which they use their voices. Their actual range may be no greater, but they use all of it, instead of restricting their speech to a narrow segment. Within this range, they display greater variety, that is, they utilize a greater number of different levels of emphasis. But most important of all, their use of their voices is fully, richly, accurately, and precisely adjusted to the meanings and emotions they have discovered in their lines or have developed as supplements to the script. The result, for the listener, is an impression of greater involvement, of heightened interest, of an intenser aliveness and awareness, of a richer and more varied experience—all those things that contribute to the impression of glamor. An actor who can develop a command of his voice that will create such an impression will be able to speak with striking effectiveness. And his fundamental vocal equipment is much less significant than the achievement of full control of it, just as an accomplished violinist can perform more effectively on a cheap fiddle then a person with no musical training or ability could on a Stradivarius.

13/Meaning and Emotion

The discussion of the use of voice and body in the two preceding chapters has been mainly technical, and mastery of this aspect of production is essential for every director. But techniques have no value in themselves; their only purpose is to assist in communicating meaning and emotion, that is, in creating the desired experience for the audience.

THE IMAGINATIVE CREATION OF THE FINISHED PERFORMANCE

The director's preliminary analysis of the script, and his work on blocking, will have resulted in the development of a picture of the finished production, which grows steadily more vivid and detailed as he works. Even designing the apparently isolated pattern of blocking will have required his analyzing the emotions and meanings of the lines, and at least adumbrating how they will be read. Directors vary in the completeness, vividness, and detail incorporated in this mental record of the play. Some directors wait to discover its final details until they have been worked out in rehearsals; others visualize every gesture, every bit of business, every change in facial expression, and hear in their imagination every vocal inflection. The result is a kind of imaginary television tape recording of the full performance.

Each of the two extreme treatments has advantages and disadvantages. The imaginative creation of a performance in full detail in advance of the start of rehearsals requires a great deal of time, intense concentration, and a level of ability in visual and auditory imagination that is rare even among theater artists. Its most serious danger is that the pattern developed fails to take into

335

account the actors who will perform in the play. Each of them will have his own special limitations, and the readings as imagined may require abilities of the actors that they do not have. In addition, each actor will bring his own strengths to his role, his own special insights and skills, which the director can discover and exploit only after rehearsals have begun. When his preconception of the performance is detailed, its apparent completeness may tend to close his mind to the actors' contributions, and may make it harder for him to incorporate them in the play, so that the final production will lack a richness and variety that would have been possible with a less rigid preparation.

The major advantage of the full plan is that it reduces the demands on the director's attention and judgment during rehearsals. Since he will already have made thousands of decisions about the play, he will be able to concentrate his attention more fully on the actors' performance. Furthermore, the study necessary for a full imaginative creation of the play guarantees that he will have become totally familiar with it, that he will have absorbed it so completely that every aspect of it will lie at the front of his mind, and he will find it easy to pull together all of the information provided by the script that is relevant to any problem that develops. The feeling of assurance and command that such preparation produces is not only gratifying to the director but enables him to conduct rehearsals more efficiently.

The factors that should govern the director's choice of planning method are his personal preferences, the time available, and his ability to rework the plan so as to incorporate the actors' contributions.

RECORDING THE ANALYSES OF EMOTIONS

Directors also differ in their methods of recording their analyses of the lines. Almost all directors make fairly complete notes of their blocking designs, but most do not record their analyses of emotion in any detail, probably because the emotional decisions are easier to remember than the blocking and need not be dictated to the actors. Even if the emotional analyses are recorded in full, they are primarily for the use of the director himself. It is presumed that each actor will work out the emotional implications of his own part, and discussion is limited to especially difficult lines. The attempt to write down the emotions which the director feels should be expressed by the actors reveals one major source of difficulty, the poverty of the emotional terms in the language. The director will constantly visualize shades and degrees of emotions for which there seem to be no words in the language. Often he will have to be satisfied with an approximation, with terms that will remind him of his analysis, even though they may not express it with precise accuracy.

As an example of the most detailed type of planning, the second scene of Shakespeare's *Twelfth Night* is reproduced below, with the annotations made by one director as a preparation for rehearsal. The scene is reproduced exactly, with sound, light, and blocking instructions, as well as emotional interpretations. The director's notes are given in italics and enclosed in brackets. As with blocking, the emotional notations in each case are inserted in the speeches immediately before the passage to which they apply. The speeches have been numbered in the left margin to make it easier to identify them in rehearsal; this director included the light and sound directions in the number scheme.

As with every play, the interpretation of the lines depends on the director's understanding of the style and purpose of the play as a whole. Although other directors might have analyzed *Twelfth Night* differently, an attempt will be made to describe the concept of the play developed by the director who prepared the plans from which this scene is taken. The following description is not intended as a definitive analysis of the play, but rather as a report of how one director saw it.

Twelfth Night is a tragicomedy; it has a happy ending, and is generally bright in tone, with some passages of low comedy, but there are occasional overtones of violence and even cruelty, which prevent its being classified simply as a comedy. It is a stylish play in all senses of the word. It has a vivid and varied style of its own, glittering with figures of speech and other types of word play, and it presents a group of characters who are self consciously mannered and artificial, who are playing a game of fashion. The play has some of the characteristics of a "comedy of manners"; the high style artificiality of the aristocratic characters is made more striking by contrasting it with the riotous earthiness of the servants and Belch and Aguecheek. Viola is a kind of bridge between the two groups; essentially aristocratic, she appears as a servant throughout most of the play.

Sir Toby Belch and Maria are the most sympathetic characters, with Viola most attractive among the aristocrats. Duke Orsino is an excessively artificial poseur, in love with love, and playing the part of a fashionable suitor to Olivia, who is busily enacting a conventionally sentimental role based on the recent death of her brother. The play ends not simply with hero and heroine united, but in an exaggeration of the traditional happy ending, with three marriages in prospect. Viola's capture of Orsino breaks through the pattern of artificial pretense; the play thus seems to be an attack on artificiality and an advocacy of true love.

The second scene introduces Viola, and is the only one in which she appears dressed as a woman. Throughout all the rest of the play she is disguised as a young man, although she is finally recognized in the last scene. Viola is a pert soubrette, interesting, vivid, pretty, and charming. She is skillful at manipulating people, especially men, and although she makes some attempt to adopt the fashionable poses, her natural vivacity and high spirits keep breaking through the pretense. In this scene, she has just escaped from shipwreck and has been cast up on the shore with the old captain of the ship. They appear on stage in the middle of their search for help. The scene is essentially expository; it not only provides information about what has happened before the play began, but it is essential in establishing Viola's personality and femininity, since for the rest of the play she will be disguised as a man. Consequently the director felt that such elements as her natural timidity and her charm and flirtatiousness should be displayed as clearly as possible. The plan for the scene as worked out by the director is as follows.

TWELFTH NIGHT, Act I, Scene 2

1	SOUND:	[*Bridge music up full*]
2	LIGHTS:	[*Fade lights in area 3 to about a third of their original level; fade area 2 lights down about half. Area 4 remains up full. The red streak along the horizon has been faded to half its original level during the preceding scene; continue to fade it slowly during this scene; it should be entirely out by the end of the scene*]
3		[*As soon as the bridge music is up full, Viola enters up right followed by the Captain, and they walk slowly along the street to up center, then downstage*]
4	SOUND:	[*Fast fade on bridge music as Viola reaches the center of area 4, then out*]
5	VIOLA:	[*Stops just below the center of area 4; looks about her, down left and down right. Speaks with a touch of wonder and apprehension*] What country, friend, is this?
6	CAPTAIN:	[*Steps down almost level with her, on her right. Speaks over her shoulder; speaks deferentially and gently*] This is Illyria, lady.
7	VIOLA:	[*Walks quickly to the down-left edge of area 4; speaks irritably*] And what should I do in Illyria? [*Plaintively*] My brother, he is in Elysium. [*Turns right, speaks with sudden plaintive eagerness*] Perchance he is not drowned. What think you, captain?
8	CAPTAIN:	[*Steps down almost level with her; speaks gently, with gentle emphasis on the pun*] It was per chance that you yourself were saved.
9	VIOLA:	[*Turns left, covers her face with her hands, speaks as if ready to break down*] Oh, my poor brother! [*Turns right suddenly, speaks to the captain with a touch of pert defiance*] And so perchance may he be!
10	CAPTAIN:	[*Steps level with her; speaks soothingly*] True, madam, and to *comfort* you with chance Assure yourself, after our ship did split, When you and those poor number saved with you

Hung on our driving boat, I saw your brother,
    [*Sententiously*]
Most provident in peril, bind himself—
    [*Sententiously*]
Courage and hope both teaching him the practice,
    [*Points down right*]
To a strong mast that *lived* upon the sea;
    [*With a touch of the dramatic, gesturing*]
Where, like Arion on the dolphin's back,
I saw him hold acquaintance with the waves
So long as I could see. [*Lets his hand drop*]

11 VIOLA: [*Snatches coin from her purse, and steps quickly to him, holding her right hand outstretched; speaks with plaintive joy*]
For saying so, there's gold!
    [*The Captain takes the coin, bows, bites it, and slips it into his purse. Viola turns left, speaks with plaintive animation*]
Mine own escape unfoldeth to my hope,
Whereto thy speech serves for authority,
The *like* of him. [*Turns back to him suddenly, speaks suddenly*]
Know'st thou this country?

12 CAPTAIN: [*Takes a step down right, nods his head wisely*]
Aye, madam, well; [*Points off stage, down right*] for I was bred and born
Not three hours' travel from this very place.

13 VIOLA: [*Looking about her, down right and down left, speaks curiously*]
Who governs here?

14 CAPTAIN: [*Respectfully—the perfect gentleman's gentleman*]
A noble duke, in nature as in name.

15 VIOLA: [*Turns to him; speaks with curiosity—always interested in a bit of gossip*]
What is his name?

16 CAPTAIN: [*Clips off the name in a self-satisfied manner: he knows about all the best people*]
Orsino!

17 VIOLA: [*Squealing with delight and amazement*]
Orsino! I have heard my father name him!
    [*Coyly, speculatively—never overlook an eligible male*]
He was a *bachelor—then!*

18 CAPTAIN: [*Sententiously*]
And so is now, [*Carelessly*] or was so, very late;
    [*Points down right*]
For but a month ago I went from hence,
    [*Conspiratorially—a practiced hand at backstairs gossip*]
And then 'twas fresh in murmur, [*Deprecatingly*] —as you know,
    [*With self-satisfied sententiousness*]
What great ones do, the less will prattle of—
    [*Lowers his voice to a stage whisper, moves close to her—this is a really juicy morsel*]

That he did seek the love of fair Olivia!

19   VIOLA: [*Draws back offended—let the other girls keep their hands off her prospects! Even so, that "what" instead of "who" is just a little more than we would expect of our heroine*]
What's *she?*

20   CAPTAIN: [*Smugly—he only gossips about the* toniest *people*]
A virtuous maid, the daughter of a *count*
[*With sanctimonious regret*]
That died some twelvemonth since; [*Picking up the story, with relish*] then leaving her
In the protection of his son, her brother,
[*Shaking his head sadly*]
Who shortly also died; [*Picking it up, with relish*] for whose dear love,
They say, [*Really tickled with this juicy item*] she hath abjured the company
And *sight* of *men!*

21   VIOLA: [*Her unwillingness to admit her admiration for such nobility gives her reply a touch of snippishness*]
                     Oh, that *I* served that lady,
[*With a touch of plaintiveness—nobody can outdo* her *when it comes to mourning brothers*]
And might not be delivered to the world,
Till I had made mine own occasion mellow,
What my estate is!

22   CAPTAIN: [*A little snappishly; she didn't have to try to top his story, did she?*]
                     That were hard to compass,
Because she will admit no kind of suit,
[*Amazement*]
No, not the *Duke's!*

23   VIOLA: [*Realizing she has gone a shade too far, and anxious not to offend a man—however ineligible—turns on all her charm, of which she has more than enough; moves to him, slips her right hand under his arm, looks sweetly up into his face, turns on the flattery; coos*]
There is a fair behavior in thee, Captain;
[*Fruitily, sententiously*]
And though that nature with a beauteous wall
Doth oft close in pollution, yet of thee
I well believe thou hast a mind that suits
[*Almost unconsciously, her left hand lays itself on horny hand, and he melts. She speaks sweetly*]
With this thy fair and outward character.
[*She has won—let's not waste the honey on the trapped fly; she shifts to a businesslike note*]
I prithee— [*Warningly*] and I'll pay thee bounteously,
[*Pleading, with intensity*]

Conceal me what I am, and be my aid
For such disguise as haply shall become
The form of my intent. [*With determination*] I'll *serve* this Duke!
   [*Swings away from him at arm's length, her right hand still
   under his arm; speaks excitedly*]
Thou shalt present me to him as a boy!;
   [*Coquettishly*]
It may be worth thy pains; [*Spreads her skirt with her left hand;
   speaks brightly, argumentatively*] for I can *sing*,
And *speak* to him in many sort of music,
   [*Modestly, coquettishly*]
That will allow me very worth his service.
   [*Playfully*]
What else may hap, to time I will commit;
   [*Swings right, close to him, laying her hand on his arm; begging
   him with childish eagerness*]
Only shape thou thy *silence* [*Coquettishly*] to my wit.

24 CAPTAIN: [*Completely taken in, wags his head in pleased embarrassment,
            speaks with honest emphasis*]
Be you his *boy*, and I your *mute* will be;
   [*Points to his tongue and eyes, nods his head wisely*]
When my tongue blabs, then let mine eyes not see!

25 VIOLA: [*Eagerly, but making it clear she's not the boss; takes his hand
            in both of hers and gives it just the gentlest tug*]
I thank thee; lead me on.
   [*Viola and the Captain walk down right and exit along the
   street*]

26 SOUND: [*As Viola and the Captain start down right, bring in bridge
            music*]

27 LIGHTS: [*As Viola and the Captain start down right, simultaneously
            fade as follows: area 4 out, area 3 out, area 2 up, area 1 up*]

The director's handling of this scene will repay study. Often emotions are suggested indirectly, sometimes by mentioning a relevant phase of the character's personality: "the perfect gentleman's gentleman," "a practiced hand at backstairs gossip," "never overlook an eligible male." A good deal of emotional interpretation has been added to the scene beyond that clearly indicated by the script, although the director has been careful to make his additions fit harmoniously with what has been included in the lines themselves. As much emotional variety as possible has been provided, and contrast between the personalities of the two characters has been emphasized rather than reduced. Movement and business have been invented not only to support Viola's vivacity, but to assist both actors in expressing the emotions and the meaning of the lines.

Seldom is the reading of lines planned in as great detail by the director as is demonstrated in this example; in fact this director has carried his planning beyond the stage for which he is fully responsible. Presumably each actor will work up his own lines in this detail, and in fact the final performance should be still richer, since even this description does not include all possible shades of meaning or emotion, all variations in gesture and voice. Even with their own lines, actors seldom record their analyses as fully as has been done in this script, but they are responsible for making an even larger number of decisions, still more subtle and detailed, and memorizing them during rehearsals and their independent study of the play.

The Development of Reading During Rehearsals

Actors usually give quite flat, uninflected, and physically static performances during the early rehearsals. As their study continues, they acquire a growing understanding of their roles and are able to steadily enrich them. That process should go on at an accelerating rate through at least the first half of the rehearsal period. By the beginning of the blending rehearsals, it should be almost completed, and only a few new details can be expected to appear during the blending and polishing rehearsals. During the fixing rehearsals, it is assumed that no further changes in the performances will take place.

The director should watch this pattern of development carefully. Even though it may proceed very well during early rehearsals, an actor often strikes a plateau and may make no further improvement in his interpretation. Although he might recover spontaneously and begin again to enrich his performance, the danger of his being permanently stopped is too great to risk, and the director should provide assistance immediately.

Two techniques are available in this circumstance. One is to discuss the meaning and emotion of key lines with the actor, carrying the analysis one level deeper than he has expressed in his performance. Although this should be a true discussion, its purpose is to stimulate the actor to continue the analysis on his own, and so it is more effective to ask him questions than simply to deepen the analysis for him. The alternative technique is to ask him to work over specific lines during the rehearsal, trying various readings and analyzing the implications of each; usually that will force him to consider subtler shades of meaning.

The director's push should always be in the direction of the fullest, richest, most alive performance possible. Since this involves an emotional and ideational amplification beyond the limits of ordinary conversation (analogous to visual and vocal projection), inexperienced actors are likely to have some difficulty in achieving it. As with vocal projection, when they reach the limit of the scale of vividness within which they normally operate outside the theater, they are likely to resist taking the next step. This familiar limit, however, is something like the sound barrier that airplanes must confront: It is difficult to break through it, but once it is past, further progress is fairly easy. Actors who have reached this point must consequently be given all of the encouragement possible by the director, so that their final performances will not remain at the level of insipidity and uncommunicativeness that is common in ordinary life, and may even be acceptable there, but which is not enough in the theater.

HANDLING ELEVATED SPEECH

Figures of speech, or any language of special vividness or brilliance, appear in ordinary conversation only as an expression of high emotion. When they are included in actors' lines, they can be made to seem natural only if the actors support them with animated delivery and with the greatest intensity of emotion the situation will allow. Elevated material spoken in ordinary conversational style seems absurdly pompous and silly. In a civic production of a play—which shall be nameless—the heroine's speeches alternated between two styles, one very ordinary, the other decorated, figurative, and inflated, apparently intended by the playwright to sound poetic. Since the play was unimaginative claptrap, neither style was effective, so that reading the lines acceptably presented a major problem. The actress who played the part had sufficient good taste to be embarrassed by the pseudopoetic passages and tried to soften them by underplaying them; when she reached a commonplace line, she was so relieved that she delivered it with unnatural fervor. Although understandable, this pattern of reading was exactly the opposite of the safest performance. The understated lines should have been read casually, and the inflated material supported by as intense a reading as possible. Probably nothing could have saved this production, but that treatment would have helped conceal the clumsiness of the attempt at poetry, especially if the actress had spoken the lines as fast as possible, so as to give the audience less time to analyze them. At least her own embarrassment would have been concealed and would not have been picked up and shared by the audience.

The recommendation that elevated language should be strongly supported by the actor does not apply simply to clumsy attempts at decoration; it is equally important for passages that are genuinely effective and in good taste.

The emotion used to lift up such lines may be of any type: playfulness, as in Mercutio's famous Queen Mab speech in *Romeo and Juliet,* self-loathing, as in Medea's monologue after her interview with the king, in Euripides' play; or sheer delight in life, as in Countess Aurelia's argument as to why life is worth living, in the first act of *The Madwoman of Chaillot.*

VOCAL TECHNIQUES

A number of specific techniques affect the communication of meaning and emotion, and the director will find it necessary to explain them to the actors. A few of them will be discussed.

VARIETY IN CHARACTERIZATION

Since contrast and conflict are almost the essence of drama, and variety is necessary for any work of art, the director should attempt to get the actors to express as wide and varied a range of emotions as possible. The empathy and sensitivity that are fundamental parts of the actor's personality often trap him into copying the mood and delivery of the speech preceding his own, rather than responding to it. To the extent that that happens, he alters his character and adopts that of the other person in the scene. If all of the actors pick up their reading styles from each other, contrast disappears, interest lags, and meaning and characterizations are obscured. Each speech should (with occasional exceptions) be a response to the preceding one, but it should contrast with it rather than echo it. If the characters are well drawn, analyzing the lines closely should demonstrate clear differences in their characteristic reactions, and those differences should be exploited fully. The director should encourage the actors to supplement the clues in the script with any harmonious sources of contrast. If one actor speaks loudly and quickly, the next can respond slowly and quietly; if one is elated, the second can express skepticism; if one speaks at a low pitch, the other can raise his pitch. Of course, the specific techniques used should be carefully chosen to harmonize with the personalities of the characters, the situation, and their lines.

CRESCENDO EFFECTS

One particular pattern of response is common enough that it is likely to appear in almost every play. It is used when a scene must build in intensity. A steady crescendo is produced if each speaker will deliver his speech at a higher level of intensity than the preceding speech. Intensity then builds by a series of steps, the size of which can be adjusted to control the speed of crescendo. This device is called "topping," and the director's instruction to the actors in this case is "Each speech should top the one before it."

If the crescendo must extend over a fairly long scene, there is some danger that the actors will reach the limit of their range of intensity in the middle of the scene and be unable to continue the rise throughout the rest of the scene. Three methods can be used to correct that problem. The actors can be instructed to drop the level of intensity lower at the beginning of the scene, to build by smaller steps, and to delay the start of the crescendo until about a fourth of the scene has been played. The second of those techniques is the most desirable, the first is next in acceptability; the third should be used only if the other two methods do not solve the problem.

PLOT LINES

Just as an actor must sometimes make crosses designed to serve the play as a whole but not clearly motivated by his speeches, so he must sometimes give particular lines an emphasis greater than the situation or the character justifies. This usually involves impressing on the audience a piece of information which has little significance at the moment, but which will later be seen to be important. Such lines are referred to as "plot lines," that is, they are lines that have a special importance in helping the audience understand later plot development, but that do not have equal significance for the character as he speaks them.

The problem is to make plot lines memorable without seeming to emphasize them, to say them apparently casually, and yet make them clear to the audience. Probably the best way to handle plot lines is by the exaggerated use of time. Pausing before the line gives it emphasis, saying it slowly, especially stretching the key words, and phrasing it as meaningfully as possible, marking the phrases with slightly longer pauses than usual, are likely to make it fully communicative. Of course, the words should be enunciated with special clarity. Concern is usually accompanied by an increase in pitch and loudness; casual speech is usually delivered toward the bottom of the pitch and loudness ranges. By holding these two vocal elements low, the plot line is made to seem casual, and at the same time the rate emphasis calls attention to it and communicates what is said clearly, so that the double requirement of unobtrusiveness and emphasis is achieved by this technique.

THROWAWAY LINES

A similar technique is frequently applicable to lines at which the audience is expected to laugh. Very often a laugh line is most effective if it is spoken very casually; an actor who does that is said to "throw it away." In this case, the reading should be placed at the bottom of all three ranges, time as well as pitch and loudness. Of course the line must be heard and understood, but a skillful use of the devices for vocal projection should make it possible to communicate such a line clearly while still creating an impression of casualness. If the actor can devise a turn, a short cross, or a piece of business that will turn his head directly toward the audience at the moment he speaks the line, projection will be greatly improved. One actor in a university production was disturbed by the fact that the audiences at the first two performances of a play had failed to respond to a line he felt was sure to get a laugh. When he asked for the director's advice, he was told "You're trying too hard; throw it away next time." At the third performance, he followed the advice, speaking the line as if it were of no importance—and was greeted by a roar of laughter.

PRODUCING LAUGHTER

Handling audience laughter involves a special set of techniques, and an understanding of the psychology of humor. Unfortunately, although humor

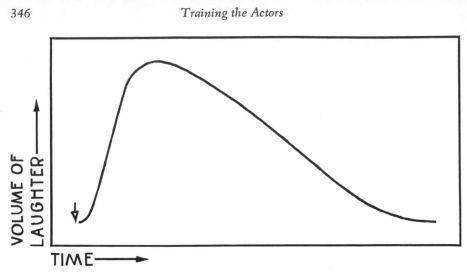

Figure 47. The pattern of laughter. The open arrow indicates the point at which the punch line of the joke was completed (or whatever instantaneous stimulus served to complete the laugh pattern).

has been studied at some length, the conclusions reached are feeble and inadequate. However, enough is known about the pattern of laughter to provide the actor with a basis for controlling it. Since few actors can be expected to be familiar with this pattern, it is desirable for the director to discuss it with each cast appearing in a comedy.

Laughter depends on a high level of tension. In stimulating an audience to laugh, then, the actor must provide a steady crescendo of tension. This can be done by increasing the amount of physical movement, by increasing the speed, pitch, and loudness of the voice, and by displaying a rising emotion or intensity on the part of the character who is being represented. The higher the level of tension, the more enthusiastic the laugh will be. However, there is a limit to the amount of tension that an audience can sustain, and after it has been passed, they will laugh spontaneously, even though the punch line of the joke has not yet been reached. It is consequently important that the actor sense this critical point, and not raise the tension past it before he reaches the moment where it is intended that the laugh occur.

Unless the tension level is held for an unbearable length of time, however, laughter requires a second element: the tension must be broken very quickly, almost instantaneously. If it is reduced slowly no laughter will occur.

The pattern of performance that will cause an audience to laugh, then, is one that produces a steady increase in tension over a measurable length of time, as high as possible short of the breaking point, and then an instantaneous stimulus designed to break the tension, usually including an element of surprise.

BUILDING LAUGHS

This fundamental pattern is subject to many variations. A special one that is occasionally useful is a technique called "building laughs." Let us suppose that an actor has a speech containing three points at which moderate laughter might be expected from the audience, based on three feeble jokes (feeble because none of them creates a sufficiently high level of tension to produce a

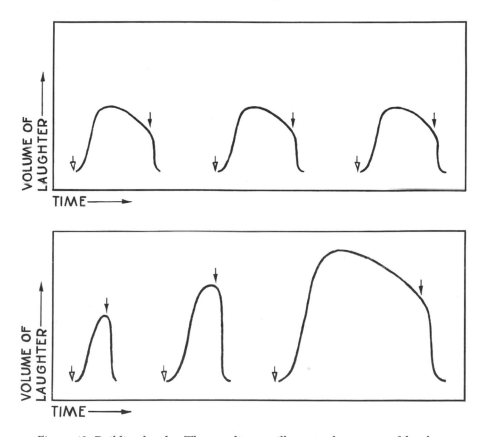

Figure 48. Building laughs. The top diagram illustrates the pattern of laughter when three weak jokes are handled in the usual way. The open arrows indicate the punch lines of the jokes, and the solid arrows mark the point at which the actor recommenced his speech, resulting in a quick suppression of the audience's laughter. The bottom diagram illustrates the process of building laughs. For the first two jokes, the actor recommences his line earlier than normal, so that the audience is prevented from dissipating the tension that has been built up; as a result, tension continues to rise, producing a stronger laugh in response to the third joke, which the actor treats in the normal way, delaying his line until the laughter has begun to die down spontaneously.

hearty laugh). As he tells the first joke, the tension of the audience mounts to a moderate level, and at the end their tension is dissipated by a mild laugh; the same pattern is repeated for the second and third jokes. However, there is another way of handling such a trio. The actor runs through the first joke in the same way as he had done before; however, instead of allowing the tension to be dissipated by laughter, he breaks into the audience's response as soon as it has well begun, gets their attention by topping them, and then starts the second joke. Since only a little of the tension created by the first joke has been allowed to dissipate, the second starts from a higher level of tension and moves upward. The laughter at the end of the second joke is cut off in the same way, and the third joke is used to carry the accumulated tension still higher. At the final punch line, the audience bursts into a roar of laughter.

HOLDING FOR LAUGHS

One vital rule in comedy may seem to contradict the technique of building laughs: An audience must never be prevented from laughing if they want to. The building pattern does not prevent the laughter, however, but simply delays it. The error consists of cutting it off altogether. If the actors do not wait for a laugh to die down, but continue with the scene, part of the lines will be missed. Since the members of the audience are anxious to follow the entire play, they will inhibit their laughter the next time so as not to miss anything. Cutting off a single big laugh early in a show can dampen audience response throughout the rest of the evening to an astonishing degree, reducing the total number of laughs by as much as fifty percent.

Psychologically a very peculiar thing happens to an audience when they laugh: they have the illusion that time stands still for the duration of the laughter. Even if a laugh should last for a full two or three minutes, the audience has no feeling that the play has stopped or been interrupted. When the laugh has died down and the actors resume, the audience interpret the action as having continued without pause. For that reason, actors must learn to "hold" for laughs, that is, to stop the play and hold their positions without speech or movement, until the audience is ready to watch them and listen to them again.

But although it is important not to cut off a laugh too soon, it is equally dangerous to hold too long before starting the action again. Even a fraction of a second's pause after a laugh has finished is interpreted by the audience as a break in the continuity of the performance. Skilled actors must learn to listen closely to audiences' laughter, to identify its pattern, and to resume the play at exactly the right moment.

Audience laughter follows a typical pattern. A laugh is started by a few members of the audience who are especially perceptive; their laughter serves as

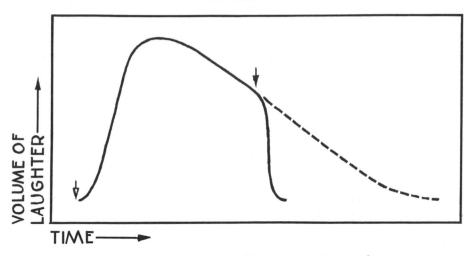

Figure 49. Handling laughter. The dashed line indicates the pattern of laughter when it is allowed to subside without interference. The normal treatment is for the actor to resume his speech at the point marked by the second arrow; the solid line traces the path of laughter resulting from that treatment.

a cue to the rest of the audience, who join in. The initial section of the laugh pattern thus has the form of a steeply rising curve. The curve rounds off to a level, and then begins to drop. The last section has the shape of a falling curve, but one drawn at a gentler angle than the first section. In this last part of the pattern, individual members of the audience gradually stop laughing, and those who continue to laugh reduce their volume. At a point about a third of the way along this section of the curve, from a third to half the audience have stopped laughing. It is at this point that the actors must cut in and resume the performance.

Since there is still a considerable volume of laughter, the actors must override it in order to catch the attention of the audience. They should top it by using extreme projection, and in this case should jump up the volume as well as using the more familiar projection techniques. The effect is to kill the remaining laughter very quickly. As it dies, the actors should ride down with it, pulling their speech down to normal stage level by the time the laughter has disappeared. Sometimes the audience may have begun to laugh slightly past the expected point, and an actor may have begun his next sentence by the time the laughter started. Having interrupted it to hold for the laugh, he should start again not at the point at which it was interrupted but at the beginning of the phrase or sentence. Like the pause for the laugh, this is not sensed as a repetition by the audience; their feeling is that the play is continuing without a break.

Avoiding Laughs

The pattern that elicits laughter is so powerful that it must be most carefully avoided in tragedy or wherever laughter is not wanted. Tension is so fundamental to tragedy that the laugh pattern can be created unintentionally, with disastrous effect on a crucial scene. The critical fact is that laughter depends on two factors: the creation of high tension, and the sudden surprising breaking of the tension, especially by an instantaneous stimulus. It is not possible to avoid tension in tragedy, but care should be taken that it not be held too high too long, and that means be provided for its slow reduction over a considerable period of time. In particular, any sudden or unexpected stimulus should be avoided when the tension is high.

One director decided that it would increase the horror of Medea's murder of her children if an actor were to bring in their heads in a cloth bag. Unfortunately the dummy heads supplied by the prop crew were made of some elastic material, so that when the bag was thrown down on stage they bounced inside it. The taste of the director can be questioned even on the basis of his first decision, but when he introduced at a moment of extreme tension the startlingly unexpected and comic touch of bouncing heads, he was asking for the laughter he got. Any sudden movement, even a quick technical effect such as a clap of thunder or a flash of lightning, may complete the laugh pattern and leave a tragedy in chaos. If such an effect is unavoidable, then the audience should be prepared for it as fully as possible, to soften its suddenness and surprise: at least some quiet rolls of thunder should have been introduced earlier.

The otherwise admirable professional production of *A Man for All Seasons* contained a pure example of the misuse of the laugh pattern. At the end of the play, Sir Thomas More slowly mounted a long, curving flight of stairs, at the top of which a headsman waited with an ax to execute him. As he moved up the steps, the tension of the audience mounted with him; and then just as he reached the executioner, the lights were snapped off, and out of the darkness came the stimulus that released the tension—the sudden, sharp, unmistakably comic sound of the ax striking the chopping block.

A study of dramatic masterpieces will usually reveal the care with which great playwrights have avoided such effects. Seldom in Shakespeare does a tragedy end with a sound like an ax chop; rather, the tension is allowed to subside during a quiet final scene. Such study will also make clear the good sense underlying the practice of the ancient Greeks of having all sudden and violent deaths take place off stage; only quiet deaths without sudden stimuli were ever permitted in the sight of the audience.

Predicting Laughs

It is the director's responsibility to attempt to predict the response of the audience to the performance. In analyzing the script of a comedy, he should devote one reading to searching for examples of the tension-stimulus pattern that provokes laughter. One director regularly draws a red star in his comedy scripts at each point at which he expects the audience to laugh. Of course, no such prediction is totally accurate, and often a director will try for more laughs than he actually expects to get, but the careful development and re-hearsal of the tension-stimulus laugh pattern is an essential part of directing any comedy.

INDIVIDUAL VARIATIONS

The actor's voice and body, personality, attitudes, and experiences are so centrally involved in his work that the director must take them into account at every moment. To a great extent, they are the raw material with which he, too, must work. Furthermore, since actors differ so much, if the director's comments to them are to produce the intended result, they must be carefully adjusted to each individual performer. A suggestion that might improve one actor's han-dling of a line might destroy the effectiveness of another actor's performance. A comment that one actor might respond to readily might produce no change in the work of a different actor.

In the middle of the second week of rehearsals for a particular play, the director was confronted by six actors all of whom read their lines woodenly and without ex-pression or meaning. Even to a careful listener, the six readings seemed almost in-distinguishable, but in fact the ineffectiveness of each actor's reading was due to an individual cause, different from each of the others'.

Andy Foe was suffering from extreme stage fright, which so paralyzed his mind and his vocal mechanism that he was unable to control his speech.

Cy Amus had just learned that his brother had been injured in a fall from a ladder, was in the hospital being operated on, and that it would not be known how seriously he was hurt until some hours later. Cy's worry about his brother made it impossible to keep his mind on the rehearsal, or even to make sense out of his lines.

Leo Nida was tone deaf and read woodenly primarily because he could not hear or control variations in pitch.

Artie Mona had neglected to study his lines, although he had had plenty of free time. His problem was simple laziness.

Nick Obulus found his speeches difficult to understand because they were written in a dialect unfamiliar to him. Since he had not been able to dig out their meanings, he did not know what to express, and so read expressionlessly.

Phil Oxenus felt he was wasted in his part. He was sure that he could perform better with two rehearsals than the rest of the cast after six weeks, and so he was purposely "walking through" the part, not bothering to act or to make the lines mean-ingful.

The director's problem in working with these six actors was to find the comment which was appropriate to each, which would result in each one's achieving an expressive, meaningful, and theatrically effective reading.

Andy's apprehension would have to be reduced before he could work freely.

The problem was to reassure him, to reduce the tension and emotional pressure he felt, so that he could move and speak without constraint.

Cy could not reasonably be expected to perform well at this particular rehearsal. He either should be excused entirely, or instructed simply to walk through the part, with the understanding that his work could be resumed when the worry about his brother had been resolved.

Leo can be helped most by scheduling one or more private rehearsals, at which the director can work with him line by line, exploiting whatever pitch variety he is able to achieve and developing the fullest possible use of variety in rate and loudness.

Artie and Phil, in contrast with Andy, need to be stimulated by increased pressure.

Nick's problem is the easiest of all to solve. Probably the best way to handle it is to schedule an individual conference, at which the meaning of his lines can be discussed and clarified.

It is obvious that, even though all six performances are apparently similar, the instructions must be different for each actor. Once the reason for a problem has been identified, the solution is usually immediately apparent; the difficulty is identifying the causal factors. In this case, if the director had analyzed the actors incorrectly and had, for instance, increased the pressure on Andy and attempted to reduce it for Phil by reassuring him, Andy's potential might have been destroyed, at least as far as this play is concerned, and Phil's work would either have been unaffected or made worse.

The director's major resource in handling such individual differences is the familiar one of empathy. In his guidance of the actor, his task is to produce a behavioral change in the use of the voice and body. He must start with the performance that the actor brings to the first rehearsal and then help him alter it to match that of the character he is to portray. Regularly, then, he evaluates each detail of the actor's performance by watching and listening very closely, and by matching it against the conception which he has developed in his mind, in order to define the differences. Having identified them, if he is to help the actor in making the necessary change, he must devise instructions that will produce the desired effect.

The director not only watches the actor's performance, he attempts to empathize with him as fully as possible, to understand what he is feeling and thinking, to identify the inhibitions or difficulties that interfere with his work. He asks himself at each moment, "If I were on stage, and had read this line in this way, what would I be thinking and feeling, what factors would influence my reading, and what might be said to me that would alter my reading so as to bring it closer to that which is needed for the scene and the character?"

If the director is keenly aware of the desirability of developing skill in empathy, continued experience is likely to raise his empathic ability to a level that sometimes seems almost like mind reading. Actors have frequently expressed astonishment at an experienced director's ability to describe exactly what they had been thinking and feeling. A comment to an actor such as, "Your cross to the exit was wrong because you were thinking about your path across the stage instead of the fact that you were going out to find the butler," may startle the actor with its accuracy.

To a great extent, the director's empathic analysis is based on subliminal clues—a minute vocal inflection, a faint muscular pattern. These should be supplemented with as much clear information as the director can collect. In the example discussed above, Andy's tension would have been clearly displayed in the form of muscular rigidity, in his facial expression, in the speed and direction of his glance; Phil's attitudes would have been evident in a relaxed and negligent posture, perhaps in the tone of his voice in talking to the director. As rehearsals continue, the director will learn more and more about how each actor responds to particular suggestions, so that his interpretation of their thinking can be expected to become more accurate.

VARIATIONS IN QUANTITY OF INSTRUCTION

There is a limit to the number of instructions any actor can absorb during a single rehearsal and can work on effectively between rehearsals. Some actors may profit from twenty or thirty specific instructions; others may be able to remember and apply not more than half a dozen. The director should especially watch the response of his cast members during the early rehearsals and adjust the number of his comments to the individual actors' capacities. With actors who can handle only a few suggestions, it is best to try to restrict comments to general principles, citing one or two illustrative examples for each, in the hope that the actors will be able to apply them at a series of points in their scenes.

The theatrical picture must be assembled by both actors and director like a mosaic, one piece at a time; no actor can work on all aspects of his performance at the same time. Identifying what should be mentioned immediately and what can be left safely till a later rehearsal is one of the director's most important and difficult tasks. Beginning directors probably err most often in concentrating on small and specific details; it is usually wiser to emphasize general principles, especially during the middle third of the rehearsal period. Many of the details will take care of themselves, and the director will need to correct only the few that persist.

VARIATIONS IN INTENSITY OF RESPONSE

One of the most striking differences between actors is the variation in the intensity of their response to suggestions. If two actors are both instructed to speak louder, one may increase his volume so little that the change is hardly detectable, the other may blast the listeners out of their seats. When two actors are asked to make crosses faster, one may change hardly at all, the other may cut the time of his cross to a third. As soon as such differences have been identified, the director should adjust his instructions to them. The actor who overresponds should be told, "Just a trifle louder—don't make a really recognizable change, but just run your volume up by a whisper, a faint hair's breadth." The actor who underreacts should instead be told "You'll have to say that line five times as loudly; don't just project it to the back row—say it so loudly it will startle people in the lobby."

Variations in Response to Types of Instruction

Actors also vary in the kind of terminology that communicates to them. One actor may need to have suggestions made in detail, another may respond better to a faint adumbration of the effect desired. Thus a careful analysis of his posture and movement might be best for one actor, if he needs to suggest more animation and vivacity; for another actor, it might be better to say "You're on top of the world, alert and full of energy, and looking forward to meeting your friends; you should enter and walk across the stage so as to show how you feel."

Often it is possible to communicate more clearly to a particular actor by using technical terms with which he happens to be familiar, even though they might be meaningless to another actor. Music students, for example, frequently find it easiest to respond to instructions stated in musical terminology: "That first phrase should be sforzando, not crescendo"; "This is a coloratura scene; you are playing it too legato"; "This is Mozartian drama, and you are making it Wagnerian."

Any aspect of performance can be described in two ways, emotional or mechanical. The emotional statement describes the effect on the audience; the mechanical statement identifies the operation of the voice or body that produces the effect. For example, "You've got to show more surprise when you hear the burglar say 'Stick 'em up!'" is an emotional description; in mechanical terms the director might say, "You've got to stop your cross more suddenly when you hear the burglar say 'Stick 'em up!'; then you should turn slowly left, with your eyebrows raised and your mouth a little open, and take a step backward as soon as you see him." In reading, the statement "You should sound more outraged on that line" is emotional; the statement "It would be more effective if you would emphasize the third word instead of the fifth; also you should make the line a great deal louder, and raise your pitch a little" is mechanical.

Some actors respond best to an emotional description—a statement of the effect to be produced; others find such a direction of little help, and must have mechanical instructions. Usually, the more skilled and experienced an actor is, the more appropriate is the emotional statement. The director will have to make many mechanical suggestions to beginning actors, although there are great individual differences entirely aside from experience or skill.

The speed with which actors respond to directions is also highly variable. Some actors can alter a reading or a bit of business on the first attempt after the director has made a suggestion; others must work through a series of experiments before they are able to make the desired change. One director commented on an actor whom he identified as "the best actor I have ever worked with." Yet Phil, he reported, could not change his performance at all during a rehearsal. "The first time I tried to get him to do a piece of business differently," the director said, "I worked it over and over with him without the slightest result, and finally gave up. I was dumbfounded when he showed up at the next rehearsal and went through the business exactly the way it should have been done. He had somehow accomplished just what I wanted between rehearsals, even though he couldn't do it at all the previous evening." As soon as he discovered that this was a permanent part of the actor's pattern, the director gave up all attempts to get the actor to work over a line or piece of business during rehearsal. "I would just analyze his performance for him," he said, "knowing that by the next evening he would be able to do it exactly the way I wanted him to." Other actors will show other patterns of work; some may be almost totally incapable of perfecting a reading outside rehearsal and need immediate assistance and repetition.

In addition to the emotional and mechanical descriptions of performance, a third method of communication is for the director to demonstrate the effect he wants by reading the line or performing the action. Some time ago such demonstration was forbidden; today it is commonly recognized as a legitimate method, even though a somewhat dangerous one. Its primary defect is that it may create a feeling in the actor of undue dependence on the director. He may assume that any difficulty will be handled by the director's acting the scene for him, and then the actor's copying the performance. Theoretically, the practice blurs the line between the assignments of director and actor, since it involves the director's abandonment of his role and his temporary performance as an actor.

Probably demonstration should be used as a last resort, but it may work when other techniques do not. It is probably least effective with the best actors and may even inhibit their performance instead of assisting it. It is best suited to actors who have not developed their imaginations fully, and who do not respond vividly to language. Even with such actors, it is desirable to try to prevent them from precisely copying a director's demonstration; it should be used as a communicative device rather than a model to be reproduced. That will be made more likely if the director will greatly exaggerate the effect desired, even to the point of caricature. That will not only make it clearer but will force the actor to translate it into his own vocal and muscular patterns.

Variations in Emotional Response

Actors vary greatly in their emotional reactions to criticism. Usually experienced actors are little disturbed by businesslike criticism aimed at improving their performances and stated with good manners. Occasionally an actor may find even mild criticism crushing, and if so that fact must be taken into account. A very good actor came to the office of the director before the first rehearsal of the first play they worked on together, and said "I can't stand to be criticized in public; I don't care what you say to me, but I wonder if you would be willing to give me your comments privately, instead of in front of the cast." The director agreed; only the most impersonal suggestions were ever given to the actor during rehearsal. The work proceeded smoothly, the actor was entirely cooperative, and he gave an excellent performance. It is to be hoped that such reactions would disappear when the actor had had greater experience, but the director must be alert to such differences in response among actors and try to handle them so as to get the best performances possible.

Actors' general sensitivity occasionally results in their being disturbed by things that would not bother most people. One actor was worried about breathing in bits of scene paint during a section of a play in which he had to lie face down on a platform, and asked that the top of the platform be varnished or shellacked so that the paint would not flake off. Another actor, in a different production, was disturbed by the fact that his hands became damp as a result of stage fright and that some of the paint of a railing came off and stained them slightly. Sometimes such problems cannot be solved practically; if facilities are such that some construction work must be done on stage during rehearsal, an actor who reports that he is disturbed by sawing, pounding, or the whispered conversations of the builders must be told that he will simply have to do the best he can under the circumstances. When the distraction can be removed, however, it is wise to do so, even if the request seems unreasonable, and even if most actors would not find the problem disturbing. Anything which distracts an actor's attention from his performance will damage it and should be removed if possible. At least some actors in any cast are likely to be afraid of heights; if they must perform on high platforms it is not enough that the platforms be safe, they must also feel safe. In one production, a platform eight feet high was filled in at the back with a solid wall of flats, which provided both the fact and the impression of safety. A railing ran along the front that was so strong that if an actor had run toward it and thrown his entire weight against it it would not have given way. However, it was slightly flexible, so that it felt insecure; additional stiffening was provided, not to make it actually stronger, but to make it feel stronger, so that the actors would feel no anxiety about it and could give their entire attention to the performance.

Some actors have what are almost superstitions with regard to their work. One excellent college actor, who later became the director of a theater in New York, regularly reduced his stage fright before an opening performance by standing behind the set before the play began, biting tiny bits out of a fresh cleansing tissue, and swallowing them. Another actor had the admittedly irrational belief that if his playscript was not backstage during the performance he would forget his lines. Even such absurd requirements should be met if at all possible. Supplying a tissue or helping an actor find an obscure corner backstage to hide his script may greatly reduce his anxiety and improve his performance. Probably most actors ultimately outgrow the need for such symbols of security, but unless they are impossible to provide there seems no reason not to agree to them if the performances can be thereby improved.

Every play requires the elevation of the level of animation, excitement, and clarity of the actors' performance from that of everyday life to theatrical pitch. The actors bring their ordinary manner to the first rehearsal, and it is not likely to be raised during the blocking period. Starting with the first interpretation rehearsal, all of the rest of the work should show a steady increase in vividness and animation, at least up to the beginning of the fixing rehearsals. Because the demands of the theater are so much greater than those of ordinary life, the problem of amplification must be consciously attacked. At its simplest, this involves physical and vocal projection, but almost all plays also require an enlargement of emotion and an increase in clarity.

One of the most effective ways to encourage actors in this aspect of their work is for the director himself to display the degree of energy to which they must rise. Usually it is best for the director not to leap to the final pitch immediately; rather, he should carry out his part of the rehearsal at a level slightly higher than the actors'. As they move a step upward, he can readjust so that he stays just a short distance ahead of them, until they have reached the right elevation.

This problem, like most of those in the theater, is most difficult with new actors. Especially if they lag behind the rest of the cast, it may be desirable to stop rehearsal occasionally and work directly on it. One technique is to take a scene made up of a series of short speeches and run through it, the actor who needs assistance reading his own lines, the director reading the intervening ones. The actor should be instructed to top the director each time. The director then tops the actor's first speech slightly, the actor tops the director's first speech, and the director moves up again. The speed of amplification can be controlled by the director; usually it is best to lead the actor up by very small steps. This exercise makes it much easier for the actor to raise his level of animation and can be repeated if necessary. The same method is also usable for improving simple vocal projection.

Even after the actor has reached an acceptable level of vividness and animation, he can be expected not to be able to sustain it for long periods without further assistance. The director should watch closely and try to catch the drop as soon as it occurs. If the actor is not helped immediately, he is likely to sink back steadily to his previous level, necessitating a major effort to bring him back up again. The best technique is to call out brief instructions at the first sign of a sag: "More!" or "Pick it up!"

The problem is especially severe in the opening scene of the first act. There may be distraction from late-comers' being seated, the attention of the audience has not yet been fully focused, the expository material presented at the beginning of the play may lack inherent interest, and the actors do not have the stimulus of a previous scene to react against, or an established momentum that they can sustain. A very skillful playwright will give the actors major assistance in handling the opening scene (many of Shakespeare's plays are noteworthy in this respect), but with less effective scripts, the actors may have to supplement the lines with all the animation and vividness they can command. It is desirable to work over the first page and a half or two pages of the play with attention focused on this problem.

Hyperstimulation as a Directorial Technique

Actors' achievement of projection, animation, and clarity is often strongly handicapped by their own inhibitions. An actor may exhibit a kind of vocal and physical paralysis because of fear of failure or embarrassment. Attacking that problem requires all of a director's ingenuity. The best solution is to reduce the actor's tension and apprehension, but that may require some weeks. One technique will sometimes improve the actor's work during a specific rehearsal and can be used as a supplement to longer-range methods.

The problem is that the actor's fears are so strong that his attention is concentrated on them rather than on the work of developing his performance. This technique aims at providing hyperstimulation in order to distract the actor from his inhibitions, and then turning his attention to the performance. The director should intensify the level of animation of his own movements and comments, moving quickly about the stage, describing blocking while crossing from spot to spot, speaking animatedly about a variety of aspects of the performance, in a random order that requires the actor to listen intently and to make mental leaps from one point to another, and attempting to catch the attention of the actor as fully as possible, directing it toward the performance and consequently away from his pattern of fear. The director should also attempt to create a feeling of vivacity and fun. When he senses that he has produced the desired alteration in the actor's attention, he should shift the discussion to the beginning of one of the actor's speeches, perhaps repeating the opening phrase, and then point to the actor and snap out "You say it!" This technique does not always work, but often the actor will respond with a freer reading than he has been able to achieve previously. The director may be able to sustain the new level of freedom by continuing the technique throughout the rest of the scene in less extreme form.

THE EMOTIONS OF ACTORS AND CHARACTERS

One source of inhibition is the necessity for actors to do or say things which they would avoid in ordinary life, or which would embarrass them if they were publicly displayed. One college student who directed one of his professors in a community play told him later that he had been worried about casting him because he was afraid he would not be able to swear naturally. Even the love scenes or the old nurse's bawdy lines in *Romeo and Juliet* have sometimes been difficult for actresses to handle. It may be possible to sidestep the problem by cutting the troublesome passages or by selecting a different play. However, two considerations may help the actor who tends to back away from an embarrassing line or bit of business. One is that the audience tends to empathize with the emotions that are presented to them. If the actor displays the slightest embarrassment, they will be equally embarrassed; if he treats the lines as a matter of course, they are likely to accept them without unpleasantness. The actor will be safest, then, if he handles the material with gusto and avoids any suggestion of shrinking from it. As one director told his cast, "If you can, cut the profanity; but if you have to say it, shout it out; the worst thing you could possibly do is to back away from it and act embarrassed." The other consideration is that if the actor performs effectively, no one in the audience will associate him with the character he is portraying: It will be Romeo making love in public, not the actor. Both of those facts demand the fullest, least inhibited performance. When the actor realizes that only in that way will he be truly safe, he will find it much easier to handle the scenes.

The whole question of the proper relationship between the actor's emotions and those of the character he is portraying has been discussed at wearisome length for decades, and with far more smoke than light. At one extreme, some theorists advocate encouraging every actor to live his part to the fullest, transforming himself by self-hypnosis into the character he plays. At the other extreme, it is argued that actors should be trained to perform mechanically, by the use of impersonal techniques, and that they should never feel any of the emotions they portray.

To a large extent, the discussion appears to involve a misunderstanding of the problem: the question is technical, not esthetic. From the standpoint of esthetics, it does not make the slightest difference what an actor feels: the only relevant question is what the audience feels. The purpose of a play is to create an experience for the audience, and if the intended experience occurs, the actor has performed successfully, whatever his own private emotions may have been.

From the technical standpoint, however, the actor's emotions are relevant. His understanding of his part, his insight into his character's personality, his identification of the kind of speech and behavior that his character would display in a particular situation, are all dependent on the fund of experiences and emotions he has stored in his memory. His emotions are part of the essential raw material out of which he builds his performances.

The actor's emotions are most significant in the interpretation rehearsals, and somewhat less important during the rehearsals devoted to finding the technical methods by which the desired experience is to be communicated to the audience.

Actors vary greatly in the extent to which they re-experience the emotions of their characters during the last half of the rehearsal period and through the performances. Some very fine actors continue even through a long run of a play to feel all of the emotions they portray with considerable intensity; they experience a surge of anger during a fight scene, they feel some degree of real fear when their characters are threatened, they are vividly downcast by tragedy and elated by triumph. Other actors quickly master the technical methods of communicating their parts and are able to play completely convincing love scenes while (so they report) planning what they will eat at supper after the show.

It is almost universally agreed that for an actor to totally live his part is unacceptable. No actor who did so could be trusted to play Othello—he would actually smother Desdemona, not simply pretend to. Occasionally actors have been said to be so carried away in scenes of swordplay that their opponents began to feel they were actually fighting for their lives. But even aside from such extreme instances, the theater is an art, and almost everything that contributes to it must be transformed. A madman must be played by an actor, not by an actual madman; a real deaf mute is almost unthinkable in the part of the orator in *The Chairs* or the deaf mute in *The Madwoman of Chaillot*. Actions must be displayed to the audience, not simply performed; the inner thoughts of the characters must be expressed, not simply felt by the actors. Even on the most mechanical level, speech and action must be projected. Furthermore, no performance ever goes quite smoothly; there are always minute deviations in timing, in blocking, in character relationships, in the response of the audience, which the actors must assess and adjust to. Even minor errors in properties or sound effects must be hidden or handled if the play is to continue to function as intended. At the very least, a large part of the actor's attention must be available for handling such matters. An actor who managed somehow to brainwash himself into even a temporary belief that he actually was Dracula would be not simply mad, he would be unusable.

A director who works with many different casts is likely to find actors at points scattered throughout most of the range between the two extremes of mechanical and emotional acting. To some extent, the actors' formulations may be quasisuperstitious, like chewing cleansing tissues or hiding playbooks, but if they actually help them in achieving better performances they are likely to be harmless. The director should probably encourage his actors to make the fullest possible use of their emotions during the early rehearsals, as raw material for building their characterizations, and to help them in analyzing their roles. His emphasis during the last half of the rehearsal period should be on achieving a sure technical command, with the attention shifting from the actors themselves to the responses of the audience.

The general psychological pattern that seems best for actors requires that their major attention should be given to the audience—perhaps two-thirds of their minds—and that the aspects of performance with which they must be concerned as actors require only the remaining third of their attention. In imagination, they should sit out front during the performance and watch and listen to the play from the viewpoint of the audience. Of course, reaching that proposed ideal requires extensive rehearsal, thorough study, and extreme technical control. Few casts in the educational or community theater actually achieve it, and it is not so common as it should be even in the professional theater, except in long-run plays. The total familiarity with the play that is necessary if actors are able to perform without giving undue attention to technical problems is achieved primarily during the blending, polishing, and fixing rehearsals. Since the work of preparing even a simple play is so enormous, the director is likely to feel reluctant to move into this group of rehearsals. He will be tempted throughout the rehearsal period to stretch each aspect of the study for one or two additional evenings—"If we just went over the blocking one more time, we'd really have it memorized"; "How can we go on to developing techniques when we need at least three more rehearsals on interpretation?" The director should usually resist that inevitable impulse. Lengthening the various sections of rehearsals must be compensated by shortening the period given to the final critical work. Blocking, interpretation, and the development of techniques are not dropped when the attention is turned to a different aspect of the work; they will continue to develop. If insufficient time is left for the final fixing of the actors' performances, the show will visibly suffer.

THE ILLUSION OF THE FIRST TIME

The focusing of the actor's attention on the audience is necessary in order for them to sense the rhythm and pattern of audience response, and to adjust their performance to it. Such adjustment is one of the special marks of the highest artistry in acting. But empathy with the audience assists the actor in another way, which is also extremely important.

By opening night, each actor will have gone over his lines at least twenty or thirty times in his private study, and he will have spoken each line on stage during rehearsals for a comparable number of times. All surprise will have disappeared in the process, and from his own point of view, the lines will have lost all freshness: the jokes will be stale, the triumphs and tragedies no longer moving. Yet he must be able to step out on stage on opening night and speak his first sentence as if he had never heard or seen it before; he must be able to respond to other actors' remarks as if they were fresh and new. This effect is so important that a special phrase has been created to express it: the actor must be able to create "the illusion of the first time."

That illusion can be produced by sheerly technical or mechanical means, but it is much easier to achieve it psychologically. However stale and overfamiliar the actor's first speech seems to him, it is fresh and new to the audience. They are actually hearing it for the first time. If it is a comic line, the joke is new for them; if it is a moving line, the emotion is unfamiliar. To the extent that the actor is able to assume the point of view of the audience, he will also be able to recapture his own original response to the line. If he is able to focus two-thirds of his attention on the act of empathizing with the audience, then the surprises will become again largely surprising, the jokes funny, the tragedies tragic.

The Actor's Attitude Toward the Audience

The actor's attitude toward the audience is significant in other ways too. Professional actors' remarks about audiences express both affection and fear; in fact, the actor-audience relationship is regularly ambivalent. The audience is hated and feared because the actor must submit himself and his work for its approval or disapproval, and there is no appeal from its judgment. On the other hand, the audience is loved because of the closeness of its relationship with the actor, who shares himself and his experiences with it, in a double bond of empathy.

From the point of view of the director, the important requirement is that the actor be persuaded to assume a relationship of dominance toward the audience. Audiences are passive and receptive. They give up a good deal for a play, the least important thing being the price of the ticket. They rearrange their schedule of dining, reshave or reapply their makeup, change from their ordinary clothes, arrange for baby-sitters, take the trip to the theater, sometimes through

I'm terrified of appearing in public. But the way to face the public is to think you love your audience.

Cole Porter

snow or rain. But most important of all, they give up whatever other activities are available to them for the evening—reading a book, watching television, going bowling, hooking rugs—and contribute their time to the play, on the assumption that an experience will be provided for them more exciting, interesting, or worthwhile than the experiences they would otherwise have had. It is the actor's responsibility to provide that experience; if he does not put on a show, no one else will. He must show and tell the audience what they are to think and feel for this significant portion of their lives. In this sense, the actor is an executive, directing the lives of others. He must be active and decisive; if he shrinks from that responsibility in any degree, at the very least the edge will be taken from the production, and at the worst almost nothing will happen.

The actor's typical personality pattern tends to make him reluctant to assume this attitude of dominance toward the audience. His habitual response to social situations is more likely to be submissive than dominant; he is more likely to sit quietly in the corner, hoping he will not be noticed, than he is to try to shine as the life of the party. At the same time, he feels an intense desire to overcome that habitual response; otherwise he would not have chosen to be active in the theater.

Each time I sing I feel there is someone waiting to destroy me, and I must fight like a bull to hold my own. The artist who boasts he is never nervous is not an artist—he is a liar or a fool.

ENRICO CARUSO

The director must try to reduce the actor's habit of submission and reinforce his desire to dominate and impress others. An important method of achieving that goal is for him to display the attitude toward the audience that the actor must assume. He should take advantage of any opportunity to emphasize that he, as well as the actor, is making decisions for the audience, choosing what they will watch and listen to, planning their responses for them. The handling of comic lines should be discussed not in terms like "We've got to try to make this as funny as we can and hope the audience will laugh," but "We want the audience to laugh at this point, so we've got to plan very carefully what we ought to do to make them laugh." The actor should not be told "Your speech isn't moving," but "You aren't showing the audience clearly enough what they should be moved at in this line; you've got to point out the emotional words to them or they'll never react the way they should." All of the directions should be phrased to emphasize by implication that the work of director and actors is aimed at creating an experience for the audience, not at preparing something to be passively displayed in the hope that the audience will like it. With actors who seem excessively terrified of the audience, it may even be desirable to suggest a somewhat patronizing attitude toward the audience—"Oh, they're a bunch of sheep; they'll never get the idea unless you hit them over the head with it."

Usually the experienced actors, playing the major roles, will have developed an effectively aggressive attitude toward the audience, and their example will powerfully influence the apprentice actors in the smaller roles. Even the accomplished actors, however, may need some support in this aspect of their work.

STAGE FRIGHT

The fear of the audience produces the distressing phenomenon called stage fright, which is so common as to be almost universal among actors. It varies in intensity, at its mildest being only a minor irritation, at its worst paralyzing the actor vocally and physically. It is such a constant problem that all kinds of devices have been invented in an attempt to reduce or explain it away, including the paradoxical attempt of some actors to persuade themselves that it is somehow a positive asset, and that if they were not frightened, they could not perform well. Some of these tricks, however irrational they seem, do help individual actors in reducing their fear of performances—wearing a good-luck charm or going into seclusion for a few minutes before the curtain rises for the first act. If such devices help, there is no reason an actor should not take advantage of them, but they can hardly be recommended to others as rational approaches; no one of them will help more than a few actors.

> *Audiences? No, the plural is impossible. Whether it is in Butte, Montana, or Broadway, it's an audience. The same great hulking monster with four thousand eyes and forty thousand teeth.*
>
> JOHN BARRYMORE

Stage fright is not an asset, it is a handicap; however, it is not a very great handicap. Studies of public speakers indicate that they perform best when they feel the least stage fright, but that the difference in the quality of their performance is not very great.

The primary disadvantage of stage fright is that it distracts the actor from his essential job. To the extent that his fear intrudes on his attention, he has that much less to give to the performance and the audience. The most important consideration in dealing with fear, then, is for the actor not to let it control his attention. The focus of attention can be controlled more fully than might be supposed. Actors must frequently resist distractions during rehearsals, and with conscious effort are regularly able to function very well even though members of the set crew may be pounding nails backstage, or conversations about costumes may be going on at a fairly high level out front. During the technical rehearsal, when the director may be shouting instructions to the light or sound crews during the performance, actors normally have no difficulty carrying on the scenes. Stage fright interferes about as much as a bad case of sunburn; the pain will continue throughout the evening, and if an actor keeps thinking about it, it will prevent him from performing well. Only a little effort is required to turn his attention to the work he is doing, and the pain of either the sunburn or the stage fright, although it continues, does not interfere significantly with his performance.

The discussion so far has dealt with the psychological aspects of stage fright; but it has physical effects also. As was mentioned in an earlier chapter, its primary effect is to raise the level of muscular tonus, the size of the increase matching the intensity of the fear. Nearly all of the symptoms of stage fright are the result of this increase in muscular contraction, especially the rise in vocal pitch, the inability to breath deeply, and the trembling of hands and knees. The disturbance in breathing is the most difficult of those three symptoms to control; the others are quite easy. Every speaker who can sing even a simple melody already has very delicate control of pitch; knowing that stage fright tends to raise the pitch should make it possible for an actor to move his pitch back down to the normal level at will.

Muscular tremor can be attacked in two ways. It occurs whenever any set of muscles are kept in a state of extreme contraction for a significant length of time. This can be easily demonstrated by contracting the muscles of the arm; the fist should be clenched, the forearm raised, and all of the muscles contracted as extremely as can easily be done. Tremor appears almost immediately and is directly correlated with the intensity of contraction. If the muscles are then relaxed and the arm allowed to go limp, the tremor will stop. Muscular contraction due to stage fright can be controlled almost as easily as that which has been consciously assumed, especially in the larger muscles of the arms and legs. If an actor is disturbed by trembling knees, he should consciously contract his leg as intensely as possible, bending the knee and pulling the lower part of the leg up tight against the thigh; then he should let it drop limply, consciously relaxing the muscles as much as possible. It is important that he focus on the kinesthetic sensations at the two extremes of tension. Of course, this exercise can only be carried on offstage, but as soon as the actor has clearly memorized the sensations of contraction and relaxation, a little practice should enable him to relax the muscles unobtrusively whenever he feels them beginning to tremble. The same method can be applied to the arm to reduce hand tremor.

It is a common experience of actors that stage fright is most intense just before the beginning of a performance, and that it fades during the first scene. That reduction is due to two factors. One is the fact that turning his attention to the speeches of the play distracts it from his fear; the other depends on the effect of physical movement. A familiar psychological theory is that the muscular tension produced by fear is an inheritance from primitive times and originally served to provide a sudden increase in strength that was useful in responding to dangerous situations, enabling primitive man either to run or to attack. According to this theory, the trembling and other unpleasant symptoms produced by fear in modern life are due to the fact that it is often not possible to use the muscular energy made available in response to the fear, so that it is not dissipated by action but remains in the form of a continuing contraction and rigidity of muscles. Any physical movement will help dissipate the excessive energy and will reduce the symptoms of stage fright. Before a performance, the actor can walk or even engage in formal exercises. On stage, the movement involved in the blocking pattern and in stage business itself tends to dissipate the symptoms. This is a very minor, but a real reason for designing blocking so as to provide a movement for almost every speech.

The earlier statement that an actor should have rehearsed until he is able to go through his performance almost automatically, giving it not more than a third of his attention, may have seemed exaggerated. One reason for it is that that degree of mastery enables him to carry on even when he is significantly distracted by stage fright.

All of the methods of handling stage fright discussed tend actually to reduce the actor's fear, and many actors report that it disappears altogether during their first scene on stage. It is important, however, not to encourage an actor to attempt to handle stage fright by reducing it. A direct attempt to make stage fright less severe almost always fails, and if the actor believes that his success depends on not being afraid, the fact that all of the methods of reduction that he tries seem to fail is likely to throw him into a panic that will exaggerate the symptoms rather than alleviate them. He may be told that there is some possibility that he will feel less frightened as the play goes on, but his own attack should be directed at preventing the fear from interfering with his performance and suppressing the symptoms. It is useful to remind him that the audience knows only what it can see and hear, and if the muscular tremor and rise in vocal pitch are controlled, the audience will have no way of sensing his fear at all. He will be almost as afraid—controlling symptoms has little effect on the emotion itself—but his fear will not affect his performance or the audience's experience.

Of course anything that will actually reduce actors' fear is desirable, so long as it does not otherwise harm the performance. The director should attempt to create an atmosphere of confidence, especially during the last few rehearsals and immediately before the first performance, although insincere reassurance of the actors is likely to be recognized as false, and if he does not really feel confidence in them it is probably better for him to say nothing. Some actors try to alleviate fear by the use of tranquilizers or alcohol, but the loss in clarity of mind damages the performance far more than the reduction in fear benefits it. Probably the best method of reducing stage fright, as distinguished from controlling its symptoms, is overpreparation. An actor who has memorized his lines not simply enough but much more than enough, who has analyzed his part more carefully than he could reasonably be expected to have done, who has rehearsed with greater thoroughness and concentration than could properly have been demanded, is buoyed by the feeling that he has done his best, and he will be able to perform with a degree of security that can be achieved in no other way.

A few actors are helped by the discovery that stage fright is universal. Especially when novice actors watch the experienced cast members going about their work with apparent assurance, they may assume that only they feel frightened. The director may even be able to assist them by displaying his own fear, especially by demonstrating that he can continue to function quietly and decisively in spite of it. The director who said to his cast "This play frightens me out of my wits; when I think of how difficult it is, I realize that only a superman could rise to the level of the script—and a superman I'm not yet" was not simply attempting to get sympathy or to share his emotions with the actors; rather, he was interested in demonstrating that it is possible to function calmly, rationally, and effectively even under stress of stage fright.

In summary, then, the director should attempt to help actors in reducing and handling stage fright, in whatever degree they display it. He should acquaint them with the facts about stage fright as realistically as possible.

1. Stage fright is nearly universal among good actors.

2. It damages the performance mainly to the degree that it distracts the actor's attention from its proper focus.

3. It is quite easy to learn to control the physical symptoms, and the audience then will be completely unaware of it.

4. The only really acceptable method of reducing stage fright that can be applied during the work on a particular play is to overprepare, to work as far as possible above the minimum level of acceptability.

The Actors' Attention

Especially during the blocking and technique rehearsals, the actors are concerned with details of performance—which foot to start a cross with, finding the key word to emphasize in a sentence, how to make a gesture fully visible. The concentration on such techniques must not be carried into the performance itself. Especially during the last third of the rehearsal period, the actors' attention should be turned more and more toward the experience being created for the audience and away from the means by which the experience is produced.

As rehearsals progress, the readings and movements should become so familiar that they come to seem automatic, the actors' awareness focusing more and more sharply on meaning rather than on technique. It will be noticed that the director's comments become steadily fewer as rehearsals proceed, and that they are gradually withdrawn from the performance of the scenes and reserved for intermission breaks. The actors' attention to the director's suggestions should follow the same pattern, until finally they should push them below the level of consciousness. One director, at the beginning of the fixing rehearsals, regularly says to his casts: "Now I want you to forget everything I have ever said to you, and go ahead and play the show for all it's worth." The reason for such advice is obvious; in the early rehearsals, directorial instructions may be a help, but in performance they must not be allowed to get between the actors and their concentration on the audience's experience. No actor, at the moment he is delivering a line in performance, should be thinking "Now did the director tell me to emphasize 'lost' or 'prefer'?" Rather he should feel, "I must get the audience to share intensely with me the feeling of wistfulness and regret that the character is expressing."

ADJUSTING TO THE AUDIENCE

It might be expected that the individual differences of members of an audience would cancel each other, so that one group of five hundred people would respond almost exactly like another group of the same size, age range, and educational background. That is not what happens. Instead, to a remarkable degree each audience displays a personality of its own, which may differ sharply from that of an audience attending the same play the next evening.

Audiences tend to be extremely suggestible, and in America at least extremely passive. They do not create experiences in the theater, they attend in order to have experiences created for them. The majority of the people in an audience tend to copy the responses of the few members who do not display this attitude. Thus, laughter or applause is not the spontaneous response of all of the viewers who take part in it; rather, it is typically started by a few more independent members of the audience, and the rest respond to their instruction. To some extent, then, the variation in audience response and personality from night to night can be explained by the reactions of the few more independent members, who may vary considerably from performance to performance.

Even with the most careful planning, the director cannot predict such variations. Adjusting to them is consequently entirely the responsibility of the actors, although the director should make sure that they are aware of it. Most plays are intended to be performed as if the actors were unaware of the audience, so that they must avoid looking out into the auditorium. Their evaluation of audience response therefore depends almost entirely on auditory clues. These tend to be undefined and difficult to identify consciously. Nevertheless, actors who are aware of the need to interpret such clues quickly develop a surprisingly acute sensitivity to them and may be able to assess the basic character of an audience very accurately within the space of a couple of speeches.

Certain gross audible signals are easy enough to describe and interpret. One of the most frightening is a nervous cough, most often suggestive of boredom and easily distinguishable to the ear of an actor from a real cough due to respiratory disease. Program rustling or a shifting of feet is also a signal that the audience has been, or is about to be, lost. Laughter, of course, is easily recognized, and only a little experience is needed to identify its quality, whether it is the nervous laugh of embarrassment, the painful response to excessive tension, or a hearty laugh at a comic line.

The most important clues, however, are indescribable and are interpreted subliminally by the actors, although they are usually vividly aware of their conclusions. A major factor is the general level of audience sound produced by small movements or vocal sounds too minimal to be heard individually, but which blend into a kind of audible atmosphere. The intensest concentration on the part of the audience is accompanied by what seems like total silence, and when it persists for an appreciable length of time after the fall of the curtain, before the applause begins, it is correctly interpreted by the actors as the highest compliment. Low audience sounds vary in quality and meaning, and the level of sound is not entirely (negatively) correlated with the effectiveness of the performance. In some cases a moderate stream of sound indicates closer attention on the part of the audience than a quieter sound of different character.

Every now and then, when you're on stage, you hear the best sound a player can hear. It's a sound you can't get in movies or on television. It is the sound of a wonderful, deep silence that means you've hit them where they live.

SHELLEY WINTERS

The actor has two responsibilities with regard to adjusting to audience response. The less important is to handle problem moments—when the first inattentive cough, the first shuffle of feet is heard. The proper response to such a crisis is to enrich the experience being provided for the audience, increase the clarity of the performance, and amplify the projection. There is an unfortunate tendency for actors to respond to such a situation with a panic increase in rate: lines are speeded up, actions are run faster, and the performance assumes an air of frenzy. Probably the best treatment is exactly the opposite: they should take more time for effects, phrase the lines more to make them clearer, wring each drop of emotion and meaning out of the lines. The attention of the audience is most likely to lag if their experience seems thin and insipid. Simply speeding it up will not improve it; it must be colored more brightly, expanded and enriched.

The other and more important responsibility of the actors in adjusting to the audience is to sense the pattern of audience response and adapt the performance to satisfy and exploit it. Each audience has a particular rhythm of response, and the actors should attempt to sense it and adjust to it. If the audience especially shares scenes of poetry and beauty, then they should be given special projection and emphasis. If they are caught most by conflict and tension, the performance should be shifted to focus on such scenes. Of course a play cannot be rebuilt during a performance; the effect is not so much to repaint the picture as to cast new lights on it, which pick out the details and colors that the present audience responds to most fully.

This adjustment is delicate and difficult, and the factors involved and the techniques by which they may best be handled are at present indescribable. At least, the director should make the cast aware of this aspect of performance. Even inexperienced actors can develop audience sense to a surprising degree in a single play, and one of the special characteristics of a great actor is his ability to adapt his performances to the response patterns of various audiences. Such adaptation is also one of the special characteristics of the live theater, and a source of much of its excitement and fascination. Although they are likely to be slower in their perception of the double response between themselves and the actors, the audience senses it fully when the communication flows freely in both directions, and the experience is an electrifying one, treasured by actors and audience alike.

14/The Actor's Personality as an Element of Production

Actors and directors typically work together something less than a hundred hours during rehearsals of a play, a period shorter than the time that a group of office workers spend together in three weeks. Yet in those few hours, a closer relationship is built up than might be attained by people in other circumstances who worked together for years. It is not uncommon for friendships to develop during a month's rehearsals that remain for decades, even though the people involved may never work together again. The actress who brings her husband and children back each summer for a ritual visit with a director with whom she worked in a single show a decade before is not so unusual as to be remarkable.

Perhaps the closest analogy to the group relationship that develops among the people who rehearse together is that of a family. Both types of relationship are close, both are likely to involve friction and conflict as well as affection, and both depend on significant shared experiences.

Friction is unpleasant in itself, and yet it is not necessarily destructive of a play any more than it is of a family. Just as members of a family who habitually bicker can nevertheless join forces against an outsider, or can come together to plan an important family vacation trip or to make arrangements for a member of the family who has been incapacitated by an accident, so a play cast may be able to function well together in spite of personal conflicts or even active dislike. In both cases the single requirement is that all the members of the group share the same goal: working out the plans for the most interesting itinerary through Europe, finding the best method of caring for Uncle Aspasius, or cre-

371

ating the best possible performance of the play. If such a common goal is fully accepted by each member of the group, the work can proceed smoothly. If, however, any member of the family is more concerned with thwarting Cousin Harpax than he is with helping plan for Uncle Aspasius, or any member of the cast is more interested in preventing Lora Arium from having a personal triumph in her role in the play than he is in achieving the best total performance possible, then effective functioning of the group becomes difficult or impossible.

The Actor's Involvement in His Work

Two factors explain the closeness of relationship that develops within a play cast, as well as some of the difficulties encountered. One is the fact that the medium of the actor is himself. He must learn to play the dramatist's melody not on an external piano or violin: his only instrument is his own voice and his own body. The other critical fact is that the materials out of which he creates the work of art are his own experiences and emotions, his memories, his habits of response. The actor is inescapably involved in the most intimate way in all that he does in rehearsal and performance.

At times, when the work is not going well or actors seem unreasonably resistant to direction, the director may feel that their personalities are irritating intrusions into the rehearsal. Every director occasionally sympathizes with Gordon Craig's wish that actors might be thrown out of the theater and replaced with life-sized puppets, who could be expected to move in the right direction when the proper strings were pulled. Such a momentary twinge of irritation or desperation is understandable, but it is quite wrong. The personalities of the actors, including the totality of their experiences and emotions, are the raw material out of which the performances must be built. The fact that they are unpredictable, complicated, and difficult to handle makes the director's work challenging, but it also provides him with rich resources.

Because the actor is himself on display, and because his intense struggle to reorganize the stubborn raw material of his experience into an acceptable performance must necessarily be largely ineffective, at least through the early weeks of rehearsal, he is likely to exhibit an extreme sensitivity to direction and to react to the director's comments in an excessive degree. Even the most impersonal suggestions ("Try stopping just a little farther on stage when you make that first entrance") may produce reactions that seem wildly disproportionate.

One of the most important characteristics of an effective director is the ability in an extreme degree to understand the actors' patterns of personality, their attitudes, experiences, emotions, and responses, their strains, struggles, difficulties, and tensions, their points of view—that is, the ability to empathize with them. His work is complicated by the differences between actors. An instruction that may result in an immediate improvement in one actor's performance may, if given to another actor, produce a chaotic disintegration. Not only is each actor unique, but the differences between them are probably greater than those between any similar group of nontheater people. At least the individual differences affect their functioning more than do those of people involved in most other types of work. But even though each actor presents a particular pattern of personality and skills, they nevertheless share certain characteristics, so that a generalized discussion is valuable as defining a basic pattern into which the individual variations can be fitted. These characteristics are correlated with acting ability. Great actors are likely to display the complete pattern; very bad actors or nonactors may not show it at all.

THE CHARACTERISTIC PERSONALITY OF ACTORS

Actors, then, are unusual people, as the popular legend claims. However, the common picture of them as loud-mouth show-offs, insensitive and egotistical extroverts, is so false that it is almost the opposite of the truth. If supremely self-confident and extroverted people, who see their proper relationship with other people as one of dominance, are attracted to speech performances, they are most likely to choose public speaking. In college, they prefer oratory and debate, and may be active in broadcasting (of course, other types of people also take part in these activities). Few of them try out for plays, and those who get parts are seldom very successful and seldom return. The essential difference, of course, is that in debate the student is able to display himself; in the theater he must hide himself. The success of a public speaker depends on his sharing his thinking, his experiences, and his reactions with his audience. An actor who does so is almost useless; he can only be typecast and can be used only in roles that accidentally match his own personality and that enable him to be himself on stage. Success as an actor, in fact, requires concealing the actor's own personality and replacing it with that of the character he is portraying. The director who said to his cast, "I don't want you on stage; leave yourself in the dressing room, and send up Macbeth, Lady Macbeth, and the three witches," was perhaps being unduly blunt, but he was expressing a truism of theater art.

A nonactor who had somehow stumbled into a play cast but whose major purpose was self-display, when he paused on his way up to the stage to check his appearance in a mirror after his makeup had been completed and he had put on his costume, would be dismayed at the discovery that he could not see himself, but instead saw only the character he was portraying. He would be likely to recoil with at least the subconscious protest, "But nobody will recognize me!" An actor, on the other hand, would be delighted at the discovery; the thought "Why, that isn't me at all!" would be more likely to produce a feeling of security.

A little episode may illustrate the typical actor's response. In one college production of *The Taming of the Shrew,* a specially written song was inserted in the play, sung by three of the men. The actress who played Katharine was singing the song in her room at the college dormitory, during the week of performances, when one of the freshman girls who had attended the play stopped at the door and exclaimed, "Oh, have you seen *The Taming of the Shrew?*" The point of the episode is not that the girl had failed to recognize the actress, even though she played the major woman's part in the show, but that the actress reported the anecdote as an amusing and delightful story. She was pleased, not disturbed, by the fact that she had not been recognized during the performance. The viewer's failure to connect Katharine with the girl she saw every day at the dorm was the highest compliment on her performance as an actress, but if she had been a nonactress, primarily concerned with personal display, she would have reacted to the comment with distress rather than amusement.

A fundamental personality characteristic of actors, then, is a desire to escape attention; far from being the life of the party, they are more likely to be painfully shy, to look forward with dread to a social gathering, and to hope desperately that they can escape attention. At the first rehearsal of a play, the best actor is most unlikely to be seen striding up and down the aisle putting on an impromptu performance by singing and snapping out jokes. The real actor is much more likely to be sitting well back in the auditorium, next to the wall, agonizing over the impression he is going to make when he has to go up on stage at the beginning of the rehearsal, and wondering if the sick feeling he has is going to get bad enough that he will have to make a sudden dash out to the lobby.

But the world is full of shy and uncertain people who never try out for plays, many of whom would not make good actors even if they did. Actors are characterized by a second quality: they are intensely disturbed by their shyness, desperately anxious to overcome it, and willing to endure any kind of agony if it will help them learn to make a better impression on others. It is the intensity of this desire that keeps the actor from actually running out into the lobby and on out of the theater; he stays because he feels that the work, however painful, will strengthen his ability to associate effectively with other people.

The actor, then, typically has both characteristics—he is shy, but he wants to overcome his shyness. If he simply wants to hide, he avoids performance altogether; if he simply wants to display himself, he chooses some type of performance other than drama. Only the theater satisfies his needs precisely, enabling him to hide inside his character, and to perform at the same time.

It's the way to get over a deep inferiority complex, being on stage; you become another person and shed your own frightened personality.

SHIRLEY BOOTH

This set of attitudes distinguishes between the actor and the nonactor. The degree of effectiveness achieved by the actor, however, is dependent on other characteristics, which do not always appear together in the same person and which may vary greatly in degree, with a resulting variation in the potential ability of the actor.

HYPERSENSITIVITY

A good actor is hypersensitive, in all senses of the word. He is sensitive to stimuli, to the things that happen to him. He sees, hears, tastes, vividly, precisely, and accurately; and he reacts to what he sees and hears. He is not simply a passive recorder of sensations. His response to his experiences is active: He likes or dislikes them vividly; he is moved by them; he analyzes them and notes their interrelationships; he files them permanently in his memory. As a result, when he is asked to portray an emotion or to carry out an action on the stage, he is able to supply from his own fund of experiences a large collection relevant to the demands of the role. Even if the character or the actions seem very different from his own, he is able to match them with many remembered events that are similar in kind, however much they may differ in degree. An actor's nose may not be grotesque, but he will have absorbed, analyzed, and stored in his memory enough incidents in which he was embarrassed and self-conscious to enable him to understand Cyrano's emotions. He will have had enough experiences with offensively crude and overbearing people to enable him to understand Ion's distaste during the conversation with Xuthus in Euripides' play. He will be able to draw on his own experiences of falling in love in order to play Romeo or Antony, or Marchbanks in Shaw's *Candida*.

THOROUGHNESS

The thoroughness with which he analyzes his experience is carried over into his work in the theater. He is a careful and systematic person, who makes his decisions only after thoughtful analysis. He does not perform on the basis of whim or impulse. The designer who, dramatically placing the back of her hand to her forehead and closing her eyes, said "I just *feel* that wallpaper more purple, somehow" was not really a theater artist. On the other hand, the woman who said "You analyze every emotion you feel, don't you?" was speaking to a true actor. This habit of methodical analysis seems cold and calculating, but it need not be cold at all, and for an actor cannot be. The fact that he notices how his hands tremble under stress does not prevent him from feeling the stress; it simply makes it possible for him to reproduce the effect when he needs it for a part in a play.

This conscious and systematic approach to experience prevents the actor from feeling impatient with the more mechanical aspects of rehearsal. He recognizes the necessity for precise blocking, for repeated experiment with different techniques, for the careful planning of details. The person who feels that the orderly procedure of rehearsals is an irritating interference, who says to himself "I wish we could stop fiddling with unimportant things like what direction I should face, and let me get on to showing how effectively hysterical I can be in my mad scene" is a nonactor. The cast member who looks at the director's blocking designs and asks "Why do you bother with all that work?" lacks an understanding of theater art.

In fact, one of the most unvarying characteristics of great actors is their staggering capacity for work. This is a characteristic that novice actors are especially likely to miss. Accounts of great professional actors often emphasize the more flamboyant aspects of their personalities and careers, and are likely not to devote comparable space to their long sessions of intense work. Sarah Bernhardt's gift for self-advertisement, and the vividness of her personality, may distract attention from what is far more important in her career as theater artist—the fantastic amount of work she did. One of the most significant details of her career is her regular practice of staying at the theater after the rest of the cast had been worn out by a full day's rehearsal and continuing to rehearse alone on the empty stage. Almost as an accident, Noel Coward early in his career established a reputation as a dilettante and playboy, who tossed off his theatrical performances with careless ease. How false that picture of him is can be demonstrated by simply running down a list of the plays he has written, acted in, and directed. If he had done no more than write music, his long list of hit tunes would have placed him among the major composers of popular music of the twentieth century. But a closer study of his methods of work reveals the pattern typical of great actors: an intense drive toward perfection of detail, a concentration on achieving the highest possible standards of performance, and a capacity for a sheer volume of work that would send an ordinary nontheater person to a rest home in a state of collapsed exhaustion.

The novice actor may overlook the careful preparation of the accomplished actors in the cast of the play in which he himself has a part. In one college production, few of the cast members were aware that the actor who played the leading role made special arrangements to use the theater after normal closing hours, and returned night after night to rehearse by himself on the stage, after the regular rehearsals were over.

OVERCOMPENSATION

The power that supplies the energy expended by the great theater artist comes from his intense desire to overcome his feelings of shyness, maladjustment, and inferiority. Often biographies of great actors describe childhood experiences of deprivation, although lack of money seems less significant than emotional deprivation. A surprising number of the most glamorous and successful stars of the theater were given little affection as children and were ridiculed or ostracized by the people around them. Such treatment may have varying effects. It may produce a ruthlessness and permanent alienation from others; for most people, its effect is perhaps to crush and destroy them. For people to rise from such backgrounds to positions of great achievement in the theater, it seems necessary for them to have two special characteristics: they must retain sympathy for others, and they must respond to their unfortunate experiences aggressively—they must fight back rather than submissively accept. The result is an intensity of drive that typically remains even after the childhood deprivations have been totally overcome. It seems likely that this pattern underlies the otherwise inexplicably high percentage of great theater artists in the last half of the twentieth century who come from minority groups.

EMPATHY

The sympathy for others which is so remarkable a characteristic of fine actors is not an accidental accompaniment of their work; it is absolutely essential. The actor's specific assignment in each role is to analyze and absorb the point of view of the person he is representing, to look at life through his eyes, to share his responses to experience—in a word, to empathize with him. And although sympathy and empathy are different, they are closely related. It is not an accident that actors are notably involved in movements designed to help the poor, the handicapped, and the victims of injustice. Rather, it is a natural expression of the sympathy for others without which they could not function effectively in the theater. The star who returns each year to perform for a fraction of his usual salary at the small night club that gave him his first opportunity, or who when he comes to town always stops at the unimpressive small rooming house run by the landlady who let him stay for months without paying his rent when he was struggling for a foothold in the theater, is not unusual. Such incidents could be matched by dozens of similar ones, and many more are never recorded.

In addition to these qualities, an actor needs high intelligence, quickness of mind, and skill in language.

> *How, without love and the intuition that comes from love, can a human being place himself in the situation of another human being? He must imagine, and imagination takes humility, love, and great courage.*
> CARSON MCCULLERS

Freedom from Inhibition

And finally, the great actor typical displays two characteristics that might seem inharmonious with the pattern outlined. The first is difficult to describe, but it can perhaps best be identified as a carelessness of dignity, a willingness to risk making a complete fool of himself. The preparation of a play involves weeks of trial and error. Especially during the rehearsals in which the actor is experimenting with various techniques, he may read a single line a dozen different ways, try out twenty different gestures to accompany it. Even assuming that one of these reading or gestures is the best possible, most of them will be wrong, and some of them are almost certain to be extremely, even ridiculously, wrong. An actor who shrinks from seeming foolish, who is unwilling to try a technique if there is any chance that it will be the wrong one, will not be able to function during the exploratory and experimental period of rehearsals, and, while he may avoid ever using the worst techniques, will be unable to find the best ones. The director's work, especially during the first half of the rehearsal period, involves constant evaluation and criticism of the actor's performance. At best the director must say to each actor over and over again, at least by implication, "What you just did was wrong; let's try it another way." An actor who interprets such comments as personal attacks, whose strongest motivation is to escape such criticism, is so hampered in his work that progress becomes almost impossible, and the final performance is certain to be much less effective than it would have been otherwise.

Even if the actor should by some miracle achieve the precisely right technique the first time, he would have to do many things in rehearsal that were embarrassing or ridiculous. In performance, the actor is hidden by his makeup and costume, and even by the lights, set, and properties, so that, for example, if he must cry hysterically in one scene, he can reasonably hope that the audience will attribute the hysteria to the character rather than to the actor himself. Without such assistance, an actor standing in the center of the bare stage during rehearsal, dressed in his usual clothing, with the auditorium lit and all the people fully visible, sobbing hysterically, may well feel like a complete fool.

Shaw's insistence on rehearsals' being rigidly closed to all but theater people may be intended to alleviate this difficulty. Once the members of a cast have become well acquainted, the rehearsals have developed momentum, and the pattern of the work has become familiar, each person will understand very clearly what the others are doing. When an actor tries out a piece of business that proves unsuccessful, the director analyzes it with him, and he then tries an alternative—which may be equally unsuccessful—the attitude of the other cast members is understanding and empathic, "understanding" in the literal, not the sentimental, sense of the word. They know what the other actor is doing and why he is doing it, and they recognize it as a regular and necessary part of the work. During rehearsals of one play at a large university, a photographer asked permission to shoot unposed action pictures. He used extremely sensitive film and was able to take the pictures without flash, so that the director and cast did not realize when they were taken. The results were hilarious, especially a group of pictures showing the director demonstrating bits of business appropriate to the characters but wildly inappropriate for the director himself. What made the pictures funny, however, was not the apparent ridiculousness of the director's performance but the concentrated seriousness with which the cast watched the demonstrations. No actor can go through the work of rehearsals effectively without frequently doing things that will seem undignified for him as a person, or without constantly trying things that will prove to be wrong for the performance. An actor who attempts to maintain his "cool," to preserve his dignity, to escape any hint of criticism, will simply not be able to do the job.

The director can do a great deal to assist the actors in this respect. The most important thing is for him to establish a businesslike tone for rehearsals. His work should be clearly purposeful, aimed toward the creation of the best performance possible. Even a ridiculously false handling of reading or gestures ceases to be embarrassing to the actor if the director avoids pouncing on it with cries of horror or ridicule—"No, no, that's terrible! you don't look as if you were in love, you just look as if you were coming down with the flu!"—but instead can say, directly or by implication, "Let's try to figure out all the different ways this line or gesture could be handled, then do all of them, and pick the best one."

With new actors, it is important to avoid any comment that can be interpreted as a personal attack, especially one involving ridicule. The necessity for commenting indirectly, and of softening all analyses or embedding them in complimentary contexts, involves a great waste of time, and if such procedures were followed for many actors very little would be accomplished during rehearsals. Seldom must the director function in that way, however. If he is able to create the proper atmosphere early in the rehearsal period, emphasizing the overall purpose of the work and the specific goal of each rehearsal and providing convincing demonstrations that the actors will not be embarrassed, that the work will be directed at the performance and not at the actors themselves, he should be able to carry on smoothly and without friction, and to conduct his discussions and evaluations frankly and directly.

It is wise to delay working with new actors until the tone of the rehearsals has been fully established. During the early interpretation rehearsals, it is better for the director to concentrate on the experienced actors who are playing the major roles, especially if he has worked with them before. The newer actors should be given a few instructions, so that they will not feel they are being ignored, but the directions as far as possible should concern relatively mechanical and impersonal details: "Next time, try pausing in the doorway and looking around to see who is on stage before you actually enter"; "If you will toss your hat down on the table during the first phrase of your speech, you may find it easier to turn toward the detective for the rest of the speech." Giving novice actors a chance to watch a rehearsal or two before working with them intensively will help them feel at home, will enable them to sense the general atmosphere of the rehearsals, and will demonstrate that the work of all the actors, including the most experienced, is subject to constant analysis, evaluation, and criticism, and that even the most skilled actors accept such criticism freely and cooperatively. The beginning actors are then much less likely to interpret the director's comments on their work as personal attacks, or to respond to them with embarrassment or self-defense.

THE CURSE OF TALENT

The other characteristic of great actors may seem astonishing: it is a lack of talent. Obviously, the word "talent" could mean many things; it sometimes is used simply as a synonym for "ability," and it would be absurd to suggest that great artists have no ability. The word is used here, however, in another sense, although it is a common one. Here "talent" means a kind of apparently unlearned ability, a gift from nature or the gods—the ability to perform more effectively than the ordinary person, without effort or study. A person who can "play the piano by ear" is talented in this sense; a person who can take a pencil and sketch a remarkable likeness of a friend, without ever having taken formal courses in drawing or studied it on his own, has this kind of talent. In the speech arts, talent in this sense appears as an apparently unstudied skill in mimicry, or the verbal fluency that is sometimes described as "the gift of gab." The essence of talent in this sense is that the person who displays it performs without study better than most other people who have not studied the particular activity.

> *Doing easily what others find difficult is talent; doing what is impossible for talent is genius.*
>
> HENRI-FRÉDÉRIC AMIEL

At first glance, such talent might seem a clear asset for an artist, in the theater or elsewhere. Surely, the ability to draw easily should give a student a head start in a career as an artist, as compared with others who must devote laborious months at the beginning of their study to developing the same level of skill. In fact, however, such talent seems to function as a handicap rather than a help. The person who can play the piano "by ear" may be able to provide an accompaniment for group singing at parties, but he is most unlikely to become a concert pianist. One member of a state legislature remarked that although he had taken piano lessons for an extended period as a child he had never learned to read music very well because he could not only play by ear but had a very quick musical memory, so that he was able to perform a selection from memory after having heard it a couple of times. Few twentieth-century painters could match the talent (in the sense in which we are using it here) of Norman Rockwell, but in spite of his great success as a commercial painter, his achievement as an artist is negligible. It is unlikely that he will be given much more than a footnote in future histories of modern art. So frequently is this kind of talent a handicap that at least occasionally especially successful artists do not simply lack it, they go to the opposite extreme of being less able than ordinary people to perform easily. Ted Shawn, who with his wife revolutionized modern dance in the early part of the century, and who was for many years the world's leading dancer, actually took up dancing because he was partially paralyzed. It will be seen that this is a special illustration of the fundamental motivation of actors, in which extraordinary achievement is identifiable as a kind of overcompensation for early deprivation.

Even so, it may seem puzzling that initial talent should prevent achievement. Tracing the experiences of one actor may help make this effect clearer.

Steve Anium was a good looking, dark-haired high school student who got involved in backstage work at plays toward the end of his sophomore year. When a minor injury prevented him from going out for football in his junior year, he decided to try out for the school's production of *The Fantasticks*. He had an excellent voice and was cast in the part of one of the fathers. He picked up dance steps so easily that the choreographer amplified his part, and his gift for mimicry enabled him to present a conniving father with remarkable effectiveness. He found the experience so pleasant that he tried out for the next production and developed into a leading actor. His performance as the stage manager in *Our Town* was especially successful; his assurance, ease of manner, and pleasantness of personality made him outstanding among the less talented members of the cast, even though the character he projected had little resemblance to the part as Wilder had written it. His final triumph was in the title role of *Cyrano de Bergerac*, which he found especially easy because he was able to exploit his athletic ability and his fine voice.

Steve considered very seriously majoring in drama when he went to college. Before he enrolled, he visited the campus he had chosen and met the director of the theater. He was warmly welcomed, and tried out for the first play, reading very effectively at the audition. He was astonished when the cast list was posted to discover that he had been assigned to play one of two butlers, but on inquiry he was assured by the other students that actors regularly started in small parts, and he accepted the play as a probationary experience.

He attended rehearsals faithfully and memorized his part even before the assigned deadline. He found his relationship with the director somewhat disturbing. He was asked a number of questions about his lines that puzzled him. Not only could he not answer the questions, but they seemed to be meaningless or irrelevant.

Furthermore, the director's comments seemed to be destructive rather than helpful. He suggested that Steve stand, walk, and gesture in ways that were not at all natural to him, and that he speak his lines entirely differently from the way that had proved so successful in the past. Steve's primary reaction was puzzlement, although he began to develop a dim suspicion that the director was a great deal less capable than the one under whom he had worked in high school.

Steve went to the tryouts for the second play with a feeling of relief at the discovery that it was to be directed by a different member of the staff. He was somewhat disturbed to discover that the actor who had played the second butler in the first play had been given a fairly strong supporting role, but his own part as an absent-minded retired minister was clearly more important than the role he had played in the first production. The minister was a key figure in one scene toward the end of the second act, on which the later development of the story hinged.

Steve saw the new play as important in establishing him as an actor at the college, so that he attacked it with great energy. He managed to learn his lines almost perfectly during the weekend before the first rehearsal, and although he carried his book during the blocking rehearsals, he dropped it as soon as the cast turned to interpretation. He noticed that all of the cast members, even the most experienced actors who were playing the leading roles, read their lines with little expression or force, and he seized the opportunity to emphasize his own skill by speaking with great animation and projection during the first interpretation rehearsal. The director made only a few comments on his performance, and mentioned only mechanical details of movement and position. Noticing that he had criticized the leading actors quite extensively and made numerous suggestions to them, Steve concluded that the director had recognized how effectively he was performing.

He was quite surprised when the director stopped him in the middle of one of his speeches during the second interpretation rehearsal, and asked him "What emotion do you think Reverend Senex would feel at this point?" Steve had not prepared an answer to the unexpected question, but after a moment's thought he said "Why, I would think he would be angry." "Well," the director replied, "there are thousands of ways of being angry. Exactly what kind of anger would Senex feel?" Steve was obviously puzzled by the question, and the director broke in after a moment's pause to say "Maybe that was an unfair question. It's difficult to describe a particular shade of emotion. But how angry would he be? would he be so furious he could hardly talk, or would he be only mildly irritated?" Steve, trying for a safe answer, said "Well, I don't think he would be really furious; I'd say he would be fairly angry." "What exactly is it that has made him angry?" the director asked. This one Steve had an answer for: "He thinks someone has been opening his mail and reading it, and he is angry because he comes in and sees the landlady with the mail in her hand." "Would anger be his only emotion?" the director continued: "Does he have some important secret he does not want discovered, and is he consequently afraid? or is he just touchy about being the object of curiosity? Aside from this particular scene, what kinds of things usually make him angry? What about his life entirely outside the play, during the years before the beginning of the play? How do you think he usually reacted to other people? Would you say anger is a frequent emotion for him, or that it is very rare?" Before Steve had a chance to reply, he went on: "Those questions are too difficult to answer at this stage of the work. But the script has a lot of hints about Reverend Senex, and as you continue to study the part you will pick them up. Be sure to look at what the other characters say about him, and don't even neglect the scenes in which he is apparently not involved at all. For instance, at the beginning of

Act III, the maid is terribly afraid that someone will see her leaving the house. Who is she afraid of? Is it Reverend Senex, and if so why? Should she really be afraid of him, or has she misunderstood what he has said and done? I know this isn't easy—nothing in drama is easy, and acting is at least the third most difficult of the arts that have to be combined to make a production. But work it out as thoroughly as you can, and let me help if you find any specially difficult problems."

The rehearsal proceeded, and the director did not bother Steve again, but after the general comments had been finished and the cast was getting ready to leave, the director strolled over toward him, calling out, "Oh, Steve!" and when he got close he said "I think you may be trying a little too hard. You don't have to give a perform-ance yet, you know; we've only just started working on the play. I really appreciate your memorizing the lines so quickly, but for the next week or so try to dig out all the meaning in the speeches you can possibly manage. You've got to make yourself the expert on Reverend Senex. You ought to get to know him inside and out, and that means you'll have to find every single item of information the playwright has given you, even the subtlest hints."

When Steve got to his room, he took out his playbook and restudied the speech that the director had interrupted. It began "Ah—I didn't hear the mailman. Is that today's mail?" Try as he could, Steve could find no clear suggestion of anger in the speech, although of course the minister did tell one of the other roomers later in the scene that he had been upset. Steve ran through all of his lines, but they seemed very ordinary; except for a word or two, which he checked with the dictionary, he could easily tell what they meant. Considerably baffled, he finally gave up and went to bed, but he decided that he'd better go over to the theater the next afternoon and run through the lines by himself, so he could get the feel of them.

He began his rehearsal with a feeling of uncertainty; the reading seemed lifeless and ineffective. Finally he decided he could do better without the playbook, and as soon as he laid it down he got into stride. He was able to make his first entrance really dramatic and to project his speeches all the way to the back row. His move-ments were easy, and he could feel the vividness and aliveness in his reading that had been so effective in his performance as Cyrano. He ended the rehearsal convinced that he had finally regained his grasp on acting, that he was back on the right track.

He was stunned that evening when the director interrupted him in the middle of his first phrase by calling out "Wait a minute!" The director got up out of his seat in the first row and walked to the edge of the stage. "Why did you come into the living room?" he asked. Steve pulled his script out of his back pocket and opened it to the scene; "Why, that was my cue," he said, "I'm supposed to come on when Pam says 'I'd better get back to my bread baking.' " One of the actors started to laugh, but the director broke in to say "I'm sorry; I didn't make myself clear. What I meant to ask was not why you entered as an actor, but why your character entered; why did Reverend Senex come in just at that time?" "Well, I don't know," Steve said, "the script says for him to." "But he didn't have any script to read," the director went on. "He must have had a reason of his own. Maybe it was an accident—maybe he was on his way to the kitchen for a cup of coffee; or maybe he was worried because he hadn't heard the mailman and came down to check; or maybe he was trying to catch whoever had been tampering with his mail." "Well, I don't see what difference it makes," Steve protested. "He has to enter then anyhow."

The director jumped up on stage without even bothering to walk around to the stairs. He crossed up to the living-room door and asked Steve if he wouldn't step aside so he could demonstrate. "It makes all the difference in the world," he said.

"If Reverend Senex is going to the kitchen for coffee, and just happens to glance in and see the landlady with his mail as he is passing the door, then his entrance has to be done one way."

He went backstage, and then walked along past the door, behind the scenery. Just as he got to the center of the doorway he glanced in and stopped suddenly; then he turned and took a couple of steps down toward the landlady, and stopped again, and paused for a moment as if he were trying to keep from blurting out something. When he spoke, he said quite mildly, "Ah—I didn't hear the mailman. Is that today's mail?"

"But you see," said the director, "he might not be going for coffee at all; maybe he is trying to catch someone opening the mail; then he would behave very differently." He went back offstage behind the set and returned walking diagonally toward the door, moving very quietly and stretching his head forward to look around the edge of the opening. He stopped in the doorway, and said, very suddenly and rather sternly, "Ah—I didn't hear the mailman!" Even though the actress who was playing the part of the landlady was watching the demonstration, she jumped and gave a little exclamation. The director walked over very quickly to her and snatched the letters out of her hand, and snapped "Is that today's mail?"

He turned to Steve. "You see," he said, "the reason why Reverend Senex entered makes an enormous difference in the way you should walk and speak the line. What's more, it isn't enough just to do what he would do; you have to communicate it to the audience. You have to say to them, if you assume he is going for coffee, 'Look: I'm not coming into the living room at all; I'm just on my way to the kitchen. But—wait a minute; I just happened to see that someone is handling the mail; it looks as though I've caught her red-handed, and here I am coming in to confront her. But I'd better be careful; this looks suspicious, but I'd better find out for sure before I let anyone know how upset I am.' You see, everything about the way you perform this little scene depends on what Reverend Senex's motivation is, and what is going on in his mind. Even when he stands still or walks, as well as what part of the stage he walks to, depends on what he is thinking and feeling. You can't hope to do the business or the speech right until you have analyzed the part and know exactly what he is thinking at this moment."

"But he wouldn't stop in the door the way you did," Steve protested; he isn't even supposed to go over and take the letters out of her hand; when we were doing the blocking you told me I was supposed to go over to the table when I came in, and look in the drawer."

"That's right," said the director. "Reverend Senex isn't really going for coffee, and he isn't really creeping into the room to try to catch someone opening his mail. Both of the ways I did the entrance are wrong. I purposely avoided demonstrating the actual motivation of the entrance because I don't want you just to mimic me. If you'll look at the scene that follows this one, after Reverend Senex has exited, you'll find out exactly what he was doing and thinking. Of course, we could stop the rehearsal and work out his whole character and motivation, especially as it applies to this entrance, but that isn't what rehearsals are for. Every actor is supposed to do that when he is studying his part by himself. What's more, this is an easy one; the second scene of Act III is the tough one, so you're going to have to do a lot more careful analysis before you can handle it. Of course, if you get in trouble with any particular point, I'll be glad to help, but if we had to work out the meaning of every line here in rehearsal, it would take us a whole month to get through the first act, and the play would go down the drain."

The director said little more to Steve that evening. He continued to find rehearsals disturbing; often the director's comments seemed to make very little sense, and over and over again, when Steve was sure he was performing at his best, the director would stop him and suggest some change in the way he was moving or speaking.

During the performance of the play he was able to do a little better, when he was not being interfered with by the director. The first scene did not go very well, but as soon as he gained some momentum he was able to "take the stage"; as soon as he could move freely and let go with his voice, he felt really at home. Buoyed up by the glow of the spotlights and the excitement of having an audience, he could feel himself swinging out with the same kind of performance that had wowed them in *The Fantasticks* and *Cyrano*. His parents thought he was wonderful, his mother in particular, and his roommate said he was "great," even though he unfortunately added, "but I really thought that part you had as a butler was funny; that was terrific, man!"

The guidance given Steve by the directors who worked with him has of course only been illustrated; it totaled hundreds of hours, extending over months, and involved assistance in acting on levels ranging from the broadest to the most specific. In addition, Steve was given personal counseling by his directors, some of whom were also his teachers, and by the counseling bureau of the college. Even so, he was unable to move from the wrong path on which he had been started to the path which would have led to sound growth as an actor.

Steve's later career as an actor puzzled him. His third part was as a walk-on, and though he struggled hard to make it as impressive as possible, the director kept frustrating his attempts by blocking him at the back of the stage behind other actors, so that the audience could hardly see him. He got better parts now and then, but he was baffled by the fact that other actors who had started at the same time he did, and who he knew had been less effective at the beginning, had moved up past him to supporting roles, and finally to leads. When he redoubled his attempts to use the techniques that had originally been successful, amplifying his gestures, displaying his personality even more fully, and speaking with even better voice quality and more animation, the only result was that he seemed to fall farther and farther behind. One of the things that puzzled him most was how directors who knew so little about their job could get positions in college, while his high school director knew so well how to help him give starring performances. Finally deciding that there was no opportunity for him in the college theater, he withdrew from drama altogether, and started working on the campus newspaper.

Far from being unusual, Steve's story is typical of the "talented" performer. Every director who works for any length of time in the theater is likely to run into many performers who follow the same pattern. It may be helpful to summarize the key factors in this tragicomedy.

Steve experienced an early easy success because he was a member of a cast made up of ordinary people without training or experience. His talent, in the sense in which the word is used here, enabled him to perform without study or understanding better than most people who had neither talent nor study.

His success was due to qualities that he had not analyzed or practiced, and that he consequently could neither control nor alter.

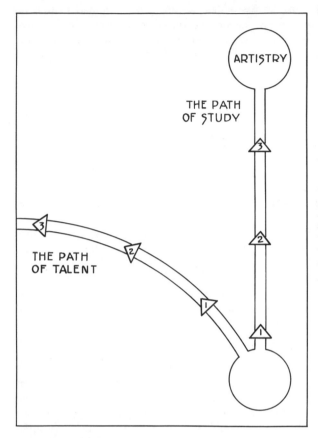

ARTISTRY

THE PATH
OF STUDY

3

2

1

THE PATH
OF TALENT

3

2

1

Figure 50. The paths of talent and artistry. The talented actor starts out ahead of the ordinary actor, actually somewhat closer to the goal of artistry (triangles 1). As each proceeds along his path, however, the actor following the path that leads directly toward artistic achievement soon passes the actor who relies on talent alone (triangles 2), and the farther each travels, the more strikingly the sound artist surpasses the merely talented performer.

His performances were acting only in the least precise sense of the word. He did not portray the father in *The Fantasticks,* or the Stage-Manager in *Our Town,* or Cyrano; he simply displayed himself, his good looks, his pleasant personality, his animation, and his attractive voice. His closest approach to acting consisted of some minimal mimicry of the mannerisms of others.

His performances, however effective, were not in any degree works of art. They did not represent an analysis of life, or even of a playscript; they did not result from the organization of experience into a unified pattern. Their appeal was almost entirely sensory, minimally emotional, and intellectual not at all.

Not only did Steve's experience not provide him with any techniques or methods of working, but it persuaded him that success was to be achieved by a completely false approach, limited to the display of personal characteristics, such as voice and appearance, that were only accidentally related to the roles to which he would be assigned. When he attempted to improve his performance, the only method he knew was to exaggerate the effects he had used in the past, but since they were unsuited to the various parts available to him, exaggerating them made his performances worse instead of better.

The destructive aspect of the easy-talent success is that it sets the actor on the wrong path; the farther he moves along it, the farther he gets from the goal of producing a work of art. The two paths, however, start out close together. An actor who is just starting on the journey toward becoming an artist may be far behind the performer who has the advantage of the initial push given him by his talent. As each moves along his own path, the actor will soon pass the talented performer, who, if he tries to catch up by moving farther along the wrong path, moves steadily farther from the goal, while the actor continues to approach it.

It has always seemed that the kind of talent that leads to an easy and accidental success for an actor should be usable in the theater; if an actor could be persuaded to take the small step from the wrong path to the right one, to study the sound methods by which artistry must be developed, the talent would then be a source of strength and not a handicap. As one university director who has worked with thousands of actors has said, "I have always expected that some day I would find an outstandingly talented actor for whom the first steps were natural and easy, who would be able and willing to learn the techniques and accept the discipline necessary to achieve great artistry, and that his talent would then give him momentum and enable him to move farther and faster than he would have without it; I can only say that in thirty years I have never found such an actor."

It is clear, then, why this particular kind of talent has been called a curse.

HUMILITY

The element of effort has not been sufficiently emphasized in this discussion; it is more important, at least as a clue to an actor's ability, than has been suggested. The theater, as has been said, is the most complex of the arts. The actor's task is surpassed in difficulty probably only by those of the playwright and director. The detail with which so simple an action as an entrance must be analyzed has been suggested by the preceding narrative. No actor with even a minor speaking part can hope to explore all of the possible ways in which the part might be played, and so can never be sure that he has found the best one. Any actor who feels that his part is unworthy of his best effort is unaware of most of the work and decisions which acting involves. It would be appropriate to apply to any such actor the burlesque revision of Kipling's "If": "If you can keep your head when those about you are losing theirs, you don't understand the situation."

The actor who is thoroughly familiar with the demands of his art is likely to view each acting assignment as an impossibly difficult task, for which he is totally unprepared. The fine actor is typically reluctant to audition for a play because he feels that any part he might get would be too difficult to handle. He is likely to be astonished at any role in which he is cast because the director has placed such heavy reliance on him.

Late in the afternoon of the day when the cast list has been posted for one production, a college actress stopped by the scene shop where the director was working and said "Somebody told me I got a major part in the play." "But Dorrie," said the director, "didn't you go over to check the cast list?" "No," she replied; "I just assumed I wouldn't get a part." Such modesty may seem excessive, but it was no accident that her performance in the play was one of the most effective. On the other hand, the self-confident actor who bounces in to audition as a mere gesture of etiquette, convinced that if the director has any sense at all he will be assigned the lead automatically, will be found, a thousand times out of a thousand, only barely capable of handling a walk-on. Few directors would want actors to express deference or humility toward them: subservience is one of the least attractive of human relationships, but an actor who does not feel humility toward the art of the theater is so ignorant of the difficulties and complexities of his job that he is not ready to undertake it.

That is the test of the true artist, always being dissatisfied, always doubting one's own ability.

AUGUSTE RODIN, QUOTED BY
LENORE CISNEY AND JOHN REDDY

DECISION MAKING

The director is, of course, organizationally in control of rehearsal. He is responsible for planning the series of rehearsals as a whole, for setting the goal for each rehearsal, and for guiding the work that is done. Inevitably, he must give directions to the actors. If he does not fulfill those responsibilities he fails to function as a director. He also bears the primary responsibility of setting the tone of the work. It is important, therefore, that he should not simply function: he should display his pattern of work. Just as novice actors copy the style of work of the more experienced actors, all actors tend to reproduce the director's attitudes and methods of attack.

The director plans, evaluates, and gives instructions. All of his various activities can be summarized by saying that his job is to make a long series of decisions, and the quality of his work depends on the quality of his decisions. His most important indirect training of the actors consists of the display of his methods of making decisions.

The factors that the director must consider in making decisions are even more numerous and more complex than those with which the actors must be concerned. Sound decisions are based on the thorough collection of all the relevant evidence, careful analysis of it, evaluation of it in terms of the purpose of the production, and an imaginative search for alternative techniques. The factor most likely to cause difficulty is the director's realization that it is literally impossible for him to collect all of the information he needs or to identify all of the possible techniques that might be available. As a result, he may be so terrified that he finds it impossible to make decisions at all. Or he may abandon the collection and analysis of evidence, since he cannot hope to complete it, and begin to make decisions on the basis of whim or coin flipping. Either reaction is destructive to his work. An indecisive director is no director at all, and a director who decides where an actor should stand, or how a line should be read, only on the basis of whim or hunch is likely to be wrong in the vast majority of cases. The director must, therefore, carry his collection and analysis of evidence as far as possible, within the limits of the available time and his own abilities, and then he must make firm decisions. This combination of decisiveness with open-mindedness—the ability to formulate and carry out plans, coupled with a vivid awareness of the fact that they are, and must inevitably be, inadequately based —is a rare one.

Actors must share these qualities, and an actor who errs in either direction will be as ineffective as a whimsical or indecisive director. When the director suspects that an actor has adopted a technique—a piece of business or a line reading—without a careful analysis of the relevant evidence, he should challenge the actor by asking for a summary of the evidence and the process of reasoning on which the selection of technique was based. If the director finds an actor unable to make a decision about how a line should be read, he should run over the essential factors affecting the decision, and should then encourage the actor to identify as many alternative readings as possible and to perform each of the readings. They can then be evaluated in discussion, and the actor encouraged to select the most effective. Usually it is easy to eliminate most of them immediately, and to reduce the possibilities to two or three. These can be reperformed, and then a second evaluation made, which will nearly always make it possible for the actor to choose the best one. These treatments would, of course, take too much time if they were applied to every gesture and line. Their purpose, however, is not so much to assist in the immediate problem as to demonstrate to the actor the proper method of attack. After two or three such demonstrations, the technique should be clear to the entire cast, and as they apply it in their study outside rehearsal, their work will steadily improve.

The most important method of teaching such an approach, however, is for the director to display it himself. He should take what opportunities occur, and they will be many, to explain some of the reasons for a decision; to indicate the enormous number of factors or alternatives that it has been impossible for him to explore; and to state his decisions with clarity and firmness. Beginning directors are often afraid that revealing the degree of their uncertainty will damage their authority and make it impossible to retain control of the rehearsal procedure. That happens only if the director is both uncertain and indecisive; a realistic demonstration of the actual conditions and methods of work is beneficial, not harmful. Especially the better actors are likely to be so terrified of the complexities that face them that they cannot bring themselves to make firm decisions. The director's repeated demonstration that it is possible to work decisively and at the same time retain full awareness of the difficulties of the problems is reassuring to them and gives them a technique for carrying on their own work.

Inevitably the actors develop some attitude of dependence toward the director. He is at least as dependent on them, but that fact tends to be concealed by the fact that he is executive, guide, and judge of their work. The tensions that good actors bring to their work as a result of their fundamental pattern of personality, and the fact that their experiences and emotions are the raw material with which they work, necessarily make the actor-director relationship emotional. The interrelationships of the cast members are also affective, although less intensely so for obvious reasons. Furthermore, because the actor must, in his work, submit his skills, experiences, and emotions for the director's evaluation and analysis, he is extremely vulnerable to destructive criticism.

The director cannot ignore such factors. The emotions of the actors are not irrelevant to the work, and their presence is not an irritating intrusion, as it might be for instance in office work; they are central to the production of the play. The director must not simply take them into account, he must work with them centrally. If he handles them improperly, he will destroy the production; and if he fails to make use of them, he will fail to function as a director.

INSTRUCTING THE ACTORS

There is a tendency among beginning directors to think of their work as consisting primarily of identifying what actors are doing wrong and making them stop it. Such directors' comments to the cast consist of long lists of errors. Even if the errors actually exist, such comments can be devastatingly destructive of the actors' self-confidence and morale. Sensing that fact, the new director may attempt to sugar-coat the medicine by including favorable items on his list; if so, he is likely to be dismayed at how little effect the change has.

This method is wrong, not simply emotionally but in its approach to the act of esthetic creation. The development of the production as a work of art involves a long series of steps, spread out over a month or six weeks, starting with analysis, then moving through a period during which technical resources are explored, toward the selection of the most effective techniques, and ending with the polishing and making permanent of the pattern that has been developed. Especially during the period of technical exploration, the actor who tries

first one and then another way of reading a line is not at fault; he is functioning exactly as he should. For the director to point out to him in the middle of
this process that much that he has been doing is wrong and must be discarded
is an absurd repetition of a truism, and is as useless as to stop an actor in the
middle of a cross and point out to him that he is walking from one position
on stage to another. Actors' uncertainty is most extreme during this group of
rehearsals; they are vividly aware that much of what they are doing will prove
unacceptable, and must be replaced with other techniques. Being unnecessarily
reminded of that fact is likely to inhibit further exploration and cannot possibly
facilitate it.

> *For it is much more easie to find Faults than it is to discern Beauties. To
> do the first requires but common Sence, but to do the last a Man must
> have Genius.*
>
> DENNIS, *The Impartial Critick*

The primary goal of rehearsals, then, should be to find the right thing and
learn to do it, rather than to find what is wrong and eliminate it. Attention
should be focused on the final goal of the best performance possible, not on the
momentary jogs in the path by which it is reached. Actors who are making clear
progress at an acceptable rate should be left alone. If their work can be accelerated by the director, so much the better; but his method should match their
own—it should be aimed at identifying the best techniques, rather than concentrating on experiments that have proved unacceptable.

Dr. Frank Whiting, an outstanding director of the educational theater,
reports an amusing incident that occured early in his career:

There had been a time in my life when, quite unconsciously, I had felt that the
director's function was to see how many things he could find wrong with the rehearsal, then point these out to the players. Fortunately an old-timer set me right
with the advice, "Let 'em have their heads, boy. No one can get his mind on the play
up there with you yappin' all the time." Anyone can watch an average rehearsal and
fill many pages with little notations of things that are wrong. It often requires a
genius, however, to decide which notations should be mentioned, which ignored, and
which lumped together around some basic principle.[1]

One teacher of directing made the same point when he told his class that
one of the most important things a director must know is what not to mention to
the actors. Only continued experience can enable him to judge accurately what
not to discuss, but a useful rule for a director at any stage of his experience is,
if unsure about mentioning something, keep quiet.

1. Frank M. Whiting, *An Introduction to the Theatre,* Harper & Row, Publishers,
New York, 1969, p. 179.

It is particularly distressing to an actor to be told by the director that his performance is unacceptable, without at the same time being given some suggestions for improving it. It is easy enough to recognize when a scene is not going well, but to identify the cause of its ineffectiveness and to prescribe changes which will improve it are much more difficult. Nearly always, the director should withhold comment until he has specific suggestions. Usually the methods of improving a scene will become clear at a later rehearsal, and the director can then discuss them with the actors.

Actors' Development

The breadth and complexity of the art of acting provides such a large space for growth that no actor can achieve his full potential in a lifetime: there is always something more to learn, a new area to master. Each actor begins his rehearsal of a play with an area of mastery that has an individual shape. One actor may have learned to handle low comedy effectively, but not tragedy; another may be effective at romantic drama, yet find it difficult to handle verse; a third may be able to express subtle effects in quiet scenes, but find it hard to rise to climaxes. Each actor actually will have dozens of skills, and as many effects that he has not yet mastered.

Growth in ability occurs just beyond the edge of the area of mastery, and an actor may extend his skill greatly during a month's rehearsals. For every actor, however, there is a limit to what can be achieved during the rehearsals for a single play. It is desirable that his growth should be as great as possible, and the director should provide constant stimulus, assistance, and encouragement, but it is important not to try to push an actor out farther than he can actually move. If the actor cannot learn to produce an effect during the current rehearsals, it is frustrating, agonizing, and wasteful for the director to persist in demanding it of him. Assessing how far an actor can be moved in rehearsal is difficult, and probably it is better to err in demanding a little more of him than he can actually achieve, rather than asking too little; but to make unrealistic demands will produce emotional disturbance and will distract the actor from work on other skills where rehearsal might be more fruitful.

It is to be expected that the actors' performances will grow steadily richer throughout the rehearsal period. They bring blank canvases to the first rehearsal and fill in the picture with one stroke of the brush at a time. If an actor is able to communicate only a few speeches effectively in an early rehearsal, the director need not be disturbed, especially if he retains his effective readings and adds more at each following rehearsal. An actor who stops progressing needs help; but so long as he is moving toward a finished performance, the director can usually assist him best by staying out of his way.

Far more disturbing is the actor who shows up at an early rehearsal with his canvas filled with colors splashed across it, before he has had time to analyze the play and his part in it. The posture, movements, gestures, and vocal expressions displayed by such an actor are likely to be left over from a previous play, and consequently are almost certain to be unsuited to the present one. The actress who had received great applause for her performance as a cripple in a high school play, and who persisted in trying to use the same method of walking in every later play, was a ridiculously extreme example. But it is not uncommon for actors to attempt to achieve instant characterizations when they have not earned the right to fill in their picture by intensive study. Such actors should be stopped immediately. This approach is not aimed at finding the best techniques; instead, it operates to prevent the necessary study and exploration, since the actor is most likely to feel that he has already achieved all of the animation and excitement the performance requires. Allowing such an actor to carry his irrelevant performance through even a single rehearsal will fix it still more firmly in his mind. He must be moved to the right path at the earliest moment possible. (It will be seen that this is related to the curse of talent.)

IDENTIFYING SUCCESSES

The critical moments, then, are those in which the right effect is finally achieved, when a reading is fully and accurately expressive, when a gesture or movement is communicative and in character. To a very great extent, the entire work of rehearsals can be described as the process of finding such moments of success, and then learning to repeat them.

Actors find it very difficult to evaluate the effectiveness of what they do. Even experienced actors are likely to have only a vague and uncertain feeling of which reading actually communicates as it should. The director, sitting where the audience will be placed, and free of the distractions of performing, is in the best situation for making such judgments. One of his most important functions is to identify every moment in a rehearsal when the right effect is produced, whether by accident or as a result of the actor's systematic experimentation, and to report each one as he finds it. In order to do that, he must watch the performance with the greatest concentration, listening intensely for the moment when a line, a sentence, or even a phrase suddenly rings true, looking at each cross, each gesture, so that whenever one is made effectively, he catches it. Usually he will dictate a note to the assistant director so that he can mention the point in his general comments to the cast. Especially during the early rehearsals, it may be preferable to stop the rehearsal and analyze what has been done immediately, while it is still fresh in the actor's mind.

Sometimes a particularly effective bit of business or reading is not isolated, but is the result of a shift in the actor's point of view, or of a sudden insight into the character. In that case, the actor may continue to perform at a new high level, and if so, it is important that the director not interrupt the flow of the scene and destroy the actor's momentum. Even in an early rehearsal it is better to wait for a moment after an effective bit and allow the actor to continue as long as he can maintain the same level of performance. The rehearsal should be stopped for an immediate analysis, however, as soon as it is clear that the actor has dropped back to his previous level. If the outstanding detail involves speech, it is especially useful to be able to play a tape recording of it immediately, so that the actor's memory of what he has done can be reinforced by hearing it again.

It is recommended that rehearsals not be interrupted past the middle of the rehearsal period. Even when the scenes are being run straight through, however, it is often desirable for the director to continue to identify the moments of special success without waiting for intermission breaks. If this is to be done, the actors should be warned in advance and should be instructed to continue their performance without pause. Even at this point in the rehearsals, each actor is likely to be still searching for the best techniques for handling individual lines or business. When one of these problem moments is handled effectively, the director can inform the actor by shouting "Good!" immediately. Such single-word comments do not interrupt the scene, and actors report they find them helpful and not distracting. It is to be expected that even these infinitesimal comments will become fewer and fewer as rehearsals progress. They must not be continued during the fixing rehearsals and should be entirely or nearly absent from the polishing rehearsals.

It will be seen that the focus on achievement rather than error is recommended on grounds of esthetic efficiency: it produces better performances. It is not recommended simply in order to promote sweetness of group relationships; rehearsals are work sessions, not social occasions whose primary purpose is ensuring that cast and director can all be happy together. Even praise of actors should be directed at the improvement of the performance, not at just being pleasant.

SINCERITY

Above all, the director should avoid praising work which does not deserve approval. According to legend, actors discount criticism and accept as deserved even the grossest flattery. Actually, exactly the opposite is true. Actors' basic personality leads them to be extremely self-critical and to be very suspicious of praise. For a director to praise a reading or a performance that the actor knows

---

Every actor in his heart believes everything bad that's printed about him.
                                                          ORSON WELLES

does not justify the approval not only creates a communication barrier between the two, but will lead the actor to disbelieve anything the director might say to him in the future.

That does not mean that the director can only praise perfection, or that he must echo the actor's own self-doubts. The important requirement is that the director's praise be sincere. There will be many times when the actor will feel he has performed badly and the director will evaluate his performance more favorably; such a difference of opinion should disturb no one—it is no part of theater work that there should be constant agreement—and the director may on occasion simply be wrong. It is important, however, that he say what he believes. Actors are extremely sensitive to pretense, since their work necessarily makes them experts at it.

It is unusual for an actor to work through a rehearsal without displaying some details that the director can genuinely praise. Even if not a single speech has been delivered acceptably, there is certain to be some variation in effectiveness, and the director can point out the few speeches that came closest to being right. Any improvement should be noted. Even if an actor has simply found new techniques to try, the fact that he is struggling with the problem can be mentioned favorably. Remarks such as "I thought you came closest to the right performance in your last scene in Act I," or "I think you're doing a good job of looking for the right way to handle that third speech; I don't think you've found it yet, but if you keep trying different approaches, as you were tonight, I feel sure you will get it eventually" are pleasant and believable, and they are genuinely helpful in guiding the actor as he continues his work. At the very least, the director can say, "I really appreciate the care and hard work that you bring to rehearsals; your concentration is an example for everybody who works on the play" (assuming, of course, that that is the truth).

Actors do not want to be babied or coddled; they do not want to be tricked by insincere praise. On the other hand, they do not want to be humiliated or savagely attacked. They will accept almost any analysis of their work, even if they do not agree with it, that is clearly motivated by a desire to help them improve their performance, and consequently to make them look better to the audience. Good relations with theater people are achieved in the same way as good relations with people outside the theater. The only differences are that the director is inevitably in an executive position in rehearsal, and so bears the major responsibility for the relationships; that actors are necessarily unusually sensitive to comments; and that their work involves them as persons more intensely than in most situations outside the theater.

The Director at Performance

It is desirable for the director to join the cast before the rise of the curtain on opening night, but he should be there as a friend and well-wisher, and he should resist any impulse to repeat an instruction or give a new one. He can help the actors most by speaking a pleasant word or two to them, by engaging in casual conversations, preferably on subjects not connected with the play, and by establishing a mood of relaxed good humor.

It is customary for the director to address the cast as a group fifteen or twenty minutes before curtain time. His remarks should be general and pleasant, an extension of his individual conversations. He may properly express his enjoyment of his work with them, but he should avoid suggestions about the coming performance. He might end his comments by remarking that he is looking forward at last to being able to simply enjoy the show, instead of having to work at it.

Some directors write an individual thank-you note to each actor; these are then distributed by the assistant director or stage manager just before the final performance. This is a pleasant gesture, which is more appreciated by actors than might be expected; many of them are treasured for years.

Preparing the notes is an irksome and sometimes difficult job. Since actors are sure to read each other's notes, each one must be individual; a form letter is probably worse than none at all. Any special achievement or effort of an actor can be mentioned, attendance at a rehearsal which happened to be difficult for the actor, unusual dedication, especially hard work. The real problem is with actors who have not worked well, or who have been unfriendly or uncooperative. The director's comments must be pleasant, but it is important that they be sincere. At worst, he can fall back on the trick of identifying the most effective detail of the actor's performance, on mentioning improvement, or on recalling the rehearsal when the actor worked best. In these problem letters, comments like the following may be made: "I especially enjoyed the pantomime business in the third act, when you juggled the tray, and nearly dropped it each evening"; "Your improvement, especially during the last two weeks, was really striking; I'm looking forward to your continued growth as an actor"; "I heard one member of the audience say he thought your second scene in Act III was one of the high points in the play." (This last device is a very useful one; it is pleasant and yet does not force the director to express his own approval; of course it may be difficult to find someone to provide a quotable comment.)

Many directors, in published accounts and in private conversations, have reported their reactions to opening night. The actor's stage fright may be no more severe than the director's offstage fright. He has the advantage that he need not be physically present, but the agonizing realization that whatever happens is now beyond his control. Each director reacts in his own way; none is typical. However, four examples may be cited as illustrative.

Ronald Arcturus is beginning his second year of high school teaching. He spent most of his first year developing a solid foundation for drama at his school, starting a drama club, training students in building scenery, working up a group of experienced actors. Tonight is the opening of this season's first play. He has been very busy during the two hours before show time. He has been back stage, in the makeup room, checking the box office, handling problems as they were brought to him. When the ten-minute warning came, he made the rounds of the cast to give them a final word of encouragement, and then raced to the lobby, slipping into his seat beside his wife just as the lights finished dimming, too exhausted to wonder how the play would go.

Geoffrey Carmidy has been a high school teacher for ten years, and is directing his first production in college. He is still directing it, although the curtain rose twenty minutes ago, and the first act is well along. He has just crept behind the set, crouching down so he would not be seen by the audience through the window in the back wall, to deliver six more instructions to the stage manager. He is afraid he had forgotten to give him one of the instructions, and since he isn't sure which one, he feels it would be safer if he repeated them all. Passing an actor waiting in the wings, he stops to give him a few final suggestions, with the result that the actor's entrance is delayed. Later, Jeff will be disturbed by a feeling of uncertainty about the show, resulting from the fact that he never actually got to see it.

Frank Demonies has directed one Broadway hit, and another play that got good reviews but bad attendance. Although he is only in his late thirties, he feels time slipping fast; and in the chancy world of the theater, he has concluded that his current production is a critical one. It is opening in the Village. If it is a smash, it's going to Broadway, and he'll be on top—with two Broadway hits, and a reputation. If it is even just fairly successful, it will stay where it is, and he'll be a has-been—a mediocre director who got lucky once. It is opening night, but Frank is not at the theater; he is in his apartment, and he has put three albums of electronic music—the most cacophonous he could find on the phonograph, with the volume turned as high as the neighbors will allow. The television is on, with the sound turned to zero; he has a best-selling novel in his lap, has poured himself a stiff drink, and is wondering whether he can nerve himself to go to the cast party after the show, at which everyone will try to hide the anxiety with which they are waiting for the reviews in the morning papers.

William Labrax is starting his eleventh year as a director of university theater. When he was an undergraduate, his director said something to him that he still remembers. Bill had commented one night that the director seemed unusually calm before a performance. "I'm through," the director replied. "I've been working on this show for six weeks, counting a month's rehearsals; I've done the best I could, and even if I hadn't it's too late now. If the scenery started to fall down, I couldn't run up on stage and hold it up; if an actor forgets a line, I can't prompt him. I'm going to sit here and enjoy the show like everybody else, for once without having to analyze and evaluate and take hundreds of notes. Why should the audience have all the fun?" Bill found that philosophy so sensible and so comfortable that he adopted it for his own. He, too, has a show opening, but after a pleasant word with each of the cast members at the beginning of the makeup session, he left with his wife for a light supper, and has not been backstage since. After supper, they spent a half hour in the lobby chatting with friends attending the show, and then took their seats in the audience, in pleasant anticipation of watching an enjoyable performance of a play.

And so, directors react to their shows, each in his own way. Of these four, Carmidy's is the worst, and Labrax's the best—if the director can manage it.

Having finished his work, the director is free to take his seat out front among the audience, to relax and enjoy the show for the first time. He will have operated for six weeks or two months so close to the production that he may have been unable to see the forest for the trees; indeed, much of his time may have been occupied in digging around under the bushes, so that he could hardly see the trees. On opening night, he is finally able to look at the show literally from the viewpoint of the audience, and he is likely to find not only that his response is surprisingly fresh and new, but that what has been work has suddenly become fun. At later performances, he may want to re-evaluate his work, to try to identify direction that produced the result he intended, scenes in which his work was not successful, and methods by which he might have improved his handling of the cast and the play. But for the first performance, he should relax and have fun.

> *A drama director, they say,*
> *Long longed for an increase in pay;*
> *But they laughingly said,*
> *"You should pay us instead,*
> *For you know that your work is all play."*

As soon as the curtain goes up on opening night, the director's work is finished; he has become totally dispensable. The audience is most likely to be unaware of all that he has done. They may congratulate him if the performance is effective, and may have some dim feeling that he must have had *something* to do with it; but even if they are theater fans, they are unlikely to be able to assess his contribution accurately. Was a particularly effective bit of business, an especially moving passage of dialog, the result of the director's work, or the actors'? Probably not a single person in the audience will be able to guess.

THE DIRECTOR AS ARTIST

The director's importance in the production, however, is overwhelming. He alone sees it as a whole, in advance of performances. He traces its broad outlines and supervises the filling in of the details. In his triple function of executive, teacher, and artist, his skill, judgment, and taste are reflected in every detail of the production. The work is dependent on his ability to respond empathically to the intentions of the playwright, the characters in the play, the actors themselves, and the audience, whose experience he must be able to predict and guide for weeks before they have assembled.

The director's growth as an artist is a source of continuing gratification. No lifetime is long enough to master the art, but conversely he is assured the opportunity of lifelong development. As a human being, the empathic function of the director ensures a steady increase in his ability to share the experiences and viewpoints of other people, and consequently a continued enlargement of his sympathy and understanding.

And finally, the experience of working concentratedly with fellow artists for a period of weeks produces a closeness of relationship that most often results in permanent friendships. If playwriting is the most difficult of the theatrical subarts, and acting the most glamorous, directing is at least as rewarding as either.

A Few Technical Terms

Expressions frequently used by directors in giving instructions to actors are indicated by enclosing them in quotation marks.

"ACT!"—an instruction to read lines with more emotion and projection

"AD LIB"—(movement) to improvise business or blocking not specified by the script or the director; actors who must pace throughout a long speech are often told to ad lib their movements; actors in crowd scenes involving extreme movement and intended to create an impression of confusion are often instructed to ad lib their blocking

—(lines) to speak lines not included in the script; actors who form crowds on stage are often told to ad lib their responses; in emergencies, when a technical error has occurred or when an actor has skipped a passage in the script, it is sometimes necessary for actors to insert ad-libbed speeches in order to handle the problem

APRON—the area of the stage in front of the act curtain

APRON STAGE—a stage with a large apron, which is used as an important part of the acting area, the actors performing both in front of and behind the curtain line

ARENA (OR CENTRAL) STAGING—a theatrical arrangement in which the audience surrounds the acting area on all sides, the rows of seats having the shape of concentric circles, interrupted by radial aisles, the seats all pointed toward the center

"ARTICULATE!"—an instruction to the actor to differentiate more clearly between speech sounds

AUDITIONS—sessions at which actors are examined in order to determine their suitability for parts in a play

BLOCKING—the design of the patterns of arrangement and movement of the actors on stage; rehearsals at which this design is studied are called blocking rehearsals

"BREAK!"—a signal that a pause has been held the maximum length of time, and that the audience's attention will wander if it is extended

BUILDING LAUGHS—a technique for amplifying laughter by delaying it through a series of laugh points, with a resulting increase of tension that produces a fuller laugh at the end of the series

BUSINESS—meaningful movement on stage larger than gesture and smaller than blocking; Hedda Gabler's burning the book manuscript in the fireplace is an example of business; inventing business is primarily the responsibility of the actor, although some business is specified by the script and some by the director

CAMP—drama in which defects are presented as things to be enjoyed; nineteenth-century melodramas are now usually treated as camp; the musical *The Boy Friend* is largely camp, and it appears in many other plays, for instance the death scenes in *The Fantasticks*

"CHEAT!"—to alter the angle from what would be most natural in a similar scene offstage, turning slightly more toward the audience; a pair of actors engaged in conversation are usually instructed to cheat so that the audience will get a better view of them than straight profiles; cheating is done minimally, in the hope that the audience will not be aware of it

CLOSED REHEARSALS—rehearsals at which only those who are involved in the production of the play are allowed to be present

"COUNTER"—an instruction given to an actor to move in the opposite direction at the instant that another actor crosses below him; the counter usually incorporates a small turn in the direction of the crossing actor

COVER—to hide from the sight of the audience; an actor is momentarily covered when another crosses in front of him

"CROSS"—to move from one spot on stage to another

CUE—the signal for a stage effect; actors' cues sometimes consist of sound effects (the ringing of a telephone is the cue for answering it), changes in lighting, or bits of business; most often the cue for a line is the last phrase of the preceding line, which is regularly marked by the actor in his script and memorized along with his own line

CURTAIN CALL—a ceremony during which the cast assemble on stage immediately after the end of the play to acknowledge the applause of the audience

DIDACTIC DRAMA—drama intended to produce a change in the attitudes, beliefs, or behavior of the audience that will persist after they have left the theater

DIRECTIONAL TERMINOLOGY—used in describing actors' positions and movements; the same terms as those used in stage geography are employed, with the exception of center; three additional terms are used to describe the relative distances of actors or scenic elements from the audience: above—farther from the audience; below—closer to the audience; and level—the same distance from the audience

DOUBLE-CASTING—assigning two actors to play the same role, usually on alternate evenings

DOUBLING—assigning two roles in the same play to a single actor

"DRESS THE STAGE"—an instruction to actors to make minor shifts in position so as to improve the stage picture, and in particular to provide the audience with maximum visibility; actors regularly dress the stage constantly throughout a performance

EMPATHY—the act of sharing someone else's experiences or emotions

EXPOSITION—the section of a play containing information about the characters or the events that took place before the opening of the first act, necessary to the audience in order to follow the story of the play; usually included in the first half of the first act

FALSE INTENSIVES—words that once served to make a statement emphatic, but that have lost that function; examples are "very," "quite," "certainly," and "awfully"

FOURTH WALL—the imaginary wall which is needed to complete the stage set so as to form a fully enclosed room; architecturally, it would stand on stage at the curtain line; psychologically, it would be placed immediately behind the seat of each spectator; in practice, for director and actors it is located at the back of the auditorium; although the term is derived from box sets representing the interior of rooms, it is also used for other types of scenery

"FREEZE"—to stop movement; actors are usually instructed to freeze while another actor is speaking, and while an audience laughs

"GIVE!"—synonymous with "Act!"

"HOLD"—to delay (a speech or an action); for instance: "Hold the cross until the doorbell rings"; "Hold the line until the butler has set down the tray"

"HOLD FOR LAUGHS"—stop the performance to give the audience time to laugh

THE ILLUSION OF THE FIRST TIME—speaking and moving in such a way that the lines and business seem spontaneous and unrehearsed

JELL—an occurrence during the rehearsal series in which the performance takes on an effect of continuity; jelling normally occurs during the blending rehearsals; previously, the play is worked on in fragments; achieving continuity is a major purpose of the blending process

KITSCH—drama that imitates the superficial mannerisms of plays of higher quality

LAUGH PATTERN—an emotional formula involving the raising of tension followed by an instantaneous releasing stimulus; the pattern is nearly always present in some form or degree when the audience laughs

LINE—(in prose drama) a speech; (in verse drama) a verse unit printed as a single line in the script

MAKEUP—paint, nose putty, false hair, etc., applied to actors to alter their appearance

    STRAIGHT MAKEUP—designed to counteract the changes in appearance of actors produced by the special lighting used in the theater and the greater distance from which they are viewed by the audience

    CHARACTER MAKEUP—designed to achieve the same results as straight makeup, and in addition to make the actor look different from his normal appearance, often to alter his apparent age, facial configuration, and personality

"MILK IT!"—an instruction to express and emphasize all the meaning and emotion possible

"MOTIVATE"—identify or invent a reason for a blocking movement, business, or a line which is suited to the character involved; also, to provide an appropriate stimulus for another actor's line; usually, each line is intended to motivate the one which follows it

"MOVE ON THE LINE"—cross while the line is being spoken; a fundamental (although often suspended) rule is that an actor should move only on his own line, not on another actor's

OPEN REHEARSALS—rehearsals at which visitors are permitted who are not involved in the production of the play

"OVERPREPARE"—to carry on work more fully than required for simple adequacy

PACE—to adjust the apparent speeds at which successive scenes of a play are performed so as to form a smooth and effective progression; pacing the play is usually done during the polishing rehearsals

PART—a role in a play

"PHRASE IT!"—break the sentences into shorter units, and mark them more distinctly for the audience

"PICK IT UP!"—to act with more animation and excitement

"PICK UP YOUR CUES!"—to avoid pauses between successive lines

PLOT LINE—a line containing information that the audience must remember in order to understand the later development of the plot; the term is usually restricted to a line which because of its significance to the plot must be given greater emphasis than would be natural for the character

PRODUCTION SCHEDULE—a list of dates of conferences and deadlines for technical work

"PROJECT!"—an instruction to an actor to make his speech intelligible at a greater distance

PROJECTION—the alteration of theatrical elements in order to compensate for the greater distance between the stage and audience, as compared with viewing distances outside the theater; all elements are regularly projected in the theater: makeup, costumes, scenery, properties, business and gesture, voice, and sound effects

PROMPTING—supplying an actor with speeches that he has forgotten

PROSCENIUM STAGE—a theatrical arrangement in which the acting area and the audience are placed in adjoining rooms, separated by a wall (the proscenium), in which an opening is cut (the proscenium arch) through which the audience can watch the action of the play

REHEARSAL—a performance of a play without an audience, usually aimed at improving the actors' work

REHEARSAL SCHEDULE—a list of dates of rehearsals, describing the types of work to be done at each, and including deadlines, especially for memorization

SCENE—a division of a play shorter than an act

    PLAYWRIGHT'S SCENE—a division of an act marked in the script and usually indicated in performance by closing the curtain

    DIRECTOR'S SCENE—a natural division of an act, identified for purposes of planning or rehearsal, but not necessarily marked for the audience in performance

    FRENCH SCENE—a section of an act during which no character enters or exits; marked in scripts of French plays but seldom indicated for the audience in performance, and often not an organic unit

SPEECH—the section of a play during which an actor speaks without being interrupted by a comment from another actor; a speech may be very short (the second speech in *Who's Afraid of Virginia Woolf?* is "Sh!"), or it can be very long (Lucky's long speech in *Waiting for Godot* extends for several pages in the script)

STAGE FRIGHT—a fear of failure in performance, producing physiological changes, an increase in tonus, trembling of hands and knees, shortness of breath, a rise in vocal pitch, an increase in the secretion of sweat, and a reduction in saliva; psychologically, stage fright results in some degree of disorientation, a kind of mental paralysis, and a distraction of attention

STAGE GEOGRAPHY—imaginary divisions of the stage floor used in giving actors directions; in the most familiar arrangement, nine areas are defined, center, up center, down center, up right, right center, down right, up left, left center, and down left; right and left are named from a position facing the audience, and up and down indicate away from and toward the audience

STEALING A SCENE—the distraction of the attention of the audience by some actor other than the one who is most important at the moment to the progress of the play

STRIKE—to remove from the stage and place in storage; properties used for Act I are struck during the intermission, and replaced with the properties for Act II; at the end of the last performance, scenery, costumes, properties, makeup, sound equipment, and lighting instruments are struck and stored for use in the next production

STUDY—a quick study is an actor who memorizes lines easily and quickly; a slow study is one who has difficulty in memorizing lines

"TAKE THE STAGE"—move to a strong position on stage and act vigorously so as to dominate the scene

TECHNICAL REHEARSAL—a rehearsal devoted to checking and working with the technical staff

TECHNICAL STAFF—all theater workers who influence the esthetic experience of the audience, directly or indirectly (excluding administrative, business, and maintenance personnel), except the playwright, director, and actors

TECHNIQUES—the methods by which the desired experience is produced for the audience; directorial techniques are the methods by which the director produces the desired changes in the performances of the actors

"THROW IT AWAY"—to speak a line casually

THRUST STAGE—a theatrical arrangement in which the stage is backed by a wall and the audience surrounds the acting area on three sides

TONUS—the degree of muscular contraction of the body as a whole; low tonus is associated with a low level of emotion, high tonus with excitement

"TOP"—to speak at a higher level of excitement or projection than something; actors are instructed to top laughter as it begins to fade; if a line which is spoken simultaneously with a sound effect or a passage of music must be heard, the actor is told he must top the sound; if a scene is to be played in crescendo, the actors are told that each speech must top the one preceding it

TRYOUTS—auditions

"TURN"—to change the angle of the face or body with relation to the front edge of the stage; an actor may turn without moving from his position on stage, or a turn can be combined with a cross

CLOSED TURN—a turn during which the actor faces the audience less than half the time

OPEN TURN—a turn during which the actor faces the audience more than half the time; open turns are nearly always to be preferred to closed turns

TYPE CASTING—the assignment of an actor to a part in which his own appearance, voice, and personality can be used on stage without great alteration

UNDERSTUDY—an actor who memorizes the lines and blocking of a part assigned to another actor, so that in an emergency he would be ready to perform as a substitute

UNITY—the organization of the elements included in a work of art so as to form an integrated pattern; Ibsen's *Ghosts* is somewhat more unified than his *Peer Gynt;*

Marlowe's *Dr. Faustus* is more unified than Goethe's *Faust;* Gounod's opera is more unified than either; both high unity and high variety are considered desirable in a work of art

UPSTAGING—a movement by an actor away from the audience, forcing other actors in the scene to weaken their positions by turning toward the back wall in order to carry on a conversation with him; an actor who takes up a position below another actor is said to upstage himself

VARIETY—the number of different elements included in a work of art; related to the scope of a play

VEHICLE—a play designed to display the personality and skill of an actor to advantage

VOCAL PATTERNS

PRIMER PATTERN—a vocal treatment of a sentence in which all words are given a uniform strong emphasis except the last word, which is sharply dropped

JACK-AND-JILL PATTERN—a vocal treatment in which each word in a sentence is given less emphasis than the word preceding it

NORMAL PATTERN—a vocal treatment characterized by randomness in the distribution of levels of emphasis, which are adjusted to the importance of the various words rather than to their order in the sentence

GLACIATED PATTERN—a vocal treatment which combines the primer and normal patterns; all words are spoken as in the normal pattern except the few most important, which are all given identical emphasis

MONOTONY—a vocal treatment in which the words of a sentence are spoken at a single level, or at fewer levels than in normal speech; any one, any two, or all three of the vocal elements may be handled monotonously, producing monorate, monopitch, and monotonous loudness; the levels used in monotonous speech may be placed anywhere in the vocal range, resulting, for example, in a low monopitch, a high monopitch, or monopitch somewhere in the center of the actor's pitch range

WALK-ON—a part in a play in which the actor has no lines to speak

WALK THROUGH—to read lines during a rehearsal without expressing emotion or communicating more than their surface meaning

WINGS—the area of the stage to the left and right of the scenery, invisible to the audience

Acknowledgements

I am most grateful to the many people quoted in the text, and to their publishers, for permitting the use of their material. The figures in parentheses indicate the pages in this book on which the quotations may be found. Mr. Wilder disclaims responsibility for the statement attributed to him, but has graciously granted permission for its use, suggesting that it be qualified by the phrase "Mr. Wilder is reported to have said. . . ."

ANGUS, SYLVIA, "It's Pretty, but is it Art?" *Saturday Review*, September 2, 1967, p. 15 (6, 25, 30)

BENTLEY, ERIC, *In Search of Theater*. New York: Alfred A. Knopf, Inc., 1953, pp. 120–121 (43), 216 (13), and 393 (22)

———, *The Playwright as Thinker*. New York: Harcourt Brace Jovanovitch, Inc., pp. 39 (306), 52 (306), and 169 (29); "Afterword" (37)

© BERNSTEIN, LEONARD, "What Makes Opera Grand?" *Vogue*, December, 1958, p. 159 (4)

BOOTH, SHIRLEY, *The New York Journal-American*, October 30, 1956 (374)

BOUCICAULT, DION, *Educational Theatre Journal*, December, 1957, p. 279 (287)

BROOKS, CLEANTH, and HEILMAN, ROBERT B., *Understanding Drama*. New York: Holt, Rinehart & Winston, Inc., 1963, p. 12 (305)

CABELL, JAMES BRANCH, *Jurgen, A Comedy of Justice*. Robert M. McBride & Company, 1920, p. 333 (27)

CISNEY, LENORE, and REDDY, JOHN, "Steichen: Dissatisfied Genius." *Saturday Review*, December 14, 1957, p. 9 (388)

DENNIS, JOHN, *Educational Theatre Journal*, December, 1961, p. 263 (391)

McCULLERS, CARSON, "The Flowering Dream, Notes on Writing." *Esquire*, December, 1959, p. 163 (377)

OLD PEKING PROMPTER, *Educational Theatre Journal*, October, 1958, p. 292 (321), and December, 1958, p. 376 (317)

WHITING, FRANK M., *An Introduction to the Theatre*. New York: Harper & Row Publishers, Inc., 1969, p. 179 (391)

WILDER, THORNTON, quoted in the *New York Mirror,* July 13, 1956 (270)

WINTERS, SHELLEY, "That Wonderful, Deep Silence." *Theatre Arts,* June, 1956, p. 85 (369)

YOUNG, STARK, quoted in Eric Bentley, *In Search of Theater*. New York: Alfred A. Knopf, Inc., 1953, p. 255 (32)

Index

The page numbers of illustrations are given in italics. For individual actors, directors, photographers, plays, and playwrights, look under the general headings "Actors, individual," "Directors," "Plays," etc.; composers of musical plays are included under "Playwrights." Authors of boxed quotations are listed under "Quotations." Fictional names of characters mentioned in illustrative anecdotes are enclosed in quotation marks.